WITHDRAWN

Past

by JEANETTA BOSWELL

ruined Ilion...

A bibliography of English and American literature based on Greco-Roman mythology

THE SCARECROW PRESS, INC.
Metuchen, N.J., & London MCMLXXXII

Also by Jeanetta Boswell:

Ralph Waldo Emerson and the Critics (1979)
Walt Whitman and the Critics (1980)
Herman Melville and the Critics (1981)
Henry David Thoreau and the Critics (with Sarah Crouch) (1981)
Nathaniel Hawthorne and the Critics (1982)

What Men or Gods Are These? A Genealogical Approach to
Classical Mythology (with Fred Boswell) (1980)

Library of Congress Cataloging in Publication Data

Boswell, Jeanetta, 1922-.
  "Past ruined Ilion--".

  Includes index.
  1. English literature--Bibliography. 2. American
literature--Bibliography. 3. Mythology, Classical,
in literature--Bibliography. 4. Mythology in
literature--Bibliography. 5. English literature--
Stories, plots, etc. 6. American literature--
Stories, plots, etc. I. Title.
Z2011.B67 [PR149.M95]   016.82'08'015   82-5541
ISBN 0-8108-1549-4   AACR2

Once again, to the memory of
my husband and fellow student,

Fred P. Boswell _____

CONTENTS

Past ruined Ilion Helen lives,
　　Alcestis rises from the shades;
Verse calls them forth--'tis verse that gives
　　Immortal youth to mortal maids.

Soon shall oblivion's deepening veil
　　Hide all the peopled hills you see,
The gay, the proud, while lovers hail
　　In distant ages you and me.

The tear for fading beauty check,
　　For passing glory cease to sigh:
One form shall rise above the wreck,
　　One name, Ianthe, shall not die.

--Walter Savage Landor

The objective of this work is quite simple: to collect and arrange alphabetically by author a wide selection of literature--mostly poems, with a few plays and novels--written on Greco-Roman mythological themes. Landor affirmed in his poem that "past ruined Ilion Helen lives," and this work supports the contention that not only does Helen live, but also Achilles and Hector, Orestes and Orpheus, Penelope and Odysseus, and a hundred others whose names have become standard words in the English vocabulary. The scope of this bibliography is principally the eighteenth, nineteenth, and twentieth centuries of English and American literature, but there are one or two items from the seventeenth century, and I have included a few selections from contemporary European literature in translation. For example, Jean Cocteau's "The Infernal Machine," and Albert Camus's "Myth of Sisyphus," are so much a part of English literature that to omit them would seem a serious oversight.

In the main body of my work I have attempted to comment on over eleven hundred selections, fully aware that reducing some of these items to a brief statement is folly of the worst kind. I know all too well that one cannot really summarize a poem, that the poem escapes such banal treatment, leaving one with only a handful of words. In these commentaries the objective has been not so much to summarize the work as to indicate its mythological basis and the use that the author has made of the myth.

Readers will note variation in the spelling of proper names. In each case I have followed the spelling used in the work being described. Also, I have not always cited the first appearance of a poem or story, preferring instead to give an edition that is easier to locate.

In addition to the selections in the main body of

the work I have listed another twelve hundred or so in
an Appendix. The basis for relegating these items to
an Appendix is varied, but in no case is it because I
felt they were inferior in quality. In some cases the
text was not available, in other instances the mythological
relation was too slight to require comment; some of the authors in the Appendix are partially represented, although
this is true also of some of the authors in the main text.
Finally, the most practical reason is that the book would
have been too long had I commented on all the selections.
Beyond the Appendix I have constructed a subject index
based on mythological themes and characters. In using
this index one must know the myth in order to find all
available material. For instance, in many of the "Cassandra" works there is much allusion to Apollo, and
these Cassandra items are not listed under Apollo. I
contemplated an index that would include all cross-
referencing, but again the length became prohibitive.
In working with this index I was able to establish the
frequency with which authors have used the Greco-Roman
myths, and I learned that Aphrodite has far exceeded all
others. And why not? Surely the concept of Aphrodite,
"the laughter-loving goddess of Love," is one of the best
creations of all time for all humankind!

Nothing is entirely original, and this work is no
exception. It has grown on the shoulders of other works,
some perhaps better, some worse, but has the advan-
tage of being the most recent attempt to assess the value
of Greco-Roman mythology on English literature. In
1932, now fifty years ago, Douglas Bush published Mythology and the Renaissance Tradition in English Poetry,
a comprehensive survey that has not been superseded.
In 1937 Bush published the work that most closely relates to my study: Mythology and the Romantic Tradition
in English Poetry. Still earlier studies include those by
H. Brown, "A Bibliography of Classical Influence on English Literature" (Harvard Studies in Philology, 1935);
William Chislett, The Classical Influence in English Literature in the Nineteenth Century (Boston, 1918); Helen
Law, Bibliography of Greek Myth in English Poetry (New
York, 1932), and Eileen O'Rourke, The Use of Mythological Subjects in Modern Poetry (London, 1912). Indis-
pensable to any study of this subject are Gilbert Highet,
The Classical Tradition (London, 1949), and Gilbert Murray, The Classical Tradition in Poetry (Cambridge, 1927).
For anyone fortunate enough to have a copy the old favorite, Gayley's Classic Myths in English Literature
(Boston, 1900), is still an important book. More recently Dan Norton and Peters Rushton published Classical
Myths in English Literature (New York, 1952), which is
similar in format to Gayley's work. All of these and
others have contributed to this bibliography, and I could
not have begun without them.

In conclusion I must thank all those who have so generously cooperated with me in my endeavors. This book belongs to the library of the University of Texas at Arlington, and particularly to the interlibrary-loan department, without which I could not have worked at all. Most of the material I have used is no longer in general circulation and is available only in rare-book collections at a few colleges and universities. Mary Alice Price, Becky Gomez, and Lila Hedrick of the interlibrary-loan division at Arlington have brought in books by the score and have put them into my hands. Thanks to them for making this work possible. I am, as always, in debt to my friends and family for their best wishes and support. This book has been one of the most interesting that I have pursued, and I shall not soon forget the hours and the labors that I have expended.

Jeanetta Boswell

Arlington, Texas
January 1982

"PAST RUINED ILION ..."

A Bibliography of English and American Literature
Based on Greco-Roman Mythology

ANONYMOUS

1   "Euripides," in Euripides: Plays, Vol. I, trans. by A. S. Way,
       with Introduction by John Warrington. London: Dent, 1956.
       Page v, Frontispiece.
    This sonnet expresses a good deal of the sentiment the average
    critic has for the Greek playwright (485-406 B.C.). He deals
    with great conflicts of human emotions and the tragedies of
    human existence; he portrays an uncompromising realism of
    common people and common problems; he expresses hatred
    for aggressive war and for inequality of woman and races; and
    he expresses undisguised scorn for the evils of religion, ora-
    cles, soothsaying, and the disgusting behavior of the gods.

ABBEY, Henry (1842-1911, American)

2   "Bellerophon," in The Poems of Henry Abbey. Kingston, N.Y.:
       Privately printed by the author, 1886.
    The story of Bellerophon is used to a moralistic purpose of
    pointing out that "great zeal for any good/ Begets a narrow-
    ness that leads to ill," and that the "gad-fly stings the flying
    horse, / And hurls the rider back to common ground." After
    the wife of Proetus, whom Abbey calls Anteia, tried to seduce
    Bellerophon and failed, she told her husband that he had tried
    to violate her. The king sent Bellerophon elsewhere with a
    letter instructing his neighbor king to kill the young man. In-
    stead Bellerophon distinguished himself in many uncommon en-
    counters, becoming a great hero of the people. At the end of
    his life he attempted to climb the heights to Olympus on Pega-
    sus, the flying horse, to tell the gods of his pure and noble
    life. In anger at his presumption Zeus sent a gadfly that stung
    Pegasus, and Bellerophon was hurled back to earth.

3   _____. "The King and the Naiad," in The Poems (1886), is
    told of Sous, a king of Sparta who conquered his enemy by
    not giving in to the pleasures of thirst. He then agreed to
    give up his conquests if he and all his men drank of a foun-
    tain. When it came his turn to drink, he refused, and thus
    forfeited his promise to cease fighting.

ABBEY, continued

4 _____. "Phaethon, " in Phaethon, With Three Other Stories.
Kingston, N. Y.: Styles and Kiersted, 1901.
This narrative is presented in seven parts, each one a stage
in the destruction and ruin of the beautiful but precocious son
of Apollo, or Phoebus, as he called in this poem. Doubtful
of his parentage, Phaeton persuades his father to prove himself by granting any request that he should make. Apollo
agrees, and then bitterly regrets his promise when Phaethon
wishes to take the fiery chariot of the sun across the heavens.
It is a dangerous journey, not a pleasant road with "springs
and groves to loiter in, " and the four horses are not "pliant
to control. " In spite of all warnings, however, Phaethon in-
sists on fulfilling the promise, and he undertakes to make the
journey across the heavens. The chariot goes out of control,
and the earth is scorched and rivers are dried up. Zeus intervenes, and in spite of Apollo's plea for his son's life, the
youth is hurled into "the vast abyss, " and "vanished in the
night. "

ABERCROMBIE, Lascelles (1881-1938, English)

5 "The Olympians, " in The Poems of Lascelles Abercrombie.
London: Oxford University Press, 1930.
An old woman and her son of Crete are approached by a man
with a wrapped-up dead child. In disguise, these two are revealed as the god Apollo and Zeus, the dead infant, to be
buried on Crete. These gods have come to the end of their
regime, and are now being replaced by one who calls himself
Dionysus.

6 _____. "Phoenix, " in The Poems (1930), is a play that takes
place before the Trojan War and tells the story of King Amyntor, who degraded his wife by bringing a bought woman into
the house. Phoenix, the king's son, is persuaded by his mother to lay with this woman and in consequence the father drives
him into exile. The play ends at this point in the story. Other
details of this myth are given in the Iliad, Book IX, lines 430-
495: Phoenix is at Troy in company with Achilles, acting as
adviser and counselor. Homer does not refer to the incident
of Phoenix' blindness, but one version has it that Amyntor put
out his son's eyes. Another says it was the gods who blinded
Phoenix.

7 _____. "Zagreus, " in The Poems (1930), is the god "who
lies in hell/ Imagining mankind. " The son of Zeus and Persephone, he is also identified as Dionysus Zagreus, the god
who was destroyed by the Titans and restored to life by his
father, Zeus. In Abercrombie's poem, however, the imagery
more accurately could be applied to Prometheus, the god who
defied the other gods to help man, and who subsequently was
punished in the hell of Tartarus.

4

ABSE, Dannie (1923- , English)

8   "The Ballad of Oedipus Sex, " in Collected Poems: 1948-1976.
        Pittsburgh: University of Pittsburgh Press, 1977.
        "The Ballad ... ," in eleven eight-line stanzas, combines the
        story of Oedipus and his mother with that of Hamlet and his
        mother, and suggests in a rather bizarre fashion that the
        love relation of a son and mother, and the killing of the
        father for that love, is one of the "human laws" and is the
        substance of most newspaper headlines. As Abse says:
        "Oedipus wrote the headlines/ for longer than a week." The
        poem is appropriately controlled by imagery of violence and
        blood.

9   _____. "The Victim of Aulis, " in Collected Poems (1977),
        is an eighty-line, free-verse composition detailing the fate
        of the hapless daughter of Agamemnon. Iphegenia was sac-
        rificed on the altar of Artemis because her father had of-
        fended the goddess, who becalmed the Greek fleet in the port
        of Aulis on its journey to the Trojan War. The emphasis,
        however, is on "the child, " victim of the parent, asking
        "why ... ?" the question of the "young-to-be-slain. "

ADCOCK, Arthur St. John (1864-1930, English)

10   "Gods in Exile, " in The Divine Tragedy. London: Selwyn and
        Blount, 1922.
        The gods are described in this poem as existing in a world
        "far from the world of man, " and where "life in eternal au-
        tumn lies embalmed. " They have lost their rule in the
        world, exiled by the coming of Christ, the god who lured
        their followers away and built altars on their fallen ones.
        The people call this god the Prince of Peace, yet, as Zeus
        says, "never was earth so rent with hate as now it lies. "
        Zeus refers to a biblical prophecy concerning the second
        coming of Christ, and predicts that when he does return he
        will be so disappointed in humankind that he will go into
        exile. The Olympians will then be called back to "remould
        the world. " This thought gives them joy, and "for the first
        time in exile, the gods laughed. "

AIKEN, Conrad (1889-1973, American)

11   "Electra, " in Collected Poems. New York: Oxford University
        Press, 1953.
        This poem details the character development of a princess
        who is cruel, sadistic, and a killer. It is not a retelling
        of the story of Agamemnon's daughter, Electra, but the im-
        agery is strongly suggestive of the classical Electra, who
        finally helped kill her mother, Clytemnestra, ostensibly be-
        cause of her love for the father who had been earlier mur-
        dered by her mother.

AIKEN, continued

12 _____. "Medusa," in John Deth and Other Poems. New York: Scribner, 1930.
This work derives its title from the staring, stonelike face of the woman in the poem. It is a sordid love story, the trial of a murderess who has killed the wife of a man who lied to her and betrayed her faith and confidence. Told in a stream-of-consciousness manner, the trial comes in and out of her thoughts, as she hears those who accuse her and those who defend her. She seems quite out of the whole thing, as though it is something taking place with other people in another time and place.

13 _____. "Priapus and the Pool," in Collected Poems (1953), is a poem of nearly four hundred lines that raises and debates the question of our physical and sexual nature: did God play "some trick upon us" by creating us in the image of Priapus, the Greek god of copulation?

14 _____. "Venus Anadyomene," is Part IV of the larger narrative John Deth, in which the forces of evil seek the temple of Venus in order that they may crucify the goddess "Venus Anadyomene," "Foam-born Venus, cold as the sea." The crucifixion goes forward, and the goddess dies, "twisting in death, and burning"; but as she dies she vows that she will "live in the hearts that crucify."

15 _____. "The Wedding," in Collected Poems (1953), is the story of Arachne, the spider, and Tithonus, the grasshopper. The myth of Tithonus is usually interwoven with Eos, the Dawn, whose lover he was until she turned him into a grasshopper. The myth of Arachne, the vain girl who dared to challenge Athena in a contest of weaving and was changed into a spider, is the subject of Tithonus' song in Aiken's poem. Later Arachne poisons and eats her lover.

AITKEN, Isabella T. (?-?, American)

16 _____. "Adonis," in Bohemia and Other Poems. Philadelphia: Lippincott, 1891.
The death of Adonis and the grief of the goddess Venus is the focal point of this poem. At his death Adonis became immortalized in the blood-red flower that we call the anemone. When he went into the Underworld, the queen of Hades, Persephone, also fell in love with Adonis but agreed to allow him to spend six months a year with Venus.

17 _____. "Cyprus," in Bohemia (1891), describes the beauty of the island that was the first home of the sea-born goddess Venus, or Aphrodite. Sometimes the goddess is called the Cyprian after this island.

6

18 _____. "Orpheus and Eurydice," in Bohemia (1891), is based
on the traditional mythology of Eurydice, who was bitten by
a snake, died, and went into the Underworld, whence her
husband was allowed to bring her back to the living. As is
always the case, Orpheus looks back and she disappears once
again into the kingdom of the dead. In this poem Orpheus
is killed and torn to pieces by Maenad women, but the severed head continues to sing the name "Eurydice," as it floats
down the Hebrus river.

19 _____. "Pandora," in Bohemia (1891), tells how the wrath-
ful Jupiter determined to punish man by creating a woman
who would plague him for all time to come. All the gods
had a part in this creation: Vulcan molded the form; Venus
gave it beauty; the Graces taught her to smile and to laugh;
Apollo gave music to her voice; Mercury gave eloquence;
Minerva brought gold and jewels; and Jupiter gave her a box
that contained all the ills of humanity. Prometheus had fore-
knowledge of the box and refused to open it, but his foolish
brother, Epimetheus, opened the box at once and out flew
all the evils that we know. Juno, however, secretly had put
Hope in the box, and this alone remained.

20 _____. "The Sea-Nymph," in Bohemia (1891), is a dream
related by the poet-narrator. He falls asleep on the beach
and dreams that a sea-nymph, a mermaid "tinged with the
brightest crimson, green, and blue," comes to him and sings.
When he wakes up, all that is left is an old gray stone, but
he comes back to the spot often, hoping the dream will come
again.

AKENSIDE, Mark (1721-1770, English)

21 "Hymn to the Naiads," in The Poetical Works of Mark Akenside,
ed. with Memoir and Critical Dissertation by Rev. George
Gilfillan. Edinburgh: James Nichol, 1857.
First published in 1746, "The Naiads" is the longest (some
three hundred lines) and the most directly mythological of
Akenside's poems. The naiads, who preside over various
forms of water, are addressed at daybreak and are honored
in the poem as deities who are closely connected with moral
and physical well-being. The naiads are referred to as the
daughters of Tethys, in keeping with standard mythological
lore. However, Akenside affirms that Love was the eldest
god, thus differing from Hesiod, who makes Chaos the first
of beings.

22 _____. "Ode II: To Sleep," in Poetical Works (1857), is
only vaguely mythological, although Sleep is called a "God of
kind shadows and of healing dews" and is identified as Mor-
pheus, the son of Midnight. The poem deals mainly with the
poet's yearning for a restful sleep, devoid of horrible dreams
and terrifying visions.

7

23 _____. "To the Evening Star," in Poetical Works (1857), is an invocation, or ode, to Hesper, the bright star to whom "it is given/ A while to rule the vacant sky. " The poem abounds in romantic images of nature and sentiment. An alternate title for this poem is "The Nightingale," which designates the song of the nightingale, a prominent theme in Akenside's composition.

24 _____. "To the Muse," in Poetical Works (1857), begins with a series of questions as to why the goddess of poetic inspiration "hast ... withdrawn thy aid. " In the concluding verse the poet once again feels her return and hails "the fair immortal guest. "

25 _____. "The Wood Nymph," in Poetical Works (1857), is narrated by the "dryad of ... the hoary things," who has lived to see two ages of change in "human things," and has now grown old and expert in "the paths of wisdom. " She relates how a noble youth, presumably the poet, comes and sits beneath her boughs, and how she prompts him, "unseen," in thoughts of "forms of good. "

AKERS, Elizabeth (Allen, Elizabeth Ann Chase Akers, 1832-1911, American)

26 "Ode to Aphrodite," in The Sun-set Song and Other Verses. Boston: Lee and Shepard, 1902. This appeal to the goddess of love is made in the first person, as of the poet Sappho speaking. It is a cry for help by the girl in love.

27 _____. "Phaon, the Ferryman," in Sun-set Song (1902), refers to the youth for whom Sappho is said to have died. In this poem he is very old but still keeps his ferry for those in need of his service. One day "came a gray-haired woman ... in mean apparel, --/ Old and unlovely. " Phaon helped her gently into his boat and rowed her safely over. When she stepped onto the bank, she was transfigured into the goddess--Aphrodite, Artemis, or possibly Demeter-- which was her true identity. Because of his kindness to her Phaon's youth was restored and he was given "beauty immortal. "

28 _____. "The Pipe of Pan," in Sun-set Song (1902), is a tribute to a time "when the earth was young and gay, " and the music of Pan is used to suggest this earlier, happier world. The poet calls on the god to play his "mystic pipe" again, even in a world that is "dull and sordid. " The imagery of the work appeals to nature, the woods, the streams, the winds--all comprising the world in which Pan had his existence.

AKINS, Zoe (1886-1958, American)

29 "Calypso," in Interpretations: A Book of First Poems. Lon-
      don: Richards, 1912.
      Calypso has little mythology except in connection with Odys-
      seus, and most of these details are incorporated into Zoe
      Akins's poem: she loves the shipwrecked Odysseus for seven
      years, until the gods command her to let him go; she offers
      to make Odysseus immortal if he will stay with her and not
      return to Penelope; and she is the daughter of Oceanus, and,
      in this poem, Thetis, the mother of Achilles. When Odys-
      seus leaves her, she is disconsolate.

30 _____. "Circe," in Interpretations (1912), is a kind of chant
      by Circe, the sorceress who is well known for her ability to
      change men into swine. She, like Calypso, loved Odysseus,
      who spent one year with her on the island of Aeaea.

31 _____. "Sappho to a Swallow on the Ground," in Interpreta-
      tions (1912), is a lyric poem with the image of the bird cen-
      tral to its meaning. The swallow, although now on the
      ground, will fly again to the tree. The poet-narrator says
      she too will rise, but her flight shall not return to earth.
      It is said that Sappho died by leaping into the sea; this poem
      says, "The Lesbian Sea shall be my funeral urn."

ALDINGTON, Richard (1892-1943, English)

32 "Argyria," in The Complete Poems of Richard Aldington. Lon-
      don: Wingate, 1948.
      The title refers to a nymph who was loved by a shepherd
      and who was later changed into a fountain. The poem says
      that Pan mourns for the nymph who has hidden in the "white
      waters."

33 _____. "At Mitylene," in Complete Poems (1948), makes
      use of the modern name for the ancient island of Lesbos,
      where the women "have laid out a purple cloth" to honor the
      goddess Artemis, whom they pray will come to the island
      for their protection.

34 _____. "Bromios," in The Poems of Richard Aldington.
      New York: Doubleday, Doran, 1934.
      Bromios, which means Thunderer, was one of the many
      names associated with the god Dionysus. In this poem he
      urges his followers, the drunken maenads, to more orgiastic
      behavior.

35 _____. "Choricos," in Complete Poems (1948), which sim-
      ply means "choric," with reference to the Greek theater,
      sets the mood and form of Aldington's poem, which is a song
      to Death, to whom we finally turn "singing/ One last song."

9

Death is envisioned as a "chaste woman" with "thin cold hands," who turns us gently from "the Cyprian's breasts" (Love) and from Phoebus Apollo (Light) to "the dark streams of Persephone."

36 _____. "Daughter of Zeus," in Complete Poems (1948), is a tribute to the moon, Artemis, who is called "the fairest of the daughters of Zeus." Although she is very pale, "she is still a frail lily," "still a tall lady comforting our human despair."

37 _____. "An Earth Goddess," in Complete Poems (1948), is narrated by the sister of the earth goddess, and their common parent is referred to as the "great Earth-Mother," possibly Cybele, Gaea, or Rhea. The earth goddess is not named, but the imagery describing her is parallel to that of Queen Jocasta, mother of Oedipus, when she saw that "both her sons were dead."

38 _____. "Eros and Psyche," in Complete Poems (1948), makes use of a striking contrast in imagery to convey the difference between the ideal and the real, the ancient and the modern. The scene is Camden Town, a borough of London, and the time is the present. In the midst of "steam and smoke and dirt" stands a statue of Psyche and Eros. The scene is sordid beyond belief, full of "clamour and filth," and the poet-narrator questions, "What are they doing here?" The poem concludes with the dreary prospect of seeing them grow "older / And sadder / And greyer."

39 _____. "Eumenides," in Complete Poems (1948), relates more directly to Aldington's experiences in World War I than to Greek mythology, but there is some slight connection. The narrator, "staring with sleepless eyes," remembers all the horror of death and the dying that he has seen in the war. And yet it is not for the dead that he is agonizing: "They are quiet," he says. It is rather for his own "murdered self" that the Furies, the Eumenides, torment him, demanding atonement.

40 _____. "The Faun Captive," in The Poems (1934), is based largely on the imagery of the faun, or satyr as the Greeks called them, who is free in the woods to roam and do as he pleases. After he is captured, however, after he is "snared and bound and dragged" out of his woods, he vows that "one night I shall break these thongs / And kill, kill, kill in sharp revenge."

41 _____. "Hermes, Leader of the Dead," in Complete Poems (1948), is an address to the winged god, who at the end of life conducts the weary and aged to the realms of Persephone.

10

The narrator says, "We, who loved Eos (the Dawn) ... " and "loved the midday heat," now "hold forth trembling hands / To thee, Hermes. "

42 _____. "Lesbia," in The Poems (1934), derives its title from the name of the woman whom the Roman poet Catullus loved. Her real name was Clodia, but he addressed her as "Lesbia" in twenty-five poems. Aldington's poem is a love lyric addressed to his own version of Lesbia.

43 _____. "Stele," in Complete Poems (1948), is a plaintive comment on an oread, a nymph of a mountain, who weeps "in the stony olive-garden/ On the hillside," because Pan has broken "her little reed," under his rough hoofs. The title of this poem means a stone, monument, or pillar.

44 _____. "To a Greek Marble," in Complete Poems (1948), is a brief love poem addressed to "Potnia," a word meaning mistress or lady, in this case a goddess of the mother-fertility type. The goddess in this poem is a grave monument, made of Parian marble, loved by another monument made of the same material.

45 _____. "Troy's Down," in The Poems (1934), tells the story of Electra, the daughter of Agamemnon, as she is portrayed in Euripides' tragedy "Electra. " In the play Electra is principally the killer of her mother, and later she is married to a peasant and sent into exile. In Aldington's poem Electra is an old woman who "nods in the sun" and reflects on her bitter life. At the end the poet says, "Troy's down/ long down/ and an old woman trembles in the sun"--an image of pathos and futility.

46 _____. Addenda: Other works by Aldington of mythological interest are A Fool i' the Forest (London: Allen and Unwin, (1925) and The Eaten Heart (London: Chatto and Windus, 1933). In A Fool ... the poems form a continuous narrative and except for Section VI, "The Voyage of Telemachus," do not stand alone. In this poem Telemachus is an old man who desires to consult with the ghost of his long-dead father, Odysseus. His journey is to the "end of the earth," where he performs the ritual for communicating with the dead, but for him no ghost appears: "There came no sight and no sound, only infinite darkness and silence. " Other poems in A Fool ... containing mythology are "Greek Art--The Conflict of Reflections," "Virgil," "The Manifestation of Pallas," "The Gods," and "Greek Science--Pagan Sensuality. " The Eaten Heart makes some use of the Philoctetes myth in parallel imagery of the wounded hero cast out on the island of Lemnos.

11

ALDRICH, Thomas Bailey (1836-1907, American)

47 "Andromeda," in The Poems of Thomas Bailey Aldrich. Bos-
    ton: Houghton Mifflin, 1915.
    This poem is less about the mythological heroine than the
    "slim girl figure fettered to dark shame / That nightly haunts
    the park." The poet says he is no longer "beguiled" by
    Grecian myths like that of Andromeda and Perseus, but that
    reality brings far greater anguish and woe to his mind.

48 _____. "The Flight of the Goddess," in The Poems (1915),
    is a tribute to the poet's Muse, the poetic inspiration that
    causes rhymes to spring up "thicker than clover." So long
    as he lived in a garret, and had little of the world's com-
    fort, the goddess was his constant companion, but when he
    married, acquired friends, and a house, the goddess took
    flight, and he fears "she will never return."

49 _____. "Invita Minerva," in The Poems (1915), is a sonnet
    written to the goddess, inviting her to bring inspiration for
    poetic creation. The poet, however, realizes that the god-
    dess seldom comes when invited, and usually "unsought she
    comes."

50 _____. "Lamia," in XXXVI Lyrics and XII Sonnets. Bos-
    ton: Houghton, Mifflin, 1881.
    In ballad form, this poem makes some use of the myth that
    Lamia, a daughter of Belus, who was beloved of Zeus, was
    deformed by jealous Hera into a creature with the face and
    breasts of a woman and the body of a serpent. Unable to
    avenge herself on Hera, Lamia went about luring strangers
    to their deaths. One myth has it that Hera killed Lamia's
    children, and subsequently the bereaved mother went about
    snatching those of other women; however, this story has no
    part in Aldrich's poem. In the poem here the narrator tells
    of meeting a woman who was beautiful beyond description un-
    til she "melted in the air," and nothing was left but a "writh-
    ing serpent."

ALLEN, Grant (1848-1891, English)

51 "The Attis," in The Attis of Caius Valerius Catullus. London:
    Nutt, 1892.
    Grant Allen's work can be considered a translation or an
    adaptation of the poem by Catullus. In either case it is based
    on a unique subject, one that does not often find expression.
    Attis, the young consort of the Phrygian goddess Cybele,
    castrates himself and dies rather than be enslaved to the
    goddess. In his notes to the poem Allen says, "Alone of
    Greek or Roman poems it preserves for us some tincture of
    that orgiastic spirit which strikes the keynote of Asiatic, and
    especially of Phrygian and Syrian religion."

52 _____. "The Return of Aphrodite," in The Lower Slopes.
London: Mathews and Lane; Chicago: Stone and Kimball, 1894.
The structure of this poem is built around the history of the
love goddess from the time she first appeared on the foam
of the ocean to the present time, when, the poet says, "back
to the nations again/ Comes Aphrodite. " In legendary times
she was worshiped as one of the mightiest and most beautiful of deities, and then came "hordes of ascetics," referring
to the periods of history when sex and love were considered
sinful.

ALLEN, Hervey (1889-1949, American)

53 "Bacchus Is Gone," in Wampum and Old Gold.   New Haven:
Yale University Press, 1921.
This poem is a lament for the passing of the god of "dancing
Folly. " In a choruslike effect the lines "Bacchus is gone"
and "Bacchus is dead" are repeated throughout.   At the end,
however, the narrator says, "He is not dead," but has fled
to a friendlier land that he knew in "days of old. " Here he
still reigns with "spotted beasts and maidens by his car. "

54 _____. "The Fire Thief," in Earth Moods and Other Poems.
New York: Harper, 1925.
Prometheus as a young man, part god, is the subject of this
narrative.   Described as the son of a giant and a maiden
who served the sun, this boy "was born with love for man
and hate of gods. " He loved the sun and envied the stars
until eventually he decided that earth must have "the gift of
fire," and it was his destiny "to snare the sun," to "strike
a fatal gash in night!" The remainder of the story is simple: he climbed into the heavens and stole a spark, which
was seen that night as a falling star.   Now "old men around
the hearth/ Would laugh and chuckle grimly at the tale/ Of
one who lost himself among the stars. "

55 _____. "Hylas," in Wampum (1921), tells the story of Hercules and the beautiful youth whom he abducted to be his
companion and lover.   The story belongs largely to Apollonius
Rhodius and is told in the Argonautica.   When the ship Argo
stopped near Cius in Mysia, Hylas wandered off into the
woods and was drowned when a nymph pulled him under the
water and would not let him go.   Bereaved and angered,
Hercules gave orders that the Cians should continue their
search for Hylas.   "Centuries have fled away," but the people still go about the countryside shouting "Hylas, Hylas,
Alas!"

56 _____. "The Wingless Victory," in Wampum (1921), refers
to Nike, the Greek goddess of victory, whose statue was
created in the second century B. C. on Samothrace.   Although

ALLEN, continued

called "the wingless Victory, " this statue does have wings,
as Allen's poem says.   It is "our Nike that has no wings, "
apparently referring to the American Statue of Liberty; and
"Time will hate her face, " for instead of ensuring victory
and liberty, it "has turned the world's hope/ Into stone. "

ANDERSON, Maxwell (1888-1959, American)

57   "The Fire Is Out in Acheron, " in You Who Have Dreams.
      New York: Simon and Schuster, 1925.
      This poem develops the idea that humanity has outgrown the
      gods and the concept of a burning hell, but not content to
      live independently, will "snatch a terror from afar" and "dig
      up the sunken gods again. "

58   _____. "Lucifer, " in You Who Have Dreams (1925), is prin-
      cipally a song that "the king of hell came singing. " He af-
      firms that all gods are but Lucifers grown older, that he is
      indeed king of youth and "the mornings. " Finally, however,
      he says that his son Prometheus shall rise against him, and
      assume his name.

59   _____. "Telemachus Muses, " in You Who Have Dreams
      (1925), is a reverie by the son of Odysseus, remembering
      his father as in a dream. "The old Ulysses, " according to
      one myth did not stay long in Ithaca after his return, but
      soon gathered his followers about him and cast off again,
      dreaming of a new adventure, a new Circe's island, a new
      cyclops' cave. In his vision Telemachus sees them all again
      "with unfleshed arms, " and then they fade as the wind rises
      "with rain and wind. "

60   _____. "The Wingless Victory, " a play related to the Jason-
      Medea story, in Eleven Verse Plays, 1929-1939. New
      York: Harcourt, Brace, 1940. Reprinted in Sanderson,
      James L. , and Everett Zimmerman, eds. , Medea: Myth
      and Dramatic Form. Boston: Houghton Mifflin, 1967.
      First printed Washington, D. C. : Anderson House, 1936.
      One critic has said of this play, "it is, in an interestingly
      muted fashion, a dramatization of the ancient Greek myth of
      the abandoned Medea" (Sanderson, p. 182). The time of this
      play is around 1800 in the American town of Salem. The
      conflict develops around a family with stern Puritan concepts
      of religion and morality, and their rejection of a Malay prin-
      cess whom one of the sons has married and brought home.
      The woman Oparre has saved the life of her husband, and in
      marrying him has deserted her own people and land. To re-
      turn is to face death for herself and her two children. When
      she is rejected by the Puritan family, including the husband,
      who weakly defends her, she returns to the ship Wingless

14

Victory, where she kills the two children, her servant woman, and herself. The parallels between this play and the ancient story of Medea and her tragedy are not exact, and yet in a broader sense, it is the same theme developed once again: racial bigotry and religious self-righteousness.

ANOUILH, Jean (1910-   , French)

61 "Antigone" (1942), trans. by Lewis Galantiere, in Four Contemporary French Plays. New York: Random House, 1946. Reprinted New York: Hill and Wang, 1958.
The play is in one long act in which the characters and basic action remain the same as in the classic myth. The details, however, have been modernized and vulgarized. The boys "smoke cigarettes," drive cars, and use coarse language. Polynices and Eteocles are both "rotten," but one had to be made a hero for the sake of the people. Creon is sorry for Antigone, urging her to live, to marry his son Haemon and be happy. However, the tragedy goes relentlessly forward, and ends on a despairing and indifferent note: "all dead: stiff, useless, rotting. And those who have survived will now begin quietly to forget the dead." Antigone "has played her part," and the drama ends with the guards "playing a game of cards."

62 _____. "Eurydice" (1941), trans. by Kitty Black, in Anouilh, Five Plays, Vol. I. New York: Random House, 1946. Reprinted New York: Hill and Wang, 1958.
The action of this three-act play takes place in the refreshment room of a French provincial railway station, a hotel bedroom in Marseilles, and later in the station restaurant again. In Anouilh's version of the myth Eurydice is killed in a bus accident; Orpheus is allowed to bring her back to life, but must not look at her until morning. Jealous, he does not restrain himself; he sees her again, loses her, as in the original myth, but then joins her in death, "for only in death can lovers keep eternal faith." Theirs is an idealized love, but surrounded by shabby, dirty, modernized details.

63 _____. "Médée" (1946), trans. by Luce and Arthur Klein, in Anouilh, Seven Plays, Vol. III. New York: Random House, 1946. Reprinted New York: Hill and Wang, 1957.
This one-act play reverses the importance of the characters of Medea and Jason from the mythological version, and Jason becomes the main character, wanting to abandon Medea's "black world," "horror and death," and "rage to destroy." The action is similar to Euripides' play, except that Medea immolates herself and the two murdered sons. At the end Jason is calmer and more rational than any other Anouilh character: He says: "I shall forget you, building up again

15

my wretched little human framework beneath the indifferent eye of the powers that be...." Anouilh's Medea has been criticized by Gilbert Highet, who writes: "... it would lessen Medea's tragic grandeur if, instead of being a great lady spurned, an exile beggared, a comrade deceived, and a proud woman humbled, she were shown mainly as a half-savage girl writhing in the frustration of lust ... she appears as a foul-mouthed Russian gipsy, and at the end burns in her own caravan like the subject of a cheap crime passionnel" (The Classical Tradition, 1949, p. 527).

64 _____. "Oresté" (1946), in Five Plays, Vol. III (1946), is a short one-act fragment that may have been a trial run for "Antigone." Aegisthus, portrayed as a realist, tries to dissuade Orestes from avenging his father's death with further murder: there arc other ways of proving one's manhood. As the fragment ends, Electra emerges as the one who will not concede.

ARMSTRONG, George Francis (Savage-Armstrong, George Francis, 1845-1906, English)

65 "The Closing of the Oracle," in A Garland from Greece. London: Longmans, Green, 1882.
Armstrong's poem is based on the historical action of banning all pagan worship. This occurred during the reign of Theodosius the Great, A.D. 379-395, when Christianity became the state religion. Much is said in the poem on the subject of a dying religion: "... the gods of Greece are dead"; "Sleep, then, ye vanquished deities of Greece"; etc. The principal theme of the poem, however, concerns the five old men who have served all their lives in Apollo's temple. The closing of the oracle is the end of life as they have known it, they have given their lives to nothing, and now they face "the night and mist and doubt and gloom."

66 _____. "Orithyia," in A Garland (1882), is narrated in the first person by the Athenian maiden who was carried off by Boreas, the North Wind, while she was dancing by the Ilyssus river. The story of her abduction is rather traditional mythology, but the poem concludes with Orithyia mourning the loss of her home in Athens and wishing regretfully that she could return to "the hands that caressed me, the faces that over me smiled."

67 _____. "The Satyr," in A Garland (1882), is looked upon as a creature "in whose being meet and mingle/ Man's motions with the life of dumb dull things." The satyr was a half-man, half-goat being generally associated with the god Dionysus. Armstrong's poem is a description of this being as

something that is still a part of nature, and yet has touched on
the boundary of human dominion. There is a kind of pathos in
the lines "In sooth he seems the sport of all the gods," and
"He laughs with them that laugh at him."

68 _____. "Selemnos," in A Garland (1882), is based on the
traditional mythology of a youth who loved the sea-nymph
Argyra. She loved him, or at least pretended to, for awhile
but soon left him, and he died of grief. Aphrodite changed
him into a river, but he continued to remember his love and
was no happier than before. Finally the goddess granted
him forgetfulness. The poem concludes by saying:

> there runs a little stream
> Bickering to the ocean; and 't is said
> His life who drinks of it becomes a dream,
> And all his past as formless as the night;
> And it is called Selemnos, or The Bright.

ARNOLD, Sir Edwin (1832-1904, English)

69 "Atalanta," in Lotus and Jewel with Other Poems. Boston:
Roberts Brothers, 1887.
Although "Atalanta" is the title of the poem, the emphasis is
on Hippomenes, the suitor who challenged Atalanta to a race
and won her. Had he lost he would have died. Arnold sees
this race to win Atalanta as life: "Life is that course," and
the outcome is always "joy or death."

70 _____. "The Hymn of the Priestess of Diana," in The Secret
of Death with Some Collected Poems. Boston: Roberts
Brothers, 1886.
The hymn is a praise of purity, and Diana is addressed as
"Queen of the quiet sky." Images of calm and cool are used
throughout to contrast with "her of Cyprus"--that is, Aphrodite, who is the goddess of passions and love.

71 _____. "Iphigenia," in Poems: Narrrative and Lyrical.
Oxford: MacPherson, 1853.
This poem comprises a single portrait, that of Iphigenia, the
daughter of Agamemnon, who was sacrificed at Aulis on the
altar of Artemis. This portrait of the girl is drawn a few
minutes before her death. She is described as beautiful, but
"so very, very still," and the scene itself is still. She appeared to see nothing, as her breath came "fast and tremu-
lous." And then she moved to "Dian's shrine," with a "quiet
step and tearless eye," and a "proud sorrow" that she could
die for a cause.

72 _____. "The Lost Pleiad: A Story of the Stars," in The
Secret of Death (1886), consists of a short introduction by
the poet-narrator and then a long blank-verse monologue

17

spoken by Merope, bewailing the sin that caused her to lose her light. In mythological tradition, Merope's sin was co-habiting with a human (she married the mortal Sisyphus), but Arnold's Christianized version is punishment by God for turning a deaf ear to the prayer of a woman in distress. Perhaps the most effective feature of the poem is a refrain that recurs with slight variations:

> ... light bearers, I am Merope,
> Merope, heaven-exiled Merope,
> Who stood between God's lowest and God's love.

73 _____. "The Sirens," in Poems (1853), is a simple account of the three sisters, the Sirens, whose song is so inviting and enticing that the weary mariner can hardly resist its call. To do so, however, is fatal, as witness a "ghastly heap of white bones, bleaching" on the shores of the Sirens' "Golden Isle, the Home of happy rest."

ARNOLD, Matthew (1822-1888, English)

74 "Bacchanalia: or, the New Age," in Poetical Works, ed. by N. H. Dole. New York: Crowell, 1897. This poem is a Dionysianlike chant, somewhat frenzied in tone and structure, celebrating the arrival of a new age. Nothing remains of the old, and the dancers, "maenads," trample "over tombs, amid graves," "clearing a stage," "scattering the past about." Only the poet remembers.

75 _____. "Empedocles on Aetna [Etna]," in Poetical Works (1897) was regarded by Robert Browning as one of Arnold's very great compositions, and it remains one of the author's most frequently anthologized pieces in spite of its length. It is a dramatic poem in two acts, both of which take place on Mt. Etna. The characters are Empedocles, a philosopher, poet, and historian who lived around 444 B.C.; Pausanias, a physician; and Callicles, a young harp-player. The facts surrounding Empedocles' death are somewhat controversial: one source has it that his curiosity to visit the flames of the crater on Etna proved fatal to him. Others say that he wished to be thought a god, and therefore threw himself into the flames in order that his death remain unknown to anyone. A less dramatic version of his death is that he lived to an ex-treme old age, and died in the sea. Arnold's character will-ingly perishes in the flames of Mt. Etna because he cannot live in a world he feels no longer exists for him; he has out-lived his time and will have no more of a life in which he feels enslaved.

76 _____. "Euphrosyne," in Poetical Works (1897), derives its

title from one of the Graces, daughters of Zeus and Eury-
nome, whose name means joy. The poem is clearly written
to compliment a woman whose office seems to be to "bring
us light and warmth and joy." It is a companion piece to
"Urania," discussed below.

77 _____. "Fragment of an Antigone," in Poetical Works (1897),
is a brief exchange between the Chrous and Haemon, just before Antigone's death. The Chrous sets the somber mood of
this tragic story: "Well hath he done who hath seized happi-
ness/ For little do the all-containing hours ... freely give,"
and Haemon responds, "Ah me!--honorest more than thy
lover, / O Antigone!/ A dead, ignorant, thankless corpse."

78 _____. "Fragment of Chorus of a Dejaneira," in Poetical
Works (1897), makes little direct use of mythology, although
the character of Hercules is suggested in the concluding verse,
as the poet praises one "on whom, in the prime/ Of life,
with vigor undimmed, / With unspent mind, and a soul/ Un-
worn, undebased, undecayed ..." the gates of the city of
death close forever. Such was the case of Hercules as portrayed in Sophocles' play "The Trachinian Women," in which
Dejaneira, the hero's wife, causes his death.

79 _____. "Merope," a play written in 1858, in Poetical Works
(1897), consists of well over a hundred pages. It tells the
story of Merope, the widow of Cresphontes, who has been
dead for twenty years. At the time of her husband's death
Merope's children were also slain and the tyrant Polyphontes
enthroned. Now, it turns out, one of the sons did survive
and returns. He is nearly killed by his mother, but then
she recognizes him and knows he has come to avenge the
death of his father. The question of revenge is debated at
length, but goes forward anyway, and Polyphontes is killed.
It has been said that Arnold's attempt to get in English the
effect of the old Greek dialogue and choruses was "difficult
and probably unwise." Arnold had just become Professor of
Poetry at Oxford, and attempted to inaugurate himself with
dignity. The drama "Merope" was close "to being frozen
with dignity" (Dolc, "Notes," in Poetical Works, 1897).

80 _____. "The New Sirens," in Poetical Works (1897), is a
narrative of two hundred lines that develops too excessively
the theme of the lost past and the great difference between
the past and present. As is often said of Arnold, he uses
a mythological framework to gloss over his own personal
sense of loss and melancholy in a modern, less-than-ideal
world. The Sirens who sang to Ulysses are no longer cruel
or dazzling, or "death-embracing," nor do they sing with
such impelling beauty as they did to the Greek hero.

81 _____. "Palladium," in Poetical Works (1897), refers to the
statue of Pallas Athene, or the temple in which the statue

19

was housed. It was said to have been sent by Zeus to Dardanus, the founder of Troy. Although Athene did not support the Trojans in their war with the Greeks, they nonetheless believed that so long as their city possessed the Palladium, it was safe from utter destruction. The Palladium at Troy was abducted by Odysseus and Diomedes, an atrocity that provoked the wrath of the goddess, who had previously supported their cause.

82 _____. "Philomela," in Poetical Works (1897), is a poetic accomplishment comparable to Arnold's "Dover Beach," a nonmythological work generally thought to be nearly perfect in development and style. "Philomela" is a tribute to the unbelievable beauty of the nightingale's song, and a subtle retelling of the myth of Philomela and Procne, daughters of Pandion, King of Athens. Procne was the wife of Tereus, King of Thrace. Tereus raped Philomela, and then cut out her tongue that she might not tell what he had done; but Philomela wove the story into a piece of tapestry, which she gave to her sister. Procne then killed her son, Itys, served him as food to his father, and fled with Philomela. On being pursued by Tereus, the sisters prayed to the gods and were changed into birds--Philomela into a nightingale and Procne into a swallow. In his poem Matthew Arnold quite logically reverses the position of the sisters, and Procne becomes the sister without a tongue.

83 _____. "The Strayed Reveller," in Poetical Works (1897), portrays a youth who strays into Circe's palace, drinks of her magic wine, and sees fabulous visions, such as Tiresias and the doom of Thebes, the centaurs of Pelion, heroes nearing the Happy Islands, and Hercules, "Alcmena's dreadful son." The youth admits that the bards can see as much, but with great pain and suffering to themselves, whereas he has sat all day long "without pain, without labor," and has seen "the wild, thronging train/ The bright procession/ of eddying forms."

84 _____. "Thyrsis," in Poetical Works (1897), was written to commemorate the death of Arnold's friend Arthur Hugh Clough, who died at Florence in 1861. It is cast as a pastoral elegy, with Arnold as "Corydon" and Clough as "Thyrsis," both names derived from traditional pastoral poetry, as in Virgil and Milton. As in Milton's "Lycidas" and Shelley's "Adonais," the personal grief is muted and made bearable by recreating it in the language of shepherds, flocks, and pipes. As Swinburne said, "The crude and naked sorrow is veiled and chastened with soft shadows and sounds of a 'land that is very far off'; because the verse remembers and retains a perfume and an echo of Grecian flutes and flowers" (Swinburne, Complete Works, 1925-1927, Vol. 15, p. 92).

85 _____. "Urania," in Poetical Works (1897), is another
       tribute to a woman, her name derived from one of the Muses,
       who is quite in contrast with Euphrosyne: Urania "coldly
       mocks the sons of men" and shows nothing but "pure, un-
       wavering, deep disdain." In mythology Urania is the muse
       of astronomy and means "heavenly."

ASHE, Thomas (1836-1889, English)

86 "Acis," in Poems by Thomas Ashe. London: Bell, 1886.
       Complete edition.
       The focus in this poem is on Acis, killed by the Cyclops
       who was also in love with Galatea, the Nereid. At his
       death he became a fountain of pure spring water, and Galatea
       still loved him. She came to his banks to lie in the tall
       growing grass, and sometimes went bathing in the crystal
       water.

87 _____. "Cleobis and Biton," in Poems (1886), tells the tra-
       ditional story of the two brothers, sons of Cydippe, a priest-
       ess of Hera's temple. On a festival day, when the oxen
       would not draw Cydippe to the temple, the two sons, Cleobis
       and Biton, took the place of the animals. Their actions won
       wide acclaim, and the mother asked the goddess Hera to give
       them a gift. This the goddess did: everlasting sleep--death
       --which she said was the best gift.

88 _____. "Delos," in Poems (1886), a small island in the
       Cyclades, was the birthplace of the god Apollo. As such it
       was one of the most honored and sacred places in Greece.
       In this poem the narrator says that, "though the god him-
       self be dead," it is still a hallowed place, and something of
       an aura of the past continues to cling about it.

89 _____. "Dryope," in Poems (1886), narrates the story of
       the girl who was transformed into the lotus tree. She was
       loved by the god Apollo and bore him a son, but finally she
       was ordered to marry the Prince Andraemon. In grief and
       despair she escaped into the forest, where the hamadryads
       changed her. Once after that she met the god Apollo, but
       he did not recognize her, and she scarcely grieved for him.

90 _____. "Eros," in Dryope and Other Poems. London:
       Bell and Doldy, 1861.
       In two parts, this composition has little mythology, but it
       does relate the nature of Love. In youth love "flutters down"
       on us and we find it more glorious "than anything we have
       dream'd in dreams." Later we put it aside, saying "wither'd
       thing." Yet if we persist, Love will "shed a holier light,
       and leave his youthful play," and make us his, "as he made
       Psyche his."

91 _____ . "The Gift of Herè," in Poems (1886), tells the story
of Deiopea, one of Hera's nymphs, whom Hera gave to King
Aeolus for his help in blowing Aeneas off-course to Italy, and
also of "a little comb of pearl," which Hera gave to Deiopea,
a magic object that caused the girl to be aware of her beauty
and glad of her marriage to Aeolus.

92 _____ . "Lost Eros," in Poems (1886), tells of a spring
when Love came, but was sent away. Now the narrator
dreams in vain, because the god has not come again.

93 _____ . "Merope," in Poems (1886), is the familiar story
of the daughter of Pleione and Atlas who married Sisyphus,
the mortal. In the beginning Sisyphus was a noble king, and
Merope was proud to be his wife. Later he "stoop'd to
meanness," the poem says, and Merope suffered in sympathy
with him until her beauty became darkened with a cloud of
tears. As one of the Pleiads in the constellation, she is invisible.

94 _____ . "The Myth of Prometheus," in Poems (1886), questions the reality of the story in which the god made humans
immortal by giving them fire, "that spark, that makes the
clay god-like." This gift should have put them at ease, in
the midst of strife and tears, yet it acts more like the vulture that ate of the god's liver, making man the creature
never at rest, at ease with neither immortality nor mortality.

95 _____ . "Pictures of Psyche," in Poems (1886), is a series
of "eight little pictures, drawn in words," separated by bits
of conversation between a man and woman. These pictures
tell the story of Eros and Psyche, the beautiful princess who
was loved by the god of love. Ashe's poem is a brief but
nonetheless complete version of the story in that it ends with
Psyche being made one of the immortals and married to the
god Eros.

96 _____ . "The Pleiads," in Poems (1886), presents the narrator in a mood of hopelessness and despair, but when he
looks up and sees the Pleiads, the seven sisters, and his
courage is renewed. He sees the lost Pleiad, Merope, as
"an image of God's pity," this deity sad because of her love
for a mortal.

97 _____ . "Psamathe," in Poems (1886), tells the story of the
Nereïd who married Aeacus and had a son by him. The
boy's half-brothers, Telamon and Peleus, hated him and eventually killed him, intentionally or accidentally, in a game of
quoits. In either case they did not care, nor did Aeacus.
After this, Psamathe, who had been much deceived by human
beings, went back to her sisters and father in the depths of

the sea, but not before she had laid a curse on the sons of Telamon and Peleus--Ajax, who would die a suicide, and Achilles, who would die at the hands of Apollo.

98 _____. "The Sorrows of Hypsipyle," in Poems (1886), is a play presented in two parts with seven scenes in each. The mythology of Hypsipyle, queen of Lemnos, is very brief, and for the most part Ashe's play differs from any standard accounts of her life and death. In the Argonautica Jason and his crew stop at the Island of Lemnos, and Jason and Hypsipyle become lovers. Prior to this the Lemnian women have massacred all the male population of Lemnos, and they are now afraid their crime will be punished. Thoas, the father of Hypsipyle, was spared, and the Queen sent him away under cover of darkness. In Ashe's play the crew of the Argo spends two years on Lemnos, and when they depart Thoas goes with them. On their way home the Argonauts again stop at Lemnos, and Thoas sees his daughter just after she dies of a broken heart. He also lies down beside her and dies.

99 _____. "Typhoeus," in Poems (1886), consists of dialogue spoken by the giant Typhoeus and a group of Watchers who react to and comment on what the giant says, but do not speak to him. In mythology Typhoeus attempts to overthrow Zeus, and for this is cast into Tartarus, where he became the source of all harmful winds. Most of the giants in Greek mythology are believed to have been the personification of terrifying natural phenomena, such as volcanoes and storms.

AUDEN, W. H. (Wystan Hugh, 1907-1973, English)

100 "Atlantis," in Collected Shorter Poems: 1927-1957. London: Faber and Faber, 1966.
Atlantis is a legendary island, or continent, that is reputed to have been sunk into the sea by a world-shattering earthquake. Atlantis plays no role in mythology, and the term is sometimes believed to be of Plato's coinage. The story appears in two works by Plato, and in no other source. From a legendary point of view Atlantis was located beyond the Pillars of Hercules in the Atlantic Ocean. It was populated by a prosperous and extremely powerful race of people descended from Poseidon. In Auden's poem the term is equated with the ideal, or the lost ideal, the end of the quest, and such related matters. He says that one should be proud "just to peep at Atlantis," and then to lie down and give thanks, "having seen your salvation."

101 _____. "The Epigoni," in Collected Shorter Poems (1966), is a satiric account of the unheroic fall of Rome. The title is derived from the mythological event in which the sons

23

of the Seven Against Thebes returned to that city and defeated it in retaliation for the deaths of their fathers in the
first war of Thebes. The word means "later born," and
is used by Auden to refer to the "sons" of Rome who were
defeated by the Goths in the fifth century A.D.

102 _____. "Ganymede," in Collected Shorter Poems: 1927-
1957 (1966), is based on the myth of Zeus taking the Trojan
boy Ganymede to be his companion on Olympus. In Auden's
poem nothing appeals to the boy, neither honor nor glory
nor the love of truth, until Zeus sends his eagle, who is
able to teach the boy "so many ways of killing."

103 _____. "Homage to Clio," in Homage to Clio and Other
Poems. London: Faber and Faber, 1960.
The title poem of this collection is a tribute to Clio, the
muse of time and history, in contrast to the goddesses
Artemis and Aphrodite, who control plant and animal life,
transient and impermanent.

104 _____. "Musée des Beaux Arts," in Collected Shorter
Poems: 1930-1944. London: Faber and Faber, 1950.
The story of Icarus as painted by Pieter Brueghel the Elder
(c. 1520-1569), demonstrates how indifferent humanity goes
on in the midst of tragedy. The boy falls out of the sky,
drowns in the sea, but the ploughman continues, the ship
sails "calmly on," and the sun shines "as it had to."

105 _____. "Ode to Gaea," in The Shield of Achilles and Other
Poems. New York: Random House, 1955.
Although written many years before we knew what the earth
looked like from space--that is, before astronauts looked at
the blue planet from the Moon, this poem is a description
of Earth, Gaea, as seen from the air. As Auden says,
"we finally see ... what our Mother, the/ Nicest daughter
of Chaos, would/ Admire could she look in a glass."

106 _____. "The Shield of Achilles," in The Shield of Achilles
(1955), is perhaps one of the most skillful and powerful of
all poems based on mythological subjects. Auden's poem
is an ironic and bitter version of Book XVIII, lines 478-
608, of Homer's Iliad. In this section of the epic Achilles
is mourning the loss of his friend Patroclus, who had been
slain by Hector. Achilles' armor, which Patroclus was
wearing, has also been taken by the victors. Thetis, the
sea-goddess mother of Achilles, has gone to Olympus to
beg Hephaestus, the smith-god, to make her son another
shield. Both Hephaestus and Thetis know that Achilles is
fated to die soon, and so they desire the most marvelous
shield the world has ever seen. Hephaestus creates the
shield of gold and silver and other precious metals and

depicts on it all the scenes of life--war and peace, country and city, laughter and sadness, a wedding and a trial-by-law, the heavens and earth, and around them all a blue border, the Ocean Stream. Thus Homer writes. In Auden's poem, however, Thetis looks over Hephaestus' shoulder and sees quite a different set of images: modern warfare, total devastation of mankind, killing of civilians, children naked and hungry, and other grim reminders of twentieth-century warfare.

107 _____. "The Sphinx," in Collected Shorter Poems: 1930-1944 (1950), is based on the subject of the Egyptian sphinx as it perceived in modern times: a huge hurt face, impervious to humanity, distress, love, learning. It simply lies, "turning a vast behind on shrill America," where success and prosperity are held to be life itself.

108 _____. "Venus Will Now Say a Few Words," in The Collected Poetry of W. H. Auden. New York: Random House, 1945.
Venus is created here as a form of Nature, or evolutionary life force, addressing the common man and informing him that he will become obsolete, and that she will "select another form" to fill his vacancy. Venus, the goddess of love, speaks coldly and objectively, like a scientist giving a lecture to a class in zoology.

109 _____. Addenda: "The Bacchae," an opera libretto with music by Hans Werner Henze.

AUSLANDER, Joseph (1897-?, American)

110 "After Atlantis," in Cyclops' Eye. New York and London: Harper, 1926.
This poem is a question and a statement: Have the archeologists uncovered Tartary, Antioch, the dead Egyptian dynasty? No matter, they will not find Atlantis, for this is "ono untampered lock/ They shall not finger."

111 _____. "Ixion," in Cyclops' Eye (1926), incorporates the imagery of the spinning wheel, the agony and torment of endless turning, but affirms that "you" to whom the poem is addressed, will have to break the wheel, "spoke by spoke" before you break "me," the narrator of the poem.

112 _____. "Medusa," in Cyclops' Eye (1926), is another love poem, similar to "Ixion," in which the narrator describes his lady as a "Medusa." In spite of this ugly image, however, he says, "I love the hissing in your hair" and "I shall always stare at you and turn/ To stone for ever."

113 _____. "Mother of Helen," in Cyclops' Eye (1926), is a

short, impressionistic account of Zeus' visit to Leda in the form of a swan, her conception of Helen, the birth of Helen, and the bitter aftermath of Helen's abduction, which led to the Trojan War.

114 _____. "There Was a Trial in Athens," in Cyclops' Eye (1926), refers to the trial and execution of Socrates. The character of Socrates is revealed best in contrast to that of the jailer, who offers the cup of hemlock, "sobbing brokenly/ like a sick child," whereas Socrates "approached the dead/ With some cool gesture of philosophy."

115 _____. "Ulysses in Autumn," in Cyclops' Eye (1926), is narrated by Ulysses as he remembers the adventurous, heroic details of his life--Circe, Achilles, Calypso, Troy, Helen--and longs to return to this life. Now his existence consists of plowing in the field, Penelope, "the stale cup of repose." He knows that one day he will not be able to resist the call of the sea, and something will hurl him "headlong to the ships."

116 _____. Addenda: "Letter to Sappho," in Letters to Women (New York: Harper, 1929), is of slight mythological inter-est, being an address to the poet of Lesbos, who became one of the immortals because of her lyrics and her capacity for great love.

BAGGORRE, Sir Reed Gooch (Carr, George Shoobridge, 1837-?, English)

117 "Alcestis," in Mythological Rhymes. London: Hodgson, 1912. The familiar story of Alcestis' taking her husband's place when Death came for him is narrated in this poem, and also the less familiar story of Admetus' winning the hand of Alcestis in marriage. At the beginning Alcestis' father imposed a hard condition, that Admetus come to claim his bride in a chariot drawn by a boar and a lion. Admetus sought the help of Apollo, who tamed such creatures for the occasion, and Alcestis was won. Later, when Death comes for Admetus, it is again Apollo who persuades the Fates to accept a substitute if one can be found.

118 _____. "Apollo," in Mythological Rhymes (1912), is an overall view of the god's birth and the nature of his being. When his mother, Leto, was denied any place to give birth, the island of Delos was formed, and the twins Apollo and Artemis were born there. Later Apollo quarreled with Zeus, his father, and was sentenced to serve a mortal for nine years. This he did in the service of Admetus, whom the god always loved for his kindness to one "from heaven exiled."

119 _____. "The Argonauts," in Mythological Rhymes (1912), tells the entire story as told by Apollonius of Rhodes, and perhaps with some improvement, since Baggorre's poem is shorter and spares the reader some of the endless diversions in which the ancient writer indulged. The crew sail with Jason in search of the Golden Fleece; engage in numerous adventures along the way; reach Colchis, where they capture the Fleece; and leave for home with Jason now in love with Medea, the sorceress daughter of King Aeetes.

120 _____. "Cacus," in Mythological Rhymes (1912), concerns the three-headed monstrous son of Bulcan and Medusa, whom Heracles killed because the monster stole and ate his cattle. Thereafter the people of the region honored Heracles because the monster had also stolen and eaten them.

121 _____. "Cadmus," in Mythological Rhymes (1912), focuses on the dragon that Cadmus slew when he founded the city of Thebes and on the dragon's teeth, which he planted to produce a new race of people.

122 _____. "Endymion," in Mythological Rhymes (1912), is a five-line poem that states that Endymion asked for eternal youth and "sleep's delight" and received these gifts from Jove. Now he is loved and wooed by Diana.

123 _____. "The Fates," in Mythological Rhymes (1912), are presented as the "arbiters of human life," the three sisters Clotho, Lachesis, and Atropus, the "aged crone who wields the shears ... ends its sorrows, joys, and fears."

124 _____. "Genesis of the Gods," in Mythological Rhymes (1912), consists of two parts, devoted to the primordial gods "Coelus and Terra," and the Olympian "Zeus." The first tells the story of the Heavens and the Earth, how Gaea plotted with her son Cronos to castrate Uranus and cast the severed part into the ocean. This Cronos did, and from the foam "sweet Aphrodite came." Part Two continues the story, with Cronos now fearful that his sons may rise against him as he had risen against his own father. He swallows his children as they are born, except for Zeus, who was hidden away on the island of Crete. In due course Zeus warred with the Titans and became the supreme god. The remainder of the poem is a catalog of Zeus' wives and the offspring they bore by him, including Helen, who was his daughter by Leda.

125 _____. "The Golden Fleece," in Mythological Rhymes (1912), begins the story of Jason and the Argonauts by telling how the nymph Theophane bore the ram with the golden fleece. In the meantime the son and daughter of Athamas

were threatened by a stepmother's jealousy, and their escape was planned by means of the ram. This winged animal carried them to Colchis, where later the son lost his
life because of the king's fear of losing the golden fleece.

126 _____. "Heracles," in <u>Mythological Rhymes</u> (1912), is a
review of the birth, life, and death of the great hero. Beginning with his birth as the son of Alcmena and Zeus, the
poem tells of his Twelve Labors; the madness in which he
killed his wife, Megara, and their children; and finally his
own death, which was caused by his wife Dejanira. Heracles is viewed as a great hero who gave his life to fighting
evils and stamping out wrongs.

127 _____. "Iphigeneia," in <u>Mythological Rhymes</u> (1912), presents the version of the story that Iphigeneia was spirited
away from the altar of sacrifice and taken to Tauris, where
she was forced to serve as a priestess until her brother
Orestes recognized her and took her away.

128 _____. "Jason," in <u>Mythological Rhymes</u> (1912), is the
second in chronological sequence of the poems on the Golden
Fleece theme (see "The Argonauts," and "The Golden
Fleece" discussed above). "Jason" tells how the hero was
chosen as leader of the Argo crew and gives his background,
which will qualify him to be the leader of this great expedition.

129 _____. "Menippe and Metioche," in <u>Mythological Rhymes</u>
(1912), is the story of two sisters, daughters of Merope
and the giant Orion, who gave their lives to save their land
from a plague. It is uncertain whether theirs was a genuine interest in saving the land, or whether they were moti-
vated by vanity and self-esteem.

130 _____. "Minos the First," in <u>Mythological Rhymes</u> (1912),
is based on the myth that Minos, the king of Crete, was a
"favorite of the gods," and that when he died he became a
judge of the dead in "Pluto's realm."

131 _____. "Orion," in <u>Mythological Rhymes</u> (1912), begins
with the story of how the giant was created by the gods for
the peasant Hyrieus, how he fell in love with Merope, the
daughter Oenopian, how he was blinded by his father-in-
law, and finally how Apollo conspired to have Artemis kill
him. At his death, however, he became immortalized as
the Orion constellation, the hunter, and his dog became
the constellation Canis Major.

132 _____. "Pelops," in <u>Mythological Rhymes</u> (1912), is a simple retelling of the myth that Pelops, the son of Tantalus,

was killed and served to the gods at a banquet. In horror the gods realized what they were about to eat and punished Tantalus in Hades by putting him near a banquet of food and drink that he would never partake of. Unwilling that Pelops should lose his life, they restored him and gave him an ivory shoulder to replace the one that had been eaten.

133 _____. "Perseus," in Mythological Rhymes (1912), tells the entire story of the hero, beginning with his birth to Danae, the daughter of King Acrisius of Argos. Later, the king of Seriphos, desiring to wed Danae, set Perseus the task of procuring the Medusa'a head, a task that the king thought would kill Perseus. However, with the help of Hades, Hermes, and Athena he not only succeeded in killing the Medusa but also a sea monster that threatened the lovely girl Andromeda, whom he married. It was Perseus' fate to kill his grandfather Acrisius; this came about quite by accident, in a game of quoits, when Perseus struck the old man, not knowing who he was. At his death Perseus became a demigod, and he and Andromeda became constellations. Cepheus and Cassiopeia, the parents of Andromeda, also became stars.

134 _____. "Theseus," in Mythological Rhymes (1912), begins with the birth of the great hero-king of Athens and ends with the death of Aegeus, the father of Theseus. For the most part the poem enumerates the adventures of Theseus in his early years, including the killing of the Minotaur of the labyrinth in Crete. It was this adventure that indirectly caused the death of his father, Aegeus. If successful, Theseus was to have flown a white flag on his ship as he came home to Athens from Crete. He forgot to change the black flag that the ship regularly flew, and Aegeus thought his son dead. He therefore jumped into the sea and died. The Aegean Sea was named in his honor by the mourning Athenians.

135 _____. "The War with the Giants," in Mythological Rhymes (1912), is a brief account of the war that was initiated by the giant Typhoeus, the son of Gaea and Tartarus. He took his war to Olympus, where the frightened gods fled to Egypt for safety. With Heracles' help, however, the giants were defeated and hurled into Tartarus. This was the last Olympic war in which mortals and immortals were engaged.

BAILY, William Entriken (?-?, American)

136 "Andromache in Captivity," in Dramatic Poems. Philadelphia: Privately printed for the author, 1894.
    After the Greeks captured Troy and burned the city, the women, including Hector's widow, Andromache, were taken

into bondage. Pyrrhus, the son of Achilles, took Andromache home with him to Epirus. Baily's dramatic poem
deals with the tragedy of war as it effects the lives of the
innocent. Pyrrhus is depicted as an essentially honorable
man who feels pity for Andromache and regrets that she
cannot forget the grief that she feels for her husband and
lost country.

137 _____. "Aurora," in Classical Poems. Cincinnati: Clarke,
1892.
Aurora is the Roman name for Eos, goddess of the dawn.
This poem is in praise of dawn: always the sign of a new
beginning and hope for another day.

138 _____. "The Birth of Venus," in Classical Poems (1892),
is based on the myth of the goddess emerging from the sea
foam, "impearled about and robed in humid splendor." It
is a beautiful poem, capturing the loveliness of the goddess
and the sea.

139 _____. "The Choice of Alcides," in Classical Poems (1892),
refers to Hercules, Alcides being a name derived from his
grandfather Alcaeus. The choice referred to is between a
life devoted to pleasure and the joys of living, or a life devoted to humanity and service. He chose the latter, and
as a result gained favor of the gods, particularly Athene,
who loved him and helped him in all of his hard endeavors.
At the end of his life he became a god and received reward
for all the hardships he had endured.

140 _____. "The Daughters of Oedipus," in Dramatic Poems
(1892), is principally a dialogue between Antigone and Is-
mene, in which they discuss the matter of Polynices' burial.
The only action occurs at the end, when the guards take
Antigone away for having defied Creon and performed burial
rites for her brother. The characterization of the two
daughters is clearly the same as that developed by Sophocles
in his drama "Antigone."

141 _____. "Pomona," in Classical Poems (1892), deals with
the Roman goddess of fruit trees. The poem celebrates
her abundance of bloom and fruit, the bounty of the harvest,
the richness of the apple and the grape. She is, and should
be, worshiped throughout the Earth.

142 _____. "Priam, King of Troy," in Dramatic Poems (1894),
encompasses a short segment of time shortly before the
death of Hector at the hands of Achilles. Priam sends
Aeneas as his ambassador to the Greeks and offers to set-
tle the war on peaceful terms. The offer is temporarily,
at least, rejected, and then Achilles sends a challenge to

Hector for single combat. Hector accepts the offer, and
is killed. The peace offer is never reopened, and the oracle tells Aeneas that the end is near, warning him to prepare for escape since Troy's doom is not to be his doom
also.

143 _____. "The Sacrifice of Iphigenia," in Dramatic Poems
(1894), takes place near the time for Iphigenia to die, and
she already knows what her fate is to be. Clytemnestra,
her mother, is bitter and angry that Agamemnon would
pledge their daughter to die for such a cause as Helen, but
Iphigenia is obedient to her father's pledge, and although
very sorrowful, accepts her doom. Agamemnon is also
bitter that he has been forced into such a position, but accepts the duty that must be his as king. Achilles considers
intervention on behalf of Iphigenia, but cannot go against
Calchas, the prophet, who has said that Agamemnon must
make the sacrifice if he would appease the goddess Artemis.
In the end the frightened Iphigenia goes forth to the altar.

BARING, Maurice (1874-1945, English)

144 "After Euripides' 'Electra,' " in Diminutive Dramas. London:
Constable, 1911.
This is a short play about a play, as the title indicates.
The characters, friends of the playwright, including the
philosopher Socrates, have gathered at the house of Cinyras
after the performance and are discussing the merits of the
new play. They argue one way and another, all agreeing
that Clytemnestra deserved killing, but not in accord over
Electra's doing the murder. There is not much disagree-
ment over the character of Orestes, whom Euripides portrayed as somewhat less than a heroic avenger.

145 _____. "Ariadne in Naxos," in Diminutive Dramas (1911),
is a unique version of what happened between Theseus and
Ariadne on the island of Naxos. In this short play the matter becomes almost a comedy routine, with Ariadne as the
girl who is about to have two lovers come face to face, in
this case Theseus and Dionysus. It is traditionally said
that Theseus abandoned Ariadne on Naxos, but in Baring's
work, Ariadne abandons him for the favors of the god.

146 _____. "The Aulis Difficulty," in Diminutive Dramas
(1911), turns into a domestic quarrel between Clytemnestra
and Agamemnon, and finally Iphigenia declaring that she is
"old enough to judge what I can do and what I can't do."
Presumably the sacrifice goes forward, but the play uses
the language and atmosphere of comedy, not tragedy, and
one can conclude only that Baring regarded this myth as a
highly ridiculous and improbable state of events.

147 _____. "Circe," in Collected Poems. London: Lane,
     1911. Reprinted New York: AMS, 1979.
     A sense of nostalgia pervades Baring's poem as he develops
     the theme of "fallen gods." Circe, much changed since the
     days of the heroic Greeks, is still the eternally beautiful
     enchantress whom men will seek "until they sink into their
     grave," or "till Death upon their tir'd eyes sheddeth rest."

148 _____. "Jason and Medea," in Diminutive Dramas (1911),
     is perhaps the most ironic of Baring's short mythological
     dramas. Again, it has the tone and atmosphere of a do-
     mestic conversation: Medea is arranging a dinner party
     and needs an extra "single woman." She suggests Glauce,
     the king's daughter, with whom Jason has entered into a
     marriage contract. When Jason tells his wife, Medea, of
     the arrangement, she quietly accepts the state of affairs,
     and goes out, saying, "I am going out to buy Glauce a
     present." Jason sits down and writes Glauce a note: "She
     has taken it too wonderfully well. We must ask her to
     stay with us, later...."

149 _____. "Pious Aeneas," in Diminutive Dramas (1911), is
     based on Book IV of Virgil's Aeneid, in which Aeneas
     leaves Carthage and pursues his quest of a new land for
     his followers. It is also at the end of Book IV that Dido
     builds her own funeral pyre and dies because of her be-
     trayal, and her loss of Aeneas. Baring's play is an argu-
     ment between Dido and Aeneas over his leaving Carthage.
     He says that it is "Jove's will" that he leave, but she in-
     sists that he is going because he "is tired of her." It is
     a domestic quarrel in every sense of the word, with hus-
     band and wife insulting and tormenting each other.

150 _____. "Proserpine: A Masque," in Collected Poems
     (1911), is in three acts, one each for Spring, Summer,
     and Autumn. Although rich in details and descriptive
     imagery, the story is simple: a prince falls in love with
     Rosemary, who is Persephone disguised as a mortal maid-
     en. During the Spring and Summer all is well, but when
     the Autumn comes, and it is time for Persephone to re-
     turn to the Underworld, the Prince must choose between
     life and death. She offers him the "apple or the slumber-
     ous pomegranate," and tells him to wait until Spring to
     make his choice:

> If on that day you still shall crave the dark,
> The silence and the sorrow of my dream,
> Taste the pomegranate; ... but is smiling life
> Be sweet to you, then taste the golden fruit ...

Unlike the plays in Baring's Diminutive Dramas (1911),

there is no satire or irony in "Proserpine." The language
and the characterization are consistent with a serious and
beautiful dramatization.

BARKER, George (1913-   , English)

151 "Daedalus," in Collected Poems: 1930-1955. London: Faber
       and Faber, 1957.
       The narrator in this poem assumes the role of Daedalus,
       the father of Icarus, who was drowned when his wax wings
       melted and he fell into the sea. The narrator also assumes
       the grief of the father for a lost son and, "totally bereft,"
       will not be consoled in any way.

152 _____. "Narcissus," in Collected Poems (1957), makes
       use of modern imagery but incorporates all the details of
       the basic Narcissus myth: the boy who became infatuated
       with his own image in a pool of water, grieved wildly to
       obtain that image, and finally drowned in an effort to reach
       it. In Barker's poem the windshield of an automobile takes
       the place of the pool of water.

BARNES, William (1801-1886, English)

153 "The Death of Adonis," in Vol. I, The Poems of William
       Barnes. Carbondale: Southern Illinois University
       Press, 1962.
       Adonis was killed while hunting a wild boar, and was sub-
       sequently mourned by the goddess Venus, or Aphrodite,
       who loved him better than any other mortal. This story
       is basic to Barnes's poem, which also adds the detail of
       the "sweet Anemone," the flower that sprang up where
       drops of Adonis' blood fell to the earth.

BEATTIE, James (1735-1803, English)

154 "The Judgment of Paris," in Poetical Works, ed by Rev.
       Alexander Dyce. London: Bell and Doldy; Bos-
       ton: Little, Brown, 1854. Aldine edition.
       Beattie's poem, a narrative of some five hundred lines,
       tells the story of the carefree shepherd Paris. He is ap-
       proached by three goddesses--Juno, Minerva, and Venus--
       and asked to choose which one of them should receive the
       prize of Beauty. The length of the poem is achieved through
       the elaborate descriptions of nature, and the overembellished
       speeches of the goddesses, each one greatly intent on pre-
       senting herself as the most likely candidate. In the end
       Paris chooses the "Queen of unrivalled charms, and match-
       less joy," Venus, and the poet remarks on the choice:

O blind to fate, felicity, and truth!--
But such are they whom Pleasure's snares decoy.

BEDDOES, Thomas Lovell (1803-1849, English)

155 "Pygmalion, the Cyprian Statuary," in Poems and Plays of
      Thomas Lovell Beddoes, ed. by H. W. Donner. Lon-
      don: Routledge and Kegan Paul, 1935.
      Beddoes describes the character of the sculptor Pygmalion,
      who carved the beautiful woman from the stone and later
      saw her come to life. As the sculptor comes and goes,
      he is repeatedly described as lonely and unloved, though
      surrounded by riches and beauty. The intensity with which
      he prays to the gods to give life to his statue is notable,
      and at the end he emerges clearly as he is "quietly / Weep-
      ing the tears of his felicity. "

156 _____. "Silenus in Proteus," in Poems and Plays (1935),
      is narrated by Silenus and is a tribute to his ass, which
      has died. Silenus, however, says "I too / Shall ride thee
      soon about the Elysian meadow. " In mythology Silenus, a
      demigod, was the nurse and teacher of the god Dionysus,
      and he is generally represented as a fat old man, riding on
      an ass and always drunk. These details are incorporated
      into Beddoes's poem.

157 _____. "Song of the Stygian Naiades," in Poems and Plays
      (1935), is a fanciful version of Pluto's infidelity to Proser-
      pine. Naiades (or naiads) are nymphs of springs, lakes,
      brooks, and rivers, in this case of the Styx, the principal
      river in the Underworld.

BELLOC, Hilaire (1870-1953, English)

158 "But oh! not Lovely Helen ...," in Sonnets and Verse. Lon-
      don: Duckworth, 1923.
      This untitled sonnet begins by evoking the image of "lovely
      Helen," but is principally about the death of Hector. This
      event, the poet says, surpassed all other events of the
      Trojan War. He "was the city's buttress," and yet his
      "dreadful day" came, and "unremembering fate / Felled
      him at last with all his armour on. "

159 _____. "When you to Acheron's ugly water come," in
      Sonnets (1924) is only slightly related to mythology: there
      is an allusion to Acheron, the river crossing into the Under-
      world. Belloc's poem is a study of death and the "pale
      dead," tortured "by nothingness and longing. "

160 _____. "The Winged Horse," in Sonnets (1923), refers to
Pegasus, the winged horse of mythology which carried the
hero Bellerophon during his famous exploits. In this poem
the hero is an ordinary man, and his exploits are all in
his consciousness, but he too rides a Pegasus, a winged
horse of the imagination.

BENÉT, Stephen Vincent (1898-1943, American)

161 "The First Vision of Helen," in Heavens and Earth. New
York: Holt, 1920. Reprinted in Benét, Ballads and
Poems: 1915-1930. Garden City, N.Y.: Doubleday,
1931.
There is no mythological basis for this poem, although it
has all the action and details of myth. Helen is pursued
by Itys, designated as prince of the centaurs, until he is
killed by Helen's brother Pollux. It is said that Helen was
first pursued by Theseus, the king of Athens, and that her
brothers Castor and Pollux rescued her from this abduction.
This incident is supposed to have happened when Helen was
very young, before she married Menelaus.

162 _____. "The Last Vision of Helen," in Heavens and Earth
(1920). Reprinted in Ballads and Poems (1931).
Again there is no mythological basis for this poem, although
it is presented as myth. After the fall of Troy, Helen goes
to Egypt, where she ceases to exist as Helen. She and the
Sphinx become "one forever, stone and ghost and dream."
There is one story that Helen and Menelaus were thrown
off course as they sailed homeward, and came ashore at
Egypt. Here they stayed for some time, but eventually
went back to Sparta. There is no record that Helen ended
her existence by becoming one with the Sphinx.

163 _____. "Winged Man," in The Young Adventure. New
Haven: Yale University Press, 1918. Reprinted in
Ballads and Poems (1931).
Daedalus and his young son, Icarus, are the subjects of
this poem, a tribute to the first human beings who equipped
themselves with wings and flew. In a larger sense it is a
tribute to humanity: "absurd, gigantic, eager for impossible
Romance."

BENÉT, William Rose (1886-1950, American)

164 "The Argo's Chanty," in Merchants from Cathay. New York:
Appleton-Century, 1919.
As suggested by the title, the poem is a chanty in form, a
song that sailors sing in rhythm with their work. A good
deal of the story of Jason and the Argonauts is embodied
in the verse, including the names of several of the heroes

who sailed on the Argo: Orpheus, Hercules, Castor, Pollux, Lynceus, Tiphys, Zetes, and Calais. Several events are also included: the Clashing Islands, the spot where Prometheus was chained, the adventures on the island of Lemnos, the boxing match at Bebrycia.

165   . "Brigand of Eleusis," in The Stairway of Surprise. New York: Knopf, 1947.
Benét bases his poem on the story of Procrustes, the brutal giant who victimized all travelers on the road to Athens by stretching them to fit an iron bed, or lopping off arms and legs if the victim was too large. Theseus killed this giant on his way from Eleusis to Athens. This basic myth is used to comment on the subject of equality: the giant claims that his infamous bed is the Equalizer, the instrument that regulates all. Theseus stands for individuality, and he is on his way to Athens, the city that stood for individual rights in the ancient world.

166   . "The Centaur's Farewell," in Merchants (1919), is narrated by Chiron, the ancient centaur who was the tutor of many of the great heroes--Peleus, Heracles, Jason, Orpheus--and is now the teacher of the youth Achilles. He bids farewell to these great heroes as they are outward bound for Colchis, and knows that the young Achilles is the last of the great ones he will tutor, his own death being at the hands of Heracles, "the flower of my sons."

167   . "Endymion in London," in The Stairway (1947), is a tribute to John Keats, who wrote the great English poem "Endymion."

168   . "Fastidious Artemis," in Starry Harness and Other Poems. New York: Duffield and Green, 1933.
The dual character of this goddess is pointed up in the imagery of Benét's poem: the Huntress who pursues her quarry, and yet turns aside to a "hare in the quicken," the goddess of the moon who kneels "to the earth's distress."

169   . "For Hellas," in Day of Deliverance: A Book of Poems in Wartime. New York: Knopf, 1944.
In order to commemorate the role the Greeks played in World War II, all the heroic episodes of the past are remembered as the narrator pauses on the steps of the Acropolis.

170   . "Ganymede," in The Stairway (1947), the Trojan boy who was abducted by Zeus' eagle and carried to the heavens, is used as the image of aspiration, an example of "mortal beauty hoisted to the skies." The poet does

not believe that we should "propitiate poetic ghosts" or
"appease the dead."

171 _____. "Ghost Actaeon," in Starry Harness (1933), remembers the episode in which he came upon Diana in her bath
and was changed into a stag. He says, however, that he
has forgotten the legend and the pain. The only thing he
remembers is the "beauty beyond bearing."

172 _____. "The Guests of Phineus," in Merchants (1919), is
a brief treatment of the myth in which the winged sons of
Boreas drive the harpies away from the tables of Phineus,
the Thracian king. The narrator sees this myth as indicat-
ing the "dark enigmas of this universe" which cloud our
feasts, and prays for the courage of the "wingèd Twins"
to face and rend despair as they hurled the harpies to
"whirlwind ruin."

173 _____. "The Halcyon Birds," in Merchants (1919), is the
story of Ceyx and his wife, Halcyone, who loved each other
very much. In time Ceyx was drowned at sea, and Halcyone grieved until one of the gods took pity and changed
her into a bird, as Ceyx has been changed into a bird at
his death. According to the myth Aeolus, the king of winds,
calms the sea for a period of time while Ceyx and Halcyone
build their nest on the waves once a year.

174 _____. "The Lost Gods Abiding," in Merchants (1919), affirms that the old gods, "the bright and glorious gods of a
world at dawn," are not dead, but have fled into the mountains and hills of our world. The poet wishes that once
more they might reveal themselves in lightnings and thunder, and in the majesty of the sea.

175 _____. "Marsyas in Autumn," in The Stairway (1947),
treats the story of the satyr Marsyas, who lost a flute
contest with Apollo and was flayed alive, as a dying vegetation myth. Marsyas is Autumn, "the fiery fading year,"
which is "flayed" of leaves and vegetation, and his music
is the wind as it plays on the trees.

176 _____. "Pelops," in The Stairway (1947), the son of Tantalus, was served by his father at a banquet for the gods.
Later the gods restored him to life and gave him an ivory
shoulder to replace the one that Demeter had eaten. Benét
sees Pelops as the "image of Man and all Man's years,"
as food for the gods, but given one strong shoulder where-
by to prolong hope.

177 _____. "Riddle for Polyphemus," in Golden Fleece. New
York: Dodd, Mead, 1935.
The riddle in this poem is the question of how the ugly,
malformed cyclops with his brutal and bloody ways would

37

dare love Galatea, the "Queen of the crystal deep," or expect his love to be returned. When humanity has freed itself of the brutality represented by the cyclops, it can expect to look upon the lovely lady rising from the sea.

178 _____. "Song of the Satyrs to Ariadne," in Merchants (1919), is lyric in form and content. Theseus has deserted Ariadne on the island of Naxos, where the god Dionysus has then chosen her for his bride. The song of the satyrs, followers of Dionysus, is one of praise and anticipation of forthcoming happiness in marriage and in the bacchic festivities.

179 _____. "Sung to Persephone," in Golden Fleece (1935), views the goddess as the spirit of Spring, when she returns to earth, and sometimes makes man feel young again. The poet sees Spring as the renewal of life for those who were "sick for their graves," and the "incredible thing / Happened that sometimes saves."

180 _____. "The Winning of Pomona," in Merchants (1919), is a narrative in which the fruit-goddess Pomona was sought in marriage by the fertility-god Vertumnus. She rejected his suit until, disguised as an old woman, he pleaded his cause so eloquently that she accepted him, and cried, "This is the hour for which my life was made."

181 _____. "Young Apollo," in Starry Harness (1933), creates the young god as the embodiment of light and truth and beauty, not unlike the young Adam, who was God's creation. The only element missing in his nature is Love, which came to life when he looked upon Eve, and "soft breathed her name." This was the gift of Aphrodite, and thus Heaven "first to Paradise came."

BINYON, Robert Laurence (1869-1943, English)

182 "Amasis," in Odes. London: Unicorn, 1901.
This story has its basis in Herodotus and is at least partially historical. The ruler of Samos, Polycrates, who lived about 525 B. C., was told by Amasis, the King of Egypt, that he should sacrifice something of great value to himself. This Polycrates did by casting an enormous emerald into the sea. Sometime later one of the ruler's fishermen caught a fish that had the great emerald in its belly. Amasis then rejected Polycrates' friendship, saying the gods were displeased with his offering, and that the ruler of Samos would be punished. The prophecy was shortly fulfilled when Polycrates fell into the hands of the Persians, and was crucified as an enemy. The emerald became the possession of the Persian ruler.

183   . "The Bacchanal of Alexander," in Odes (1901), is descriptive of an incident in the career of Alexander. Returning from his conquest of India, Alexander came upon the pleasant country of the Carmanians, where he entered the city in a chariot and his soldiers followed with dances and singing in imitation of the ancient ritual parades of Dionysus. The citizens hailed Alexander as they might have welcomed the god in legendary times.

184   . "The Dryad," in Odes (1901), praises the beauty and simplicity of the wood-nymph, who lives in nature and is a part of nature. The narrator is, in effect, describing a lovely woman whom he knows.

185   . "Memnon," in Three Short Plays. London: Sidgwick and Jackson, 1930.
Memnon, the king of Ethiopia, was the son of Eos, goddess of the dawn, and Tithonus, the brother of Priam. When the Trojan War broke out, Memnon felt compelled to aid his uncle in the struggle. This play deals with the king's decision to lead an army to Troy, although an oracle has warned that he will die in battle. He was, indeed, killed by Achilles.

186   . "Niobe," in Lyric Poems. London: Mathews, 1894.
This composition begins with a lengthy section in which Niobe laments the death of her children, crying that the gods are too stern and pitiless. The children remain unburied for nine days, but on the tenth night the gods came down and buried them while the town slept. Later Niobe was changed into a marble fountain, and in this form she continues to weep, silently and tragically, but does not feel the pain of her overwhelming loss.

187   . "On a Figure of Justice with Bound Eyes," in Lyric Poems (1894), refers to Dike, one of the daughters of Zeus and Themis. This poem questions why she must be sightless; if she could see there might be greater wrongs redressed and justice far better served.

188   . "Orpheus in Thrace," in Odes (1901), is an account of Orpheus after the death of Eurydice and his futile attempt to return her from the kingdom of death. He now turns to the "bleak North," to Thrace, a traveler without hope. He encounters a group of frenzied maenads, in their worship of Bacchus, who set upon him and kill him. When they come to their senses, they cannot believe they have killed one whom they loved.

189   . Paris and Oenone, a one-act play. London: Constable, 1906. Originally published in Fortnightly Review, 1905.
The scene is Mount Ida; the characters are limited to Paris

and Oenone, with several attendants, and, at the end, Helen.
Paris comes to Oenone knowing that she alone can cure him
of a mortal wound he has sustained. She hesitates to help
him, and allows his pain to worsen. Finally she rushes
out and goes to gather herbs that will cure him. Paris in
the meantime instructs his attendants to carry him to his
funeral pyre, and light it as soon as he breathes his last.
Helen arrives from Troy just as Oenone is returning from
gathering the life-giving herbs, and the two women see the
flames of his funeral pyre in the distance. Oenone challenges Helen to show her love for Paris by joining him in
death. Helen shudders as Oenone disappears down the hill,
and the flames leap higher as she throws herself into them.

190   . Penthesilea: A Poem. London: Constable, 1905.
The story told here is basic to the mythology of this character. The Amazon queen Penthesilea accidentally killed
her own sister and in atonement vowed that she would give
her own life to the Trojan cause. At first Achilles refuses
to fight in a war with women, but when Penthesilea and her
warriors rout the Greeks back to their ships, he joins in
the battle, and in single combat kills the lovely Amazon.
He then falls in love with her beauty and watches as her
spirit is liberated, "where he might not follow. "

191   . Persephone. Oxford: Blackwell; London: Simpkin,
Marshall, 1890.
The emphasis in this work is on the change that came over
Persephone as a result of the time she spent in the Underworld. Persephone is taken away by Hades to his gloomy
world; she is the queen in this shadowy existence; Hermes
arrives to lead her back to her mother and the earth, where
she will spend half of the year. But now, she says, she
sees "with alter'd eyes. " She does not know how it came
about, but she pities these poor mortals whose lives are
so brief and always darkened by their approaching doom.
Her stay on earth is also brief, but she will live in the sun
and beauty until the day comes for her to return "to that
dark home, " and her lord below.

192   . "Psyche, " in Lyric Poems (1894), derives its title
from mythology, but does not incorporate the details of the
story. The narrator equates Psyche with soul, or that
which is immortal, and in this instance it is a woman he
loves.

193   . "Queen Venus, " in The Death of Adam and Other
Poems. London: Methuen, 1904.
One day Queen Venus left her splendid palace on Olympus
and went to the topmost peak of a mountain where wind and
water beat roughly against the shore. On this day she

wanted to be alone with the elements that first gave her birth, remembering how she came "from deep-moved waters tossing and uptorn. " The conclusion of the poem draws a parallel between this story and the human search for our true nature. If we had the courage to reject our daily surroundings and return to our origins, we would find peace.

194   . The Sirens: An Ode. London: Macmillan, 1925. The Sirens is a free-verse, stream-of-consciousness work that celebrates the human odyssey. The Sirens are those forces that "flatter, threaten, foil, betray," but man continues and at last comes triumphantly home. The poem is distinguished by its great variety of water imagery and its structure of increasing intensity as man sails deeper and deeper into the unknown.

BISHOP, John Peale (1892-1944, American)

195 "And When the Net Was Unwound Venus Was Found Ravelled with Mars, " in The Collected Poems of John Peale Bishop, ed. with Preface and Personal Memoir by Allen Tate. New York: Scribner, 1948. This is a title based on a story that Homer tells in Book VIII of the Odyssey. Aphrodite (Venus) and Ares (Mars) were notorious in their love-making episodes, much to the shame and disgrace of Hephaestos, Aphrodite's husband. Eventually Hephaestos laid a plan to entrap them. He fastened a net above the bed and waited for the moment when the lovers would be in a compromising position. Then he loosened the net and caught them, inviting the other gods to come and see what he had caught. Bishop's poem is about a girl and a soldier who make love in a tawdry, cheap hotel room, the modern equivalent of Love and War in their lustful escapades.

196   . "Another Actaeon," in Collected Poems (1948). The time sequence of this poem seems to be divided between a "then" and "now. " The narrator presents all the imagery of the mythological Actaeon, who saw Diana in hor bath and was torn to pieces by his own hounds, but says that perhaps he did not die. The questions "What have I fled from?" and "What do I ask for?" point up the confusion and shame of the narrator in flight from punishment for crimes he only half-understands.

197   . "The Coming of Persephone," in Collected Poems (1948), is an invocation to the coming of Spring, April, when Demeter's daughter once more comes into the sunlight and nature is won "from the underworld. "

198   . "The Death of the Last Centaur," in The Undertaker's Garland and Other Poems, with Introduction by

Edmund Wilson. New York: Knopf, 1922. Decorations by Boris Artzybasheff.
The centaur in this poem is Eurytion, who led a band of centaurs in a drunken attempt to carry off Hippodamia at her wedding with Pirithous. Most of the centaurs were killed or driven from the region of Pelion. Mythology indicates that Eurytion was killed by Heracles, but in Bishop's poem he escapes and is cured of his wounds by Cheiron, the wisest and best of the centaurs. Endowed with a kind of immortality, the centaur comes to a new world, once the heroes and gods are gone from the ancient world, but he finds only "monstrous bulk and terrible sound." Now it is time for him to die, since he has no place except a "cold and fetid stall." His death will be ignoble; he will have not even a burial.

199 _____. "Emily in Hades," in Undertaker's Garland (1922), is a short story in which Emily, the main character, dies of influenza and finds that she has entered the land of the dead, having been ferried over a river by an old man. She learns that Hades is not Heaven or Hell, and that neither of these places exists. It is simply a place of being, the dead for the most part just sitting about, thinking nothing, feeling nothing, saying nothing. Not satisfied to stay with people whom she knows, Emily is taken to a place that is identified as seventh-century B.C. Greece. Here she meets Sappho and begs the poet to teach her about love, this being the only thing she bitterly regrets missing in life. The poet weeps, not because Emily is dead but because she will never be able to learn about love.

200 _____. "Endymion in a Shack," in Collected Poems (1948), is a modern youth who lives in a windowless shack and loves the "white body of the moon," as he feels she loves him. The moon is described as a beautiful woman who comes in the silent night and brings love to the heart of this most unloved man.

201 _____. "Epilogue," in Undertaker's Garland (1922), is the conclusion of this volume, all parts of which have dealt with death, death of the body and death of the spirit. In the epilogue the poet cries that he has "dwelt with death too long," and prays to Phoebus Apollo, the god of light and life to direct him as he goes forward.

202 _____. "Farewell to Many Cities," in Collected Poems (1948), commemorates the "nine sea-cities/ Of Ilion's lineage," each of which was great in its time, but passed into oblivion before the great Ilion of Trojan War fame. Now the ninth Ilion is gone.

203 _____. "Hecuba's Rage," in Collected Poems (1948), is a
contrast between the anger and outrage felt by an old, barren woman, and the lust and passion felt by a young woman,
Helen, for the old woman's son. Most bitterly and ironically, it is the love of the young woman that the world remembers, and not the tears of the old woman, even though
her cause was right and just.

204 _____. "Lucifer," in Undertaker's Garland (1922), is based
on the narrator's belief that the god of the sun, "god of the
silver bow, divine Apollo," did not die when Hellas died.
The god, whom the narrator mistook for Apollo, says, "I
am that other/ Who sang. For me the morning star was
named." The reference is to Lucifer, the brightest one,
who later became Satan in the Christian religion.

205 _____. "Narcissus," in Collected Poems (1948), poses the
question of what could the youth do but plunge into the depths
of the water in which he saw his own reflection. The constant, gleaming motion of the water produced a reality beyond grasp, and could not be resisted by the boy.

206 _____. "Phaeton," in Collected Poems (1948), is based on
the myth of the son of Apollo who tried to take the chariot
of the sun across the heavens, lost control of the fierce
horses, and was finally brought down to his death by Zeus.
In Bishop's poem the role of Phaeton is apparently assumed
by young pilots in a war, and their hope is that the plane
will not plunge to its destruction.

207 _____. "To Helen," in Collected Poems (1948), is a slight
poem in which the narrator expresses a question of when
will come his "own true love, / The flame-encircled nympho-
lept?"--the unattainable.

208 _____. "Whom the Gods Love," in Collected Poems (1948),
is ironic and bitter toward the proverbial wisdom that the
gods love those who die young. Take Achilles, for example,
who died young and a great hero. On the other hand, take
Tithonus, who was loved by a goddess and given immortality.
He grew old but could not die.

209 _____. "Why They Waged War," in Collected Poems (1948),
is a commentary on the reasons for war, as in the Trojan
War, for example. The Greeks charged the Trojans with
Paris' abduction of Helen. As Ulysses pointed out, however,
it is not wise to have gods covered with gold and a king as
old and wealthy as Priam.

BLACKBURN, Thomas (1916- , English)

210 "Bacchae," in In the Fire. London: Putnam, 1956.

Although compact, Blackburn's poem manages to tell the
story of Pentheus and his mother, Agave, the violent and
bloody myth that is the basis of "The Bacchae," by Euripides. To avenge himself for their disbelief, the god Dionysus throws a spell of drunken frenzy on his worshipers,
who include Agave, and they tear Pentheus to pieces. At
the end Agave returns with her son's head, under the delu-
sion that she has the head of a lion.

211 _____. "Eros and Agape," in In the Fire (1956), is a contrast of the two forms of love, divine or spiritual (Agape),
and sensual or sexual (Eros). It questions the difficulty of
Agape, when man is essentially a physical being, flesh and
mortality.

212 _____. "Oedipus," in The Outer Darkness. London: Hand
and Flower, 1951.
This study of Oedipus is an impressionistic, stream-of-
consciousness poem that makes reference to all the grim
details of the mythological hero: his mother's bed, his
blindness, Jocasta's suicide, and finally "as he stumbles
to the desert sands, / Bleeding and helpless as the newly
born, / His daughters leading him with childish hands."

213 _____. "Orpheus," in In the Fire (1956), develops the
theme of the magic in Orpheus' singing, how "wild beasts
and women," "dog and harlot," sought him because his
singing "could unlock/ Their moment for a breathing space."
Even after his death "his sacred essence walks abroad,"
and he is still followed.

214 _____. "Orpheus and Eurydice," in In the Fire (1956), is
narrated in the future sometime after Orpheus looks back
at his wife and she turns to stone. Perhaps had Orpheus
understood that his "wife was omnipresent" he would not
have sought her in the "shadow underground." The narrator
says that Orpheus nearly understood this one bitter evening
as he "walked away half smiling from her tombstone." But
then "the emptiness grew large and whimpered round him,"
he wants her body, her physical being, and not finding this
he howls and raves and gnashes his teeth like a dog.

BLACKIE, John Stuart (1809-1895, Scottish)

215 "Aeschylus," in Lays and Legends of Ancient Greece with Other
Poems. Edinburgh: Sutherland and Knox, 1857.
The son of Euphorion is visited by Dionysus during Demeter's
festival at Eleusis. The god informs the youth--who is
Aeschylus--that he will become the bard of Apollo and Diony-
sus. In the remainder of the poem the god tells Aeschylus

what he will write about: Agamemnon, Clytemnestra, and Orestes; the war against Thebes; Prometheus; etc. In effect these are the subjects of the extant dramas of Aeschylus. Blackie even manages to incorporate a remark attributed to Aeschylus: that all the dramas were crumbs dropped from Homer's banquet.

216 _____. "Ariadne," in Lays and Legends (1857), is the story of Ariadne's desertion by Theseus on the island of Naxos and her subsequent marriage to Dionysus. The preparations for her arrival on Olympus are described in elaborate detail, as she is borne heavenward in a chariot drawn by a "spotted pard."

217 _____. "Bellerophon," in Lays and Legends (1857), tells a complete story of the mythological hero's exploits, but uses the story to point up a simple moral: "Pride was not made for man." At the end of his life, not content with his mortal lot, Bellerophon tried to "scale the sky." The gods would have none of this, and frightened Pegasus, the winged horse, which plunged earthward and injured Bellerophon. Henceforth, the hero wandered about the world, "dejected and alone."

218 _____. "Galatea," in Lays and Legends (1857), is less about the "lovely Galatea" than it is about the "ugly Polypheme," the cyclops who fell in love with her. As the story is told, Polypheme has his revenge on Acis, the shepherd whom Galatea loved, by crushing him under a rock, and Galatea became a fountain of water that flows over the rock.

219 _____. "Iphigenia," in Lays and Legends (1857), begins at the point at which Calchas tells the Greek leaders that there must be a sacrifice to appease the goddess Artemis. It continues through the sad business of bringing Iphigenia to Aulis and ends with the priest binding the girl and laying her on the altar, where her throat is cut. In the concluding stanza the narrator describes the blue sky free from clouds, the sun beaming down, and the Greek fleet sailing northward. As for Agamemnon, he sailed "with a sad heart/ For he had lost a daughter."

220 _____. "The Judgment of Paris," in Lays and Legends (1857), emphasizes the striking contrast between the simple, happy shepherd boy that Paris was before the goddesses approached him, and the great ceremonial grandeur of the goddesses themselves. When Paris sees "golden Aphrodite," he exclaims, "Thou art fair," and vows that henceforth he will worship beauty. The importance of his decision is made clear when "Jove's thunder .../ Rolled ominous in his ear."

221 _____ . "The Naming of Athens," in Lays and Legends
(1857), is based on the myth in which Poseidon and Athena
struggled for possession of "the city of Cecrops." Athena
won and "gave Athens her name, and terrestrial/ Joy, from
the oil of the green olive-tree."

222 _____ . "Pandora," in Lays and Legends (1857), is based
on Hesiod's version of the myth, in which Zeus and all the
other gods create the woman Pandora and send her to
Prometheus, who promply rejects her. Epimetheus, however, accepts her as his wife. Later she produces a box,
which Epimetheus opens and allows all the evils to escape.
Hope alone remained in the box.

223 _____ . "Prometheus," in Lays and Legends (1857), attributes the creation of men and women to this god, who made
them out of the earth and then equipped them with fire in
order that they would not be totally "weak and defenceless."

224 _____ . "Wail of an Idol," in Lays and Legends (1857),
creates a mood and atmosphere of darkness and despair--
as well it might, since the setting is the kingdom of Hades.
One of the most notable features of the place is inertia and
stagnation. Even the throne of Persephone and Hades is
described as "dark, drear, alone," and they are the "stern,
relentless pair." At the end the narrator is plagued with
questions: "Where is the bustle of many-winged life?" He
prays to Hermes, leader of the dead, to bring him to
"Lethe's silent stream," where he may drink and forget,
"where Memory lives no more!"

BLACKMUR, Richard P. (1904-1965, American)

225 "Alma Venus," in Poems of R. P. Blackmur, with Introduction
by Denis Donoghue. Princeton: Princeton University
Press, 1977.
The title of Blackmur's poem means "nourishing, cherish-
ing, fostering" Venus, and basically describes the content
of the composition. As the poet says: "I'll say she is
more powerful/ And far more wise/ Than any Socrates and
Hercules."

226 _____ . "The Bull," in Poems (1977), is only slightly mythological, suggesting rather than saying anything specifically
related to the Bull-Europa episode. The imagery of the
animal, however, is in godlike terms--the "lightning," the
"thunder claps," "thunder-seed."

227 _____ . "The Rape of Europa," in Poems (1977), uses the
myth of Europa and the "foam-white bull" to say something

about World War II, a "six years' bout" that has left Europe "mauled, battered and barren," "trod and torn, grossness itself defiled."

BLAKE, William (1757-1827, English)

228 "To the Muses," in The Poetical Works of William Blake, ed.
      by Edwin J. Ellis. London: Chatto and Windus, 1906.
      Unlike a great many poems addressed to the Muse, or
      Muses, Blake's composition is specific. He refers to the
      "Fair Nine," "Ida's shady brow," the home of the Muses
      of mythology, and "the bards of old." Blake questions
      where they have gone; poets no longer write the way the
      ancients did. Now, he says, "the sound is forced, the
      notes are few!"

BLUNDEN, Edmund (1896-1974, English)

229 "An Ancient Goddess," in The Poems of Edmund Blunden:
      1914-1930. London: Cobden-Sanderson, 1930.
      The ancient goddess in this poem is Phoebe, a name given
      to Diana, or the moon, because of the brightness of her
      light. Blunden's poem is a description of the effects caused
      by moonlight. He calls her "the ghost, the dying lady and
      dead star," and proceeds to describe all the beautiful objects that her light enhances.

BLUNT, Wilfred Scawen (1840-1922, English)

230 "Adonis," in Poetical Works of Wilfred Scawen Blunt. London:
      Macmillan, 1914.
      The emphasis here is on the fact that Adonis died young,
      even though the gods loved him. Where he lay dead "was
      white with blossoms," but he was gone. The theme is further enunciated in the line, "A man fills but the measure
      of his destiny."

231 _____. "Venus of Milo," in Poetical Works (1914), is
      praise for the statue found on the island of Melos, the ancient name for Milos, in 1820. The poet sees the statue
      as "Earth's archetypal Eve. All womanhood."

BOGAN, Louise (1897-1970, American)

231a "Cassandra," in Dark Summer (1929). Reprinted in Collected
      Poems: 1923-1953. New York: Noonday, 1954.
      Cassandra, the Trojan prophetess, narrates this poem and
      reveals her plight as she refers to "madness," "the shrieking heaven," and the "dumb earth." When she says, "This

flesh will never give a child its mother," she refers to her
virginity, as the priestess-prophetess of Apollo's temple.

232 _____. "Medusa," in Body of This Death (1923). Reprinted
in Collected Poems (1954).
The narrator in this poem describes a scene in which
"everything moved," a bell hung ready to strike, a water-
fall gushed, grass was growing. Then the Medusa appeared
--hissing hair, stiff bald eyes, serpents--and the scene became dead. Nothing will ever stir again. Apparently the
symbol of the hideous Medusa is used to designate a person
or possibly an event that simply stopped life.

233 _____. "The Sleeping Fury," in The Sleeping Fury and
Other Poems (1937). Reprinted in Collected Poems
(1954).
The Furies, or Erinyes, were spirits whose function it was
to punish the guilty of some serious offense. In one sense
they represented the guilty conscience of an individual, and
sometimes hounded the person into madness. In Bogan's
poem the guilt has been laid to rest; the fury is sleeping
in peace, and so is the narrator.

BREND, Charles Cunninghame (?-?, English)

234 "Before the Harvest," in Freshets of the Hills. London:
Methuen, 1915.
This poem is a brief chant addressed to "Sweet Ceres," to
"make ripe the corn." The narrator makes several references to poverty, "short fare," "stint of bread," and "little
store," but prays that now Ceres will be generous and give
him a bountiful harvest.

235 _____. "The Centaur," in Freshets (1915), describes an
encounter with a centaur, "vast, black ...," his locks
streaming behind him. He disappears, but the narrator
still hears him, "his hoofs and voice, that wrought long
thunders down the dale."

236 _____. "The Cretan Fisherman," in Freshets (1915), is
based on the story of Britomartis, a Cretan maid who was
pursued by Minos. To escape him she leaped into the sea
and was caught in the nets of some fishermen, who abused
her and threatened to return her to Minos. Artemis transformed her into a sea-goddess, Dictynna, meaning "Lady
of the Nets." In the poem she avenges herself on the fishermen, by causing the fish to swim away from their nets.

237 _____. "Endymion," in Freshets (1915), is a study of the
four seasons--Spring, Summer, Autumn, Winter--as they

come and go on Latmos, where Endymion sleeps forever, "beautiful and calm," no matter what the season or the weather.

238 _____. "Erigone," in Freshets (1915), is a fragmentary drama, which nonetheless manages to tell most of the myth concerning Erigone and her father, Icarius. They welcomed the god Dionysus, and he taught them the art of cultivating the vine and making wine. Icarius in turn set out with a load of wine to tell everyone. The peasants drank themselves into a stupor and killed him. At this point Brend's poem stops, but subsequently Erigone hanged herself, and Dionysus avenged himself for the deaths of his faithful followers by sending a madness on the peasants, who hanged themselves from trees.

239 _____. "The Faun at Sunset," in Freshets (1915), is a simple description of a faun, or satyr, frolicking on the beach at sunset; he "dabbled his goat-feet, and splashed up the spray."

240 _____. "The Faun in the Garden," in Freshets (1915), is a colorful nature poem describing the faun in a garden, with its abundance of flowers, fruits, and greenery that fauns would delight to eat.

241 _____. "Faunus and the Woodcutter," in Freshets (1915), recounts an incident of a woodcutter disturbing Faunus as he rests in a shelter made of tree limbs and fallen boughs. Faunus is a Roman god, somewhat like Pan, with considerable influence over the fertility of both flocks and crops. After he disturbs Faunus, the woodcutter is fearful and prays to the god that he will not withhold his blessings.

242 _____. "Helios and the Water-Nymph," in Freshets (1915), points up the irony of a water-nymph in love with Helios, the sun, whose rays make bright with color the sparkling waves, and yet who dries up the water, and destroys the nymph.

243 _____. "Hymn to Mercury," in Freshets (1915), is a dramatic exchange between the god and the poet. The poet prays for guidance in writing poems that will be profitable, but Mercury, who was the Roman god of merchants, rebukes the poet and scorns him: "Poet--pah!" he says. With this the poet tells the god to "fall down and break his neck," and bids farewell.

244 _____. "Icarius," in Freshets (1915), deals principally with the favors shown to Icarius by the god Bacchus in planting and growing the wine-producing grape. The poem is a happy one with dancing and chanting, and does not touch on the tragedy that later befell Icarius, when the

49

drunken peasants killed him, and his daughter hanged herself.

245 _____. "Marsyas," in Freshets (1915), tells briefly the story of the satyr Marsyas, who found the flute that Athena had thrown away with a curse on anyone who picked it up. The contest between Marsyas and Apollo is foreshadowed in Brend's poem, with a repeated line: "Ah! the flute will cost you dear." The loser of this contest was, of course, Marsyas, who was hanged from a pine tree and flayed alive.

246 _____. "The Naiads," in Freshets (1915), is a song to the water-nymphs, and a warning to the poet not to sing of woods and bough and bush.

247 _____. "Pan and Pindar," in Freshets (1915), is based on the saying that Pan loved Pindar, and would sing only this poet's works. The narrator here is certain that the "forest King" would not notice his own songs, but he hopes that some lesser faun might take up the verse.

248 _____. "The Pleiads," in Freshets (1915), is a retelling of the familiar story of the seven sisters, daughters of Atlas, six of whom married great heroes or gods. The seventh, Merope, married "Sisyphus of evil name," and now hides her face in "solitary shame." She is the star that cannot be seen in the constellation.

249 _____. "The Rain-Bringers," in Freshets (1915), is an allusion to the Hyades, or "rainy kids," as they have been called, the ancients believing that the rising and setting of the Hyades were accompanied by much rain. The myth is that the five sisters pined away in grief and tears over the death of their brother, Hyas, who was killed by a wild boar. Zeus pitied them and transformed them into stars.

250 _____. "The Sirens," in Freshets (1915), points up the soothing, mesmerizing effect the Sirens' song, or in this case probably just the sound of the sea, can have on a weary shipwrecked sailor. The sound is one of "Whirling round and round and home, / Round and home."

BRIDGES, Robert (1844-1930, English)

251 Achilles in Scyros. London: Bell, 1912. Reprint of 1890 edition.
When the warriors and ships began gathering to sail against Troy, Thetis, the mother of Achilles, hid her son on the island of Scyros disguised as a girl, to prevent his being pressed into the war. Thetis knew that Achilles' fate was

to die young if he became a great hero. In this play Ulysses and Diomede come looking for Achilles at the court of Lycomedes, and Ulysses tricks him into revealing himself as a young warrior. Before he leaves for war, Achilles marries the daughter of Lycomedes, Deidamia.

252 _____. "Demeter, A Mask," in The Poetical Works of Robert Bridges, ed. by Humphrey Milford. London: Oxford University Press, 1914.
This is a standard version of the Demeter-Persephone myth, told in dramatic form in three acts. In the first act Hades finds Persephone alone and carries her off to be his queen. In the second act, which takes place ten days later, Demeter has learned the fate of her daughter and plans to compel Zeus to have her restored. Zeus sends Hermes to command Demeter to return to Olympus, but she is defiant and vows to win Poseidon to her cause. The third act takes place one year later, when Hermes brings Persephone from the Underworld. Demeter is reconciled to the terms of Persephone's restoration, and the play ends with the Chorus singing and crowning Persephone with flowers.

253 _____. The Feast of Bacchus. Oxford: Privately printed by H. Daniel, 1889.
Except for the title, which designates the occasion represented in the drama, the work has no relation to mythology. It is based on a comedy by the Latin poet Terence, which in turn is based on a play by the Greek poet Menander. The action involves two fathers and their two sons, and the attendant difficulties of getting the sons happily and suitably married.

254 _____. "I heard great Hector," in Poetical Works (1914), is number 53 in a sonnet sequence, The Growth of Love. In this segment of the work the narrator sees, as in a vision, the ghost of Hector still sounding "war's alarms," and urging his people on to victory in spite of their lost cause. But there is very little enthusiasm in the call, his words seeming dull and created from mere routine.

255 _____. "The Isle of Achilles," in Poetical Works (1914), is designated by Bridges as "from the Greek," and represents a poetic retelling of a prose work by Philostratus (c. A.D. 215), the Latin author of Heroicus. This curious work purports to be the "real" story of the Trojan War, and the composition by Bridges accounts for what happened to Achilles after he was killed at Troy. Although the Homeric tradition says that Achilles went to the Underworld, as did all the dead, a later tradition says that the hero went to Leuké, or the White Island, where he enjoyed a form of immortality and was worshiped as a deity.

256 _____. "Narcissus," in Poetical Works of Robert Bridges.

London: Oxford University Press, 1936. This edition
includes poems from October and Other Poems, in
which "Narcissus" originally appeared, 1920.
This poem regards the Narcissus myth as essentially the
symbol of humanity itself. All that we have done, whether
in creative arts of scientific discovery, has been done in
the image of that which we see reflected as ourselves. In
the end, however, the poet says, "Look again! Thou seest
a shadow and not thyself."

257 _____. "Prometheus, the Fire-Giver," in Poetical Works
(1914), recreates the episode in which Prometheus gives
fire to humanity. The occasion is a festival of Zeus, with
the setting in Argos. Inachus, the ruler of Argos, has
been chosen by Prometheus as the one most fitting to receive the high gift from the gods--fire. His wife, Argeia,
is afraid that they will be punished for impiety, but finally
Prometheus persuades them to accept the gift, after he has
instilled hope in their hearts. Most of the play is given to
foreshadowing what will happen to Prometheus for stealing
the fire, and to other mythological characters connected
with the myth; Io, the daughter of Inachus, and Heracles,
for example.

258 _____. The Return of Ulysses. London: Bumpus, 1890.
In a note appended to this work Robert Bridges says that
it is a "dramatising of the chief scenes in Homer's Odyssey,
and not a recast of the story in dramatic form." The entire play is laid in Ithaca, with Act I on the seashore just
after Ulysses has arrived home; Act II in the hut of Eumaeus,
the faithful swineherd to whom Ulysses reveals himself, re-
questing that his identity be kept a secret until the propitious
moment arrives; and Acts III, IV, and V, in the halls of
Ulysses' palace. The action focuses on Ulysses' return as
a beggar, his revealing himself in the bow and arrow contest, and finally the battle with the suitors who have wasted
his goods and destroyed his property. The battle is offstage,
with the killing being reported to Penelope by a maid who
looks through a window and tells the queen how things go
with her son, Telemachus. In conclusion Penelope and Ulysses are reunited, and the goddess Athena wishes them well.

BROOKE, Rupert (1887-1915, English)

259 "Ante Aram," in Collected Poems, ed. by George Edward
Woodbury. New York: Dodd, Mead, 1915.
This is a chantlike poem addressed to the goddess "on her
throne of tears and faint low sighs," the goddess of "cool
deep silence" and "pale Lethean wine." The poet expresses
a great tiredness of body and spirit, and longs for death
and oblivion.

260 _____. "The Goddess in the Wood," in Collected Poems
(1915), is "Lady Venus," or Aphrodite, who loved the beautiful youth Adonis. He, however, cared very little for her,
preferring the hunt. She warned him to beware of large
game, a warning that went unheeded, and he was killed by
a boar. Brooke's poem is based on the incident of Adonis'
death; Aphrodite's "immortal eyes" looked on the death of
her mortal lover.

261 _____. "Menelaus and Helen," in Collected Poems (1915),
has the perfect blending of imagery and narrative that makes
a memorable poem. In Part I Troy falls, and Menelaus,
"sword in hand," could not wait to confront Helen. But he
had forgotten that "she was so fair." He threw away his
sword and "knelt before her there." In Part II Menelaus
and Helen have grown old. The poet had no problem with
the incidents in Part I; but now he must deal with such
matters as "that journey home," "the long connubial years,"
and how Helen bears "child on child" and finally becomes
a scold. He must deal with a Menelaus who sacks a hundred Troys between noon and supper, who becomes "garru-
lous" and deaf. In conclusion Brooke says that Menelaus
often wonders "why on earth" did he ever go to Troy, and
why did "poor Paris" come to Sparta. In the meantime
"Menelaus nagged; and Helen cried" and Paris "slept on by
Scamander's side."

BROOKE, Stopford Augustus (1832-1916, English)

262 "Endymion," in Poems. London: Macmillan, 1888.
This version of the Endymion story changes Selene to Dian,
but she remains the goddess of the moon, and Endymion is
a young shepherd "driving his fleecy crew." The Moon
approaches him and tells him to meet her "in Latmos'
deepest dell." The poem ends with a question: "Who can
tell what happened then/ When they met within the glen?"
Endymion's immortal sleep on Latmos is not mentioned in
this work.

263 _____. "The Faun and the Dryad," in Poems (1888), is a
brief exchange of remarks between the dryad, the nymph of
the tree, and a faun. After he has slept "under thy tree,"
he asks her love. She replies that he should not have
slept: "Night has gone, and the Dawn/ Gleams on the lawn/
Farewell, foolish Faun."

264 _____. "Glaucon," in Poems (1888), or Glaucus, was a
minor sea-god who was originally a fisherman. In Brooke's
poem he gives up his ship: "my ship is laid/ In port," he
says. Ironically he concludes, "I have escaped the sea."
Mythology relates that later he ate a magic herb and could
not resist plunging into the sea; hence the gods made him
a sea-deity.

265 _____. "Hylas," in Poems (1888), adds nothing innovative
to the basic myth of the beautiful youth, beloved of Hercules,
who went wandering into the woods and was captured by a
naiad, a water-nymph, who kissed him and then pulled him
under the water to live with her forever.

266 _____. "Phoebus the Herdsman," in Poems (1888), takes
place during the time that Apollo had been sentenced to
serve the king Admetus. The god fell in love with a woman,
who loved him at first, and then deserted him for a "rustic
boy." Apollo considered revenge: he could kill them both,
but instead he fell in love with a naiad, and afterward the
music he played was so beautiful that it inspired all lovers'
hearts. The woman he first loved could not hear the music,
and he soon forgot her name.

267 _____. "Proteus," in Poems (1888), is a mildly ironic comment on the fickleness in a maiden's heart. Proteus, the
old man of the sea, who can change his shape and color at
will, thinks that he himself is the most changeful creature
in the universe, but he is mistaken: it is woman.

BROWNING, Elizabeth Barrett (1806-1861, English)

268 "The Battle of Marathon," in The Poetical Works of Elizabeth
Barrett Browning. London: Oxford University Press,
1913.
In the Preface to her very long narrative poem Mrs. Browning says, "The Battle of Marathon is not, perhaps, a subject
calculated to exercise the powers of the imagination, or of
poetic fancy, the incidents being so limited; but is a subject
every way formed to call forth the passions of the soul."
She further writes, "I have chosen Homer for a model," and
in this respect her poem draws heavily on mythology: the
gods, the battle, and the heroism all sound like an imitation
of the Greek epic. However, Marathon is history, the scene
of a decisive defeat of the Persians by the Athenians in
490 B.C., and for the most part Elizabeth Browning's poem
reflects this historical event.

269 _____. "The Dead Pan," in Poetical Works (1913), is based
on a legend, having its origin in Plutarch, that at the moment of Christ's death, the news went out that "Great Pan
is dead." It is uncertain whether this cry was intended to
identify Pan as Christ, or (as Mrs. Browning unequivocally
says) to signal that the gods of antiquity were no more:

> Earth outgrows the mythic fancies
> Sung beside her in her youth:
> And those debonaire romances

Sound but dull beside the truth.
Phoebus' chariot-course is run!
Look up, poets, to the sun!
Pan, Pan is dead.

270   _____ . "A Musical Instrument," in Poetical Works (1913),
describes "the great god Pan" as he creates a musical instrument from the reeds in the river. He cut it short,
then drew out the pith and "notched the poor, dry, empty
thing/ In holes as he sat by the river." The music that
he played on the reed was so sweet that "The sun on the
hill forgot to die, / And the lilies revived, and the dragon-
fly/ Came back to dream on the river."

271   _____ . "Wine of Cyprus," in Poetical Works (1913), is
simultaneously about the famous wine from the island of
Cyprus and about reading the Greek classics. In the poem
the narrator sips a glass of wine, recalling the ancient authors and describing each in terms of intoxication: Aeschylus, Sophocles, Euripides, and Plato; and such characters
as Cassandra, Medea, Prometheus, and Oedipus. At the
end the reader is made aware that the narrator and a friend
are sitting together and that "the poets poured" the wine.

BROWNING, Robert (1812-1889, English)

272   "Apollo and the Fates," in The Complete Poetical Works of
Robert Browning, ed. by Augustine Birrell. New York:
Macmillan, 1915.
This dialogue served as the Introduction to Browning's book
Parleyings with Certain People of Importance in Their Day
(1887), in which the poet discusses the seven major interests in his life: philosophy, history, poetry, painting, politics, Greek, and music. (See W. C. DeVane, Browning's
Parleyings: the Autobiography of a Mind [Yale University
Press, 1927].) The story of Admetus and his reprieve
from death is an appropriate introduction to such a work,
for Apollo's argument with the Fates--Clotho, Lachesis,
and Atropos--is indeed an argument on the interests in
life, and the value of living as opposed to death.

273   _____ . "Artemis Prologizes," in Poetical Works (1915),
is a dramatic monologue in which the goddess recounts the
story of Hippolytus, the son of Theseus, and how he met
his death at the hands of a sea-monster sent by Poseidon
at the curse of Theseus. This poem makes use of the
myth that Artemis snatched Hippolytus from his funeral
pyre and transported him to a forest near Athens, where
the god Asclepius cured him. While presenting the basic
story of Hippolytus, Artemis also incorporates a good deal
of mythology surrounding herself into the poem. Artemis
is sometimes referred to as the Triple Goddess. As a

55

goddess of the heavens, she is associated with the moon; as a goddess associated with the dead, she is generally identified as Hecate; and as a goddess of earth, her functions are to care for the animals and birds that inhabit the forest.

274 _____. "Eurydice to Orpheus: A Picture by Frederick Leighton, R.A.," in Poetical Works (1915), is a plea by Eurydice for Orpheus to look at her. She says, "One look now/ Will lap me round forever," and will compensate for all the "woe that was" and all "terror that may be."

275 _____. "Ixion," in Poetical Works (1915), is a repudiation of the gods, especially Zeus and Hera, for their treatment of this hero. The story is that the gods invited Ixion to their banquets, welcoming him as one of them. Zeus even told him that if Hera attracted him, "then--as thy heart may suggest." Ixion was overcome with joy, but the smiles of the gods soon changed to fury, and he was thrown into Tartarus, where he was chained to an ever-revolving wheel. Browning's poem concludes with Ixion affirming his triumph over the gods, "past Zeus to the Potency o'er him." Most studies of Ixion do not show him in the generous light of Browning's poem but describe him as arrogant and wicked.

275a _____. "Pan and Luna," in Poetical Works (1915), in spite of its length and number of extraneous details, is a simple retelling of the myth. Luna, the Roman goddess of the moon, felt quite naked and tried to hide herself behind a fleecy cloud. Actually the cloud had been prepared by Pan, who was hiding in it. When Luna slipped into the cloud, she fell into the god's embrace, not too unwillingly.

276 _____. Addenda: Other works by Browning with some interest in mythology are Balaustion's Adventure (1871), in which Euripides' Alcestis plays a prominent role; Aristophanes' Apology (1875), in which Euripides' Heracles figures; and a translation of the Agamemnon, by Aeschylus (1877). These works may be found in Complete Works, edited with Introduction and notes by Charlotte Porter and Helen A. Clarke. New York: Crowell, 1898; and in Works, edited with Introduction by F. G. Kenyon. London: Smith, Elder, 1912. Centenary edition.

BUCHANAN, Robert Williams (1841-1901, English)

277 "Ades, King of Hell," in Vol. I, The Complete Poetical Works of Robert Williams Buchanan. London: Chatto and Windus, 1901. Reprinted New York: AMS, 1976. This poem, narrated by Ades (Hades), is unique in that it

emphasizes the loneliness, darkness, and coldness that Hades felt before he abducted Persephone to be his queen in the Underworld, and later the joy he felt that at least through Persephone he was still connected to life, to the warm and bountiful earth.

278 _____. "Euphrosyne; or The Prospect," in Poetical Works (1901), takes its title from the Grace whose name means Joy. In this poem someone is reading to a seventeen-year-old girl and instructing her that in heaven there will be no grief and pain, no appetites of the flesh, no love. The girl then took the book and buried it in the hollow of a tree, exclaiming with joy, "I love the earth, and life, and thee!"

279 _____. "The Gift of Eos," in Poetical Works (1901), is the gift of immortality to Tithonus, her lover. Now he has grown old, withered, and sere, but he cannot die. Every morning he watches as Eos opens the gates for the sun, Apollo and his golden chariot, and his old heart thrills to a new day, but he is so old and so tired.

280 _____. "The Groves of Faun," in Poetical Works (1901), is a narrative of a dreamlike experience in which the night wanderer stumbles into a wood "Where Faunus leads his legions ruminant;/ And where Selene, with soft silvern feet/ Walks every summer night." Later in the poem he is rewarded by a vision of Eros and Psyche, as they meet deep in the forest at Psyche's castle. Everything is in the narrator's consciousness, but for him it is nonetheless real while it lasts.

281 _____. "Iris the Rainbow," in Poetical Works (1901), is a description by Iris of her activities after the storm. In mythology she is the daughter of Thaumas, a sea-god, and the Oceanid Electra, and is therefore associated with the storms and winds of the sea. In Homer she is a messenger of the gods, but later her office consists of making peace between warring factions, as indeed the rainbow is a sign of the subsiding storm.

282 _____. "Mnemosyne: or, The Restrospect," in Poetical Works (1901), is a complement to "Euphrosyne" (see above). In "Mnemosyne" the young girl has grown old and is near the end of her life. Now she looks back and remembers, and feels that "this life we live/ In this strange haunted planet," could not be the last. Mnemosyne was the goddess of memory in mythology, and in this poem she is described as "large, lustrous-eyed, and white--/ The twilight goddess."

283 _____. "The Naiad," in Poetical Works (1901), is a water-nymph who has her shrine deep within Diana's wood, and

is grateful to the goddess for allowing her this quiet beauty, this place of unbroken solitude. By serving Diana faithfully, the naiad hopes "to earn a place divine/ Among the white-robed deities."

284 _____. "Orpheus the Musician," in Poetical Works (1901), is an incident narrated by Orpheus in which his music charms the naiads, satyrs, fauns, and even Silenus, who is completely lulled by the enchanting music.

285 _____. "Pan," in Poetical Works (1901), is based on a rather tenuous myth that the name "Pan" means All, and that the god was finally considered the universal god, the Great All. Most mythologists say that the name is related to the Latin term for "to eat, to graze, to pasture," which seems likely since Pan was above all a shepherd-god of flocks and pastures. In Buchanan's poem Pan prophesies that he will outlive all the other gods. He says: "Some power more piteous, yet a part of me, / Shall hurl ye from Olumpos to the depths, / And bruise ye back to that great darkness whence/ Ye blossom'd thick as flowers...."

286 _____. "Penelope," in Poetical Works (1901), is a dramatic monologue in which Penelope, the long-waiting wife of Odysseus, ponders the absence of her husband and silently implores him to return. She has grown old, she thinks, and no longer young and beautiful, but then he too has grown old, his hair "threaded with the silver foam."

287 _____. "Polypheme's Passion," in Poetical Works (1901), is a dialogue between the cyclops Polypheme and Silenus. Polypheme is in a very loquacious mood and tells the drunken Silenus all about his love for Galatea, the sea-nymph who thus far has scorned all his advances. At the end Silenus grossly advises the man-eating cyclops to "make a meal of trouble--that is, eat her!"

288 _____. "Proteus," in Poetical Works (1901), derives its title from the god of the sea who could change his shape as he liked. In this poem Proteus is conceived of as far more than a god, and is the living element in all things. In a kind of history of humankind--Adam and Eve, the Trojan War, the Christ child, the crucified Christ, the fall of the Roman Empire--Proteus says he was always there, "change on change." Finally he says, "I am the change that is not change, for I/ Am deathless, being Death," referring to the idea that inherent in life is the certainty of death.

289 _____. "Pygmalion, the Sculptor," in Poetical Works (1901), deals with the basic story of the Cyprian sculptor

but adds several details not found in the myth. In Buchanan's poem Pygmalion's betrothed, Psyche, has died, and he carves the woman-statue to take her place. Once the statue has been given life, however, his love for her becomes lascivious and orgiastic, until a plague comes and kills her. The sculptor then flees, "a homeless man."

290 _____. "Sappho: On the Leucadian Rock," in Poetical Works (1901), is a song by Sappho in which she laments her love for Phaon, a ferryman in Lesbos, made so handsome by Aphrodite that all the women loved him. The story has it that Sappho finally jumped off the Leucadian Rock for his sake. This detail is not a part of Buchanan's poem.

291 _____. "The Satyr," in Poetical Works (1901), is a songlike poem in which a satyr describes his life: romping in the woods, making love to the water-nymphs, sometimes drinking with Silenus, but most of all being under the protection of a bright star that shines above him and loves him.

292 _____. "Selene the Moon," in Poetical Works (1901), is an expression of the love that Selene, the moon, has for Endymion. As she glides across the sky, she cries, "Awake! Awake Endymion," but he never stirs and her cries are in vain. Not even Zeus hears her plea to awaken the sleeping Endymion.

293 _____. "The Swan-Song of Apollo," in Poetical Works (1901), is narrated by Apollo, who sings farewell for the gods, the "great pale gods" who now sit still, and are being replaced by "a mortal shape ... / Bearing a heavy cross and crown'd with thorn." At the end of the song he fades away and is gone forever.

294 _____. "The Syren," in Poetical Works (1901), is a conversation between the Syren (usually spelled "Siren") and Eumolpus, a son of Poseidon. The Siren sings to Eumolpus and tells him she will be whatever he wishes her to be: "Call me Love or call me Fame/ Call me Death or Poesy/ Call me by whatever name/ Seemeth sweetest unto thee...."

295 _____. "Venus on the Sun-Car," in Poetical Works (1901), tells of Venus riding with Apollo in his sun chariot, and asking when will Adonis awaken. As they travel about the world, she questions the frost-filled woods, the spirit of the sun, the "silver-winged Moon," to stir the sleep of Adonis, her beloved who is dead.

BURKE, Kenneth (1897- , American)

296 "Atlantis," in Collected Poems, 1915-1967. Los Angeles: University of California Press, 1968.

59

Burke's poem describes the "island of Antiquity," as it emitted a "huge geologic sigh," lurched, and "gently sank beneath the sea." Now it lies there, "aimless," the houses "bearded with sea-growth," and fish peering through the doors.

297 _____. "Of Rome and Carthage," in Collected Poems (1968), is a comic performance based on Virgil's Aeneid, Book IV. Burke says that Virgil explains "how Dido gave what Aeneas took," and later that "Aeneas took what Dido gave," mockingly referring to the scene in the Aeneid in which Dido and Aeneas are caught in a cave during a storm and make love; or expressed in another way: "Aeneas and Dido, in stormy weather, / Put their snails together."

BUTLER, Arthur Gray (1832-1909, English)

298 "The Choice of Achilles," in The Choice of Achilles and Other Poems. London: Frowde, 1900.
This narrative is related largely by Achilles as he debates whether he will take his men and ships and go to the Trojan War. The question is really one of "long life and ease, or glory and the grave, / Still in my prime!" He raises the issue of doing battle for another's wrong, saying, "What to me / Is Helen? What Atrides?" But on the other hand, if he does not go to Troy, Hector will triumph, and all Greece will lament the absence of her bravest son. As he is making his decision to go to Troy, he identifies with Heracles, saying:

> Mine is to build a name
> To shine like Heracles, and mount the stars,
> Beyond all hope, all envy, all desire,
> Whose short-lived splendour shall outlast the world.

At the conclusion Achilles is in arms, crying, "Hector, I come."

299 _____. "The Choice of Heracles," in The Choice of Achilles (1900), is not one of life and death, as was Achilles', but rather between a life of pleasure, sensuality, riches, and other wordly offerings, or a life of suffering and dedication. The choices are presented in symbolic terms represented as two young women, sisters who look exactly alike. One, however, is the Temptress, who offers him the life of pleasure, and the other is a modest, pale maiden, who offers him a pure life. When he makes his choice, Heracles says:

> I am thine ...
> Be life though weary, yet not long:
> I will with suffering fill it to the close.

The poem concludes with Heracles going forth "knowing his old self dead." Beyond the scope of this poem, but part of the Heracles mythology, is the story that he became one of the immortals at his death and married the beautiful goddess Hebe, symbol of youth.

BYNNER, Harold Witter (1881-1968, American)

300 "A Canticle of Bacchus," in A Canticle of Pan and Other
     Poems. New York: Knopf, 1920.
     A canticle is a song or chant with a religious or biblical
     connotation. In this case it is the god Bacchus, and his
     drunken companion Silenus, who are praised for their con-
     tribution to humankind. Wine, it is argued, is that which
     sets us free and gives us joy; the other side, however,
     opposes and does not believe that we should ply ourselves
     with drink.

301 _____. "A Canticle of Pan," in A Canticle of Pan (1920),
     presents a reconciliation of Christianity as represented by
     Christ and the pagan gods as represented by Pan. The
     goat-god stands for Nature, and the Christian god stands
     for peace. These two concepts do not contradict each
     other, and unlike the legend that said "Pan is dead," when
     Christ was born, this poem holds that such was not the
     case.

302 _____. "Captain's Table," in Guest Book. New York:
     Knopf, 1935.
     The opening line, "Cassandra, treading the Titanic deck,"
     very well indicates the nature of this sonnet, with its
     ironic forecast of wreck and disaster and a crew that was
     rich and pleasure-loving and foolish to believe that the
     ship was invulnerable to disaster.

303 _____. "Faun," in Guest Book (1935), is a slight work,
     both in form and substance. It is a portrait of a faunlike
     man, irresponsible, trying to attract attention, and eager
     for approval. Such were the creatures of mythology.

304 _____. "The Faun That Went to War," in A Canticle of
     Pan (1920), is a contrast of the natural, peace-loving ways
     of the faun, and the unnatural business of war. The faun,
     a creature of nature, goes to war and kills, performing an
     act that he does not understand.

305 _____. "Ganymede," in Guest Book (1935), is a portrait
     of the beautiful Trojan boy as he goes about his business
     of playing among the flowers, rejoicing in the Spring.
     Then the eagle circles, and he is carried away to greater
     things on Olympus, but he is not happier for the change.

306 _____. "Iphigenia in Tauris, " in A Book of Plays. New
York: Knopf, 1922.
This work is for the most part a translation, following the
story of the play by Euripides, but the language is straight-
forward free-verse English, with no attempt to recreate
the Greek dramatic form. According to the story told in
this play, Iphigenia did not die at Aulis, but rather was
transported to the land of the Taurians, where she served
as priestess in the temple of Artemis. It was the custom
of the half-savage Taurians to sacrifice all foreigners who
came to their shores on the altar of Artemis, and it was
Iphigenia's duty to prepare the victims for the sacrifice.
When her brother, Orestes, and his friend Pylades come
to Tauris, Iphigenia, who had believed him to be dead,
recognizes him and plans for all three of them to escape.
The plan is successful, and the goddess Athena appears at
the end to instruct the Taurian king that the gods wish the
image of Artemis to rest in Athens, where the rites will
no longer be performed with human sacrifice.

307 _____. "Pan, " in Grenstone Poems. New York: Stokes,
1917.
This quatrain manages to convey a good deal of irony and
wit in few words and one well-defined scene: a farmer is
chopping down trees and asks the narrator what he is reading. Pan Is Dead, the narrator says, at which the farmer
laughs, "What a name, " and keeps on hacking away at the
trees.

308 _____. "The Singing Faun, " in A Canticle of Pan (1920),
is a study of contrasts: the singing faun who has "come
down from the hill of trees" and the world of civilization
with its weapons and killings.

BYRON, George Gordon, Lord (1788-1824, English)

309 "The Curse of Minerva, " in The Complete Poetical Works of
Lord Byron, ed. by Paul Elmer More. Boston: Houghton, Mifflin, 1905.
This satire is based on the myth that Odysseus and some
other impious Greeks abducted the statue of Pallas Athena
--the Palladium--from a temple in Troy, and for that sac-
rilege were severely punished by Athena, who had heretofore been their patron goddess. In Byron's poem it is
Thomas Bruce (1766-1841), the Earl of Elgin, who carried
off the Greek sculpture from the Parthenon in Athens during the years 1803-1812. These famous pieces have subsequently been known as "the Elgin Marbles" (see poem by
Keats, below). Byron, who was intensely pro-Greece, vig-
orously objected to this action, and wrote his poem in

Athens, March 1811. The "sacriledge" was further intensified by the fact that some of the carvings were destroyed
in the process of attempting to remove them from the Parthenon.

310 _____. "Prometheus, " in Poetical Works (1905), is a praise
of the god "Titan, " who did not despise the sufferings of
mortals. Byron says, "Thy Godlike crime was to be kind, "
to help humanity in its wretchedness. It is pointed out
that the punishment was not only "the rock, the vulture,
and the chain, " but the immortality of the god, whose punishment will not end, the gods can torture "where they cannot kill. " It has been pointed out by Paul Elmer More
that the character of Prometheus early and strongly attracted Byron--as it did Shelley--and there are many allusions to the god in his later works. Indeed his mind wav-
ered almost to the end between the heroic defiance of
Prometheus and the cynical defiance of Don Juan.

CALL, Wathen Mark Wilks (1817-1890, English)

311 "Admetus, " in Reverberations. London: Trübner, 1876.
This poem, a sequel to "Alcestis" (below), tells of Hercules rescuing Alcestis from "King Death" and restoring
her to her husband and children.

312 _____. "Alcestis, " in Reverberations (1876), based on the
myth of the death of Alcestis, consists largely of her
leavetaking of the earth, her husband, and her children.
This poem, together with "Admetus, " discussed above,
fairly well cover the events given in Euripides' play
"Alcestis. "

313 _____. "The Legend of Ariadne, " in Golden Histories.
London: Smith, Elder, 1871.
For all its length and seeming complexity, six books in
some seventy pages, "The Legend ..." consists primarily
of embroidery and unrelated details. The story line is
simple: after he kills the Minotaur, Theseus sails from
Crete, taking with him Ariadne and her young sister,
Phaedre. Later he abandons Ariadne, and she is chosen
by Bacchus to be his wife. Much of the poem is taken up
with description of Bacchus, his followers, and his glory
as a god. At the conclusion they are married, and "Ariadne
is crown'd by deathless hands, " sitting on a "celestial
throne. "

CALVERLY, Charles Stuart (1831-1884, English)

314 Although this poet did not write any mythological poems, he
is included in this study because of the interest in his

63

translations from Greek into English, and from English into Latin. See The Complete Works of C. S. Calverly, with a biography by Sir Walter J. Sendell (London: Bell, 1901), which contains Milton's "Lycidas," Tennyson's "Oenone," and Landor's "Nereid Maids," translated into Latin from English. Calverly's best work, however, is a translation of Theocritus, a third-century B.C. Greek poet, into English verse. This work contains poems on a number of well-known mythological themes: "The Death of Daphnis"; "The Sorceress" (Circe); "The Triumph of Daphnis"; "Hylas"; "The Festival of Adonis"; "The Sons of Leda" (Castor and Pollux); "The Infant Heracles"; "Heracles, the Lion Slayer"; "The Bacchanals"; and "The Death of Adonis."

CAMPBELL, Thomas (1777-1844, English)

315 "Song of the Greeks," in The Poetical Works of Thomas Campbell, ed. by Rev. W. A. Hill. London: Moxon, 1854.
Although not strictly mythological, Campbell's poem does evoke some images of ancient Greek mythology. He calls the Greeks "Achaians," refers to them as sprung from the gods, and says that the Nine (muses) shall again inhabit the land. The poem was written around 1821 on the occasion of the insurrection of the Greeks against the Turks --"crescent," "Mahomet's slaves," "the turban," "yon Mussulman," are all referred to in the poem. After six years of fighting alone ("no succour advances, / Nor Christendom's chivalrous lances/ Are stretched to our aid") European countries intervened, and Greece was declared free. This poem, with Campbell's "The Battle of the Baltic," was studied by George Saintsbury in "English War-Songs--Campbell," in Essays and Papers, Vol. I, pp. 330-355.

CAMUS, Albert (1913-1960, French)

316 "Helen's Exile," an essay (first published in French in 1948), in The Myth of Sisyphus and Other Essays, trans. by Justin O'Brien. New York: Knopf, 1955.
Helen in this work stands for beauty, which Camus says the modern world has exiled. "Our time, has fed its despair on ugliness and convulsions." Only the artist still struggles for freedom, and those who are struggling for freedom are ultimately fighting for beauty. In conclusion Camus says that we may hope for victory: "The Trojan war is being fought far from the battlefields! Once more the dreadful walls of the modern city will fall to deliver up the beauty of Helen."

317 _____. "The Minotaur: or, the Stop in Oran," an essay
        (first published in French in 1939), in The Myth ... (1955),
        is an analysis of Oran, a city in Northwest Algeria, which
        attracts much tourist interest. In his description of the
        city Camus describes a labyrinthine affair, saying that it
        is a "walled town that turns its back to the sea," and "has
        been built up by turning back on itself like a snail." Oran
        is a great "circular yellow wall covered with a leaden sky,"
        a real labyrinth, in which you turn round and round in the
        "pale oppressive streets," and are eventually devoured by
        the Minotaur," the Minotaur being boredom. He concludes
        by saying that the citizens of Oran "have given up wander-
        ing. They have accepted being eaten."

318 _____. "The Myth of Sisyphus," an essay (first published
        in French in 1943), in The Myth ... (1955), is one of the
        truly brilliant compositions in which theme and form com-
        bine to make a perfect whole. The subject is, of course,
        Sisyphus, whom the gods condemned to roll a rock to the
        top of a mountain, whence the stone would immediately fall
        back. Camus says that for some reason the gods had
        thought that "there is no more dreadful punishment than
        futile and hopeless labor." The reasons for Sisyphus' pun-
        ishment are somewhat varied: one myth has it that he
        stole the secrets of the gods and was guilty of a "certain
        levity" in regard to the august beings; Homer says that
        Sisyphus put Death in chains, and Hades could not endure
        this effrontery; still another myth says that Sisyphus died
        and went into the Underworld. He obtained permission
        from Hades to return to earth in order to punish his wife
        for not paying proper respect to his body. Once on earth,
        he could not bring himself to return to the infernal dark-
        ness, and stayed many years enjoying the sun, the spar-
        kling sea, and all the other wonderful bounties of life.
        Eventually the gods sent for him and returned him to the
        Underworld, where "his rock was ready for him."
            Camus sees Sisyphus as the prototype of the modern
        absurd hero: we discover that there is no correspondence
        between the human mind, which needs meaning and coher-
        ence, and the world, which is without intelligence or mean-
        ing. Sisyphus is such a man, conscious of the meaningless
        task that he has been given to perform, and yet "superior
        to his fate." He is stronger than his rock, since there is
        "no fate that cannot be surmounted by scorn."

CARMAN, Bliss (1861-1929, Canadian)

319 "At Phaedra's Tomb," in The Pipes of Pan: Vol. I, From
        the Book of Myths. Boston: Page, 1904.
        The narrator here is "one more passer-by," who stops
        and looks at the old grey ruin of a tomb and a temple,
        the tomb that of Phaedra, the wife of Theseus who loved

Hippolytus, and the temple built by Phaedra to Aphrodite in hopes of winning the love of Hippolytus. Now it is all gone, and Phaedra is but a "name, a story, and a tomb."

320 _____. "Daphne," in The Pipes of Pan (1904), is written of the girl who was changed into a laurel tree when the god Apollo pursued her. The narrator here recognizes her in the laurel tree, as if she is about "to shed the flowery guise" and be herself once more. He begs her to do so, and promises her a greater love in return.

321 _____. "The Dead Faun," in The Pipes of Pan (1904), begins with the question, "Who hath done this thing?," referring to the killing of the faun. From this point the poem is descriptive of all aspects of death: the eyes shall look no more, the fingers play no more, the sensitive ears hear no more, the feet rove no more. The image of the dead faun is all the more pathetic because the faun was a creature that knew nothing but joy and playful mirth in the woodlands, but now he is dead.

322 _____. "Hylas," in The Pipes of Pan (1904), is a short narrative of the youth loved by a water-nymph, who pulled him under to his death. He was never found, but in the springtime the villagers of that country still call, "Hylas, Hylas!"

323 _____. "Legends of the Reed," in The Pipes of Pan (1904), consists of four separate poems that deal with the history of the wood-pipe, or reed. In "Marsyas" the satyr finds the instrument that Athena tossed away because it made her face disagreeable when she puckered her lips to play it. It suits the satyr perfectly, and he plays for all the woodland creatures. In "Syrinx" the story is told of the nymph who tried to elude the amorous grasp of the god Pan, and was changed into a reed that Pan then fashioned into the musical pipes. "The Magic Flute" is an Egyptian folktale of the lover who played his flute-strain to win his love, but without success. His memory still lingers, however, in the rain and wind and other mournful sounds that nature makes. "A Shepherd in Lesbos," concludes the sequence of poems, and deals with a "mad young shepherd" whose music stops all travelers as they pass his cabin. They listen to mournful, strange sounds, but they do not understand.

324 _____. "The Lost Dryad," in The Pipes of Pan (1904), is Daphne, who became the laurel tree and is now lost. Her lover seeks her in all regions, praying to Mother Earth that he will soon find her.

325 _____. "The Pipes of Pan," in The Pipes of Pan (1904),
is the story of how Pan's music came to be the way it is:
"Something sad and calm and old, / Like an eerie minor
strain." Pan has experienced all the sadness that life has
to offer, and yet he, like nature, renews himself and continues to pipe songs that are always new. In conclusion
the poet says, "the world is growing old," but its joys
grow greater as they come and go.

326 _____. "The Urban Pan," in Bliss Carman's Poems. New
York: Dodd, Mead, 1931.
The setting of this poem is the city in the Spring, and the
narrator awakes to a fanciful vision of a "smiling swarthy,
hairy man/ With kindling eye," whom he immediately recognizes as Pan. In reality it is the hurdy-gurdy man, but
the children follow him and listen to the music, and they
are enchanted by the magic.

327 _____. "A Young Pan's Prayer," in The Pipes of Pan
(1904), is the concluding poem of this volume, and is in
effect the poet's prayer that his poems, his "music," be
all that the "Pipes of Pan" stand for: the magic, the enchantment, the songs of earth and life and nature, the
"strength of the hills and the strength of the sea."

CARPENTER, Edward (1844-1929, English)

328 "Narcissus," in Narcissus and Other Poems. London: King,
1873.
This version of the Narcissus myth focuses on the story of
Echo, the maiden who loved Narcissus and was rejected by
him in favor of his own image, which he found so attractive
in a pool of water. Echo had already been punished by
Hera by being condemned to repeat the last words said by
others. After Narcissus scorned her love, she wasted
away and became just a voice.

329 _____. "Persephone," in Narcissus (1873), is a long narrative that tells the story of Demeter's daughter as she
was carried away by Hades to be his queen in the Underworld. However, the emphasis in this poem is not so much
the story as it is the changes that occurred as a result of
the event. Heretofore humanity had known only the growing
season, but after Persephone became the Queen of Hades,
the seasons were divided, as was her life divided between
being his wife and the daughter of Demeter, the Earth.
Now there was a growing season, Spring and Summer, and
a season of rest and quiet, Autumn and Winter.

330 _____. "Sleeping Venus," in Narcissus (1873), is presented
as a painting, describing one feature at a time--her face,

her lips, the flowing limbs, her forehead--all indescribably beautiful.

331 _____. "The Veiled Isis, or the Nature Worshipper," in Narcissus (1873), refers to the Egyptian goddess, who with her brother Osiris encompassed the totality of nature. On her statues were these words: "I am all that has been, that shall be, and none among mortals has hitherto taken off my veil." In Carpenter's poem the narrator praises and worships all the facets of nature, but has never seen beneath its appearances. In the end we will go to our death and become a part of nature, but we will still not see the face of "mother Isis."

332 _____. "Venus Aphrodite," in Narcissus (1873), is a detailed description of the birth of Venus, the goddess of Love, rising from the sea-foam, near the island of Cyprus. There are several myths of the origin of this goddess, but the most popular has always been that of her emerging from the waves. The word "Aphrodite" means sea-foam.

CARRYL, Guy Wetmore (1873-1904, American)

333 "Atlantis," in The Garden of Years and Other Poems. New York and London: Putnam, 1904.
The lost continent of Atlantis is described as though it exists at the bottom of the sea, sleeping in the "dim, dead calm," where there is no night or day, no seasons, no change. In conclusion the poet compares Atlantis to the many sunken ships of the ages, and says they sleep side by side "until the sea shall render up her dead."

334 _____. "Hesperia," in The Garden (1904), was an imaginary western land, meaning "Land of Evening." The poet sees it as the land of peace, and longs to "claim" it as his.

335 _____. "Narcissus," in The Garden (1904), the son of the river-god Cephissus, fell in love with his own image as reflected in a pool of water. He ignored all advances of love, and since he could not embrace the image in the pool of water, he lay beside it until he wasted away and died. For him nothing else existed, neither "time's swift flight, the dawn, and the noon, and the night, / The sun's gold glory, the moon's white mystery."

336 _____. "The Passing of Pan," in The Garden (1904), commemorates all the creatures--naiads, hamadryads, nymphs, woodmaidens--who adore Pan and run before him as he passes.

337 _____. "Phoebus Apollo," in The Garden (1904), is a
     prayer to the god by a modern narrator, who says that
     "we have hearkened to creeds unnumbered," and have found
     that the Delphic creed is best. Apollo is called "Monarch
     of light and laughter, honor, and trust, and truth, / God of
     all inspiration, King of eternal youth."

338 _____. "Pompeii," in The Garden (1904), is only slightly
     mythological, being mostly a historical account of the vol-
     cano that erupted and destroyed the city in the first cen-
     tury A.D. Mythologically speaking, the town was built by
     Hercules, and the volcano that destroyed it was regarded
     as a sleeping giant. The city prospered and made itself
     beautiful, and "still the giant slept." Then one day every-
     thing was gone, and "the giant sleeps again."

CATHER, Willa (1873-1947, American)

339 "Antinous," in April Twilights and Other Poems. New York:
     Knopf, 1903. Reprinted and ed. with a new Introduc-
     tion by Bernice Slote. Lincoln: University of Nebraska
     Press, 1962.
     Antinous was a youth of Bithynia of whom the emperor Ha-
     drian (A.D. 76-138) was so fond that at his death he erected
     a temple to him, and required his subjects to pay homage
     to his memory. One account of Antinous' death is that he
     offered himself as a sacrificial victim to honor the emperor.
     Willa Cather's poem describes the youth as nearly godlike,
     but flawed with a "frowning brow" and a "sick soul."

340 _____. "Lament for Marsyas," in April Twilights (1962)
     refers to the satyr who lost a musical contest with Apollo
     and was brutally killed by the god. This brief poem is
     simply a lament for his death, telling the maidens that they
     need not wait for him; he will not come again.

341 _____. "Winter at Delphi," in April Twilights (1962), is
     spoken by the priestess who attends Apollo's temple and
     waits for the god to return The Spring will return, Pan
     will return, but will Apollo return? The answer seems to
     be that he will not, since he is the "god who never comes
     back."

CAWEIN, Madison Julius (1865-1914, American)

342 "Aphrodite," in Blooms of the Berry. Louisville, Ky.: Mor-
     ton, 1887.
     Cawein's poem is a description of the goddess rising from
     the sea-foam. Details of the ocean, the wind, the stars,
     and the night are abundant and beautiful. Her birth is at-
     tended by various other forms of sea-life, Tritons, Oceanids,

dolphins, Nereids--all in attendance on this "child of the airy foam and queen of love."

343 _____. "Apollo," in Intimations of the Beautiful. New York: Putnam, 1894.
Developed in three parts, this poem begins with a series of praises for Apollo as the god of music and song. His songs have embraced a variety of life forces, and none else are comparable. In the concluding section, however, the poet strangely moves to another subject, the song of "a Nation," America presumably, and praises the song of liberty and equality that this nation sings.

344 _____. "Argonauts," in Intimations (1894), makes use of all the imagery connected with Jason and his search for the Golden Fleece to draw a parallel between the mythological hero and the ideal searcher, whose "purpose steers afar," whose Golden Fleece is the "farthest star."

345 _____. "Artemis," in The Triumph of Music and Other Lyrics. Louisville, Ky.: Morton, 1888.
For the most part "Artemis" is an overview of the functions of this goddess, as the huntress, as the maiden goddess, as the moon. In conclusion the myth of Endymion is referred to, and the poet exclaims that after looking full upon the goddess, nothing was left to Endymion but death. The older goddess Selene is usually associated with the Endymion story.

346 _____. "Before the Temple," in Intimations (1894), does not name the goddess who is described, but it is probably Thetis, the Nereid mother of Achilles, who has assumed a mortal form to sit on the steps of the temple and watch the parade of heroic soldiers, which includes Achilles, as they march "towards the siege of Troy."

347 _____. "Circe," in Intimations (1894), is based on the myth that this goddess had the ability to turn human beings into swine. The narrator here reflects that once a beautiful woman whom he loved also turned him into a "brute" and a "beast."

348 _____. "The Dead Faun," in Intimations (1894), represents the animal-like creature as a type of total innocence and happiness. He lived in the joy of nature and took each day for its worth. When it came time to die, he lay down in the "long-loved woods" and passed into nature.

349 _____. "The Dead Oread," in Blooms of the Berry (1887), is similar to "The Dead Faun," in that it portrays the oread, the mountain nymph, as a natural and happy creature.

Even her death is not without its blessing: she will no
longer be chased by some "unhallowed Pan with lust," or
have to flee the "bacchanals that mock, / Wine-wild, the
long, mad nights."

350 _____. "Demeter," in Blooms of the Berry (1887), is an
account of the goddess as she travels over the earth seeking her lost daughter, Persephone, who had been abducted
by Hades to be his queen in the Underworld. The theme
of the composition is built around the universality of suffering, life, and death.

351 _____. "Dionysia," in Myth and Romance. New York:
Putnam; London: Knickerbocker, 1899.
The title refers to the drunken celebrations in honor of
Dionysus, the god of wine and fertility. This poem, however, portrays a vision of the narrator, as he imagines
that once again he sees a woman whom he has loved, and
they are together, carried away into frenzied heights of
passion, as the maenads of the Dionysia were overcome
with passion and irrationality.

352 _____. "Dionysus," in Blooms of the Berry (1887), praises
the universality of the god and suggests that perhaps he is
the most powerful of all from "India to the flooding Nile."
Several gods outside Greek mythology are referred to, and
their powers are also subservient to Dionysus.

353 _____. "The Dryad," in The Triumph of Music (1888), is
a slight description of the dryad, a nymph of the woods,
how her beauty flashes here and there, and how finally she
is chased and sometimes assaulted by the "amorous Pan."

354 _____. "Eleusinian," in Intimations (1894), is derived from
the name Eleusis, the town associated with the rites of
Demeter and Persephone. The word, however, has a
broader application, and came to be almost synonymous
with "mysteries," which were celebrated throughout Greece
and honored many of the gods.

355 _____. "Hylas," in New Poems. London: Richards, 1909.
Cawein's poem is unique in its point of view, that of Hylas
from the shadowy, watery world of the nymph who had pulled
him under. He remembers his master Heracles, the Argonauts, the Mysian shore, the wood of Cyzicus. This recollection is presented by way of the singing of the hylas, or
the tree-frogs who inhabit the woods.

356 _____. "Leander to Hero," in Accolon of Gaul with Other
Poems. Louisville, Ky.: Morton, 1889.
This poem represents the lover Leander as he is taking
leave of the maiden Hero. He says, ironically, that she
will follow him, meaning in thought and love. Finally she
does follow him, in death after Leander has drowned.

357 _____. "Lethe," in Intimations (1894), has little mythology other than the title, which refers to the river Lethe in the Underworld. It is the river of forgetfulness, and this poem focuses on the hell of remembering before forgetfulness comes.

358 _____. "Lotus," in Intimations (1894), another poem that calls upon mythology for its title, develops a personal story of a man and woman who loved each other until she died. After her death he reflects that "she and I were shadows / And all our world, a dream." The lotus is referred to in the Odyssey as a fruit that produces a dreamlike state of existence, pleasant but unreal.

359 _____. "Mnemosyne," in The Triumph of Music (1888), is a four-line description of a statue of Memory, the goddess Mnemosyne. She is said to have "love and hate" chiseled on her brow as she sits with "dead roses in her hands."

360 _____. "Moly," in Intimations (1894), refers to the magic herb that Hermes gave to Odysseus to save him from the enchantments of Circe. The poet uses the allusion to say that he prefers to "lean upon" realities and not be enchanted by the magic of vision and imagination.

361 _____. "Myth and Romance," in Myth and Romance (1899), is a fantasy of nature as the poet looks forth "to greet the glad-faced Spring." Perhaps he will see a dryad, a naiad, an oread, a satyr. He may even encounter Pan or Sylvanus. In any case, he says, wherever he goes, "Myth, Romance ... reach out bewildering arms," and compel him to follow.

362 _____. "The Naiad," in Intimations (1894), is a description of the water-nymph as she sits among the irises and sings her beautiful song. She herself is beautiful in face and limb, but no one will ever see her who is not wise with love for nature.

363 _____. "Pan," in The Triumph of Music (1888), pays tribute to the god of the woods, the piper of hidden mountain places, the ruler of nature, "Pan of many faces."

364 _____. "The Paphian Venus," in Intimations (1894), portrays the Venus Mylitta, or the Assyrian-Babylonian deity also called Astarte. It is brought out in the poem that this is a most unidealized form of love-goddess and that the maidens of her temple were allowed to practice prostitution. This Venus, however, was destined to be replaced by Venus Aphrodite, a more idealized form of love.

365 _____. "Persephone," in Blooms of the Berry (1887), is a

dirgelike poem for the beautiful young goddess who was
carried to the "horrid gulfs below," as the queen of the
shadowy Underworld.   The poet-narrator calls Hades and
Zeus "false gods" who would give away the maiden without
"a mother's sanction or her knowledge." With Persephone's
leaving, all nature was the loser.

366   _____. "Sibylline," in Intimations (1894), suggests rather
than specifies a mythological theme.   The imagery consists
principally of apple blossoms as they are whirled about in
a storm, and this suggests the leaves of the Sibyl, the
priestess of Apollo, as she tosses her leaves about, reading the future in their random falling.

367   _____. "The Sirens," in The Triumph of Music (1888), is
well contained in two four-line stanzas.   The narrator
makes a comparison between himself and Odysseus and
tells the Sirens to sing on.   They cannot distract him, for
there is one sweet voice in his heart that gently, firmly
draws him home.

368   _____. "Thamus," in Red Leaves and Roses.   New York:
Putnam; London: Knickerbocker, 1893.
The name "Thamus" has no mythological basis, but the
narrative of Cawein's poem is a well-known legend that
has its origin in Plutarch.   It is said that at the moment
of Christ's birth, the news was carried throughout the
Pagan world, "great Pan is dead," "Pan is dead." Thamus
of this poem is told by a mysterious voice to spread this
word.   At first he ignores the command; then, as he sees
the great shrines crumbling and the gods and goddesses in
ruin, he fearfully cries out.

369   _____. "Wood Myths," in New Poems (1909), is a romantic
composition in which the narrator tells what he saw on a
moonlight night: all the creatures of the forest, nymph,
oread, faun, satyr, even "old Pan himself." He further
adds, "suddenly Diana stood, / Slim as a shaft of moonlight," and concludes that the "gods are not dead"; they
remain, "the unseen forces" of nature.

CHURCH, Richard (1893-1972, English)

370   "As Plato Says," in The Collected Poems of Richard Church.
London: Dent, 1948.
This poem contains less mythology than philosophy, but
does make use of one important mythological allusion to
Apollo as "Soul of Earth's soul, the solar spirit." The
principal theme of the poem is a contrast between the ideal
world as envisioned by Plato and the real world.   In that
"world behind the world," the world of Plato's ideal forms
and images, everything that humanity dreams of may be
true, and our "eternal tale of hope is heard."

371 _____. "Atlantis," in Collected Poems (1948), like the poem above, examines the differences between the ideal and the real, the ideal in this case being Atlantis "lost under the waves."

372 _____. "Endymion by Day," in Collected Poems (1948), tells of the "moon-queen" coming to Endymion "in the heat of noon," for love when no one can see her, but he continued to sleep and dream.

373 _____. "Narcissus," in Collected Poems (1948), is based on the myth of the lad who gazed at himself in a pool, infatuated with the image he saw, until he fell in and drowned. This poem suggests that we close our eyes and "gaze up and inward" to our minds. Here each of us may discover either a universe or a dunce. If we discover a universe, we will dream that we are a king--unless we indeed be a dunce.

374 _____. "Niobe," in Collected Poems (1948), is a grief-stricken cry by the mother who has lost all her children to the wrath of Artemis, who killed the girls, and Apollo, who killed the boys. In this poem Niobe offers the father one of their daughters and bids him to "grieve." Bitterly and ironically, she says "I was her mother; I dare not mourn."

CIARDI, John (1916- , American)

375 "Of Heroes Home from Troy and More Coming," in 39 Poems by John Ciardi. New Brunswick, N.J.: Rutgers State University Press, 1959.
This brief poem reduces the heroes of Troy, and by implication of any other war, to the status of "boys," small ones at that, and having not at all the stature that legend and song attribute to them. The difficulty becomes apparent when one tries to imagine these heroes "home from Troy" with the war over and heroics gone.

376 _____. "Ulysses," in 39 Poems (1959), is a perfect combination of subject and imagery. By focusing on the hero Ulysses at the end of his journey, Ciardi effectively illustrates the difference between the real and the imaginary. As Ulysses is nearly home, he turns to "remember the sea," and it was not the sea of his memory. He encounters an old man, "an oaf chewing a stalk of garlic"; he offers to pay the old man for one of his goats and then wants to be left alone. The old man simply "stayed," "would not be scared off, and would not be whipped off." In anger that the gods would send such a sorry man in his

path, Ulysses prayed for him to leave, but he would not.
Ulysses killed him and then all his goats and piled them
on one funeral pyre. In utter disgust he lost his way and
knew that he could never return. All that he loved was
dead, and he "was woven to the dead men. "

CLOUGH, Arthur Hugh (1819-1861, English)

377 "Actaeon," in The Poems of Arthur Hugh Clough, ed. by H. F.
        Lowry, A. L. P. Norrington, and F. L. Mulhauser.
        Oxford: Clarendon, 1951.
        Clough's is a traditional account of the unfortunate hunter
        who comes upon Artemis while she is bathing, and the out-
        raged goddess changes him into an "antlered stag," which
        his own hounds set upon and tear to pieces. The poem
        closes with an image of Artemis as a divinity indifferent
        to her devotee's fate. The early lines of the poem are
        perhaps too rich with details of the natural setting, the
        trees overshadowing the pool of clear water, the oleanders,
        the white poplars, fig-tree, and other images of "green
        herbage. "

378 _____. "Selene," in The Poems (1951), listed in the sec-
        tion on "Unfinished Poems," is somewhat chaotic and lack-
        ing in unity, but it seems to be a love song of the Sun to
        the Moon, Selene. The principal image throughout the com-
        position is one of motion, the lover--the Sun--and the be-
        loved--the Moon--drawn inevitably upon the same line but
        never touching.

379 _____. "Uranus," in The Poems (1951), is about the planet
        named for the primordial god, the seventh planet in our
        solar system, identified in 1781. In this poem Clough
        speculates on the possibility of life on other planets, "men
        of other frame than ours. "

COCTEAU, Jean (1889-1963, French)

380 "Antigone," adapted from the Greek tragedy by Sophocles.
        Trans. by Carl Wildman, in Five Plays by Jean Cocteau.
        New York: Hill and Wang, 1961.
        This play was produced in 1928, with scenery by Picasso,
        a musical score by Honegger, costumes by Chanel, and
        masks by the author himself. Although it follows the story
        laid down by Sophocles, Cocteau's play is meant to appeal
        to the "unconscious" and therefore dispenses with traditional
        dialogue. The characters speak as though no one else were
        present. The problems of Antigone, a young girl, are
        translated into problems of the adolescent, the rebellion
        against authority and the search for personal identity.

381 _____. "Bacchus," trans. by Mary Hoeck, in The Infernal
Machine and Other Plays by Jean Cocteau. New York:
New Directions, 1963.
First produced in 1951, this play has its setting in a small
German town in the sixteenth century. A custom in this
town gives a boy or man absolute power for one week, a
parallel version of the ancient ritual of Bacchus-Dionysus
that made someone king for a year and was killed or sacrificed at the end of his reign. In Cocteau's play Hans, the
village idiot, is elected to be Bacchus, and he turns out to
be a revolutionary, a hater of leaders and the Church. The
conflict develops between Hans and a cardinal, sent from
Rome to investigate heresy. Hans is arrested and later
dies. His friends at first are proud of him because he did
not recant, but when the cardinal lies and says he did recant, they become bitter and cynical, and the play ends on
this note.

382 _____. "The Infernal Machine," trans. by Albert Bermel,
in Other Plays (1963), was first performed in Paris in
1934 (in a translation by Carl Wildman); the Bermel translation was performed in New York in 1958. It is called a
"cycle," which means it consists of four acts, each one a
complete play within itself. In the first act Jocasta, an
aging woman, is warned by the ghost of her husband that a
young conqueror is soon to arrive in Thebes. Act II brings
Oedipus to a confrontation with the Sphinx, who tells him
the answer to her riddle, knowing the fate that is ultimately
to be his. Act III is the wedding-night of Oedipus and Jocasta, and in the final act, seventeen years later, the tragedy of Sophocles unfolds.
    The play begins with a Voice telling the audience
what is about to transpire. The language is memorable:
"Watch now, spectator. Before you is a fully wound machine. Slowly its spring will unwind the entire span of
human life. It is one of the most perfect machines devised
by the infernal gods for the mathematical annihilation of a
mortal. "

383 _____. "King Oedipus," in Five Plays (1961), is the libretto
for an opera-oratorio with music by Igor Stravinsky. It was
produced in Paris in 1928 and translated into English in
1949. The content is similar to Act IV of The Infernal
Machine.

384 _____. "Orphée," trans. by Carl Wildman, in Five Plays
(1961), is regarded as Cocteau's masterpiece. It was written in 1925 and first performed in Paris in June 1926. An
English translation was performed in London in 1928. The
play is presented in thirteen consecutive scenes, and follows
the basic story of Orpheus and the death of Eurydice. Carl

Wildman, the translator, has said that it has the effect of music on people. On the other hand, it has been called "clever but silly." Death in the form of a very beautiful young woman wears a bright pink evening dress and fur cloak, while her assistants wear uniform linen masks and the rubber gloves of operating surgeons, as they attend the dying Eurydice. Orpheus later submits an obscene poem to a contest and when he loses he is torn to pieces and cast into a river. The last scene takes place in heaven, where he is searching for Eurydice.

COFFIN, Robert P. Tristram (1892-1955, American)

385 "The House of Jason," in Dew and Bronze. New York: Boni, 1927.
The house of Jason in this poem is that of the poet's neighbor, which he had passed "a thousand, thousand times or more," but he had never noticed "the horned head of a golden ram." The Golden Fleece myth is used metaphorically to say that the neighbor has been through an extraordinary crisis of some sort, "as far as Hell / And back that day," and is now celebrating with a festival.

386 _____. "Lamps Once Were Being Lit in Troy," in Dew and Bronze (1927). Reprinted in Collected Poems. New York: Macmillan, 1939.
The simple imagery of this poem, the lighting of the lamps, gives a dimension of reality to Troy that is sometimes lost in a large-scale epic. The mythological characters for a moment seem real--Paris, Helen, Andromache, Hector-- and Troy "was urns and dust and dreams / Three thousand years ago."

COLERIDGE, Ernest Hartley (1796-1849, English)

387 "Diana and Endymion," in The Complete Poetical Works of Hartley Coleridge, ed. with Introduction by Ramsay Colles. London: Routledge; New York: Dutton, 1908.
This sonnet calls the myth of the moon and Endymion a "quaint old Fable," and yet the poet says it is no more outrageous than the idea that the stars control human destiny.

388 _____. "Homer," in Poetical Works (1908), consists of two sonnets, which resemble two versions of the same theme. Homer is glorified as the "Great Poet of thy kind," in one poem and called "Great Poet of mankind," in the other. Further, the Greek poet is one who could describe human greatness but could also tell how "Priam wept, or shame-struck Helen pined." In the other version Coleridge says, "Death is lovely in thy tale enshrined."

COLERIDGE, continued

389 _____. "Prometheus," in Poetical Works (1908), is presented in dramatic form, with the scene in a desolate spot
where Prometheus is chained to a rock. The dialogue is
between the titan and a chorus of sylphs, who question and
comment on the situation. Prometheus reveals his offense
against the gods, but he is unrepentant and says that he
knows all, including the secret that will set him free. The
poem ends with a song of nymphs, who praise the joys and
triumphs of nature and humanity; which needs to "fear no
more."

COLERIDGE, Mary Elizabeth (1861-1907, English)

390 "Alcestis to Admetus," in Poems by Mary Elizabeth Coleridge.
London: Mathews, 1908.
This poem expresses a question that many readers of the
Alcestis-Admetus myth must have felt: after Alcestis died
in her husband's place, how long could he wait before de-
cently remarrying? Euripides' play "Alcestis" says that
Hercules brought Alcestis back from the dead, but basically
the myth is simply that she took her husband's place when
Death came for him. Miss Coleridge has Admetus waiting
a year before marrying again, and Alcestis rebukes him for
doing so.

391 _____. "On a Bas-Relief of Pelops and Hippodameia," in
Poems (1908), is mythological in title only. The subject is
the stone statue that was lost and lay many years under the
sea. The husband and wife whose forms were copies from
nature returned to nature, where the wind and waves per-
fected "those lines of beauty" until at length the work was
complete and "a perfect thing was rescued from the deep."

COWLEY, Malcolm (1898- , American)

392 "Leander," in Blue Juniata: Collected Poems. New York:
Cape and Smith, 1929.
Cowley's poem grows out of the Hero-Leander story of the
two lovers who were destined to die young. Hero was the
beautiful priestess in love with Leander, who swam the
Hellespont river in order to be with her. Finally he drowned,
and Hero in despair threw herself into the sea. Cowley's
poem deals only with the drowning, saying "the sea flung
her arms about his arms / in foam, mingled her hair with
his." As he died he sank "through immense halls of darkness, infinite / chambers of dream." The sea dressed his
body as she could: in wreaths of algae, with coral and
pearl. Now he drifts forever, "through indefinite Marquesas,"
"spinning in the typhoon," and time is a "secret frozen" in
his smile.

COX, George W. see FREEMAN, Edward Augustus

CRANCH, Christopher Pearse (1813-1892, American)

393 "Atalanta," in The Bird and the Bell. Boston: Osgood, 1875.
     Reprinted New York: Arno, 1972.
     Atalanta is best known in connection with the Calydonian
     Boar Hunt and the hero Meleager, who fell in love with
     her. The poem by Cranch, however, makes use of a sub-
     sequent episode in which Atalanta races with Melanion (or
     Hippomenes), loses because he tricks her into stopping to
     pick up three golden apples, and later marries him. Cranch
     uses the episode to moralize and warn America that "the
     fleetest in the race are lost, / If in their gold alone they
     boast. "

394 _____. "Iapis," in The Bird and the Bell (1875), in spite
     of its length, is a simple poem telling how Iapis, the son
     of Iasius of Troy, received his gift of healing from the god
     Apollo. The god would have given Iapis the gifts of music,
     prophecy, or archery, but he chose the art of healing. The
     story is derived from Virgil's Aeneid, Book XII, 391-405,
     in which Aeneas is wounded and Iapis saves him with Aphro-
     dite's help.

CRANE, Hart (1899-1932, American)

395 "Atlantis, " in Collected Poems of Hart Crane, ed. by Waldo
     Frank. New York: Liveright, 1933.
     Although "Atlantis" is the concluding poem of Crane's long
     work The Bridge, it is complete in itself and stands as the
     author's final statement on the theme of poet as a modern
     discoverer. In this case the lost continent of Atlantis is
     the symbol of the Absolute, even as the Golden Fleece was
     the ultimate goal for Jason, and Crane seems to conclude
     that the true meaning of the search is not in the thing sought,
     but in the seeking.

396 _____. "For the Marriage of Faustus and Helen, " in Com-
     plete Poems, ed. with Introduction by Brom Weber.
     Garden City, N. Y. : Doubleday, 1966.
     In this composition the poet-narrator assumes the identity
     of Faustus, standing for knowledge, and Helen is the arche-
     type of beauty. Helen, for this Faustus, is the girl he
     meets on a streetcar and pursues through a penthouse
     nightclub of a metropolitan hotel. In the concluding part
     of the poem the narrator ceases to be concerned merely
     with his own salvation by beauty and turns to a world that
     has been devastated by war. He sees this war as the mod-
     ern counterpart of the battle of Troy, and only through
     beauty can humanity rise above its little frame in time.

CREELEY, Robert (1926-   , American)

397 "The Death of Venus," in For Love: Poems 1950-1960. New
        York: Scribner, 1962.
        Creeley evokes the imagery of Venus rising from the sea-
        foam, but instead of the traditional view of the goddess as
        a beautiful ideal of love, this poem is structured around
        ugly and discordant themes. Such terms as "Sea-beast,"
        "she snorted," and "sank," point to the death of the god-
        dess of love and beauty. This work illustrates Creeley's
        theory of poetry, that there are "no ideas but in things"
        and that "things are made of words. "

398 _____. "Kore, " in For Love (1962), is an extremely mod-
        ernistic statement on the abduction of Persephone, daughter
        of the earth-goddess Demeter. The name Kore, meaning
        "Maid, " was the title of the Underworld deity as worshiped
        at Eleusis. She symbolized the fertility of crop growth.
        The "goat men" of the poem are satyrs, usually depicted
        in company with the god Dionysus. They are fertility spirits
        and thus may associate with Persephone, but it is ironic
        that they are leading her to the house of Hades, which has
        no connection with the fertility motif.

CUNNINGHAM, James Vincent (1911-   , American)

399 "The Helmsman: An Ode," in The Exclusions of a Rhyme:
        Poems and Epigrams. Denver: Swallow, 1960.
        The voyage, in this poem, is that of the soul, "through age
        to wisdom, " and the helmsman is the individual, "confiding/
        In star and wind and wave. " The figures of Odysseus,
        Aeneas, and Teucer, the half-brother of Ajax are used to
        support the idea of voyaging. Teucer, setting forth from
        his "friends and kin" said, "Drink! and, tomorrow, un-
        travelled seas!"

400 _____. "The Phoenix," in Collected Poems and Epigrams.
        Chicago: Swallow, 1971.
        The phoenix is a bird, derived from Egyptian mythology,
        which is said to live in the Arabian desert for a very long
        time, five or six hundred years, and then to destroy itself
        by fire, rising from the ashes to begin another long life.
        In Cunningham's poem it is used in a traditional sense, to
        indicate immortality.

CUSTANCE, Olive (Lady Alfred Douglas, 1874-?, English)

401 "Endymion," in The Inn of Dreams. London: Lane, 1911.
        This is an intensely personal poem, the love song of "a
        mortal girl, " whose lover she compares to "young Endymion,
        risen from the dead. " The imagery of the Moon, however,

pervades the poem, reminding the reader of the myth that Selene, the Moon, loved Endymion and granted his wish that he be allowed to sleep forever on Latmos.

402 _____. "Hyacinthus," in The Inn (1911), embodies the myth of the beautiful youth who was loved by Apollo and was accidentally killed by the god with a discus: "the fatal game that murdered thee." From the blood of the dying boy a flower sprang up, which we have called the hyacinth.

403 _____. "Hylas," in The Inn (1911), was another beautiful youth, loved by Hercules, who met his fate at an early age. In this poem he is presented as utterly happy and carefree at one with the world of youth and nature, not dreaming "of the night." In the myth Hylas is pulled under water by a nymph and drowned.

DABNEY, Julia Parker (1850-?, American)

404 "Aeolus," in Songs of Destiny and Others. New York: Dutton, 1898.
In mythology Aeolus was the keeper of the winds, it being uncertain whether he was a mortal whom Zeus so honored, or a lesser god himself. In Julia Dabney's poem the title is used to indicate simply a wind, and the poem consists of describing what things a gentle wind can do.

405 _____. "Bacchanal," in Songs of Destiny (1898), is a drinking song in praise of the gift of Dionysus. The poet says, "Raise on high the cup, / Pour the fiery wine," concluding with a choruslike effect: "Drink the perfect wine! / Drink the gift divine!"

406 _____. "A Dance of the Dryads," in Songs of Destiny (1898), is a celebration of the different nymphs of the trees, the pine, chestnut, myrtle, and others. They sing of the woodland flowers growing around them, and at night they praise "Golden Artemis," as the goddess of the forests and also as the moon that gives off "pure radiance." They also crown Dionysus "with vine and fruit," and Pan, who lurks in the woods.

407 _____. "Orpheus Sings," in Songs of Destiny (1898), is a threnody, or song of grief over death, and except for the title and one reference to Eurydice could be for any lost loved one. The mythological singer laments for his love, "I call thee and thou answerest not," and wishes for a "deadly calm wherein I too might cease." Later in the poem he speculates as to where she is, "in caverned labyrinth or dim recess" or "heavenward-flung." Wherever she is, he knows that "naught may perish." In conclusion he affirms his faith: "Wherever more thou passest--shade or day--/ I too will pass."

408 _____. "The Parcae," in Songs of Destiny (1898), is the
Roman name for the Fates, or Moerae as they were called
by the Greeks. They are usually conceived of as three
sisters responsible for spinning, measuring, and cutting
the threads of human life. In this poem the narrator comments on the brevity and futility of people's lives and
plans, and affirms that the only permanence is Time:

> There is no new nor old; and Time clasps hands
> With Time across the lapsèd centuries ...
> And aeons rolled o'er dead that is not dead
> Sift but the ashes--let the Phoenix rise!
> Then spin--and cleave--the temporary thread!--
> Spin, Sisters, spin!

409 _____. "Tithonus," in Songs of Destiny (1898), is a poem
of Autumn and a lament over the passing of Summer. One
feature of the Autumn is the singing of the grasshopper and
other insects soon to die in the blast of Winter. The myth
of Tithonus is only vaguely embodied in this poem: Eos,
the Dawn, fell in love with the Trojan Tithonus and gave
him immortality, but she forgot to make him ageless. One
story says that she shut her old lover into a room where
she would not have to look at him, but a kinder story says
that she changed him into a grasshopper, an insect that
was thought to slough off old age with its skin.

410 _____. "Tmolus," in Songs of Destiny (1898), is identified
as the oak-chapleted deity of Mount Tmolus, the son of
Ares and Theogone. With his wife, Omphale, he ruled
over the kingdom of Lydia and was the judge in the musical
contest between Pan and Apollo. The remainder of his
mythology tells of his falling in love with an attendant of
Artemis, whom he ravished on the goddess's own couch.
Artemis let loose a mad bull that killed Tmolus. Miss
Dabney's poem is based on the story of Tmolus' judging
the contest between Pan and Apollo. He gave the crown to
Apollo, and "flung his ponderous bulk" at the god's feet,
saying, "Lo! thou hast borne me a soul; art thou not king?"

DAY, Richard Edwin (1852-?, American)

411 "The Conquest of Thebes," in New Poems. New York: Graf-
ton, 1909.
The conquest in this poem is that by Dionysus, or Bacchus
as he is called. The king of Thebes, Pentheus, is a devout
believer in the gods but not in the upstart god who has come
from "across the sea." Dionysus, however, avenges himself on the nonbeliever by inspiring the drunken women, the
bacchants, to lay hands on the king and tear him to pieces.
Thus the conquest of Thebes by Dionysus is complete.

412 _____. "The Fall of Dionysus," in New Poems (1909), occurs on "pine-clad Cithaeron," when Hermes informs Dionysus that it is the will of Zeus that henceforth there will be
no further celebrations of mirth and pleasure, that "the
cross--name of terror," has taken its place, and the reign
of the gods is over.

413 _____. "The Furies to Alcmaeon," in Dante and Other
Poems. New Haven: Yale University Press, 1924.
The story of Alcmaeon is one of matricide, and his plight
is not unlike that of Orestes, who murdered his mother to
avenge his father's death. Alcmaeon murdered Eripyle,
his mother, at the orders of his father, who died in the
war of the Seven Against Thebes. The furies drove Alcmaeon mad, and only after many years of wandering was
he purified of the murder and freed from his madness.

414 _____. "The Gift of Hercules," in Dante (1924), is the
bow and arrows that Hercules bequeaths to Philoctetes as
he is approaching death. Preparing to mount the funeral
pyre, Hercules recalls one last time his many heroic exploits, but one deed he would have forgotten, the accidental
slaying of the gentle centaur Pholus.

415 _____. "Ino," in New Poems (1909), the sister of Semele,
mother of Dionysus, took care of the young god and tried
to protect him from Hera's wrath. However, Hera found
out that Dionysus was being cared for by Ino and her husband, Athamas, and sent a devastating madness upon them.
Athamas shot one of their sons, mistaking him for a deer,
and Ino leaped into the sea with the other son, Melicertes.
Ino and Melicertes were changed into sea-deities and became known as Leucothea and Palaemon.

416 _____. "Songs of Silenus," in Dante (1924), develops the
question of "human or bestial?" with regard to the race of
satyrs, followers of the god Dionysus. Silenus, who calls
himself "teacher and friend of the wine-god," explains the
dual nature of the satyrs by saying they are half-divine,
as were the first gods whom Zeus banished to the stars,
and half of the earth, the scene of the conflict in the war
of the gods and Titans. Silenus says that Earth's "mighty
breast and her nostrils flame with the breath of old wars,"
and for this reason human beings need a god who will allow
them to be "human and bestial," "hideous and beautiful."

417 _____. "The Voyage of Bacchus," in New Poems (1909),
occurs while the god is still an infant, sometime after the
deaths of Ino, his foster mother, and her son Melicertes,
whom Bacchus regarded as his playmate. In grief over
their disappearance Bacchus allows himself to be lured
aboard a ship whose crew plans to sell him into slavery.
The pilot, however, knows the child is a god and will be
protected by the gods. Near the shores of Egypt the boat

is stopped, and the crew changed into dolphins. Bacchus then sees Ino and Melicertes "robed in immortal graces," driving the dolphins.

DE VERE, Aubrey Thomas (1814-1902, English)

418   "The Acropolis of Athens," in Vol. I, Poetical Works. London: Kegan Paul, Trench, 1884.
This work consists of two sonnets, the first advising readers that if they would "seek the famed Acropolis," they must do so by means of art and the imagination; and the second addressed to Athena, patron goddess of Athens, to return in spirit and once more make her city "strong, pure, and free."

419   _____. "Aeschylus," in Poetical Works (1884), pays tribute to the great poet, saying that few can understand his "mystic meanings," but those who do will learn wisdom.

420   _____. "The 'Antigone' of Sophocles," in Poetical Works (1884), expresses the poet's notion of how Sophocles created his great play "Antigone." He sees the dramatist at Colonus, seemingly lost in meditation, until suddenly the moment on inspiration comes, "his hour of immortality," and he cries aloud, "Antigone."

421   _____. "Europa," in Poetical Works (1884), tells the story of the girl who dared to ride a beautiful white bull, not knowing that it was Zeus in disguise, and was carried away to the island of Crete, where she became the mother of kings. The poem not only tells the story but also recreates the fear and panic of the young girl when she realizes how far from home she has come. She calls on her father and her brother Cadmus to save her, but of course they cannot.

422   _____. "Lines Written Under Delphi," in Poetical Works (1884), is an elaborate treatment of a rather simple theme: the poet laments the loss of the old gods, by which he means the old traditions and standards, and deplores some of the modern gods, by which he means greed, materialism, and cowardice. The poet reviews a great many of the mythological gods, with special interest in Apollo, whom he calls the "loftiest shape of all/ That glorified the range of Grecian song."

423   _____. "The Prison of Socrates," in Poetical Works (1884), is a statement on the uselessness of venerating a spot, the prison that was a cave opposite the Acropolis, where Socrates died. His Truth and Wisdom knew no confines, and easily escaped the bonds of a prison.

424 _____. "The Search After Proserpine," in Poetical Works
(1884), begins after the goddess has been abducted by Hades,
and is presented in four scenes, each of which is one area
in which Demeter looks and searches for her daughter. In
the last scene, along the Sicilian shore where Persephone
was abducted, Hermes enters and tells the grieving mother
that her daughter has been returned to earth, and that it is
the will of Zeus that she spend half the year with Hades in
the Underworld and the other half with her mother. In an
Introduction to this work the author says that he favors this
myth perhaps above all others because it is "connected with
that great mystery of Joy and Grief, of Life and Death."

425 _____. "Sophocles," in Poetical Works (1884), pays tribute
to the dramatist by referring to his seven extant tragedies
as "seven majestic Statues." One of the statues is that of
a king, "with blinded eyes" and another was a royal maid
pressing a funeral urn to her breast. The reader, of
course, recognizes the images as those of Oedipus and his
daughter Antigone.

426 _____. "A Statue of Juno," in Poetical Works (1884), is a
description of the giant statue in which every detail is
stamped with majesty, the brow, the hands, the breast, the
eyes. Everything announces that she is the "Matron Ruler
of the World, the Queen/ Of Gods, and Mistress of the
Universe."

427 _____. "The Sun-God," in Poetical Works (1884), is a
precise and detailed description of Apollo as he brings his
chariot into the new day. It is a picture of perfect light
and beauty as the sun-god sends his brilliant shafts in pursuit of "flying Night."

428 _____. "The Theatre at Argos," in Poetical Works (1884),
is an imaginative account of the theater, no longer in existence but well populated with the spirits of the "old Homeric
hosts," Agamemnon, Menelaus, Helen, Paris, and all the
others who were embodied in the tragic drama enacted at
one time in the theater at Argos.

429 _____. "The Tomb of Agamemnon," in Poetical Works
(1884) consists of two sonnets, the first a simple description of the tomb believed to be that of the great Argive
king; and the second a reflection on just what Agamemnon's
death meant. The imagery of the first poem is hushed and
quiet, as "round the sick bed of one men fear to waken."
In the second poem the moral is drawn out that in spite of
his being "King of Men," a murderess awaited, and in truth
Agamemnon was the sacrifice of the gods.

430 _____. Addenda: In addition to these works De Vere wrote
another dozen or so poems that have slight mythological

value. These pieces were originally printed in a collection
called Recollections of Greece and reprinted in Poetical
Works (1884). These additional poems are: "An Aged
Greek," "The Dying Platonist," "Grecian Ode," "Greek
Idyls: Glaucé, Ioné, and Lycius," "A Night at Corcyra,"
"The Nightingale," "Ode to an Aeolian Harp," "The Pan-
theist," "The Platonist," "Psyche; or an Old Poet's Love,"
"The Sibyl's Cave at Cuma," "To a Greek Lady," and
"Zoe, An Athenian Child."

DIXON, Richard Watson (1833-1900, English)

431 "Apollo Pythius," in Odes and Eclogues. London: Daniel,
1884.
This poem elaborates the myth of Apollo killing a huge serpent, Python, at Delphi, where he early established his
oracle. There are varying accounts of the serpents. One
has it that it was the guardian snake of the ancient oracle,
which it defended against the young god Apollo. Dixon,
however, prefers the legend that the snake was a ravaging
monster and that Apollo did the country a great service by
killing it.

432 _____. "The Birth of Apollo," in Historical Odes and Other
Poems. London: Smith, Elder, 1864.
This writer sees the birth of Apollo as the beginning of a
new age, "the great uniter of the heaven and earth." Apollo
was the son of Zeus and the Titan goddess Leto, born on
the island of Delos. At his birth other gods and Titans
came and looked on knowing it was the end of the old order
of things. Apollo stands for the sun-god and also represents light and truth. He is the god most nearly comparable to the Christian concept of deity.

433 _____. "Cephalus and Procris," in Odes and Eclogues
(1884), details at some length the story of the wife who
followed her hunter husband into the forest and was accidentally killed by one of his arrows, he thinking that the
movement in the bush was a deer. Dixon's poem adds the
motif of the dog and spear, gifts from the goddess Artemis,
which Aurora seized upon Procris' death and would not return unless Cephalus promised to love her alone.

434 _____. "Mercury to Prometheus," in Lyrical Poems.
London: Daniel, 1887.
The effect in this poem is gained by contrasting the little
winged god with the chained Titan. Mercury says, "Like
a star I fly," which is true, but always on some errand
for the other gods. Prometheus, on the other hand, defied
the gods, for which he was punished.

435 _____. "Orpheus, " in Historical Odes (1864), focuses on
the music of Orpheus and sees it as the outgrowth of his
sorrow for Eurydice. After he failed in his quest to bring
his wife back from the Underworld, Orpheus became a
wanderer and played his music in all parts of the world.
Dixon calls it "stern and strange, " the music of "sorrow's
heart. "

436 _____. "Polyphemus, " in Odes and Eclogues (1884), is a
long narrative telling of the ugly cyclops's love for the
beautiful Galatea. Of particular interest in this poem is
the character of Polyphemus, which is presented in a somewhat more favorable light than is usual. At the end, however, he tries to destroy Acis and Galatea, but they triumph
after all: "Galatea fled beneath the wave, / And Acis issued
trembling from their cave, " he having become a spring of
water.

437 _____. "Proserpine, " in Christ's Company and Other Poems.
London: Smith, Elder, 1861. Reprinted in The Decadent Consciousness. New York: Garland, 1978.
The daughter of Demeter is abducted by "the dragon black"
while she is joyously picking flowers in the Spring. She
is taken to the dark kingdom of death, even as mortals are,
and, no less than mortals, she misses life and the beautiful world that she loses. In a prayer addressed to Proserpine the poet asks her to be merciful "in Hades to our
hopes and fears. "

438 _____. "Ulysses and Calypso, " in Lyrical Poems (1887),
is narrated by Calypso after Ulysses has left her. She
laments the loss of her lover, even though she knows that
mortals prefer to mate with mortals, and at the end of the
poem wishes that she were Penelope. Dixon's poem depicts
Calypso from a sympathetic point of view, showing that goddesses, no less than mortal men, are confronted with difficult conflicts.

439 _____. "The Vision of Thebes, " in Christ's Company (1861),
refers to the Egyptian city called Thebes by the Greeks. It
is referred to in Homer as "hundred gated, " although it was
not a walled city. It is the site of the temple of Karnak
and other monumental ruins. One remarkable statue at
Thebes is that of Memnon, the legendary king of Ethiopia
who died at Troy. In Dixon's poem Thebes is called the
"great heart ... of Egypt, " where life "throbbed mightily,
in its primeval strength. "

DOBSON, Henry Austin (1840-1921, English)

440 "A Case of Cameos, " in Complete Poetical Works. London:
Oxford University Press, 1923. Reprinted St. Clair
Shores, Mich.: Scholarly Press, 1970.

This composition comprises five ten-line poems, based on
five different gemstones: agate, chalcedony, sardonyx,
amethyst, beryl. Each stone has a cameo scene carved
into it: Eros riding a centaur; Mercury stealing Apollo's
shafts even while the powerful sun-god was lecturing his
younger brother on the wrongs of thievery; Orpheus playing
to the animals; Silenus crowned "King of Topers"; the Sirens on their rocks and a tall ship in the background drawing shoreward.

441 _____. "The Death of Procris," in Complete (1923), retells the pitiful story of the wife who went into the woods
to spy on her husband, Cephalus, the hunter. Mistaking
her for a deer, Cephalus shot Procris, and none saw her
die but her faithful dog, Lelaps. Dobson's poem is based
on a painting by Piero di Cosimo, in the National Gallery.

442 _____. "The Prayer of the Swine to Circe," in Complete
(1923), derives from Homer's Odyssey (Book X, 235-245),
in which Circe changes Odysseus' men into swine: "They
had the heads of swine and the voice and the hair/ And the
body, but the mind was steady as before. / So they were
penned in, weeping...." Dobson takes this passage and
bases most of his poem on it, in the "Prayer" of the swine
to Circe. They plead with her either to restore them to
men or else take away their consciousness of what they
have become. At the end of the poem Odysseus has arrived, and as Homer tells the story he will force the goddess to restore his men to their rightful shape.

443 _____. "A Tale of Polypheme," in Complete (1923), is a
telling of the story of the cyclops and Galatea, but with
characters of a contemporary setting: an old man with one
eye, a young woman with a child, and a boy. The child
and the boy became close friends, as the old man had developed an infatuation for the child. One day they disappeared, and "never came again." In conclusion Dobson
says:

> Therefore our Cyclops sorrowed, --not as one
>   Who can command the gamut of despair;
> But as a man who feels his days are done,
>   So dead they seem, --so desolately bare;
> For, though he'd lived a hermit, 'twas but only
> Now he discovered that his life was lonely.

444 _____. "To a Greek Girl," in Complete (1923), is a love
song addressed to someone the poet calls "Autonoe," after
the mythological figure of that name. The image of the
girl is lovely, "nymph-like head," "a girlish shape," "blithe
airs," but she appears mostly as a vision; the poet knows
that she is not real.

DODD, Lee Wilson (1879-1933, American)

445 "Adonis to Aphrodite," in A Modern Alchemist and Other
Poems. Boston: Badger, 1906.
Although Aphrodite loved Adonis as much as any god can
love a mortal, the beautiful youth did not love her very
much, or so the myth says. Dodd's poem creates an
Adonis who is outright scornful of the goddess, and boasts
arrogantly that he will not waste his life in love-making
but rather will pursue more manly sports, hunting in the
forest. Aphrodite knew he was to be killed by a wild boar,
"bristling with fury," but she did nothing to stop his death,
"she gave no sign."

446 _____. "Circe," in A Modern Alchemist (1906), depicts
the enchanting goddess as the symbol of sensuality. This
poet says most men "have sung of Circe," but he sees
"no hogs wallowing in the mire." Instead he sees "half-
green, half-gold" feline eyes; the "unsyllabled soft moan of
mating doves," "lean lovely serpents," and "voluptuous
leopards yawning with desire."

447 _____. "Cypselus," in A Modern Alchemist (1906), is
identified as a man of Corinth who killed the Bacchiade,
followers of Dionysus, and seized the ruling power. Later
the Bacchiade attempted retaliation, but were unsuccessful
because the mother of Cypselus hid him in a coffer of wine.

448 _____. "The Delphic Sybil," in A Modern Alchemist (1906),
is a description of what the poet sees in Michelangelo's
painting of the Delphic Sybil. He describes eyes that do
not seem to see, eyes that "are veiled and sad." The lips
express a wistfulness, and the brow is mournful. Yet the
poet says that she is beautiful in spite of the burden of
knowledge that she must carry.

449 _____. "Fragment of an 'Electra,'" in A Modern Alchemist
(1906), is an exchange between Electra, the daughter of
Agamemnon, and the Chorus. Had the play been finished,
the character of Electra would perhaps have resembled the
characterization in Sophocles' "Electra." Dodd's Electra
is fierce for revenge on her mother, who killed Agamemnon.
The Chorus admonishes her to restraint, but she replies
that she will not wear her "days out, sad, unhusbanded, /
Uncomforted of children!"

450 _____. "To the Gods of Greece," in A Modern Alchemist
(1906), asks why we still turn to the "long-exiled gods" of
Greece, not believing in them, "sadly, without faith," but
seeking the calm austerity that dwells "above the strangled
tide of strife." We see in them the symbols of peace,
certitude, and beauty.

DOOLITTLE, Hilda (known as H. D. , 1886-1961, American)

451 "Acon," in Collected Poems of H. D. New York: Liveright, 1925.
Although "Acon" is not based on a mythological story, the imagery of the poem creates a mythological atmosphere as a background for the slight narrative. The narrator calls on the dryads and Nereids, and later on the Pales, to bring gifts of flowers and wine to his love, "whom no god pities," who "lies panting/ drawing sharp breath/ broken with harsh sobs," apparently near death.

452 _____. "Adonis," in Collected Poems (1925), makes use of the Adonis myth of death and rebirth to say that "each of us like you/ has died once." The imagery is primarily of nature: "a drift of wood-leaves/ cracked and bent/ and tortured ... in the winter frost," and then reborn in pure gold of the "sun-fire."

453 _____. "After Troy," in Collected Poems (1925), is narrated from the Trojan point of view. They knew that their cause was lost long before the Greeks realized that "fortune had tossed to them/ her favour and her whim," yet they fought their best nevertheless.

454 _____. "At Eleusis," in Collected Poems (1925), pays tribute to Dionysus, whose rites under the name of Iacchus were celebrated in this city near the Ishthmus of Corinth. It is not said, but strongly suggested here, that the rituals were orgiastic and violent.

455 _____. "At Ithaca," in Collected Poems (1925), is Penelope's soliloquy as she weaves the scene by day and tears it out at night. In this poem she secretly admits to hoping that one of her suitors might "conquer this long waiting with a kiss," but then visions of Odysseus rise up and she continues to wait.

456 _____. "Callypso [sic] Speaks," in Selected Poems of H. D. New York: Grove, 1957.
After Odysseus has left her island, Calypso laments all that she has done for him, feeling that he was ungrateful: "he never looked back," she says, and calls him a brute and a fool. On the sea Odysseus recounts all that she has given him: water, food, wine, "an ivory comb for my hair," and, perhaps more than anything else, "peace in her cave."

457 _____. "Cassandra," in Collected Poems (1925), is a chant to Hymen by Cassandra, the unwed priestess of Apollo. Although this god, Hymen, has no genuine mythology, he was associated with the marriage rites in late classical literature.

90

458 _____. "Centaur Song," in Collected Poems (1925), develops a love-theme by means of contrasting the rough animal appearance of the centaur, half-man, half-horse, with the beauty of the night flowers, the sweet-smelling grass, and the soft winds.

459 _____. "Circe," in Collected Poems (1925), presents the goddess in a mood of regret after Odysseus has left her. She says that it is easy enough to change men into animal shapes, to summon them to her feet, to work other feats of magic, but she would exchange it all if Odysseus could return to her island.

460 _____. "Demeter," in Collected Poems (1925), is a lengthy account, spoken by Demeter herself, of her loss of the daughter, Persephone, who became "mistress of Death." The goddess complains bitterly of her greatness, which is largely ignored; hers is "the child the gods desert."

461 _____. "Eurydice," in Collected Poems (1925), is another bitter charge against Orpheus for his attempt to bring Eurydice out of the Underworld. Eurydice says, "so for your arrogance/ and your ruthlessness/ I am swept back. . . ." In this poem Eurydice has been dead for some time, and she says that she would have found peace had her husband let her alone and not attempted to bring her back to the earth, but now for his "arrogance" and "ruthlessness" she has "lost the earth/ and the flowers of the earth."

462 _____. "Evadne," in Collected Poems (1925), is based on the story of the girl who was loved by Apollo. There are several other individuals by this name--notably the wife of Capaneous who threw herself on her husband's funeral pyre --but the subject of H.D.'s poem was a daughter of Poseidon who was loved by the god Apollo and bore him a son, Iamus, who became a prophet, receiving the gift from his father.

463 _____. "Helen," in Collected Poems (1925), expresses the hatred of the Greeks for Helen, the white face, the white hands, the beauty of cool feet and slender ankles. For all the grief and heartache she has caused they would love her "if she were laid/ white ash amid funeral cypresses."

464 _____. Helen in Egypt, with Introduction by Horace Gregory. New York: Grove, 1961. Horace Gregory points out that this work is not a novel or an epic; it is a three-hundred-page poem, conceived of in three basic parts, written in a series of three-line choral stanzas, a "lyric narrative." Within the three divisions are numerous subdivisions, each change of voice introduced by a brief interlude in prose.

In Part I, "Pallinode," the story is based on the
work of the Greek lyric poet Stesichorus, who lived from
about 640 to 555 B.C. It is said that he first wrote a
poem, Helen, in which he condemned the beautiful woman
for her elopement with Paris. For this he was blinded,
and in order to regain his sight he wrote the Palinodia, a
recantation, in which he apparently created the myth that
the real Helen did not go to Troy at all, but instead a
phantom was sent by the gods, and the real Helen was sent
to Egypt.

Part II, "Leuké," refers to the White Island, one
of the Islands of the Blessed, or Elysium. It is here that
certain figures of the legendary periods were said to be
living in eternal bliss. Among those were Helen and
Achilles, who had married and bore a son, Euphorion. It
is in this section of H.D.'s poem that most of the remembered episodes and characters of the Trojan War are recounted.

Part III, "Eidolon," meaning phantom, is an attempt
to reconcile time and reality, timelessness and illusion.
How real was Paris? Paris was Eros. Helen would return to reality, but knows that reality is phantom; phantom
alone is reality.

465   _____. "Helios," in Collected Poems (1925), praises the
sun-god, and compares him with certain other gods: the
Cyprian, Athene. H.D. says, "Helios makes all things
right...."

466   _____. "Hermes of the Ways," in Collected Poems (1925),
pays tribute to the god of travelers, one of the numerous
functions of Hermes. The poet-narrator says, "I know
him/ of the triple path-ways, / Hermes/ who awaits."

467   _____. "Hermonax," in Collected Poems (1925), is a fisherman, a "caster of nets," who has come upon a "sea-
gliding creature" and now gives it back to the sea, "to thee,
Ino, / and to Palemon."

468   _____. "Hippolytus Temporizes," in Collected Poems
(1925), is a soliloquy and meditation on the goddess Artemis, whom Hippolytus loves. He says, "I worship the
greatest first," and "I worship the feet, flawless, / that
haunt the hills."

469   _____. "Hymen," in Collected Poems (1925), is a choral
arrangement of song and dance presented in front of the
temple of Hera, who was, among other things, the goddess
of marriage. Hymen, another god of marriage, is the
principal subject of this poem, however, and all the joys
and happiness of the married state are chanted and praised.

470 _____ . "Leda," in Collected Poems (1925), is unique in
that it presents the image of the swan from the swan's
point of view, not Leda's. He is described as a red swan
with red wings and coral feet, drenched in sunlight, pure
gold, pure god.

471 _____ . "Lethe," in Collected Poems (1925), is forgetfulness, and this poem says that nothing shall cover you,
nothing shelter, nothing protect, when "the roll of the full
tide," comes in "Without question/ Without kiss."

472 _____ . "Odyssey," in Collected Poems (1925), tells, as
Homer had done, the story of Odysseus' fate, "who roamed
long years/ after he had sacked/ Troy's sacred streets."
Many details of Homer's Odyssey are incorporated into
H. D.'s brief composition, but the emphasis is on the gods
and how they control human fate according to their whims
and caprices.

473 _____ . "Orion Dead," in Collected Poems (1925), describes
the great hunter as he was in life and as he now is in death.
The mythology of his death is variously given, but each version indicates that he somehow ran afoul of the goddess Artemis, who shot him dead with an arrow. Also basic to
the story is the fact that when he died he became a constellation, the Hunter.

474 _____ . "Pallas," in Selected Poems (1957), addresses
Athena, called Pallas Athena, as the goddess of war, the
defender of heroes. It is a slight poem, creating several
images of war and blood: "We have taken life," "why ask
happiness of the dead ...," and "violets throw strange fire
... gold and purple and red/ where her feet tread."

475 _____ . "Phaedra," in Collected Poems (1925), is narrated
by the queen at the point of her downfall in the Theseus-
Hippolytus story. She prays to all the gods of Crete to
hear her at this moment of great need, saying that "the
poppy that my heart was ... made to strike and gather
hearts" now "fades and shrinks," "drenched and torn in
the cold rain."

476 _____ . "Pygmalion," in Collected Poems (1925), is a
rather philosophical debate of the sculptor with himself.
He questions his power as an artist: does he carve the
stone, or does the stone carve him "for its use"? He
says, "I made god upon god/ step from the cold rock,"
and now each one cries out, "you are useless/ no marble
can bind me/ no stone suggest." At the end he says each
god has "stepped into the light," and his work is for nothing.

477 _____ . "She Contrasts with Herself Hippolyta," in Collected
Poems (1925), is spoken by Phaedra, the wife and queen of

Theseus who had a son, Hippolytus, by the Amazonian maiden Hippolyta. Phaedra sees her former rival as a strong unyielding force, who even when raped by Theseus did not break, but prayed to Artemis, the goddess of virgins, to forgive and "grant that no flower/ be grafted alien on a broken stalk." Phaedra, now in love with the son of this union, Hippolytus, says that he was "born of hate."

478 _____. "She Rebukes Hippolyta," in Collected Poems (1925), is a continuation of the Phaedra poems, in this one a questioning of the Amazon's true nature: "Was she so chaste?" The answer seems to be that she was "frail and wild," and was betrayed "by the glint/ of light on the hills."

479 _____. "Thetis," in Collected Poems (1925), in this poem is the sea-goddess reflecting on her marriage to "Pelius" [sic, Peleus] and the son, Achilles, who was born of this marriage. It is not a happy poem, the goddess bitter that she has borne a mortal son and that the father, himself a mortal, had asked for and received immortality.

480 _____. "Thetis," in Collected Poems (1925), is a description of the goddess as she steps carefully along the seasand, her white feet and the gold that binds them showing plainly. In the Iliad Thetis is usually called "silver-footed."

481 _____. "Winter Love," in Hermetic Definition. New York: New Directions, 1961.
This poem, one of the last that H.D. wrote, is a fantasy in which Helen, now old and tired and cold, remembers her life and the men whom she has loved: Menelaus, Achilles, Paris, and finally Odysseus. It is now that she dreams of Odysseus and would go with him, leaving the hated city of Sparta and the boredom and tedium of being the wife of Menelaus. By Odysseus she has had a child whom she calls "Espérance," meaning Hope. She is urged by inward voices to send the child away, but cannot do so even at the expense of her own life.

DREW, Bernard (1885-?, English)

482 "Cassandra," in Cassandra and Other Poems. London: Nutt, 1906.
Cassandra, the prophetess daughter of Priam, warns her people that Troy is soon to be overthrown, but no one listens, as Apollo had decreed that it was her fate to know the future but never be heeded. Her wild tale of doom and violence is told against a background of the last sunset that Troy would know: "Slow from the west one blood-red sea of fire/ Blazed o'er the pillar'd towers of Ilion," the poet

says, and as Cassandra continues, her dire warnings are dominated by images of blood and fire.

483 _____. "Endymion and Selene," in Helen and Other Poems.
London: Fifield, 1912.
In this poem Endymion is portrayed as sleeping all day, but at night awakening to cry out to Selene, the moon. He calls out, "Come down to me, my bride," and for "one fierce embrace" she does forsake the heavens; for "one anguished kiss" she comes to earth, but then must return.

484 _____. "Helen," in Helen (1912), is a soliloquy spoken by Helen sometime before the Greeks came to Troy. She reveals herself as a woman who is divided in soul and mind: on one hand she loves Paris because he is beautiful, the ideal lover, dressed in soft silks and perfumed; and on the other hand, she still loves Menelaus, the warrior, who delights in "battle, and the strife of swords fierce ringing." She also loves Troy, the ancient shrines, the pinnacles of palaces and temples as they "glow in crimson hues of dusk." And yet she longs for Greece, and hears a whisper from "far-off shores and valleys, and green hills." Under it all she has a vague premonition and hears a voice prophesying battle and fury and destruction.

485 _____. Helen of Troy. London: Selwyn and Blount, 1924.
This play is in four acts, with three years between Acts I and II, and nine years between Acts III and IV. The first scene is laid at the palace of Tyndarus, King of Sparta and the father of Helen, and the remaining scenes are at Troy. The cast of characters is extensive, and includes Tyndarus, Helen, Priam, Paris, Cassandra, Menelaus, Agamemnon, Suitors of Helen--Ulysses, Ajax, Patroclus, Diomedes--and other attendants, Trojans, etc. Act I, describing the choice of a husband for Helen, concludes with her marriage to Menelaus, with a grim foreshadowing of the strife and war that is to come. In Act II Paris arrives at the palace of Menelaus in Sparta, and Menelaus embarks for Crete, where urgent family affairs call. In his absence Helen and Paris fall in love, convinced that it is the gods' will, and elope for Troy. When Menelaus returns, he is overcome with jealousy and rage and vows that "vengeance shall o'ertake the towers of Troy." Act III begins with Helen remembering Greece and debating with herself over what she has done. The first scene here is almost identical with the short work "Helen" (Helen and Other Poems, 1912), making use of the same phrasing and imagery. Later the scene shifts to Priam's court, and Cassandra frantically warns Paris that he should return Helen to her husband, and himself return to Oenone on Mt. Ida. Priam calls her words "dark fantasies" and vows that he will not relent. Helen and Paris refuse to listen to the "mad-brained girl" who is obsessed "with gloom and lurid dreams." Act IV begins with much

the same sentiments as Drew expressed in the short work "Cassandra" (Cassandra and Other Poems, 1906), with the addition of Helen, who promises that on the morrow she will leave Troy and beg forgiveness for herself and pity for Troy. It is already too late, however, as Cassandra says that Troy will not see another tomorrow. At this point the Greeks come crashing through the wall that has been partly torn down. In the concluding scene Helen is confronted by Menelaus, who renews his pledge of love to her and says the rest of their lives will be as if their "parting was a dream."

486 _____. "Hymn to Demeter," in Helen (1912), is narrated by an individual who regards Earth--that is, Demeter--as the source of all life and nurture, and prays that as it is in life so it will be "in the Halls of Death," that he will still praise the hallowed Mother.

487 _____. "The Muses," in Helen (1912), is a brief poem in which the muse of poetry, Calliope, is praised as the best and most virtuous of the muses.

488 _____. "Orpheus and Eurydice," in Cassandra (1906), is a narrative that begins with the death of Eurydice, progresses through the events of Orpheus seeking Eurydice in the Underworld, and ends with his own death. The emphasis, however, is not on the story but in the details of Orpheus' grief over his loss of his wife. These details are apparent in the beginning when he finds her dead; they are intensified as he loses her the second time; and finally as he dies, he is relieved that he will once again be reunited to his lost Eurydice.

489 _____. "Penelope Forsaken," in Helen (1912), is based on the myth that after Ulysses reached Ithaca the first time, he set out on another voyage, his heart hungering "for a nameless quest." Penelope grieves at this departure, so soon after he returned home, and now she does not know if he will ever return. Her dilemma is that she has hope, and yet this hope is so near despair.

490 _____. "Prometheus Delivered," in Prometheus Delivered and Other Poems. London: Sisley, 1907. In this dramatic poem the time is eons after Prometheus has been chained to the mountain, and now Hercules has come to release him. Vulcan (Hephaestos) tries to persuade him not to defy the gods, but Hercules tells him that the Fates would have it otherwise.

491 _____. "To Homer," in Prometheus Delivered (1907), is a hymn of praise to the poet who is called the "mightiest

son of song," "monarch," and "King of the immortals."
His works are referred to as elements of nature.

492 _____. "To Virgil: A Sonnet Sequence," in Prometheus
Delivered (1907), consists of fourteen poems that review
the characters and action of Virgil's Aeneid: the fall of
Troy, the story of Carthage and Dido, the final defeat of
Turnus by Aeneas.

DURRELL, Lawrence (1912- , English)

493 "Aphrodite," in The Ikons and Other Poems. New York:
Dutton, 1967.
This is not a romantic version of Aphrodite rising from
the sea, but rather a modern and somewhat ugly presentation. Durrell says that man created "this speaking loveliness"--that is, Aphrodite--to comfort himself in the night
of storm and labor.

494 _____. "Ballad of the Oedipus Complex," in Collected
Poems. New York: Dutton, 1960.
This version of the Oedipus myth is a satire, full of sex-
uality and implicit ribaldry. The narrator affirms that
wherever Freud has followed him, he "felt Mama and Pa
go," until now he is "all Libido."

495 _____. "Blind Homer," in Collected Poems (1960), is a
tribute to a host of images that the poet can see, the winter night, the moon, six pines, signs of the coming Spring.
Blind Homer could not see these sights, and yet they are
much the same in "February 1946," as they were in Homer's time. This poet, although he is not blind, has become "more uncertain of his gift with words."

496 _____. "Eleusis," in The Ikons (1967), was the principal
center of Demeter's worship, and later it became associated
with Dionysus. Centuries after, the narrator is aware that
something still lingers about the ruins, some "echo of
truth," from the past.

497 _____. "Io," in The Ikons (1967), was the daughter of the
river-god Inachus. She was loved by Zeus, and either
through Hera's jealousy or because of Zeus' desire to con-
ceal his affair, Io was changed into a young cow. After
this she wandered over the face of the earth, trying to find
peace from the gadfly that stung her constantly. This poem
sees Io as the "contemporary street-walker," asleep in the
museums, resting in the street-corners, strolling down the
stone pathways of Athens.

498 _____. "Near Paphos," in The Ikons (1967), describes in
ugly terms the sea as it washes up twice a day to the

shores of Paphos, where Aphrodite is reputed to have
washed ashore from the sea. Lovers still walk along the
sandy shore, now unromantic, holding hands and hoping to
find something of the magic of the goddess.

499 _____. "Nemea, " in Collected Poems (1960), refers to a
city situated on an open valley on the northern borders of
Argolis. The poem creates a mood of quiet desolation,
the fury of the aftermath of the Trojan War over, all
players in that drama now passed into nature and death:
Agamemnon; his wife, Clytemnestra; the returning men
from the war--all gone now, their swords and helmets
turned to rust, and the green grass cool and quiet. This
poem, perhaps more beautifully than the others by Durrell,
combines the mythological theme with the modern, less-
than-ideal world.

500 _____. "On Ithaca Standing, " in Collected Poems (1960),
is a tribute to the small island in the Ionian sea, off the
western coast of Greece, that constituted the kingdom of
Odysseus. It is rocky and mountainous, and a most unlikely
source of so much "magic, " as presented in the Odyssey.

501 _____. "Orpheus, " in Collected Poems (1960), is regarded
as the perfect poet-musician, the model of all artists, "en-
camping among our verses, " seeking to restore a lost love.

502 _____. "Penelope, " in Collected Poems (1960), is related
in the first person by Penelope, the long-waiting wife of
Odysseus. She waited for him to return twenty years, and
in this span of time grew old. "I remained, " she says,
and watched the seasons "file their summaries, " and walked
beside the "winter sea. "

503 _____. Sappho: A Play in Verse. New York: Dutton,
1950.
This work, set in Lesbos, 650 B. C. , is in nine scenes of
uneven length. It tells the story of the young girl who became the Poet, recreating the events of her youth before
she became aware of her destiny.

504 _____. "The Sirens, " in Collected Poems (1960), are
called "glittering temptresses of distraction, " and every
poet and hero has to face them. They always appear in
their own time, when one is confronted with the most trying of circumstances, "far from home, " confronting "the
loutish sea. " Homer and Milton ignored the Sirens, and
were punished with blindness for doing so.

505 _____. "To Argos, " in Collected Poems (1960), is cast in
the form of a travelogue, the narrator heading southward

to the land that was once Argos. "In this land," he says, "one encounters always/ Agamemnon, Agamemnon." The visitors speak with the "cold sound of English idioms," and "the modern girls pose on a tomb smiling." The good and the bad have lost their meaning, and "this is what breaks the heart."

506 _____. "Troy," in The Ikons (1967), questions the worth of Helen, and the validity of the whole myth that made her the cause of "shattered cities ... defaced altars, and burning hearths." As for Paris, he was a "wild-eyed freak," who exchanged everything for this "doll," "this insipid drone." The narrator says that he is "astonished when they talk of her."

EASTER, Marguerite Elizabeth (1839-1894, American)

507 "Antigone's Farewell to Haemon," in Clytie and Other Poems. Boston: Philpott, 1891.
Antigone, the daughter of Oedipus, has been imprisoned for defying the king of Thebes and giving her brother Polynices a burial rite. She knows she has been sentenced to die, to be sealed alive in a tomb, and in this poem she bids farewell to Haemon, the son of the king, to whom she is betrothed. She also anticipates a reunion with her father and brother in the Underworld.

508 _____. "Clytie," in Clytie (1891), is the myth of the girl who loved Phoebus, the sun, but was not loved in return. She finally wasted away to her death, and was then transformed into the sunflower, or heliotrope--a flower whose head turns to follow the sun throughout the sky.

509 _____. "Selene," in Clytie (1891), is a sentimental account of the poet's love for moonlight, interwoven with the idea that the poet has lived in an earlier, mythological era and was a votary of the moon-goddess Selene. The myth of Endymion, and several other classical stories, are briefly referred to, giving the poem a definite mythological framework. The reference to Endymion seems to indicate that the mortal sleeps on Latmos in order that he may always see the moonlight.

EMERSON, Ralph Waldo (1803-1882, American)

510 "Bacchus," in Complete Works: Poems, Vol. 9, ed. by Edward W. Emerson. Boston: Houghton, Mifflin, 1903. Reprinted New York: AMS, 1968.
Bacchus in this poem is more clearly recognizable as Dionysus, the Greek god of inspiration, the imaginative powers of creativity as opposed to the powers of logic and under-

standing. In the context of the poem Bacchus as the god
of wine is also referred to, but Emerson is not invoking
this god so much as he is writing a hymn to the powers
of the imagination, the divinely poetic inspiration.

511 _____. "Nemesis," in Complete Works (1903), was originally titled "Destiny," and in this poem is used more in
this sense than in the sense of retribution. As the poet
says, "Every Man ... of his fate is never wide," and "All
our struggles and our toils/ Tighter wind the giant coils."

512 _____. "Pan," in Complete Works (1903), has very slight
mythological value, and refers to Pan as the spirit that
animates the forms of nature, these having but momentary
value. Beyond the individual form lies the great being,
permanent and abiding.

513 _____. "The Sphinx," in Complete Works (1903), is the
controlling image in a poem about the particulars and the
whole of created forms. Emerson said that if the mind
lives only in particulars, and lacks the power to see the
whole, then the world--that is, the Sphinx--poses questions
that this mind cannot answer, destroying it. On the other
hand, if the mind perceives that in all the variety of existence there is an underlying principle, then the riddle can
be answered, and the mind remains true to its ideal.

514 _____. "Terminus," in Complete Works (1903), is the
Roman god of boundaries, and this poem is about growing
old. The god came to the poet-narrator and said, "It is
time to be old," "to take in sail"--in other words, to stop
dreaming and tighten the reins on "broad ambitious branches."
The poem is not pessimistic but is simply a recognition
that we have boundaries, and as we near these boundaries
in old age, we should not waste ourselves in youthful, impossible dreams.

ERSKINE, John (1879-1951, American)

515 "Achilles and the Maiden," in Collected Poems: 1907-1922.
New York: Duffield, 1922.
The Maiden in this poem is Penthesilea, the beautiful Amazon queen who came to Troy and fought on the side of the
Trojans. She was killed in battle by Achilles, and the
other Amazon warriors were also killed, but they killed
many Greeks before they died. The story is told in the
work by Quintus of Smyrna, the Posthomerica (c. A.D. 300),
and John Erskine's poem seems to be based largely on this
work. After the fierce Achilles slays Penthesilea, he falls
in love with her beauty and is sorry that he has killed her;
he would rather have taken her home as his wife.

516   . "Actaeon, " in Actaeon and Other Poems. New
York and London: Lane, 1907.
Unlike several other poems on this subject, Erskine's treatment has its setting in the Underworld, where Actaeon, the
hunter, is approaching the river Lethe to drink of its water
and forget all happiness and sorrow alike. He is described
as one "half crazed, " who comes to the edge of the river
and then refuses to drink. He says to the others who have
gathered there:

> Ye may forget, but I
> Gazed once on beauty till her glance grew kind,
> Suffered the cost of it, drank of the bliss,
> And evermore remember.

In spite of his sufferings he will not forget how he came
upon Artemis in her bath, was changed into a great stag
by the goddess, and was killed by his own hounds.

517   . "Iphidamus, " in Actaeon (1907), is based on a
minor character and slight incident given in Homer's Iliad
(Book XI, 221-245). Iphidamus, the son of Antenor,
married Theano, and they were happy until a traveler
brought news of the Trojan War and the abduction of Helen
by Paris. From that day on there was no happiness, since
Antenor was a close friend of Priam's, and Iphidamus felt
a duty to go fight in the war. Finally he left, bidding his
lovely wife farewell. (Iphidamus, other sources relate,
was killed at Troy by Agamemnon.)

518   . "Paris, Helen's Lover, " in Collected Poems (1922),
is a sequence of six sonnets on the subject of Paris and
his relation to beauty. First he loved Oenone, and then
he saw "Queen Helen, " and would soon have turned from
her, "That fixed immortal beauty by his side, / Impeccable,
invincible, sublime, " and gone back to Oenone, "where he
could relax a little and be plain. " As to Helen's beauty,
she simply was the last and most beautiful of a long line
of beauties, one more beautiful than the last. Finally came
Leda, so beautiful that she was wooed by a god, and became
the mother of Helen. At the end Paris has been captured
by this beauty and there is no escape.

519   . "Penthesileia, " in Collected Poems (1922), describes,
largely through a conversation between Andromache and
Priam, the coming of the Amazon warrior to fight in the
Trojan cause. Hector has been killed, and Achilles is expected at any moment to come storming through the gates.
Priam has some reluctance about seeing the young girl go
into battle, and yet he says, "Were she my child, I would
not bid her stay. " She may prove the savior of the Trojans
or "she may find her grave, " the argument goes. The
poem ends with Penthesileia "young and proud, " marching
out to do battle with the Greeks.

520 _____ . The Private Life of Helen of Troy. Indianapolis:
Bobbs-Merrill, 1925. Reprinted New York: Ungar,
1954.
This five-part novel is written in stylish but ordinary English. The parts are titled Helen's Return, The Younger
Generation, Their Elders, Death and Birth, and Helen's
Beauty. The plot, in what might be called a "domestic
novel," is principally concerned with Menelaus and Helen
after the Trojan War and their problems with the marriage
of their daughter, Hermione. She wants to marry Orestes,
whom the parents dislike, and they want her to marry Pyrrhus, the son of Achilles. She first marries Pyrrhus, who
is killed by Orestes, and then marries the latter, according
to the ancient myth. The novel ends with the visit of Telemachos, son of Odysseus, who is seeking news of his father.
The young Telemachos is fascinated by Helen's beauty, seeing her for the first time in Sparta, as is related in the
Odyssey.

521 _____ . "The Sons of Metaneira," in The Shadowed Hour.
New York: Lyric, 1917.
This narrative is a retelling of a story that has its origin
in one of the Homeric Hymns to Demeter. Metaneira is
presented as a too-careful mother who is finally persuaded
by her husband, Celeus, the king of Eleusis, to allow an
old woman to share their home and take care of their children, two boys, Triptolemus and Demophoön, an infant.
The old woman, who is Demeter in disguise, teaches Trip-
tolemus all the arts of agriculture, and the infant she attempts to make immortal by nightly placing him in a fire
to burn away the mortal parts. One night Metaneira discovered what the old woman was doing, and the goddess
disappeared, leaving Demophoön "to be master of nothing,"
"a pilgrim of confusion," stranded between two worlds--
mortality and immortality--"but at rest in neither."

522 _____ . Venus: The Lonely Goddess. Illustrations by
Warren Chappell. New York: Morrow, 1949.
This short novel is based on the myth that Venus was married to Vulcan, as in the Iliad Homer depicts the goddess
of love married to the lame and ugly Hephaestos. In Erskine's work she explains why she married Vulcan: "he
could get things done," unlike some of the gods who had
no skills or talents and very little common sense. The
novel is somewhat satirical in tone, although based on the
horrors of the Trojan War and ending with the fall of Troy.
According to John Erskine the details are drawn from the
legends contained in Pierre Bayle (1647-1706), Dictionnaire
historique et critique, published in 1697.

523 _____ . "Winter Song to Pan," in Actaeon (1907), is a fan-

tasy dreamed in the middle of Winter, with nature and birds silent and wrapped in snow "whiter than a thousand years. " Pan, the half-god, is also asleep, and the poet-narrator calls on him to return with his "summer-bringing voice. "

FAWCETT, Edgar (1847-1904, American)

524 "Actaeon, " in Voices and Visions: Later Verses. London: Nash, 1903.
The narrative here is by Actaeon, the hunter who saw Artemis bathing and was turned into stag that was then torn to pieces by his own faithful hounds. In this poem Actaeon calls this a "silly and false" story, that his "faithful dogs were fired by madness. " He says:

A deadlier vengeance yet from life hath reft me:
I have drained all joy at one wild draught--
the lees alone are left me!

525 _____. "Greek Vintage Song, " in Romance and Revery. Boston: Ticknor, 1886.
The narrator of this poem is apparently the bull for whom Pasiphae of Crete conceived a wild and abnormal passion. Rejecting this possibility, the narrator is simply an individual longing and watching "the balmy moon of Crete. " Pasiphae, whose name means "she who shines for all, " was worshiped in Crete as a moon-goddess, as was her daughter Ariadne.

526 _____. "Helen Old, " in Voices and Visions (1903), portrays the world's most beautiful woman as having become a "bony and withered hag, " with "blanched lips and locks of snow. " Was it for this that Ilium was overthrown? Did Achilles slay "glorious" Hector for this old woman? Helen prays to the goddess to give her back her youth and beauty, and then if the goddess chooses, "dash me dead. "

527 _____. "La Belle Hélène, " in Fantasy and Passion. Boston: Roberts Brothers, 1878.
The title refers to an operetta by Jacques Offenbach that was produced in Paris, 1864. This work was a rather boisterous comedy, "travesty under its wildest spell, " the poet calls it. He admits to laughing as much as the others, but he also thinks it is a sorry way "to remember it all. " Yet, in conclusion, he says perhaps it is better to remember it thus than to utterly forget "here on this busy and fickle earth. "

528 _____. "Medusa, " in Fantasy and Passion (1878), was written to describe what the poet saw in a painting of the Medusa. The poem is a study in contrasts of horror and

beauty. The face of the Medusa has "olympian faultless-
ness of mold and hue" and lips "that a god were worthy
alone to woo." Her beautiful hair, the color of "tall harvest wheat," however, is alive with "coils of lean horror,"
snakes "with sharp tongues flickering in flat clammy heads!"
The mythology of the Medusa is fairly well incorporated
into this poem: she was said to be very beautiful, and
loved by the god Poseidon, until Athena changed her into
a thing of horror.

529 _____. "Oedipus and the Sphinx," in Voices and Visions
(1903), is a telling of the story at the time Oedipus con-
fronts the Sphinx. The poem is a well-developed study of
the confrontation, with many details of the landscape just
outside the city of Thebes, and much description of the
young Oedipus, almost brash in his self-confidence and
ability to defeat his powerful adversary. Finally there is
a fully portrayed Sphinx, a monster, "a lion, a bird, yet
human." When Oedipus must answer the riddle, a trancelike dream falls on him, and he tells her everything she
wants to know. The riddle in Fawcett's poem is not the
legendary one, but is rather a question of human knowledge.
The Sphinx stands for Superstition, and when confronted
with Knowledge is automatically destroyed, "whirled into
chaos whence she had come."

530 _____. "The Sphinx of Ice," in Song and Story: Later
        Poems. Boston: Osgood, 1884.
The Sphinx in this poem is the enigma of the North Pole,
where "vast huddling bergs of frozen brine/ Jut spectral
from the bitter North's gray air." Like the Sphinx in the
Oedipus story, this one also kills those who cannot answer
her riddle, in this case "venturous mariners," who are
eager to discern "her great pale shape, her secret to entice."

531 _____. "Vesta," in Fantasy and Passion (1878), was the
        Roman goddess of the hearth, whose functions were essen-
tially the same as those of the Greek goddess Hestia. In
this poem the narrator speaks of a girl by whom he is
charmed. She emerges as a tireless "little farmer," busy
with hay, and animals, and growing gardens. He calls her
"Vesta of the milking-pails and chickens!"

FLECKER, James Elroy (1884-1915, English)

532 "The Bridge of Fire," in The Collected Poems of James Elroy
        Flecker, ed. with Introduction by Sir John Squire.
        London: Secker and Warburg, 1947.
Flecker's poem is a tribute to "all great Gods to whom

men prayed or pray," and they are ranged "high on the bridge of Heaven," where nothing interferes with "their grand and timeless hours of pomp and play." The assemblage is complete: Hermes, Persephone, Cybele, Mars, Pomona, Allah, Isis, Orpheus, and others, all standing on the "bridge of fire," eternal and beyond the realm of humanity.

533 _____. "Destroyer of Ships, Men, Cities," in Collected Poems (1947), is Helen of Troy, who was the most destructive force the ancient world knew. However, "she still breaks the hearts of men," and her destruction has never ceased.

534 _____. "Epithalamion," in Collected Poems (1947), is a wedding-hymn in praise of Peleus and his sea-goddess bride, Thetis. Aphrodite is an honored guest; she arrives with Thetis from the "glimmering house where her Father dwells in the sea."

535 _____. "In Phaeacia," in Collected Poems (1947), refers to an island in the Ionian Sea near the coast of Epirus. Odysseus here was treated well by the King and his daughter, Nausicaa. The poem is descriptive of a beautiful place, with praise for the beauty of a lady who wears a gown of silver and a crown of gold.

536 _____. "Narcissus," in Collected Poems (1947), comprises two poems, one a later version of the earlier. Although slightly different in imagery and style, they are essentially a lament by the narrator for the lovely image of his youth. He remembers the face, like Narcissus, which he saw reflected in the water, now that his "happy ways have ended/ By waters of despair."

537 _____. "Ode to the Glory of Greece," in Collected Poems (1947), is a fragment related to mythology only in several allusions--Apollo, Aeolus and Boreas, the Achaeans and Trojans. Mainly the poem commemorates the "glory that was Greece," and laments the absence of Byron and Shelley, who were great nineteenth-century poets of Grecian antiquity.

538 _____. "On Turner's Polyphemus," in Collected Poems (1947) refers to the painting "Ulysses Deriding Polyphemus," by Joseph M. W. Turner. Most of the details of the painting are embodied in Flecker's poem: the sun on the horizon is a burst of red and gold spraying out across all the other forms; Polyphemus is visible only as a huge pair of legs, his body disappearing into the clouds. One art critic (John Canaday, Mainstreams of Modern Art, page 271), has remarked that Turner's "romantic vision of the world as a cosmic union or struggle between the elements, dominated by fire and water," found its fullest expression in this painting.

FLECKER, continued

539 _____ . "Philomel," in Collected Poems (1947), is an adaptation in English of a poem by the French poet Paul Fort.
The violent story of Philomel, the nightingale, is not told
in explicit terms, but is the underlying theme throughout:
is it a bird or "some immortal voice from Hell?" All
else is silence, and even "Demeter listens to the nightingale."

FLETCHER, John Gould (1886-1950, American)

540 "The Bacchanal," in The Book of Nature: 1910-1912. London:
Constable, 1913.
The occasion for celebrating is not specified, but whatever
the reason it is a joyous time, and the poet says, "We with
draughts of ruby wine make revelry today." The crowd is
laughing and dancing and drinking.

541 _____ . "The Death of Prometheus," in Parables. London:
Kegan Paul, Trench, Trübner, 1925.
This two-page prose composition sees Prometheus as the
giver of a "new and quenchless fire of divine discontent,"
after Heracles released him from the rock. But he soon
found that no one was much interested in this gift and begged him to take it back. After ten thousand years he succeeded somewhat in "filling with some measure of his own
rebellious spirit, the breasts of a few poor, sickly, and
half-cracked enthusiasts." When these appeared to threaten
the order of things, he was nailed to a cross. He did not
die, however, and next took his gift to various rich and
powerful men; they were unimpressed, and put him to work
in a factory. Finally Prometheus begged Zeus to end his
life, but "Zeus, being in an ungenerous mood," refused to
do even this, so the Titan went back to the mountain and
chained himself up again.

542 _____ . "Dionysus and Apollo," in Fire and Wine. London:
Richards, 1913.
Here the two gods are presented as striking contrasts to
each other. Dionysus, as the god of wine, is also the god
of passions and "hot folly." Apollo is the god of light and
truth, and "sits high on a summit." The poet says,

Dionysus I shall not follow,
Too drowsy and dull is his wine.
I shall sit on the heights with Apollo,
And be taught of the sacred Nine.

543 _____ . "The Flocks of Pan," in The Book of Nature (1913),
is an uncomplicated description of the flocks as they browse
and feed on the mountainside; but when the god appears they

106

"flee over rock and dell." Pan is described as red-faced,
"with horns and a rag of beard," "horrible," and "goat-
legged, amorous."

544 _____. "On a Moral Triumph," in Parables (1925), is a
short prose piece in an ironic vein on Helen's attempt to
vindicate herself after she returned home to Sparta. She
claimed that she had never been to Troy, but that the gods
had taken her to Egypt and that a phantom had gone to
Troy. When asked for proof, she produced three witnesses
who were deaf and blind, but who obliged her by saying they
had seen and heard her in Egypt. Menelaus knew that he
had been taken in, but preferred to drop the matter and not
look foolish before the people of Sparta. As for Helen, she
became the benefactress of a home for fallen women and
the Society for protection of Young Girls. She still regarded
herself as beautiful, until one day a young man yelled, "You
wrinkled old harridan!" After this Helen hanged herself,
leaving a note in which she laid all the blame on Menelaus
and his fits of bad temper.

545 _____. "Towards Olympus," in Parables (1925), is a nostalgic poem at the conclusion of the book of parables. The
gods have all gone, out of the sky, away from the earth,
out of the sea. We no longer seek the "lithe and brittle
music of swords and flame," the poet says, and "heaven is
a blank news-sheet."

FLETCHER, Phineas (1582-1650, English)

546 "Venus and Anchises (Brittain's Ida)," in Venus and Anchises
and Other Poems by Phineas Fletcher. London: Ox-
ford University Press, 1926.
This new edition has been edited from a Sion College manu-
script for the Royal Society of Literature by Ethel Seaton,
with a Preface by F. S. Boas. The volume contains seven
poems, including the one published by Thomas Walkley in
1628 as Brittain's Ida, and attributed to Edmund Spenser.
The two versions of the poem, however, have different be-
ginnings. The poem, in sixty-one eight-line stanzas, tells
the familiar story of the goddess and the Trojan boy Anchises, as related in Virgil's Aeneid.

FREEMAN, Edward Augustus, and George W. Cox (1823-1892 and
1827-1902, English)

547 "The Feast of Attaginus" (by Cox), in Poems, Legendary and
Historical. London: Longman, Brown, Green, and
Longmans, 1850.
The feast described in this poem follows the conquest of
Athens by the Persians, under the command of Mardonius.

107

In the halls of the Theban Attaginus the Persians drink and
lay waste the sacred relics of Athena. There is one among
them who has prophetic powers and knows that the gods will
soon avenge the "sons of Greece." This occurred in 490,
when the Athenians with the help of the Plateans defeated
the Persians for the first time at Marathon.

548 _____. "A Legend of Thermopylae" (Cox), in Poems (1850),
is told some fifty years after the Battle of Thermopylae, by
an old man who now opposes the coming war of Athens and
Sparta. He knows the strength and powers of both sides,
and fears the extent of bloodshed and ruin. He recalls the
Spartans at Thermopylae, how they knew for three days that
they would die, and how on the third day they dressed themselves in their festival robes and went forth to their deaths.

549 _____. "The Meed of Heroes" (Freeman), in Poems (1850),
is a hymn to the honor of the warriors who fell at Marathon. These heroes are as much deserving honor as the
fallen heroes who fought at Thebes and Troy, and they de-
serve a poet as great as Homer or Orpheus.

550 _____. "Othryades" (Freeman), in Poems (1850), is based
on the historical event in which three hundred Spartans and
three hundred Argives were sent to do battle for a disputed
territory of Thyrea. All but two Argives and one Spartan,
Othryades, were killed. The Argives went to Argos with
tidings of victory; in the meantime Othryades stayed on the
field and stripped the Argive dead. Another battle ensued
and the Argives lost. Othryades then killed himself so
that he would not outlive the countrymen who had died.

551 _____. "The Parting of Hector and Andromache" (Cox), in
Poems (1850), is based on Book VI of the Iliad, but is not
a translation. Hector arms himself to go out and fight the
Greeks, and his son is frightened of his helmet and plumes.
Andromache is fearful that she will never see Hector again,
as indeed it turns out that she does not.

552 _____. "The Persians at Delphi" (Freeman), in Poems
(1850), is a part of the expedition of Xerxes, 480 B.C.,
to conquer Greece by land and sea. He won most of central Greece, including Argos, and the oracle at Delphi.
Freeman's poem is an appeal to the god Apollo to avenge
his temple and oracle, and to protect all the sacred relics
that have been brought for dedication to the god.

553 _____. "Poseidon and Athena" (Freeman), in Poems (1850),
is a traditional myth in which Poseidon and Athena compete
for patronage of the city of Athens. The twelve Olympian
gods sat as judges, and they gave the award to Athena, who

made the olive-tree grow on the soil. Poseidon had produced a salty spring, but the gods agreed that this was not
too useful. Angered by losing the competition, Poseidon
flooded part of Attica, but he later relented and was worshiped side by side with Athena in Athens.

GARNETT, Richard (1835-1906, English)

554 "Aegisthus," in Poems by Richard Garnett. London: Mathews
    and Lane; Boston: Copeland and Day, 1893.
Aegisthus, who helped Clytemnestra murder Agamemnon, is
the narrator of this poem. He reveals himself as a fearful
man, haunted by what he has done, yet feeling that he had
suffered much wrong at the hands of Agamemnon's father.
More than anything he is aware of Clytemnestra, calling
her his "soul's insane delight" and wishing that she would
kill him.

555   . "Apollo in Tempe," in Poems (1893), is based on
the mythological episode of Apollo's being exiled to spend a
year on earth serving the mortal Admetus. As a shepherd
Apollo kept the flocks, and while doing so he played on the
flute. He always attracted a crowd of listeners--birds,
wolves, shepherds, and shepherdesses. One day Hermes
arrived and hailed Apollo as brother, announcing that his
exile from Olympus was over. When his following saw that
he was a god, they were fearful, begging his forgiveness
for treating him as a mere mortal. Apollo chides them
for their foolishness.

556   . "The Cyclop," in Iphigenia in Delphi and Other
Poems. London: Unwin, 1890.
This poem tells the familiar story of the ugly, one-eyed
cyclops who loved the sea-nymph Galatea in vain. He is
described as sitting on the sea-shore pleading with the
nymph to come forth and love him, since he cannot swim
beneath the waves. The tone of the poem is ironic, and
presents Polypheme in a comic, ridiculous light for being
so presumptious as to think the beautiful nymph could love
him.

557   . "Dian's Ways," in Poems (1893), is a slight poem,
in form and substance, that describes the goddess as she
hunts in the forest, chasing the deer as it flies before her.

558   . "The Dumb Oracle," in The Twilight of the Gods
and Other Tales. New York: Knopf, 1926.
This moralistic prose tale begins with the death of the old
priest, who had been singularly influential in the lives of
the people who paid homage to Apollo. A new priest is
chosen, but the popularity of the temple declines until there
are hardly any followers at all. The god no longer speaks

through his oracle. One day an old woman comes to the young priest and tells him she can help him restore the greatness of the oracle, for it was in reality her voice that pretended to be the voice of Apollo. The young priest leaves the temple, disgusted and believing that all the gods are frauds and do not actually exist. As he travels throughout the land, he hears rumors that a young priest bearing his name now serves at the temple, and the people follow him by the thousands. The young priest returns to see who has usurped his position and finds that it is no one less than Apollo himself who has assumed his role. Now the priest is eager to resume his office, but the god tells him that he is reserved for a greater role: anyone can serve as the god's votary, but he must become the servant of Truth and Humanity, which will endure long after Apollo and all the gods are no more.

559 _____. "Echo and Narcissus," in Poems (1893), is a short lyric that incorporates the myth of Narcissus, the youth who became so infatuated with his own image, and Echo, the nymph. She loved him but was powerless to speak except to repeat words spoken by others, in this case by Narcissus, who looked at himself and murmured, "Beautiful image."

560 _____. "Endymion," in Poems (1893), is based on the myth that Endymion, loved by the goddess Selene, chose an immortal sleep on Mount Latmos. This poem depicts an Endymion who is indifferent to the time of the world and cares for nothing but the lovely face of Selene.

561 _____. "Io in Egypt," in Poems (1893), begins with a brief summary of Io's wanderings over the face of the earth after she was changed into a cow by the jealous goddess Hera. Soon, however, she comes into Egypt, where she awakes in a flood of sunlight, finds the gadfly that had tormented her gone, and is surrounded by a chorus of women inviting her to be their queen. Egypt is described as a land of refuge, welcome to Io after her long anguished travels.

562 _____. "Iphigenia in Delphi," in Iphigenia in Delphi (1890), is a dramatic work that extends the mythology of Iphigenia beyond the traditional story and accounts for her eventual death. At Aulis, Iphigenia was about to be sacrificed on the altar of Artemis, but at the last moment the goddess substituted a hind and spirited the girl away to serve in the temple at Tauris. Here Iphigenia prepared victims for the altar, for it was the custom of the Taurians to kill all strangers who came to their shore. When her brother, Orestes, came to Tauris, fleeing from the Furies who hounded him after he killed his mother, Iphigenia recognized

him, and together they escaped. Garnett's work begins at
this point, with Hermes leading the shade of Achilles into
the Temple of Apollo at Delphi. Soon Electra, the daughter of Agamemnon who helped Orestes kill their mother,
comes into the temple bearing the axe that had killed both
Agamemnon and Clytemnestra. She lays it on the altar of
Apollo, praying that it will do no further evil to her family.
Iphigenia arrives, and she and Electra talk at length, Electra not recognizing her sister, whom she believes to be
dead. Eurycles, identified as a friend of Orestes, comes
in and falsely points to Iphigenia as the "Scythian woman"
who would have killed Orestes. Electra snatches up the
axe and strikes Iphigenia. Orestes arrives too late to
save her, but tells Electra the truth of the situation. Iphigenia dies, and the tragic story of the children of Agamemnon is finally closed. In the background Hermes is seen
departing with the shades of Achilles and Iphigenia. When
Iphigenia was brought to Aulis for the sacrifice, it was
under pretense of marrying her to Achilles; now the hero
does indeed have his bride. Although most of this drama
is the innovation of its author, it is interesting and a not-
unreasonable conclusion to the Iphigenia story.

563 _____. "The Lost Poetry of Sappho," in Poems (1893),
creates an atmosphere of gloom and melancholy with images
of change and oblivion into which all things pass. The
narrator knows that he cannot halt this inexorable march
of time, but he prays for the poetic harmony that was once
Sappho's.

564 _____. "Nausicaa," in Poems (1893), refers to the daughter of Alcinous, king of the Phaeacians, who befriended
Odysseus when he was shipwrecked and washed ashore.
In the Odyssey not much emphasis is placed on Nausicaa's
being in love with Odysseus, but in Garnett's poem this
love is increased to a glowing obsession. Nausicaa has
three choices: she must find Odysseus safe with "grey
Penelope," in which case she will become one of the queen's
serving women; she must know if Odysseus perished, in
which case she will end her life; or she will be drowned
at sea.

565 _____. "Pan's Wand," in The Twilight of the Gods (1926),
tells an elaborate story of a nymph, Iridion, whose life
was somehow magically controlled by a special lily. When
she broke the stem of the lily, her life would expire. She
went to the cave where the god Pan lived and begged his
help. By means of his magic wand he transformed the dying girl into a magnificent lily, and when Death came looking for her Pan laughed at his own trickery. Death, however, warned Pan of the consequences of joking with Death.
Later Pan reached for his wand, only to discover that
Death had taken it. In conclusion, the perfect lily of Pan's

creation disappeared, and Iridion took its place, now dead "with the faded flower of her destiny" clutched in her hand. Death had not been outwitted after all.

566 _____. "Philemon's Death," in Poems (1893), refers to the Greek poet who lived about 360-263 B.C. With the invasion of Athens by Antigonus of Macedon, the Muses took flight, and the poet finished one last drama and died.

567 _____. "The Poet of Panopolis," in The Twilight of the Gods (1926), refers to Nonnus, a Greek writer of the fifth century A.D. His chief work was the Dionysiaca, an epic-like poem in forty-eight books, mainly concerned with the adventures of Dionysus in India. Nonnus also wrote a paraphrase of the Gospel of St. John. Garnett's tale accounts for the authorship of these two unlikely works, and does so with pure satire and malice. Even though it was the fifth century of the Christian Era, the old gods still stayed about, keeping an eye on human beings and coming to their aid when the cause was great enough. On one occasion Nonnus and Pachymius, an anchorite hermit, both desired the post of bishop in Panopolis. It came to a contest of fire and water, and Nonnus was supported by Apollo with Pachymius being represented by a certain "dark stranger" whom no one recognized. Nonnus was asked to burn one of his books of the Dionysiaca, the mere thought of which he could not stand; Pachymius was asked to take a bath, the mere thought of which sent him flying back to the desert. Thus neither one became the bishop. Nonnus pleaded with Apollo to restore him to favor, promising any penance that the god should impose, even to destroying the paraphrase of St. John. The penance, however, was that Nonnus should publish the paraphrase, and thus it was that "this Homer of Egypt" came to be author of one of the world's worst compositions.

568 _____. "Polyidus," in Poems (1893), refers to a mythological physician who brought back to life Glaucus, the son of Minos, by applying to his body a certain herb with which he had seen a serpent restore life to another than was dead. This poem is a simple telling of the legend, with particular emphasis on Apollo as the god of prophets and soothsayers, as well as of the healing arts.

569 _____. "The Siren," in Poems (1893), is a title that refers to two different poems, related only in that they both deal with the mythological temptress, the Siren. In one work the sailors hear the "luring melody" and are mindful of the destruction that its charms can bring. In the other poem seven sailors embark "down a stream unknown/ On a strange voyage towards an unknown sea." The Siren bids

them come to her, and then disappears. Henceforth the
seven sailors sit in their motionless boat and "gaze for
her return," and think no more of the unknown sea.

570 _____. "Truth and Her Companions," in The Twilight of
the Gods (1926), has a mythological basis, although this
work is more elaborate than its sources. Veritas (Truth)
was the daughter of Zeus, whom he sent to earth to educate
mortals. In this dialogue Truth reports to her father, telling him how she has been treated on earth: threatened,
laughed at, sneered at, even burned at the stake. Zeus
concluded that his daughter could not manage alone, and so
gave her two companions, Discretion and Good Nature.

571 _____. "The Twilight of the Gods," in The Twilight of the
Gods (1926), a tale told in five parts, takes place in the
fourth century A.D. at about the time Apollo's oracle was
closed at Delphi and the pagan religions declared officially
dead. This story begins with the awakening of Prometheus
and his release from captivity. As he had championed human beings, so he has now become a human being himself
and soon falls in love with a beautiful young girl, the daughter of an important official in the Christian church. Before
long there are those who would kill Prometheus and his
young wife as heretics. The Christian official gets them
away, and the rumor of their residence soon spreads among
the old gods. Here all the old gods--Apollo, Athene, Zeus,
and so on--call frequently, and spend most of their time
complaining bitterly of the state into which they have fallen.
Finally Prometheus suggests they go to Elysium, and off
they go, to be "seen no more." In the rush Hermes drops
his sandals, which Prometheus picks up, straps to his own
feet, and grasping his young wife, rises to immeasurable
heights among the stars where human beings have never been.
They look back and see the "little speck of shining dust from
which they had flown."

572 _____. "Wine and Sleep," in Poems (1893), is told in something of a fable atmosphere. Bacchus, the god of wine,
boasts that he is the most powerful of gods, that he can
depend upon his worshipers always to follow him, that he
is supreme over Zeus himself. And then, one by one, the
followers of Bacchus close their eyes and go to sleep; finally Bacchus stretches his young limbs and himself falls
into a deep sleep. From Olympus comes "the sovran
laughter of supremest Zeus." Powerful though he is, Bacchus has no control over the god Sleep, who is the servant
of Zeus.

GERARD, William (?-?, English)

573 "Achilles and Helen in Elysium," in Dramatic Vistas. London:
Mathews, 1919.

In form this work is a dialogue between Achilles and Helen
after their deaths. According to the myth these two were
transported to the Elysian Fields, where they enjoyed a
form of immortality. Life, or existence, as reflected in
Gerard's poem, leaves much to be desired, however. The
atmosphere is not gloomy as in the Underworld, but the
characters are afflicted with inertia; there is nothing to do
but reflect on their past lives.

574 _____. "Hellas Once More," in Hellas Once More and
Other Poems. London: Mathews, 1925.
For all its length (some forty pages) and seeming complexity, this poem achieves very little. At the outset the narrator calls, "Hellas in spirit be here," like "a light from
afar, to illumine the dark of the present." In the verses
that follow, something of a history of Greece is given,
particularly that of Athens, and its patron goddess Athena,
who stands for freedom of thought and mind. In conclusion
the spirit of Hellas is once more invoked, and the poem is
finished by acknowledging the debts that the English owe to
the Greeks.

575 _____. "Sappho," in Dramatic Vistas (1919), portrays
Sappho alone on the high Leucadian promontory. At the
end she leaps from the rock into the sea and is killed.
In the poem Sappho reviews her short life, what she has
been and how meaningless the future looms before her.
She recalls many of the girls who loved her, Atthis over
all, and how she loved them, and how they all are gone,
"passed from my life/ As from my sight." Then she remembers the ferryman Phaon, with whom she fell hopelessly
and insanely in love, and how he scorned her. She knows
it is the work of the goddess Aphrodite, and there is no
escape from the net that the goddess has thrown around
her. So thinking, Sappho calls out one final time and leaps.

GIBSON, Wilfrid Wilson (1878-1962, English)

576 "Baccanal," in Collected Poems: 1905-1925. London:
Macmillan, 1929.
This bacchanal was written to commemorate the ending of
World War I, November 1918. It describes the "twilight
of Trafalgar Square," with lads and girls locked in wild
embraces, celebrating the end of dealing with death. The
poet narrator says, "I see the outrageous dance, / The
frantic torches and the tambourines/ Tumultuous on the
midnight hills of Thrace."

577 _____. "Prometheus," in Collected Poems (1929), depicts
an old man, "broken and blind, a shivering bag of bones,"
as he goes about the streets selling matches. At night he

crawls into some dark corner to find sleep--ironically, since he holds Promethean fire within his hands.

578 _____ . "Thessaly," in Collected Poems (1929), was a province in northern Greece, believed to be the original home of the Achaeans who came from Crete. Many events and characters are associated with Thessaly, including Jason and the Argonauts, and a large expedition from there went to Troy. Gibson describes a "sun-steeped land" and then hears a boy, himself as a lad, in "shivering Northern seas," chanting to that "dark sky the tale of Troy."

GIDE, ANDRÉ (1869-1951, French)

579 "Oedipus," in Two Legends: Oedipus and Theseus, trans. by John Russell. New York: Knopf, 1950. Reprinted New York: Vintage, 1950.
Although the story in Gide's work is basically the same myth as that given in Sophocles' plays, the emphasis or theme is not the same. Here the central conflict is between individualism, as represented by Oedipus, and religious authority, as represented by Tiresias. Oedipus is a threat to the prophet, who encourages the people to believe that the plague is due to the impiety of the king. Moreover, it is Tiresias who prompts Oedipus to investigate the past, which will lead to his downfall and the destruction of his happiness. In the end, however, Oedipus triumphs by blinding himself, and tells Tiresias, "No more can you overwhelm me with the superiority of the blind."

580 _____ . "Persephone," an opera libretto, later printed in Complete Works, ed. by L. Martin-Chauffier. Paris, Nouvelle Revue Française, 1932-1939. Has not been translated.
This opera based on Gide's libretto was presented at the State Opera in 1934, with music by Igor Stravinsky, who also conducted and directed, and with choreography by Kurt Jooss. It did not attract many favorable comments. In structure it consists of three acts, or tableaux, the first of which shows Persephone's descent into the Underworld. The second part presents the goddess in the Underworld, and emphasizes her relation with the shades of that region. Finally, in the third act, she returns to the world, the betrothed of Triptolemus, whom Demeter has taught the arts and crafts of agriculture. The last view shows the goddess as she prepared to return to Hades in the Underworld, now reconciled to her loss of the world, anticipating her return in due season.

581 _____ . "Philoctetes, or The Treatise on Three Ethics," a play, in My Theatre. New York: Knopf, 1951. Reprinted in Bens, John H., and Douglas R. Baugh, eds., Icarus: An Anthology of Literature. New York: Macmillan, 1970.

This work is based on the traditional myth of Philoctetes, the Greek who inherited the bow and poisoned arrows of Hercules, and who was abandoned by his comrades on the island of Lemnos after a festering wound disabled him. In Gide's play, set some time in the tenth year of the Trojan War, Odysseus and Neoptolemus, the young son of Achilles, have come to the island to steal the bow and arrows. Philoctetes hears them plotting the theft, and freely gives up the treasures. Largely based on philosophical speculation, rather than action, the play goes forward with the wounded hero explaining what has happened to him in his years of solitude: he is no longer devoted to Greece, or to the gods, since they are merely projections of Greek thought, and are therefore limited and national in scope. He is now devoted to what is above the gods, the exact nature of which he cannot specify, but it is a pure devotion, free of all attachments to things. After his bow and arrows are gone, he achieves this devotion utterly, and is one with nature.

582 _____. "Prometheus Misbound," in Marshlands and Prometheus Misbound: Two Satires, trans. by George D. Painter. New York: New Directions, 1953. Reprinted New York: McGraw-Hill, 1965.
The French version of this work appeared in 1899. The edition referred to here is the only English translation. The setting is Paris in the late 1800s. The plot is complicated, with a number of comic episodes, but deals mainly with Prometheus, who has tired of his mountain and comes into Paris, bringing his eagle with him. He sits about and feeds the scrawny bird a morsel of his liver, which is disgusting to the café society with whom Prometheus associates. They tell him to feed the bird in private. Later Zeus, who is portrayed as a banker, has Prometheus thrown into prison for manufacturing matches without a license. In prison he grows fat and forgets about his eagle. Finally one day he calls the bird, and it comes, thin and nearly starved. Prometheus revives it with his liver, until it is able to lift him out of prison. After this Prometheus takes to the lecture stage, but does not manage to say much. At the end he kills his eagle, and he and his friends dine on its "plump goodness."

583 _____. "Theseus," a short novel, in Two Legends (1950), retells the entire Theseus legend, but manages to do so by keeping a firm grasp on details and never forgetting that the theme of this work is, like that of "Oedipus," a search for identity. According to the myth, after the death of Hippolytus, his son, Theseus went into exile from Athens and was not heard from again. Gide's work begins near the point at which Theseus, who is the narrator of the tale,

leaves the city. It is the story of his life, as he had
planned to tell it to his son, but now the son is dead, and
he feels that his own life will soon end. His youthful exploits are accounted for--his love for Ariadne, slaying of
the Minotaur, founding the city of Athens, love for Hippolyta
the Amazon, late marriage to Phaedra, the tragedy of Hippolytus and Phaedra, and in conclusion his meeting near
Thebes with Oedipus of Thebes. Theseus calls him the
greatest man he ever met, and their meeting at Colonus
"the summit and crown" of his life. Theseus had triumphed
on the "merely human" level; Oedipus had braved the gods
and won.

GIRAUDOUX, Jean (1882-1944, French)

584 <u>Amphitryon 38</u>, trans. by Samuel N. Behrman. New York:
Random House, 1938.
Giraudoux's play follows the classical myth that is presented
in the play by Plautus (c. 200 B. C.), but makes the characters modern. Allusions to modern ideas and feelings create
an atmosphere of reality, but these elements never degen-
erate into the bizarre and offensive. Alcmena, the wife of
Amphitryon, is visited by Zeus, who assumes the form of
her husband and makes love to her during his absence.
When the real Amphitryon returns, he and Alcmena are
puzzled until she realizes what has in truth happened. In
the course of time Alcmena gives birth to twins, one of
whom is Hercules, the son of Zeus. Although the comic
atmosphere of the play is maintained, there is an underlying theme of seriousness, the intrusion of the divine upon
the human.

585 _____. The Apollo of Bellac, trans. by Maurice Valency.
New York: French, 1954.
This short work is a curious mixture of reality and fantasy
that does not quite cohere into a single effect. The plot
revolves around Agnes, a charming young girl who is searching for a secretary's job. She is exceptionally ill suited to
this work, for she is too shy to meet anyone face to face.
In a waiting room she meets a certain Monsieur de Bellac,
who tells her that she can conquer the world if she will
merely say "you are beautiful. " She begins by practicing
on a butterfly, and soon finds that the formula does indeed
work. At the end she is far from happy, however, for she
does not feel that she has ever uttered the truth. She embraces the Gentleman from Bellac, but when she opens her
eyes he has disappeared, a god whom she knows was not
real.

586 _____. Electra, trans. by Wynifred Smith, in Bentley,
Eric Russel, ed. From the Modern Repertoire,
Series II. Bloomington: Indiana University Press,
1952.

For the most part the story follows the outlines of the Electra myth as given in Euripides. Electra, bearing great hatred for her mother, encourages her brother, Orestes, to murder Clytemnestra and her lover, Aegisthus. However, Giraudoux introduces a conflict that does not exist in the classical version. Just as Orestes is about to kill his mother and her lover, it is reported that Argos is being invaded by the Corinthians who will no doubt overrun the city and kill the people. Aegisthus suddenly emerges as a great warrior, and can save Argos if Orestes will not kill him. Electra remains inflexible, determined to see "pure justice," no matter how impractical the action. And so, with the Corinthians battering down the walls of the city, and destroying everything in sight, Orestes still slays Aegisthus, who might have saved them, and his mother, Clytemnestra.

587 _____. Elpénor, trans. by Richard Howard with assistance of Renaud Bruce. New York: Noonday, 1958.
This short novel is a parody of Homer's Odyssey, and since the main character is a figure for whom there is no traditional mythology, Giraudoux is free to go as far as he wishes with inventive fun. Elpénor, a companion of Odysseus, is killed when he mistakes a window for a door, falls off a roof, and breaks his neck. Most of the original adventures of the Odyssey are incorporated into this work, the cyclops episode, the Sirens, King Alcinous and his daughter, Nausicaa. The events are experienced by Elpénor, who is mistaken for Odysseus. At the end Odysseus orders him killed, but the gods restore him to life, only to kill him themselves later quite without cause or motivation.

588 _____. The Trojan War Will Not Take Place, trans. by Christopher Fry as Tiger at the Gates. New York: Oxford University Press, 1956.
This is usually called the most brilliant of Giraudoux's works, and is by any measurement a masterpiece. The setting is the city of Troy just before the war. Negotiations are going forward in a frenzy, with Hector trying to avert the war and Ulysses trying to regain Helen for Menelaus. Ulysses, however, is not at all sure that Helen is the true motive for the war--the Trojans are rich and the countryside fertile. At the end the peace is secure, and the Trojan war will not take place. Then a violent scene erupts, and a drunken Greek makes advances to Andromache, Hector's wife. The poet screams out that the Trojans are cowards for trying to make peace, and the war is decreed by the gods. Hector, still trying to avert war, kills the poet, but too late: the Trojan War will take place, and the gods are rejoicing. In answer to the question "What is tragedy?" Giraudoux once said: "It is the affirmation of a

horrible bond between humanity and a greater-than-human
destiny; it is man yanked from his horizontal, four-footed
posture and held erect by a leash; a leash whose tyranny
is abundantly evident. but whose governing will is unknown. "

GOSSE, Edmund William (1845-1928, English)

589 "Alcyone, " in On Viol and Flute. London: Kegan Paul,
     Trench, and Trübner, 1890.
     This is a conversation between Alcyone, the wife who has
     lost her husband at sea, and the god Phoebus Apollo. Al-
     cyone mourns "her fate and loveless days, " but Phoebus
     tells her that he will give her a treasure beyond compari-
     son: he will make their story immortal in song and poem.

590 _____. "The Death of Procris, " in In Russet and Silver.
     London: Heinemann, 1894.
     The myth of Cephalus and Procris is told as an illustration
     of the woes that jealousy can bring. Procris, whose hus-
     band, Cephalus, was a devoted hunter, began to fear that
     he was spending much time with another woman. One day
     she followed him, remaining out of sight hidden in the
     bushes. Cephalus heard a noise and thinking it was a deer,
     began shooting. An arrow hit Procris and she died. The
     poem ends with the observation that she is now at peace.

591 _____. "Eros, " in On Viol and Flute (1890), is a short
     description of the "god of love. " He is found sleeping in
     a forest, his lips as red as a rose, the busy bees swarm-
     ing around him.

592 _____. "The Gifts of the Muses, " in New Poems. London:
     Kegan Paul, 1879.
     The story of this poem is that of Daphnis, a mythological
     shepherd who is said to be the first to write pastoral poe-
     try. His successor Theocritus claimed him as his literary
     master. As a simple shepherd Daphnis was happy enough
     to play his flute and be in love with a nymph named Lycoris.
     Then one day the nine Muses came by and exchanged his
     flute for a lyre, and he became a great bard, traveling
     throughout the world and playing for kings. Once he saw
     Lycoris, who had now become a queen. His music and
     poetry were very sad, and he prompted his audience to
     tears. Finally, as he was an old man and near death,
     Apollo came and spoke to him of his greatness, how his
     songs would live forever. Daphnis had one final request
     of the god: that he restore his flute and take away the
     lyre that the Muses had given him in its place.

593 _____. Hypolympia, or The Gods in the Island. New York:
     Dodd, Mead; London: Heinemann, 1901.
     The subtitle of this work calls it "an ironic fantasy, " and

in the "Preface" we are told that it takes place on an island
in a remote but temperate province of northern Europe in
the early years of the twentieth century. The characters
of the play are the gods of ancient Greece, who make their
appearance in twelve scenes. The gods have been exiled
from Olympus by someone who seized the power and drove
them from their home. They are all here--Zeus, Hera,
Apollo, Aphrodite, Ares, Persephone, Dionysus, Hermes,
Hephaestus, even Heracles, the mortal who became a god--
behaving in their characteristic manners, trying to adjust
as best they can to the change from immortality to mortality. Some of them actually improve by becoming human;
others have grown peevish and petulant. Kronos, the old
god, is really senile and hard of hearing. At the end
three white ships led by Iris, the rainbow messenger, come
for them: the interloper on Olympus has himself been overthrown, and the gods can come home. In the rush to board,
Athena forgets Pandora's box, which contains a priceless
jewel, but Hermes tells her that they will need it no more,
to forget about it. Thus Hope remains on earth for human
beings.

594   _____. "The Island of the Blest," in Firdausi in Exile and
          Other Poems. London: Kegan Paul, Trench, 1885.
        In this long sequence of sonnets the narrator tells how he
        and his shipmates were lost in a storm at sea, were finally
        washed ashore on a strange island inhabited only by the
        dead heroes of ancient times. This place was ruled by
        Rhadamanthus, who gave the strangers permission to stay
        in this idyllic place so long as they did no wrong. Life
        went well until one of the crew members tried to steal
        Helen. For this crime he was hanged and the other mor-
        tals were driven from the island. Thus the narrator can
        say "we were stunned with awe and hopeless as the dead,"
        as he and his shipmates headed into a realm of gloom and
        storm.

595   _____. "The Lost Lyre," in New Poems (1879), is a refer-
        ence to "the ivory lyre/ That Orpheus bore." The poet
        imagines that it has been lost in a forest, is covered with
        endless autumn leaves, its music lost forever. He laments
        the state of music and song in his own time, and wishes
        that the spirit of Orpheus could revive the greatness.

596   _____. "The Maenad's Grave," in The Collected Poems of
          Edmund Gosse. London: Heinemann, 1911.
        This brief but effective poem points up the difference be-
        tween life and death. In life the girl, a maenad follower
        of Dionysus, was all motion--dancing, singing, whirling in
        the madness of the wine festival. In death she lies in a
        grove of poplars near a river, and both the trees and the
        water whisper, "Farewell."

597 _____ . "The New Endymion," in On Viol and Flute (1890),
is the story of a man who has always been observant of the
moon, as it comes and goes in its monthly cycle. Eventually he finds a love that fills his heart so completely that
he forgets about the moon. Then his love, Celia, dies,
and gradually the man begins to imagine that the moon is
a being who loves him. He now spends much time out on
a hill, and always sleeps outside on the night of the full
moon. The story of this man is not unlike that of Endymion,
who was loved by the Moon and was granted immortality.

598 _____ . "The New Memnon," in In Russet and Silver (1894),
has very slight mythological value, principally with reference to the giant Egyptian statue of Memnon that was built
to face the rising sun. In mythology Memnon was the son
of Eos and Tithonus, and when he died in the Trojan War,
his ashes were returned to Egypt. At some time he became
a god to the Egyptians and they erected this huge statue,
which was said to sing as Dawn, his mother, announced the
end of night and the approach of day.

599 _____ . "Philomel in London," in In Russet and Silver
(1894), is principally concerned with the dirt and squalor
of London and the human misery that the night hides. Over
this sad and squalid scene the nightingale--that is, Philomel--
sings her beautiful but despairing song.

600 _____ . "The Praise of Artemis," in New Poems (1879), is
a songlike poem in which the attributes of the goddess are
reviewed: the fleet-footed huntress, the keeper of animals
in the forest, and finally the goddess easily stirred to anger
and relentless with those who violate her laws.

601 _____ . "The Praise of Dionysus," in On Viol and Flute
(1890), is written in the form of a chant, with each verse
ending in the line "Deathless praises to the vine-god sing."
The imagery of the poem is descriptive of the dancers and
drinkers in the Bacchic procession as they make their way
through the town and into the mountains where the rites of
Dionysus were celebrated.

602 _____ . "The Sons of Cydippe," in Firdausi in Exile (1885),
is a brief telling of the story of Cleobis and Biton, the sons
of Cydippe, who pulled their mother in a chariot to a festival at the temple of Hera. At the altar Cydippe prays to
the goddess to grant her sons "the best gift of gifts," for
their kindness in drawing the chariot to the festival. In
reply the goddess of the heavens strikes the sons dead, this
being the best of all possible gifts.

603 _____ . "Timasitheos," in Firdausi in Exile (1885), is based
on a slight story told by Pausanias. The statue of Timasitheos was created by Ageladas of Argos to commemorate
the beautiful young wrestler who won more often than anyone

else at the Olympian and Pythian games. He also distinguished himself in battle many times, but finally he died
young. He took part in an uprising against Athens, and
when he was caught he was condemned to die. Gosse uses
the story to point up a moral that the gods do not look with
favor on anyone who rises too swiftly in the pursuit of excellence; they prefer a much slower growth.

604 _____. "The Tomb of Sophocles," in On Viol and Flute
(1890), is a tribute to the greatness of the Greek playwright
and a sad reminder that "he awakes no more / Wrapped up
in silence at the grave's cold core." No one in the history
of literature has made more poignant remarks about the nature of death than Sophocles, and now he himself is dead.

605 _____. "The Waking of Eurydice," in New Poems (1879),
begins with a conversation between Orpheus and Persephone
as he approaches the goddess in the Underworld. He pleads
for permission to return to life with his wife, Eurydice.
Persephone tells him that he must persuade Eurydice to go
with him, "Win her if thou canst with pleading." Slowly
Eurydice emerges from the shadows, but she says, "Bound-
less space and time unmeasured lie between thy voice and
me." She pleads with Orpheus to leave her, she does not
want to return to life. At the end she says, "Have pity,
Love, and leave me," or stay with her in death.

GRAVES, Robert (1895-   , English)

606 "The Ambrosia of Dionysus and Semele," in New Poems.
        Garden City, N. Y. : Doubleday, 1963.
The poem is narrated in the first-person by the poet, who
regards Semele and her "little slender lad" as the symbols
of poetic inspiration, who "have ambrosia eaten" and still
live.

607 _____. "Anchises to Aphrodite," in More Poems: 1961.
        London: Cassell, 1961.
The dilemma of the human being who is loved by a deity
is pointed up in this brief poem. Anchises, the handsome
Trojan who was loved by Aphrodite and had by her a son,
Aeneas, knew that he was simply one of the "ten-thousand
champions" whom she had loved, but he awaits her pleasure
and will be loved as long as she desires him.

608 _____. "Apollo of the Physiologists," in Poems: 1938-
        1945. New York: Creative Age, 1946.
Not much mythology finds its way into this poem, but it
does ironically remind the reader that the biological scientist, or perhaps the doctor, makes use of the symbol of

Aesculapius, the physician son of Apollo. This reminder is set against the scientific view of rejecting belief in gods or deities of any sort.

609 _____. "Damocles," in Poems and Satires: 1951. London: Cassell, 1951.
The subject of this poem is the legendary king over whose head a sword hung suspended by a single thread. He was unafraid of death, but somehow his story caught the imagination of poets and orators, and ever since has been used as a metaphor for doom and uneasiness.

610 _____. "Eurydice," in Man Does, Woman Is. Garden City, N. Y.: Doubleday, 1964.
Although making use of the basic story of Orpheus and Eurydice, Graves's poem has a highly original twist. Orpheus, who narrates the poem, is tired of death, and the neverending theme of the death of his wife, Eurydice. He would be free of her, but he knows he will never be.

611 _____. "Galatea and Pygmalion," in Collected Poems: 1961. Garden City, N. Y.: Doubleday, 1961.
In this version of the story of the sculptor and the woman whom he carved out of marble, the irony is that she, Galatea, who has been created to satisfy so much lust and passion in Pygmalion, readily turns to other men, enhancing her own reputation as a whore and not his as an artist.

612 _____. "Hercules at Nemea," in Poems About Love. Garden City, N. Y.: Doubleday, 1969.
The title refers to the first labor of Hercules, which was to kill the Nemean Lion. This he accomplished by strangling the animal with his bare hands, it being invulnerable to weapons. Graves, however, uses this incident to comment on the art of writing poetry. His Nemean lion is the Muse, who bites him through a finger, thus figuratively crippling him in his art.

613 _____. Hercules, My Shipmate. New York: Creative Age, 1945. Published in England as The Golden Fleece. London: Cassell, 1945.
For the most part Graves's long novel follows the story as told by Apollonius of Rhodes in the Argonautica, the most ancient extant work on Jason and the Golden Fleece. In this work Ancaeus, one of the Argonauts, tells the story in retrospect and concludes with a kind of epilogue, "What Became of the Argonauts." A sampling of chapter titles will indicate the familiarity of subject matter: "Orpheus Sings of the Creation," "Hylas is Lost," "King Phineus and the Harpies," "The Seizure of the Fleece," "Away from Colchis," "The Argo Comes Home," and so on. The language of the work, however, does not attempt to be formal and classical, but modern and colloquial, and the story-

telling details are frequently realistic and rowdy. The novel was reviewed favorably by most of the critics, their most frequent remark being that it was a very good story, readable and entertaining perhaps to a fault.

614 _____. "Instructions to the Orphic Adept," in Poems: 1938-1945 (1946), instructs a man as to what he must do to survive when he "descends from daylight into darkness" --that is, when he dies. He must avoid the spring of Forgetfulness, which will tempt him as he journeys through Hades, and continue to the pool of Memory. Here the guardians will ask him what he has to remember, and he must tell them that he wants to remember what he has suffered, that he is a child of Earth and of Sky, like Persephone. Then they will welcome him "with fruit and flowers," and he will become one of the lords of Hades.

615 _____. "Lament for Pasiphae," in Poems: 1938-1945 (1946), refers to the moon, or Pasiphae as a moon-goddess. The lament is that "this must be a night without a moon." The narrator pleads with the sun to "shine warm a little longer" since there will be no moon that night. In a larger sense the poem is also for a woman who is no longer there: "She who shone for all resigned her being" implies her death.

616 _____. "Leda," in Collected Poems. New York: Doubleday, 1955.
The imagery of Leda and the swan pervades the poem and is used to express disgust and revulsion of the "horror" that is lust or lasciviousness. Lust is equated with bestiality; the act of Leda in cohabiting with Zeus in the form of a swan shows humanity descending into the lowest depths.

617 _____. "Penthesileia," in Collected Poems (1961), is a short poem that nevertheless conveys a wealth of detail concerning the Amazon warrior who was killed by Achilles. Mythology says that Achilles loved the beautiful maiden in death, but this poem says he "committed Necrophily," on her in public view. This act met with the indignation and disgust of all; but one soldier, Thersites, gave an obscene snicker, and Achilles killed him on the spot. In Elysium, Achilles and Penthesileia meet, and she thanks him "for avenging her insulted womanhood / With sacrifice."

618 _____. "Prometheus," in Poems and Satires (1951), makes use of the Prometheus myth in a slight way, invoking the imagery of the god bound to the mountain, the eagle pecking away at his liver. In this poem, however, the god becomes a man, and the mountain becomes a bed in which he tosses all night. The eagle is the man's guilt, or regret, or whatever it is that prevents sleep.

619 _____. "Theseus and Ariadne," in Poems: 1938-1945
(1946), is an arrangment of two opposing points of view:
Theseus, who deserted Ariadne on the island of Naxos,
imagines that she still grieves for him, perhaps even died
for love of him. Ariadne, on the other hand, was loved
and wed by the god Dionysus after Theseus departed. She
never gives a thought to the lover who deserted her, but
now plays "the queen to nobler company."

620 _____. "To Calliope," in Collected Poems (1961), is an
address to the Muse of poetry, in which the narrator claims
he has done the best he could, but knows he has not lived
up to the utmost ideal.

621 _____. "To Ogmian Hercules," in Poems: 1965-1968.
Garden City, N. Y.: Doubleday, 1968.
This title is derived from the name Ogmius, by which the
Gauls referred to Hercules. It means Sun-Face, and the
poem is a tribute to the great hero who performed the
twelve labors and suffered a great many hardships. He is
immortal now, married to Hebe, and deserves to take his
ease, to "meditate a new Alphabet," to inspire poets, to
let others continue in war and strife.

622 _____. "Ulysses," in Poems About Love (1969), depicts
the hero as little better than a sex maniac, with all his
adventures being some form of sexual experience. Graves
says that he was "never done with woman whether gowned
as wife or whore," and he became blinded as to the dis-
tinctions between "Penelope and Circe." There were also
other women: Calypso, Scylla, Charybdis, the Sirens, and
the king's daughter Nausicaa.

623 _____. "The Weather of Olympus," in Poems: 1938-1945
(1946), is a godlike complaint about the weather. Zeus
complains that Olympus is too hot in the Summer, too cold
in the Winter. Ironically, however, the king of gods can
do nothing about the situation, since the winds are "answer-
able to Fate alone, not Zeus."

624 _____. "The White Goddess," in Collected Poems (1955),
was earlier printed as "The Destroyer," a title that best
describes the goddess. In the Spring her lovers celebrate
the "Mountain Mother," but even in November, the season
in which she destroys her lovers, the poet will still remain
faithful. The White Goddess stands for several ideas:
Nature, the poet's conscience, eternal wisdom, and perhaps
above all the pattern of death and rebirth.

GREGORY, Horace (1898- , American)

625 "Haunted Odysseus: The Last Testament," in Collected Poems.
New York: Holt, Rinehart and Winston, 1964.

In this poem the subject matter--Odysseus' visit to the
Underworld--and the language in which it is related com-
bine to produce a work of extraordinary excellence. Odysseus is the narrator, not the half-boastful hero of the Iliad
and Odyssey, but a frightened and haunted man: he has
been to the house of the dead, and the horror of the experience lingers about him still. The imagery that conveys
this experience is dark, tortured, and shot through with
cries of futility and hopelessness. When encountering his
mother among the dead, Odysseus stands like a little child
and just as helpless. At the end Odysseus is still haunted:
"at winter's midnight/ The Dead are here whispering through
snow. "

626   _____. "Homage to Circe, " in Collected Poems (1964),
       pays tribute to the beautiful "Lady" whose glass of wine
       could change a man into anything she wished, "lion, dog,
       or swine, " or create an illusion of whatever sensuous plea-
       sure she delighted in. But now it is time for death; "it is
       cold among the waters of the dead, " and the "long night
       has just begun. " This last journey "has outstepped" Circe's
       spell.

627   _____. "Medusa in Gramercy Park, " in Collected Poems
       (1964), is written in the form of a letter, by a very mod-
       ern Perseus, a traveler to all the important places in Eur-
       ope, England, and America. The letter might be to An-
       dromeda, the maiden whom the mythological Perseus res-
       cued from a monster and married. In Gregory's poem
       Perseus recalls his encounter with Medusa, in this case a
       very seductive woman, with whom he is tempted to have
       an affair, but he withstands the temptation. In his letter
       to his true love he explains that he "never touched her, "
       that rumors of rape and violence are being spread, but he
       is innocent. In order to escape the scandal he is leaving
       New York for the time, but will return.

628   _____. "New York, Cassandra, " in No Retreat: Poems.
       New York: Harcourt, Brace, 1933.
       This work is an impressionistic account of the confusion
       and suffering that accompanied the fall of the American
       economy in 1929, the beginning of the Great Depression.
       It is suggested by means of allusions and imagery that this
       great fall is not unlike the holocaust of Troy, which had its
       prophet in Cassandra but did not heed her warning. The
       poem abounds in images of unemployment, hunger, and loss
       of reason for living. Economic phrases are interwoven in
       the pattern of ruin and destruction.

629   _____. "Orpheus, " in Collected Poems (1964), recreates
       what Orpheus must have felt just before he was killed by

the maenad women. Suddenly his world was "Autumn's
afternoon, " he felt "the frost of winter" in his hair, and
the "wind was full of leaves. " It is a dreary, sunless
prospect, and when the women take him he does not care:
"His body was an empty martyrdom. "

630 _____. The Shield of Achilles: Essays on Beliefs in Poetry.
New York: Harcourt, Brace, 1944.
In his Foreword to this book of fifteen essays in literary
criticism, Gergory explains how he uses the image of "the
shield of Achilles. " This image is, of course, derived
from Homer's Iliad, Book XVIII, and refers to the huge
shield that Hephaestus made for Achilles before he went into
battle to kill Hector. For Gregory it is not so much a
question of all the descriptive details on the shield as it is
a matter of why Homer expended so much care on the
description. Perhaps it was a statement of the poet's theory of art: what the art should include and the use for
which it should be maintained. Gregory writes: "It might
be said that all the writers of whom I speak created with
variable success an Achilles' shield with which to face the
world. "

631 _____. "A Temptation of Odysseus, " in Collected Poems
(1964), refers to the Sirens, whose song of irresistible
charm was nearly the undoing of Odysseus and his men.
In this poem the emphasis is not on the sound of the Sirens'
song, but on the beauty of the paradise that is their island.
It beckons to the lonely man "lost at sea, " offers warmth
and shelter out of the storm, a haven of rest. Odysseus
says the secret of his avoiding the temptation was not just
in stopping his ears but in closing his eyes.

632 _____. "Venus and the Lute-Player, " in Collected Poems
(1964), is a picturelike description of a young man playing
a lute, creating "music with an art that angels sing. "
Such songs have power "to wake the moon, " and one might
think they would also "capture Venus. " But the goddess
stares, unmoved, as if to say she has no need of music or
any other artful means. "I am what you seek, and all you
need to know, " she says in closing.

GRIGSON, Geoffrey (1905- , English)

633 "Eurydice, " in The Collected Poems of Geoffrey Grigson:
1924-1962. London: Phoenix House, 1963.
The structure of this poem is built around the descent into
the Underworld made by Orpheus and Eurydice. The beginning and ending of the poem are controlled by imagery of
"yellow wrinkled poppies" and rain. Orpheus notes the poppies as he comes to the "gnarled entrance" of the cave,
and he sees them again when he comes out. The cave itself

127

is described in horrible images: "blackest cave," "blood not dried," "twitter and stench of urinating bats," and "damp dung of cattle." The basic story of Orpheus and Eurydice remains the same under this exceptionally ugly imagery.

HAKE, Thomas Gordon (1809-1895, English)

634 "The Birth of Venus," in New Symbols.   London: Chatto and Windus, 1876.
The birth of Venus is the traditional account of the goddess emerging from the sea-foam, but the details of Hake's poem are unusually sensuous, as well they might be, since Venus represents the principal of procreation and fertility. The birth occurs at night, and with the next dawn, a new era arrives, as the goddess is "thence upborne to the impassioned heaven."

635 _____. "The Sibyl," in Legends of the Morrow. London: Chatto and Windus, 1879.
The sibyls were prophetesses usually associated with Apollo, who lived in the shrine or temple of the god. Their lives were devoted entirely to the god they served, and they were reputed to have lived a thousand years.

636 _____. "Venus Anadyomene," in Legends (1879), is based on Praxiteles' sculpture of Venus rising from the sea. This artist, who lived in the fourth century B.C., created most of his work with his model and mistress, Phryné. In Hake's poem Praxiteles is represented as attempting to create his Venus by persuading this woman to reveal how the goddess looks in heaven. Finally, when Phryné falls in love with the sculptor, she is able to do so, and he cries, "The Venus is revealed! ... this is the immortal hour."

HEMANS, Felicia Dorothea (1793-1835, English)

637 "The Alcestis of Alfieri," in The Poetical Works of Felicia Hemans, with a Memoir by Mrs. L. H. Sigourney. Philadelphia: Porter and Coates, 1853.
This poem is an adaptation of Act I, Scene II, of the last tragedy that the Italian dramatist Vittorio Alfieri (1749-1803) is said to have composed. It is a simple scene, in which Alcestis announces to Pheres, the father of Admetus, that the oracle has provided for the son to live, that she will take his place in death.

638 _____. "Antique Greek Lament," in Poetical Works (1853), was originally called "The Lament of Alcyone." It tells

the story of Alcyone and her husband, Ceyx, who was
drowned at sea. The effect of the poem is gained largely
through a refrain: "Lonely I wander, weeping for my lost
one. "

639   . "The Death Song of Alcestis," in Poetical Works
        (1853), begins with a description of Alcestis as she comes
        forth in her splendid bridal robes, now to serve as her
        burial robes. It is a picture drawn with precise detail,
        but then she becomes aware that it is time to die, to leave
        the world, her children, even the one for whom she is go-
        ing to die, her husband, Almetus. The poem trails into
        another twelve stanzas, in which Alcestis bids farewell to
        the sun, the laurel, and the rose, and so on throughout na-
        ture. Finally she ends with a "conqueror's song," saying
        that she is glad to die for her lord.

640   . "Elysium," in Poetical Works (1853), describes the
        beauty of the mythological Elysium, the abode in which
        heroes, the fortunate, or distinguished persons spend eter-
        nity. However, the peasant, the slave, and the child had
        no such reward, and for these it was a plain that "could
        not yield one hope to sorrowing love. "

641   . "The Last Song of Sappho," in Poetical Works
        (1853), was suggested by a sketch that represented Sappho
        sitting on a rock above the sea, with her lyre cast at her
        feet. There is a desolate air about the figure, who seems
        utterly alone. In the eight stanzas of the poem Sappho ex-
        presses her love for the earth "with all its lovely things,"
        but still she invokes the sea to "bury her anguish," and at
        the end she identified with the sea-bird, saying, "I too
        come. "

642   . "The Lost Pleiad," in Poetical Works (1853), makes
        slight use of the mythological lost Pleiad, the sister who
        does not shine in the constellation, but for the most part is
        a poem of personal loss and grief. The poet has lost a
        loved one, and compares this loss to the star that has been
        lost, the one that does not shine. She concludes, however,
        that the "majestic heaven/ Shines not the less for that one
        vanished star. "

643   . "On a Leaf from the Tomb of Virgil," in Poetical
        Works (1853), describes a leaf, a "pale, withered thing,"
        that has fallen on the poet's grave. Other leaves will pre-
        sently grow in its place, and so on throughout nature; but,
        When will another poet of Virgil's stature be born? the nar-
        rator asks in conclusion.

644   . "Psyche Borne by Zephyrs to the Island of Plea-
        sure," in Poetical Works (1853), was written for a picture
        in which Psyche, on her flight upward, is represented looking

129

back sadly and anxiously to the earth. The poem, however, is more than a simple description of the mythological figure being swept heavenward; in effect it becomes a statement on the human soul, which at last must leave earth, and always does so with some regret and mourning for people and things left behind.

645 _____. "The Shade of Theseus," in Poetical Works (1853), is called "An Ancient Greek Tradition" and appears in a section titled Lays of Many Lands, each one commemorating some national celebration, popular custom, or tradition. This tale relates an incident that occurred at the battle of Marathon, which was fought between the Athenians and the Persians in 490 B. C. The Athenians were victorious, losing just under two hundred men, according to Herodotus, and the Persians losing over six thousand. The reason for this is attributed to the shade or ghost of Theseus, who fought in the battle and killed the Persians by the hundreds with his unseen sword and spear.

HEWLETT, Maurice Henry (1861-1923, English)

646 "Actaeon," in Artemision: Idylls and Songs. New York: Scribner, 1899.
"Actaeon" is a slight poem in which the narrator uses the myth of the hunter who looked upon his "Lady Artemis," and offended her with his unworthiness, as a metaphor of himself when he looks upon his lady and offends her. Yet, he says, he would rather be a "dog below her" than never to have known her.

647 _____. "Agrotera," in Artemision (1899), is a tribute to Artemis in an anniversary sacrifice of goats to the goddess at Athens.

648 _____. "The Argive Women," in Helen Redeemed and Other Poems. New York: Scribner, 1913.
These are the women who have accompanied Helen from Sparta. Cast in dramatic form, the composition was originally intended to be the first scene in "Helen Redeemed." The women live in almost total imprisonment, as indeed does Helen, and concern themselves with love-making, not the war. They are the playthings of Trojan soldiers, and they are not eager for the war to be over.

649 _____. "Ariadne Forsaken," in Songs and Meditations. Westminster: Constable, 1896.
Identified as a chorus from a play, this brief work laments the fate of Ariadne, who has been forsaken on the island of Naxos. The subject is treated fully in the play "Ariadne in Naxos," following.

650 _____. "Ariadne in Naxos," in The Agonists: A Trilogy
of God and Man. New York: Scribner, 1911.
The reason for Theseus leaving Ariadne on the island of
Naxos is variously given, but in this play it is the god
Dionysus who causes Theseus to take to his ships and sail
away. He leaves Ariadne pregnant and in company with
Dionysus. Later she is seized with remorse and refuses
to continue her relationship with the god. She seeks forgiveness in prayers to Artemis, but the goddess kills her
in a grove. The play ends with a soldier bearing Ariadne's
dead body onto the stage, and the Chorus of Cretan woman
commenting on the tragedy.

651 _____. "Arkadia," in Gai Saber: Tales and Songs. London: Mathews, 1916.
This sonnet describes "Artemis the Fleet," as she ranges
the hills of Arcadia, greeting the mountains and lakes, her
lips parted in the "sweet strong air."

652 _____. "The Ballad of Clytie," in Songs and Meditations
(1896), is the story of the hamadryad who loved and was
loved by the sun-god. In Hewlett's poem the maiden, consumed by the fierce rays of the sun, was changed into a
sunflower, which still worships the sun and follows him as
he travels across the sky.

653 _____. "The Cretan Ode," in Songs and Meditations (1896),
is a chorus that the author later used in his play "Minos
of Crete" (1911). It pays tribute to the gods and goddesses
who were favored on Crete--Apollo and Artemis, Demeter,
and several lesser deities. It is also a tribute to the beauty
of the island.

654 _____. "Daphne and Leukippos," in Gai Saber (1916), is
the story of the youth who loved Daphne and pretended to
be a girl in order to be with her as she hunted in the train
of Artemis. His pretense was discovered when he would
not strip and go swimming, and he fled away fearful of the
anger that Artemis might show toward him. One version
of the myth says that the girls fell upon him and killed him
with their hunting spears, but Hewlett's poem does not end
with such violence. Daphne was later loved by the god
Apollo, and was turned into a laurel tree to escape his advances.

655 _____. "The Death of Hippolytus," in The Agonists (1911),
is basically the same story that has been told of Phaedra
and the son of Theseus from Euripides down. Phaedra,
the wife of Theseus, conceives an uncontrollable passion
for Hippolytus, the son of Theseus by the Amazon Hippolyta.
He scorns her advances, and tries to escape. In the traditional account Phaedra tells Theseus that Hippolytus has
tried to persuade her to be unfaithful, and at this point Theseus calls down the curses of Poseidon on his son. Hippolytus

dies, and too late Theseus realizes the truth. Phaedra commits suicide. In Hewlett's version of the tragedy Phaedra prays for the destruction of Hippolytus, and then she herself is destroyed by Artemis. At the end Artemis appears and says that Hippolytus is safe "deep in the woodland, not of this world. "

As the last play of the trilogy that included "Minos of Crete, " and "Ariadne in Naxos, " this work climaxes the overall story of the destruction of the House of Minos. With the death of Phaedra, the youngest daughter, the downfall is complete, and "all the Blood of the Bull split as it was foretold. "

656 _____. "Eros-Narcissus, " in Songs and Meditations (1896), is a delightful combination of two myths, resulting in a statement on the nature of love. The narrator questions that he should pry all the secrets from his lady's heart, saying, "In her own mould she fashions Love, and he / Scarce knows himself, vested so tenderly. "

657 _____. "Hecate, " in Artemision (1899), is a tribute to the goddess who is sometimes identified with Artemis and the moon, or rather with the absence of Artemis and the moon during the dark nights of the month. She is also connected with fertility, and therefore is an earth-deity.

658 _____. "Helen Redeemed, " in Helen Redeemed (1913), is a long narrative poem about the final days of the Trojan War. The first part accounts for the death of Achilles, which had long been foretold and was his fate since he killed Hector. The second part continues with the suicide of Ajax, and the despair of the Greek army in its loss of the two great heroes. Menelaus has a dream in which he and Helen are reunited, and risking his life he goes up to the wall where Helen is sitting in the night. Parts three and four consist largely of conversation between Helen and Menelaus, recriminations and threats from him, explanations from her and finally a plea, "Come soon, come soon. " In the fifth part a council of the Greeks is held, and it is decided that Odysseus will slip into Troy, seek out Helen, and obtain information from her; this scheme is carried out in the sixth part. The remainder of the poem details the building of the Wooden Horse and the Greeks' entry into Troy. In the conclusion the Greeks overrun the city, and Paris leaves Helen for the last time, going forth to meet his death.

659 _____. "A Hymn to Artemis, " in Songs and Meditations (1896), enumerates the functions for which this goddess is responsible: to sever the thread of life when a person is dying, to aid in childbirth and labor, to light the night with the moon, to protect wild animals and creatures of the

forest, to protect virgins. In brief, her functions are so numerous that Zeus said of her birth, along with that of Apollo, "Delos the chosen is and shall be / Star-ray for all this blind and groping Earth."

660 _____. "Hypsipyle," in Helen Redeemed (1913), is the Persephone myth with a highly original turn to it. The Hypsipyle of this poem is a child whom Persephone regards as her playmate and best friend. When Hades brings the goddess to the Underworld as his queen, Hypsipyle goes with her, forsaking life and the world of the living. The Hypsipyle of this poem is not to be confused with the Queen of Lemnos whom Jason loved.

661 _____. "In the Forest," in Gai Saber (1916), is a poem of Pan, descriptive of the half-goat, half-man deity, and his needs as an animal and as a god. His is a divided world, in which he must constantly reconcile and live with his two natures.

662 _____. "Latmos," in Artemision (1899), is a lengthy treatment of the Endymion story. In this version, however, Endymion is a rather rowdy and forward youth who pursues the moon-goddess and would have her marry him and be his housemate and constant companion. This is impossible, of course, and the goddess leaves him on the island of Latmos to sleep forever. Nightly the goddess passes over the island and looks upon her lover, whom she had to abandon when he asked for too much.

663 _____. "Leto's Child," in Artemision (1899), begins with the birth of Apollo and Artemis on the island of Delos. As the twins grow into youth, Leto, their mother, sends them forth, for they are gods and must go their ways. Artemis becomes the "Gentle Shepherdess," and cares for all creatures that live in the forest. She becomes fast friends with a nymph named Callisto, and the two are like sisters until Callisto betrays the goddess. In Hewlett's poem it is Pan who fathers Arcus, Callisto's son, but the seducer is usually said to be Zeus. Artemis changes Callisto into a bear and she is hunted and shot by her son. Still unwilling to entirely abandon Callisto, Artemis made her a constellation known as the Bear.

664 _____. "Minos of Crete," in The Agonists (1911), is the first play of the trilogy that includes "Ariadne in Naxos" and "The Death of Hippolytus," three "barbarous old tales," as Hewlett called them. The background of this play is principally the Europa story, the girl who was carried away by Zeus disguised as a bull. She had given birth to three sons on the island of Crete, the oldest of whom, Minos, proclaimed himself king of that island. Pasifae, the wife of Minos, mated with a white bull that had been sent by

Poseidon to curse the house of Minos. She was the mother of the dreadful Minotaur, the half-man, half-bull creature that Theseus eventually killed in the labyrinth. As this play begins, Pasifae has killed herself, and Minos is away on a pilgrimage to Mt. Ida, where he communes with Zeus, his father. When Minos returns to Crete, his world falls apart: he learns that Pasifae is dead, that the Minotaur is her offspring by the Cretan Bull, and that his son, Androgeos, has been killed in Athens. Minos vows that henceforth Athens will pay tribute to Crete by sending its youth on a yearly voyage to feed the Minotaur, and that his people will no longer be killed by the ravening creature. The play ends with Minos thinking that he has outwitted the oracle who has said, "Woe upon woe till the blood/ Of the Bull be drained and done." In effect Minos has simply set the final stage for his house to be destroyed: Theseus will come with one shipload of Athenian youths and kill the Minotaur, he will be the cause of Ariadne's death, and finally he will be the destruction of Phaedra, the youngest of Minos' daughters. All these events occur in the other two plays of Hewlett's trilogy.

665   _____. "The Niobids," Artemision (1899), is a straight-forward narrative of Niobe and her seven sons and seven daughters, who were all slain by Apollo and Artemis. The focus of this poem is the reason for this slaying--the immense pride of Niobe, who constantly boasted of having so many fine children and scoffed at the goddess Leto for having only two, Apollo and Artemis. At the end Niobe is changed into a fountain and her tears continue to flow.

666   _____. "Oreithyia," in Helen Redeemed (1913), is the princess of Athens who was loved by the North Wind, Boreas, and was carried to "stormy Thrace," where she bore him two winged sons, Zethes and Calais.

667   _____. Pan and the Young Shepherd. London: Lane, 1899. This "Pastoral," although cast as a mythological composition, is in effect a Christian morality play. Neanias, a young shepherd, goes seeking a bride and falls in love with Aglae, one of the seven daughters of Earth. It so happens that Aglae is the beloved of Pan, who asserts himself in very powerful tones: "I am Pan, haunter of these wilds ... I am Pan, and the Earth is mine." He drives Neanias away, but the shepherd's love for Aglae is far too great to abandon her, and they escape into the forest in a cold November night. The other daughters of Earth plead for Pan to save them from the storm, and reluctantly he does so. However, Aglae and Neanias would have been saved anyway because they prayed to the Christian god and he heard their prayers. Thus the hold of Pan is broken.

668 _____. "Prometheus," in Songs and Meditations (1896), is
an unusual interpretation of the myth, and perhaps a most
meaningful one. The fire that Prometheus brought to humanity was the power of thought, which puts us "in a cage
of pain," which all our life is a "pure thin fire that beateth
against the bars and bonds" of our "grosser part." Finally,
when we are freed of the body "shatter'd and torn," we see
the futility of life and know it were "better not to be born."

669 _____. The Ruinous Face. New York: Harper, 1909.
This is a prose composition based on essentially the same
material that was to be covered in the shorter poem "Helen
Redeemed" (1913). In The Ruinous Face Hewlett departs
from basic mythology and allows Menelaus to kill Paris,
which serves poetic justice, but not the old myth in which
Paris is killed by the arrows of Philoctetes. Also, at the
end of this work Helen hangs herself in great remorse over
what she has done, which perhaps also serves poetic justice
but does not follow any known mythology of what happened
to Helen at the end of the Trojan War.

670 _____. "The Veiled Lover," in Gai Saber (1916), is a version of the Hippolytus-Artemis myth. It is always said that
Hippolytus served this goddess and scorned Aphrodite, but
it is not usually presented that Hippolytus was actually the
lover of Artemis. In this poem she veils herself and loves
the youth in a "deep wood" that was sacred to her. After
some time Hippolytus must go to Athens, where he will become involved with Phaedra and ultimately meet his death
because of her entanglement. At his death Artemis once
again takes Hippolytus to the sacred grove, where she restores his life and stays with him.

HOPE, A. D. (Alec Derwent, 1907- , Australian)

671 "Circe: After the Painting by Dosso Dossi," in Collected
Poems: 1930-1965. New York: Viking, 1966.
The details of the poem follow those of the painting by the
Italian artist Dosso Dossi (1479-1542), with the beautiful
naked form of the goddess at the center, and all the creatures she has changed around her. The most striking aspect of the painting, however, is the expression on the faces
of the animals. The poet says it is "the last human shadow
of despair," as it fades from "the sad, inquisitive, animal
eyes."

672 _____. "The End of a Journey," in Collected Poems (1966),
is an analysis of Odysseus as he slowly recognizes that his
adventure is over. First, his night with Penelope is not
very exciting, "an old man sleeping with his housekeeper";
then it is not very heroic to look on the victims of his
slaughter, particularly the housemaids who were hanged,

135

"each with a blank, small strangled face"; and finally there was the sea, no longer a threat, "the gods at last had left him." He dreams of the past, and relives hearing the song of the Sirens, Calypso singing in her haunted cave, the love of Circe. Now he is indeed a "castaway upon a cruel shore."

673 _____. "Pasiphae," in Collected Poems (1966), is based on the myth that Pasiphae, the wife of Minos of Crete, conceived an unnatural passion for a bull that Minos had failed to sacrifice to Poseidon. Daedalus created a hollow wooden cow by means of which Pasifae was able to satisfy her passion. From this encounter she gave birth to the Minotaur, half-man, half-bull, who was later confined in the labyrinth by Minos.

674 _____. "The Return of Persephone," in Collected Poems (1966), makes use of the familiar myth that Persephone returns each year to earth, leaving her dark husband in the Underworld when the god Hermes comes for her. This poem, however, goes beyond the simple story and recreates the character of Hades, the love he feels for Persephone, and the pain he feels at her return to the upper world. The poem also considers the love Persephone feels for Hades, when she sees his great pain at her leaving. These emotions are not typically a part of the legend, it being understood that Persephone was the wife of Hades through no choice of her own.

HOPKINS, Gerard Manley (1844-1889, English)

675 "Andromeda," in The Poems of Gerard Manley Hopkins, ed. by W. H. Gardner and N. H. Mackenzie. London: Oxford University Press, 1967. Based on the 1918 edition.
Andromeda, the daughter of Cepheus and Cassiope of Ethiopia, was betrothed to her uncle Phineus, when Poseidon sent a flood and a great sea-monster to ravage the country because Cassiope had boasted of her beauty and had compared herself with Hera and the Nereids. The oracle gave out that nothing could appeast Poseidon except that Andromeda to be exposed to the sea-monster. She was therefore tied to a rock, naked, and at the moment the sea-monster was about to devour her, Perseus, returning home through the air by means of Hermes' winged sandals, saw her and instantly fell in love with her. Having just come from his feat of killing Medusa, the Gordon, Perseus turned the sea-monster into stone by showing him the hideous head. The marriage of Andromeda and Perseus was opposed by Phineus, and he too was turned into stone. One myth says that Athena changed Andromeda into a constellation after her death.

676 _____. "Io," in Poems (1967), is largely descriptive of the beautiful young cow into which Io was changed because of Hera's wrath and jealousy. Only a vague shadow of her former self still remains, but she remembers her life as a woman loved by Zeus, and she suffers bitterly.

677 _____. "Spelt from Sibyl's Leaves," in Poems (1967), is based on the function of the Sibyl, a priestess of Apollo's temple, as in Virgil's Aeneid, Book VI, who reads the future of Aeneas by writing her prophecies on leaves and then scattering them to the winds. In his poem Hopkins is "spelling" a modern future, dark and torturous, filled with images of waste, loss, and death itself.

678 _____. "A Vision of the Mermaids," in Poems (1967), recreates an experience of the narrator as he rows out to sea "at the setting of the day." With the heavens ablaze at sunset, he sees six or seven mermaids rise from "the deeps to gaze on sun and heaven." They pay no attention to the man, but he perceives them to be very sad. He does not know why, but he speculates on their sadness: perhaps because they must live in the sea, "far from man," or because they ring the death knells for those seamen who die in the vast chasms of ocean. Then they begin to sing, as the day darkens. At the moment of darkness they disappear, their song becoming one "sweet, deep, heart-broken close." The narrator hopes to see them again, but never does, and knows they will come no more.

HORNE, Richard Henry [Hengist] (1803-1884, English)

679 Orion, An Epic Poem in Three Books. London: Miller, 1843. Reprinted with Introduction to Horne's Life and Works, by Eric Partridge. London: Scholartis, 1928.
For all its length and complexity, Orion is a simple story, designed to present a complicated allegory. Orion, the giant hunter, is one of a group of beings who represent elemental physical power; Orion is not entirely like the others, however, and once he falls in love with Artemis, his imagination soars upward. Later he falls in love with the beautiful daughter of King Oenopion, Merope, but this proves his undoing. The king's men take Merope away and put out the eyes of the giant. He is directed to Eos, goddess of the dawn, who restores his sight, but arouses the jealousy of Artemis, who kills him with a giant scorpion. She repents of her action, and asks Zeus to restore him to life, but this is impossible, and the best he can do is make Orion immortal by transporting him to the stars. Thus the life of the giant hunter becomes an example of one who triumphs over the nature of his being, and is finally rewarded by being made a part of the eternal order of things. He is still loved by the goddess Artemis, but especially by Eos, as he, "rising still with nightly brilliance," merges with the dawn.

HORNE, continued

680 _____ . Prometheus, the Fire-Bringer. Edinburgh: Ed-
       monston and Douglas, 1864.
       In a note at the beginning of this work Horne explains that
       he adopts the myth that Prometheus did not steal fire from
       the gods, but that the gift had been taken away from human-
       ity by an earlier Supreme Ruler. Zeus refused to return
       fire, and Prometheus undertook to obtain it for humankind.
       Otherwise, the dramatic poem is much like other versions
       of the story: Prometheus is condemned to be chained to a
       mountain, and an eagle will eternally eat of his liver. The
       lame god Hephaistos is assigned to weld the chains in place,
       but he does so very reluctantly. Horne creates the Titan
       as the "friend and instructor of Humanity,--its first Cham-
       pion, and its first Martyr; the grand old Pagan archetype,
       and providential foreshadowing of the Divine Master who
       came upon the earth many centuries afterwards. "

HOUGH, Graham (1908- , English)

681 "Andromeda," in Legends and Pastorals. London: Duckworth,
       1916.
       Without being coarse, this poem strips the Andromeda-
       Perseus myth of any heroic or romantic notions. Androm-
       eda is not chained to a rock: she is married to a monster,
       and they live in a cave that is described as dark and foul-
       smelling. When Perseus arrived, "red-hot with bravery,"
       he finds her sitting upon a damp stone, busy with her knit-
       ting, the monster asleep in the corner, and dinner simmer-
       ing on a fire of smouldering wood. The hero did not know
       what to do in the face of so much dullness, and clearly he
       saw no "thundering wrong to fight about. " He simply turns
       and leaves, and Andromeda once more turns to sweep "the
       dark sea from the door. "

682 _____ . "Children of Zeus," in Legends and Pastorals
       (1961), is a review of the numerous progeny engendered by
       Zeus, and some of the results of his encounters. Assuming
       many shapes--bull, ram, serpent, swan, golden rain--he
       beget "tall heroes, monsters, deities"; the fall of Troy;
       and a son with endless wisdom, Dionysus, "a child who was
       madness, wine, and tragic fury. " The poet questions wheth-
       er the god intended to create such variety, his own lust be-
       ing "a tale more likely. "

683 _____ . "Diana and Actaeon," in Legends and Pastorals
       (1961), retells the familiar story of Actaeon, the hunter,
       who accidentally comes upon Diana, or Artemis, in her
       bath and is changed into a stag that is hunted and killed by
       his own dogs. This poem, however, attributes the tragedy
       to a law much older and more significant than merely the

"furious routine of outraged majesty and vengeance. " In
fact, the Diana of this poem "did not really care, " and
would gladly have spared the "great innocent, " except for
the old law that "decrees whoever trips upon their [the
gods'] power must fall its prey. " The hunter who trips
upon the source of his power must become the hunted, as
is the case with Actaeon. A similar example might illus-
trate the law just as well: the warrior who violates the
source of his strength (Athene, as the goddess of warriors)
may very likely fall in battle.

HOUSMAN, A. E. (Alfred Edward, 1859-1936, English)

684 "Atys, " in Complete Poems of A. E. Housman, with an Intro-
       duction by Basil Davenport and a History of the Text
       by Tom Burns Haber. New York: Holt, Rinehart and
       Winston, 1959. Centennial edition.
     The name Atys refers to several mythological characters,
     but the one in Housman's poem is the son of Croesus, a
     king of Lydia. In this myth is the theme that one's fate
     is irrevocable and is not to be escaped. Croesus dreamed
     that his son was killed, and thereafter denied the youth all
     access to weapons. Eventually the dream became less
     vivid and Croesus allowed Atys to go with a hunting party
     in search of a wild boar that was laying waste the country.
     During this hunt he was accidentally killed by Adrastus,
     his guardian.

685 _____. "The Oracles, " in Complete Poems (1959), illus-
       trates that one of the most prominent features of the Greek
     religion was a belief in and reliance upon the prophecies
     and pronouncements of the oracles, given out to the people
     by the prophets or soothsayers. The two most famous
     oracles--both referred to in Housman's poem--were that of
     Zeus at Dodona and that of Apollo at Delphi. At Dodona
     the answers came from an oak sacred to Zeus, either
     through the sound of the wind in its leaves or from the
     sound of a spring that gushed up at its roots; this temple
     contained a large cauldron, renowned for its echoes. At
     Delphi, the answers were given by a divinely inspired
     priestess, the Pythia, who shrieked her prophecies in an
     incoherent frenzy and threw leaves of a tree into the wind.
     The stone called the Omphalos, or navel, was supposed to
     be the central point of the earth. The details of the last
     stanza are derived from the account given by Herodotus in
     his History. The Athenians had twice consulted the oracle
     at Delphi and had been forewarned of their defeat. The
     Greeks, however, remained faithful to their lands, and had
     the courage to await the coming of the Persians. The
     Spartans' combing of their hair was reported by a spy of
     Xerxes, who found it a laughable matter. He had no way
     of knowing that the Spartans were preparing themselves to
     hold the pass or die courageously.

139

HUMPHRIES, Rolfe (1894-1969, American)

686 "Aeolus," in <u>Collected Poems of Rolfe Humphries</u>. Bloomington: Indiana University Press, 1966.
Aeolus, the king of the winds, is the narrator, and he explains how he must fight "those stormy devils" to "save a world
from ruin." The winds all wish to blow at once, but it is
the office of Aeolus to see that this does not happen; he
must be "responsible and tyrannous."

687 _____. "Arachne, Penelope," in <u>Coat on a Stick</u>. Bloomington: Indiana University Press, 1969.
Of this composition Rolfe Humphries says, "A difficult poem,
which began simply with the sight of a redwinged blackbird;
then I wanted to counterpoint him with other music makers,
neither of whom was quite sure who led, who followed.
Hence, the weaving girl, Arachne. Then the idea was to
set off against them another pair, making music in some
different way, with a different kind of assistant. Ah!
Penelope, the unweaver;--her assistant? Nobody. It is
coincidental that Odysseus had told Cyclops his name was
Noman."

688 _____. "Episode in Elysium," in <u>Collected Poems</u> (1966),
recalls the visit of Aeneas to the Elysian Fields in the
Underworld where he consults with his father, Anchises.
The imagery of the first stanza suggests the <u>Aeneid</u>, the
fall of Troy, the murder of Priam and his young son, and
the long, perilous journey of Aeneas that began the night
of Troy's destruction. The second stanza suggests Virgil's
pastoral poetry, the <u>Eclogues</u> or <u>Bucolics</u> and the <u>Georgics</u>.
The last remark, "sorrowful from birth," has been inferred,
perhaps, from the fact that Virgil suffered from ill-health,
was never married, and in general expresses a melancholy,
tragic outlook in all his work. In the concluding three lines
Virgil is sorry for the poet who values life, and work, and
the eternal quest.

689 _____. "Europa," in <u>Collected Poems</u> (1966), is the Europa-
Zeus-Bull myth with a modern air. Europa is bored with
the men in her life, "polite, intelligent, and thin." She
longs for a "bull-necked savage," a real animal, as we
would say in modern terms. She finds this one who will
utterly possess her in the captain of a boat, whom she sees
as a god who has assumed the form of a bull.

690 _____. "Fragment of a Legend," in <u>Collected Poems</u> (1966),
relates the myth of Orpheus going into the Underworld to
return his beloved Eurydice to life. His music so charmed
Persephone that she gave her consent. Then Hades gave
his consent, knowing that Orpheus would look back, and that
Eurydice would be finally lost to him. Hades knew that the
"great songs rise from loss," and that this musician at the

last moment would choose to see his love fade into the darkness rather than relinquish his great power of song and music.

691 _____. "The King of the Grove," in Collected Poems (1966), is based on the myth with which Sir James G. Frazer begins his monumental work The Golden Bough. According to this legend, the priest of Diana's wood at Nemi held his office until he was murdered by his successor. He had himself obtained the office by murdering his own predecessor. Life for this "king of the wood" was a constant vigil of carrying a drawn sword and expecting at every moment to be set upon by one who wished his office. It was always kill or be killed. In Humphries's poem the challengers are of decreasing heroic stature--cowards, a eunuch, a woman, a dwarf--whom the king kills and finds disgusting. Eventually no one comes. At the end the king is challenged by a young boy who kills him and who is killed. The king dies happy, for "once more his sword has pierced a warrior's heart."

692 _____. "The Labyrinth," in Collected Poems (1966), makes use of the ancient labyrinth of Crete, the Theseus and Ariadne story, and the Minotaur to create the predicament of a modern narrator. He says, "Dark is the maze," but he has "no Ariadne at his side," he has no shield. He hears the "two-formed monster" bellow and smells him, but he has no defense and will be destroyed.

693 _____. "Proteus, or, the Shapes of Conscience," in Collected Poems (1966), refers to the sea-deity, sometimes called "the Old Man of the Sea," who had the ability to change shapes and thereby frighten or discourage anyone who would try to make him foretell the future. The secret was to "hold him down," no matter what shape he took, untill he told you what you wanted to know. This poem equates the human conscience with Proteus, and says that one must not be frightened or dismayed by the changing forms, that in time the conscience will measure up to one's own identity.

694 _____. "Theseus," in Collected Poems (1966), is a study of the hero on his way home from Crete, having faced the Minotaur. As he nears the shore, he thinks it is good to be on land once more, to have the safety of earth to hold on to. He may lie awake all night and look at the stars in pure utter space. This will once again remind him of the infinite sea and his longings for adventure. So the cycle goes, the coming in and the going out, and Theseus is the great symbol of humanity in its search for action and its need for rest.

695 _____. "The Thracian Women," in Collected Poems (1966), refers to the woman who killed Orpheus and threw his head

into the Hebrus river.   The maenads hated Orpheus because
he loved Eurydice, or man, or perhaps the art of song.
They hated everything, love and men and art.   Although
they followed the god Dionysus, their real loyalty was to
Attis, the god who castrated himself, and this "was how
they wanted men to be. "   In killing Orpheus, however, they
set his music free to float down "all the shining streams of
Time, " forever in that immortal voice.

HUNT, Leigh (1784-1859, English)

696   "Apollo and the Sunbeams, " in The Poetical Works of Leigh
            Hunt, ed. by H. S. Milford.   London: Oxford Univer-
            sity Press, 1923.
      Hunt's poem is a tribute to the sun as it is manifested in
      light, which he sees as "visible immortality, warm from
      heaven. "   As for Apollo, he still lives, nor have poets and
      painters ever thought otherwise.

697   _____. "Bacchus and Ariadne, " in Poetical Works (1923),
      follows the traditional myth in that Theseus deserts Ariadne
      on the island of Naxos, either because he wished to be free
      of her, because he had fallen in love with Ariadne's younger
      sister, Phaedra, or because the god Bacchus ordered him
      to do so.   Whatever the reason for Theseus' leaving, Bac-
      chus comes to console the grieving woman and marries her.
      The poem concludes with their wedding among the gods; at
      the end of their festive day Bacchus tosses Ariadne's crown
      into the heavens, where it becomes the constellation Corona
      Borealis.

698   _____. "Hero and Leander, " in Poetical Works (1923), for
      all its length is simple in structure and follows the usual
      story of the ill-fated lovers.   Hero, as the beautiful priest-
      ess of the temple of Venus, guided her lover with a torch
      as he nightly swam the Hellespont to be with her at Sestus.
      One night the winds and a storm blew out the light and
      Leander lost his way as he swam the river.   He was
      drowned, and the next morning when Hero sees the body of
      her lover "floating, and washed about, like a vile weed, "
      she was seized with such a panic that "she leaped, and
      joined her drowned love. "

699   _____. "The Nymphs, " in Poetical Works (1923), has been
      called Hunt's "best poem with few of his irritating faults, "
      (Douglas Bush, Mythology and the Romantic Tradition, 1937).
      It is indeed a riot of description of a world peopled with
      the lovely forms of Woman: the dryads, nymphs of the
      trees; napeads, nymphs of the hills and woods; limniads,
      nymphs of the lakes; ephydriads, nymphs of the fountains;
      oreads, nymphs of the mountains; and nepheliads, nymphs

of the clouds. In addition to this catalog, the poem abounds
with description of the area of nature over which the nymphs
preside. It is a beautiful tribute to nature, presented without moralizing or didacticism.

HUXLEY, Aldous Leonard (1894-1963, English)

700 "Leda," in Leda and Other Poems. London: Chatto and
        Windus; New York: Doran, 1920.
     The story of Leda and the swan is presented in three stages.
     First the scene is with Leda, the young wife of the king of
     Sparta, who thus far has not been made especially happy by
     being married. She says, "Love to me has brought nothing
     but pain and world of shameful thought." The next scene is
     on Olympus, with Jove brooding and restless. He sees
     earth through a rift in the clouds, and the sight of Leda as
     she is bathing inflames his passions beyond endurance. He
     must have this girl "or die." In the last scene Jove has
     assumed the form of a beautiful white swan, and has con-
     spired with Aphrodite to assume the form of an eagle who
     would attack the swan. Leda's sympathy with the beseiged
     swan is thus obtained, and gradually the rape takes place.
     This volume of poems generally fared very poorly with the
     critics, but the title poem was said to "describe the Olymp-
     ian love episode with singular beauty of diction as well as
     mundane realism."

INGELOW, Jean (1820-1897, English)

701 "Persephone," in Poems. Boston: Roberts Brothers, 1867.
     Jean Ingelow's poem is based on the familiar story of
     Demeter's daughter abducted by Hades, but this work per-
     haps makes more than common use of the role that the
     daffodil played in the affair. The daffodil here is the Nar-
     cissus, or Narkissos, of the ancients, the flower that
     sprang up when the youth of that name wasted away while
     contemplating the image of himself in the water. The
     flower was much in favor with gods and mortals. Hades
     used it to entice Persephone into his realm, or else to dull
     her senses that she would not perceive her danger. It was
     also the flower that mourners placed on the brows of the
     dead as they went into the presence of the Underworld dei-
     ties. Although a very beautiful flower, it gave off an evil
     odor that produced dullness and sometimes madness and
     even death. Narke, the Greek word from which the flower
     takes its name, means narcotic.

JACKSON, Helen Hunt (1831-1885, American)

702 "Ariadne's Farewell," in Poems. Illustrated. Boston: Roberts
        Brothers, 1892. Reprinted New York: Arno, 1972.

Ariadne's farewell is to Theseus, the king of Athens, who
has brought her to the island of Naxos and deserted her.
She is a king's daughter, and she had believed that Theseus
was a noble and honorable king himself. She has learned,
however, that his face of gold was mere tinsel, and she
scorns him as he leaves her.

703 _____. "Demeter," in Poems (1972), is based on the story
that during her grief for the lost Persephone, Demeter expressed her anger and rage by causing the death of other
children, leaving their mothers in the depths of grief. This
poet says that it is a "legend of foul shame to motherhood,"
and goes on to develop the theme that mothers, when they
have lost their young, do not take revenge against other
mothers, but "finds only joy in thought that joy is left."
This sentiment, although beautiful, ignores the nature of
the goddess-mother, for whom revenge is in the order of
things.

704 _____. "Oenone," in Poems (1972), tells the story of Paris
being wounded by one of the poisoned arrows of Hercules,
which had been brought to Troy by Philoctetes. Paris goes to
Oenone, the wife whom he deserted for Helen, knowing that
she alone can cure him of his wound. Outraged, Oenone
refuses to help Paris and he dies. This poem suggests that
had Oenone aided her fatally wounded husband, her love
would have transcended that of Helen for Paris, and thus
she would have won him back.

JARRELL, Randall (1914-1965, American)

705 "Orestes at Tauris," in The Complete Poems. New York:
    Farrar, Straus and Giroux, 1969.
    Jarrell based his poem on Euripides' play "Iphigenia
    Among the Taurians," but rejects certain unrealistic ele-
    ments of this play, constructing a primitive, violent work.
    In Euripides, Orestes and Iphigenia, brother and sister,
    recognize each other and the tragedy of sacrifice is averted.
    In this modern version, however, Iphigenia does not recog-
    nize her brother and he was killed, "his head and body"
    alongside the Taurian Artemis, the image he had come to
    take.

706 _____. "The Sphinx's Riddle to Oedipus," in Complete
    Poems (1969), deals with the horror of what it means to
    have answered the Sphinx's riddle. More than anything else,
    "to see, Blind One, is to be alone." To have answered the
    riddle means to have wed one's mother, to have killed one's
    father, to have been utterly doomed. Every event has its
    consequences, one thing leads to another, and so on to the
    bitter, tragic end.

JEFFERS, Robinson (1887-1962, American)

707 "At the Fall of an Age," in The Selected Poetry of Robinson
    Jeffers. New York: Random House, 1938.
    This dramatic poem is based on a somewhat obscure myth
    concerning Helen's death. Derived from Pausanias (Book
    III, section 19), the story follows a vengeance theme and
    accounts for Helen being worshiped on Rhodes as a tree-
    goddess. The time is some twenty years after the fall of
    Troy, and now it is truly "the fall of an age," when mor-
    tals must make sacrifice and thereby renew themselves.
    Helen, now a widow, has been exiled from Sparta and has
    sought sanctuary on the island of Rhodes. Here Polyxo,
    the widow of Tlepolemus, who died at Troy, is in sole com-
    mand. Helen falls into her power, and after much threaten-
    ing delay, is hanged. Polyxo feels that her husband's death
    is now avenged. At the end, however, Polyxo is killed by
    one who feels the need to avenge Helen's death, and the
    tragedy is complete.

708 _____. "Cassandra," in The Double Axe and Other Poems.
    New York: Random House, 1948. Reprinted New York:
    Liveright, 1977.
    The poet identified with "the mad girl" who shrieks the
    truth, but to whom none listen. "Truly men hate the truth,"
    Jeffers says; they would rather "meet a tiger on the road."
    Truth is always disgusting to both gods and mortals.

709 _____. "The Cretan Woman," in Hungerfield and Other
    Poems. New York: Random House, 1954.
    This work follows the "Hippolytus" of Euripides rather
    closely. The language is modern, but the characters have
    not undergone any basic change and external details have
    not been modernized. Phaedra, the wife of Theseus, is in
    love with Hippolytus, the son of Theseus, and their bitter
    tragedy takes its unalterable course. When Hippolytus re-
    jects her advances, Phaedra determines on an act of revenge
    and tells Theseus that the boy has tried to violate her honor.
    Theseus calls on Poseidon to come to his aid, and the god
    hastily brings ruin to Hippolytus. Too late Theseus knows
    his mistake, and in the meantime Phaedra has hanged her-
    self. At the end Aphrodite closes the play laughing at what
    fools men are.

710 _____. "The Humanist's Tragedy," in Dear Judas and Other
    Poems. New York: Random House, 1929. Reprinted
    New York: Liveright, 1977.
    First published as "The Women on Cythaeron," (Poems,
    1928), it is the story of King Pentheus of Thebes. He does
    not believe in the irrationality of the followers of the god
    Dionysus, who has been recently introduced into his country.
    When he is told that his own mother is among the crazed,
    drunken women on Mount Cythaeron, Pentheus goes to see
    for himself. The women mistake him for a lion and tear

him to pieces. His mother, unaware of what she had done, triumphantly carried his head into Thebes. Without distorting the events of the myth, Jeffers has used the Pentheus story to make a bitter comment on the forces of irrationality as they systematically overcome the rational.

711 _____. Medea. New York: Random House, 1946. Reprinted in Sanderson, James L., and Everett Zimmerman, eds., Medea: Myth and Dramatic Form. Boston: Houghton Mifflin, 1967.
This work is called a "free adaptation from the Medea of Euripides," but for the most part follows the ancient myth. The most noticeable difference is in the character of Medea, who, as Louise Bogan has pointed out, has become "a creature so obsessed by jealousy and a paranoid fear of ridicule that she passes from the normal world into the regions of insanity" (Selected Criticism, 1955). Two changes occur in the presentation of the story: the two small sons in Euripides have no speaking part, but in Jeffers they emerge as two real children, thereby making their deaths all the more shocking; and at the end Medea does not escape by means of dragon-drawn chariot: she simply walks through a door. A sampling of critical opinion seems to lead to the conclusion that Jeffers has taken an already-violent myth and turned it into an even more violent story.

712 _____. "Solstice," in Solstice and Other Poems. New York: Random House, 1935.
This work is an early version of the Medea-Jason myth, although here the characters are given new names and the story does not follow the classical version in any respect except one. The woman Madrone Bothwell, mother of two children, has been deserted by her husband. The court has given custody to the father, ruling Madrone an unfit mother. Just as the father is taking his children away, Madrone pleads for one last time with them. Then she kills them, brutally stabbing them to death. At the end she takes the dead children and escapes to the mountains.

713 _____. "The Tower Beyond Tragedy," in Selected Poetry (1938), is a long poem, part narrative, part dramatic, which makes use of the Agamemnon-Clytemnestra myth, but does not follow the Oresteia of Aeschylus very closely. Clytemnestra kills Agamemnon upon his return from the Trojan War, and later Orestes kills his mother, or rather orders one of his men to do the deed. Cassandra, the captive who returned with Agamemnon, is not killed until Orestes kills his mother. Her frenzied but meaningful ranting pervades the whole of Jeffers's work, and when her voice is finally silenced the tragedy is complete. The "tower beyond tragedy"--or philosophical detachment--is achieved by Orestes, who leaves his kingdom and dies on alien soil.

KEATS, John (1795-1821, English)

714　"Apollo to the Graces," in The Poetical Works of John Keats, ed. by H. W. Garrod. Oxford: Clarendon Press, 1939.
This is a song written to the tune of an air in the opera "Don Giovanni," in which Apollo asks which of the three Graces will ride with him that day "across the gold Autumn's whole Kingdom of corn." They all answer eagerly saying, "I will."

715　————. "Endymion: A Poetic Romance," in Poetical Works (1939), as told by Keats, although presented with a great many Romantic embellishments, is basically the myth of Endymion and the moon-goddess, Diana or Selene, who loved the handsome youth and wanted to keep him with her forever. This being impossible, Zeus gave Endymion the right to choose his own fate. He chose to sleep forever, and never grow old, journeying to a cave on Mount Latmos for his long sleep. Selene continued to love and watch over Endymion as he slept.

716　————. "Hyperion" and "The Fall of Hyperion," in Poetical Works (1939), are related, but are not sequential. According to the best evidence, "Hyperion" was begun in the Autumn of 1818 and finished by April 1819. In November and December of that year Keats was engaged in remodeling the fragment in the form of a vision poem, "The Fall of Hyperion." The subject matter of both poems is suggested by the titles, Hyperion being one of the Titans, the god of the sun. The theme is the fall and overthrow of the Titans, the older and more elementary gods, by the young Olympians, Zeus, Poseidon, and so on. The poems are particularly concerned with Apollo, the young god of poetry, who also comes to be identified with the sun, light, and truth.

717　————. "Lamia," in Poetical Works (1939), is based on the myth of a beautiful woman who was changed into a deformed serpent by Hera. Because she could not avenge herself on Hera, Lamia lured strangers to their deaths, as in Keats's poem.

718　————. "Ode on a Grecian Urn," in Poetical Works (1939), is certainly one of the best-known poems in the English language, but is dependent upon Greek mythology and legend to enrich its imagery and meaning. It abounds in description of pastoral life and activity, the festival, the sacrificial animals, the lovers, the music--all frozen in time and preserved in a kind of immortality on the urn. One tradition says that the urn that inspired this poem was preserved in the garden of Holland House, a mansion in Kensington, London. There were many such urns in the British Museum, however, any one of which could have inspired Keats to conclude that "beauty is truth, truth beauty."

719 _____ . "Ode to Apollo" (also titled "Hymn to Apollo"), in Poetical Works (1939), praises the "god of the golden bow, and of the golden lyre," the god most honored by poets.

720 _____ . "Ode to Apollo," in Poetical Works (1939), addresses the god "in his western halls of gold," and develops the ode by praising Homer, Milton, Shakespeare, Spenser, and Tasso--poets who have been honored by Apollo, "great God of Bards," who gave them birth.

721 _____ . "Ode to Psyche," in Poetical Works (1939), is loosely based on the myth contained in Apuleius' The Golden Ass (second century A.D.). It is the story of a god's love for a mortal woman, but unlike most myths based on this theme, the story of Cupid and Psyche has a happy ending: Psyche, after many hardships and trials, comes to Olympus and becomes one of the gods with her husband, Cupid.

722 _____ . "On a Leander Gem," in Poetical Works (1939), is a simple cameo description of the scene in which Leander tries to swim the Hellespont and drowns. The story on which this scene is based is that of Hero, a beautiful priestess of Sestus, and the youth Leander of Abydos. They met nightly after he swam the Hellespont, but on the last fatal night a storm swept him under and he drowned. Hero later jumped into the sea and was also drowned.

723 _____ . "On First Looking into Chapman's Homer," in Poetical Works (1939), refers to a translation of the Iliad and the Odyssey by George Chapman (c. 1559-1634), an Elizabethan dramatist and translator of the classics. Keats and his friend Charles Cowden Clark are said to have spent an entire night reading these works, after which Keats wrote his famous sonnet, comparing this reading experience to the process of adventure and discovery.

724 _____ . "On Seeing the Elgin Marbles," in Poetical Works (1939), was written in 1817, four years before Keats died. It is similar to "Ode on a Grecian Urn" and "Ode to a Nightingale" in theme: the life of art as compared with the life of humankind. As in his longer poems, Keats addresses himself to the beauty and permanence of Greek art. Thomas Bruce (1766-1841), the Earl of Elgin, was a British diplomat who collected the ancient Greek sculptures brought from the Parthenon, in Athens in 1803-1812, and placed them in the British Museum.

725 _____ . "To Homer," in Poetical Works (1939), is a sonnet in which the poet is regarded as a god-created being, blind in the physical senses but gifted with unlimited sight into the nature of creation. The poem is rich with mythological

allusions--Jove, Neptune, Pan, Dian--each of whom is
highly visible in the works of Homer.

KINGSLEY, Charles (1819-1875, English)

726 "Andromeda," in Poems, Vol. 14 of Works. New York and
        London: Co-Operative Publication Society, 1899.
     Although the story of Perseus and Andromeda is used in
     this composition, the theme of Kingsley's work is focused
     on the behavior of the gods, the capriciousness of their ac-
     tions and the utter meaninglessness of their relations to
     human beings. In the beginning Andromeda is bound to a
     rock and left to die at the hands of a sea-monster because
     her mother carelessly offended the sea-god's wife; at the
     end she is rescued by Perseus, who is beloved of Athene.
     Not only does Athene help Perseus rescue Andromeda, the
     goddess also spins a wondrous veil on which are pictured
     all the sea-creatures and gives it to Andromeda on her
     wedding day.

727 _____. Hypatia, 2 vols. in Works (1899), is a historical
     novel based on the life of a Greek philosopher and teacher.
     The principal action of the novel concerns her struggle to
     restore the Greek gods in the onslaught of Christian religion.
     She is in the end killed, in A. D. 415, by a mob that tears
     her beautiful body to pieces. Kingsley's long novel is set
     against a background of intrigue and unrest when many forces
     were struggling for human souls, pagan, Christian, and
     Jewish. In a larger sense the novel is set against the back-
     ground of the dying Roman Empire and the violence of the
     Christian religion as it struggled to gain a foothold on civili-
     zation.

728 _____. "Sappho," in Poems (1899), presents a picture of
     the young woman as she lies among the myrtles on a cliff.
     The noon sun glares above, there is no wind, it is a hot,
     sweltering day, and Sappho is consumed with a "mighty
     fever" that will not let her rest. She plucks a few chords
     of music on her lyre and tosses it away, saying that it
     mocks her with harmonies to her own discords. It sings
     of nobler natures than its own, a mere tortoise shell.

LANDON, Letitia Elizabeth (Mrs. George McLeon, "L. E. L.," 1802-
1838, English)

729 "Arion," in The Complete Works of L. E. Landon. Boston:
        Phillips, Sampson; New York: Derby, 1854.
     Arion was a Greek poet and musician who lived about
     585 B. C. on the island of Lesbos. He obtained great wealth
     in Italy, but when he tried to return to his native island,
     the sailors of the ship plotted his murder. Seeing his life

in danger, he begged that he first be allowed to play his lyre. The moment he ended the music he threw himself into the sea, where according to the tale, some dolphins took him safely home. Later the sailors were executed.

730 _____. "Bacchus and Ariadne, " in Complete Works (1854), is a conversation between a painter and his lady. He has just finished the picture of Ariadne and Bacchus, and is explaining it to his love. She disagrees that the picture is faithful to a woman's heart, to love again so quickly after one love, in this case Theseus, has been lost.

731 _____. "Calypso Watching the Ocean, " in Complete Works (1854), is a description of a painting that portrays the goddess as grieving for Odysseus, who has left her to return to his native Ithaca. Her gaze is intent upon the farthest wave of the ocean, over which Odysseus has now disappeared.

732 _____. "Head of Ariadne, " in Complete Works (1854), is less a description of a statue of Ariadne than it is a question of "why should women ever love. " The poet sees Ariadne as the symbol of woman betrayed by her love for a man, "another proof of woman's weary lot. "

733 _____. "Hebe, " in Complete Works (1854), uses the image of the Greek goddess of youth to comment on the transience of youth itself. The poet calls Hebe the "type of what may never last. "

734 _____. "Leander and Hero, " in Complete Works (1854), is a short narrative based on the story of the two young lovers who were destined to be early separated from each other. Their faithfulness to each other in the face of much adversity is the theme most emphasized in Landon's poem. After Leander drowned in the Hellespont, Hero threw herself into the sea and so shared his fate.

735 _____. "The Lost Pleiad, " in Complete Works (1854), is an innovative account of the seven daughters of Atlas, six of whom married gods. The seventh, Merope, married a mortal, the notorious Sisyphus, and it is said that she hides her face in shame for the crimes of her husband. Landon's poem deals with a Prince Cyris, who fell in love with the sad, half-veiled star of the Pleiad cluster, Merope, and so she became the maiden Cyrene, who loved him. At last he deserted her, and she learns to her regret that "Love is of heavenly birth, / But turns to death on touching earth. " As in all of Landon's poems, the theme emphasizes the betrayal of women and the unfaithfulness of their lovers.

736 _____. "A Nereid Floating on a Shell, " in Complete Works

(1854), is a slight poem that merely describes a lovely girl as she floats on the water.

737 _____. "The Queen of Cyprus, " in Complete Works (1854), has little mythological value other than being related to the island of Cyrpus, the origin of Aphrodite's worship. The poem tells of the story of Queen Irene, who abdicated her throne to a kinsman whom she loved, and who deserted her.

738 _____. "Sappho, " in Complete Works (1854), is based upon the Greek poet's love for Phaon, the handsome youth who was everything to her: "Hope, Genius, Energy, the God/ Her inmost spirit worshipp'd. " Soon, however, he left her, and Sappho cast herself into the sea. The world remembers the true love and devotion of Sappho.

LANDOR, Walter Savage (1775-1864, English)

739 "Achilles and Helena, " in Vol. 1, The Complete Works of Walter Savage Landor, 16 vols. , ed. by T. Earle Welby; Vols. 13-16 ed. by Stephen Wheeler. London: Chapman and Hall, 1927-1936. Reprinted New York: Barnes and Noble; London: Methuen, 1969.
This dialogue between Helen and Achilles occurs on Mt. Ida at some point during the Trojan War. They have been spirited away from Troy and the battle by Thetis and Aphrodite. Their discussion centers around the reasons for each of them being there: Aphrodite urged Helen to leave Menelaus, and Achilles is at Troy to win honor by killing Hector.

740 _____. "Achilles and Helena on Ida, " in Vol. 14, Complete Works (1969), is essentially the same composition as the above, with added details on the war and the situation Helen has created by being unfaithful to Menelaus.

741 _____. "Acon and Rhodope; or, Inconstancy, " in Vol. 14, Complete Works (1969), is a love story of a "Gentle Hamadryad, " who lost her lover, Rhaicos, when the oak-tree where she lived "was blasted and laid desolate. " Acon and Rhodope are another young boy and girl in love with each other. One day the hamadryad leads Acon into the wood and he dies. The inconstancy of the poem was on Acon's part, by following the hamadryad into the forest.

742 _____. "Aeschylos and Sophocles, " in Poems by Walter Savage Landor, ed. by Geoffrey Grisgon. Carbondale: Southern Illinois University Press, 1965.
Aeschylos is departing from Sophocles, leaving the younger playwright to wear "the laurel crown. " They discuss the mythology of the plays they have written, among them "Oedipus, " "Prometheus Bound, " and "The Oresteia. "

743 _____ . "The Altar of Modesty," in Vol. 14, Complete
Works (1969), consists of a long conversation between Helen
and her mother, Leda, on the subject of Helen's abduction
by Theseus of Athens, and her subsequent rescue by her
brothers, the twins Castor and Pollux. Included also is
the story of the altar where the conversation between Leda
and Helen takes place. When Penelope married Ulysses,
her father, Icarius, tried to persuade them to stay in Sparta.
But Ulysses would not abandon his lands and people in Ithaca.
Penelope then was ordered to choose between father and husband, and "covering with her veil her tearful eyes," inclined
toward her husband. The father thereafter raised "an altar
dedicate to Modesty." Ironically Leda asks Helen why she
was not present at the dedication of the altar.

744 _____ . "Ancient Idyl: Europa and her Mother," in Vol. 14,
Complete Works (1969), tells, by means of a dialogue between Europe and her mother, the story of Europa's abduction by Zeus, who had disguised himself as the white bull.
The poem presents a realistic account of the inability of a
good marriage for Europa, and the sudden tragic disappearance of the girl, carried to Crete. At the end the mother
foolishly reflects on a scarf that will be ruined in the water
as Europe rides off on the bull's back.

745 _____ . "The Children of Venus," in Vol. 14, Complete
Works (1969), apparently are the two figures with the name
Eros. The eldest brother, the Eros of which Hesiod speaks,
is the one who has "reduced the ancient Chaos," driving
darkness out of the heavens and ordering all things. The
youngest brother is the little god Cupid, also called Eros
by the Greeks, with the bows and arrows to strike love into
human hearts. At the conclusion the elder brother turns
over his office to the younger, saying that he is fully capable of persuading the sun and stars and moon to shine
brighter, the flowers to bloom sweeter, and all order in
the universe to be fulfilled.

746 _____ . "Chrysaor," in Vol. 13, Complete Works (1969),
for the most part ignores the mythology of this figure and
recreates him to the purposes of the poem. He is portrayed
as one of the giants who tries to overthrow the gods, and
seeks to become an oppressor of humankind. He is killed
by Neptune, but in his place Superstition, the daughter of
one of the Titans, is allowed to carry on another reign of
tyranny.

747 _____ . "Coresos and Callirhoe," in Vol. 14, Complete
Works (1969), retells a story of violence and human sacrifice.
Coresos, a priest of Dionysus, is in love with Callirhoe,
who scorns him. He prays to the god for help and is told

to sacrifice Callirhoe unless she could find someone willing
to die for her. She finds no one, and is dragged to the altar where Coresos is waiting. At the last moment he cannot kill her and turns the knife on himself. Later she kills
herself, and the crowd of drunken worshipers go mad with
violence.

748 _____. "Corythus," in Vol. 13, Complete Works (1969), is
a lengthy sequence of events sometimes printed as three
separate poems: "Corythus" (Parts I and II) and "The Death
of Paris and Oenone" (Part III). This story begins when
Oenone, the wife of Paris while he was still a shepherd on
Mt. Ida, sends their son Corythus into Troy to seek his
father, now living with Helen. The youth finds Helen without difficulty, and she responds with kindness and favor
toward him, she having no son and hoping to please Paris
by presenting this son to him. When Corythus is introduced
to his father, Paris falls on him thinking he is some young
suitor to Helen. Too late, the father realizes he has killed
his own son. In subsequent events Paris is mortally wounded
by an arrow from the bow of Philoctetes and is carried to
Mt. Ida, where Oenone could heal his wounds. She refuses,
however, and Paris dies. In remorse Oenone kills herself
on her husband's funeral pyre, and the tragedy of those three
is complete.

749 _____. "Cupid and Pan," in Vol. 14, Complete Works
(1969), is a contest between the god of Love and the brown,
hairy, goatlike Pan. At first Pan appears to be winning
the contest, but then Cupid blinds him, and Pan must beg
for mercy. Cupid decks him out with flowers, which the
goat-god rejects and tears away. Venus now appears and
warns "goat-foot," as she calls him, that soon another
wreath shall adorn his brow, as indeed it did with the death
of Pitys, when he thereafter wore a pine wreath.

750 _____. "The Death of Clytemnestra," in Vol. 14, Complete
Works (1969), begins a sequence of events that continues in
"The Madness of Orestes" and "The Prayer of Orestes,"
and concludes in "The Priestess of Apollo." Orestes and
Electra kill Clytemnestra, their mother, for her murder of
Agamemnon, their father. With the death of Clytemnestra
the Furies are stirred into action, and Orestes suffers madness for his matricide. He prays to Apollo, the god who
had ordered him to avenge the death of his father, and is
answered by the priestess of Apollo, who tells him to take
refuge from the Furies in the temple of Apollo at Delphi.

751 _____. "Dirce," in Vol. 16, Complete Works (1969), is a
four-line composition that is utterly complete in form and
theme, and nothing is wasted. In Greek mythology Dirce
was the second wife of Lycus, King of Thebes. She mis-
treated Antiope, his first wife, who fled and found refuge

with her twin sons, who were living as herdsmen. Dirce
ordered the young men to tie Antiope to the horns of a wild
bull; but discovering that she was their mother, they inflicted the punishment upon Dirce. In the poem she is on
the way to Hades and is being ferried across the River
Styx by Charon.

752 _____. "Dryope," in Vol. 14, Complete Works (1969), is
the girl who was loved by Apollo and bore him a son. She
and the son were later changed into lotus-trees.

753 _____. "Endymion and Selene," in Vol. 14, Complete
Works (1969), is a short conversation between the moon-
goddess and the youth to whom she gave eternal beauty by
allowing him to sleep forever on Mt. Latmos. In this exchange, however, she complains of his sleeping all the
time, and he rebukes her, saying, "How less warm art
thou than what a shepherdess gives to a shepherd."

754 _____. "The Espousals of Polyxena," in Vol. 14, Complete
Works (1969), is the segment of the story in which Polyxena,
a daughter of Priam, becomes the betrothed of Achilles.
The poem is presented by means of contrasting the happy
festivities of the proposed marriage with the grim warnings
and prophecies of Cassandra, who knows what Polyxena's
real fate is to be. At the death of Achilles, Polyxena will
be sacrificed on his funeral pyre.

755 _____. "Eucrates to the God Sleep," in Vol. 14, Complete
Works (1969), is praise for the "gentlest of Gods," among
whom none visit more often. Sleep, however, departs when
his twin brother, Death, appears.

756 _____. "A Greek to the Eumenides," in Vol. 16, Complete
Works (1969), is a narrator who would be rid of these "old
beldames," the Furies, who are always croaking the same
old "tiresome tune."

757 _____. "The Hamadryad," in Vol. 14, Complete Works
(1969), is related to "Acon and Rhodope" (above), and tells
how the oak-tree of the hamadryad was destroyed, and how
Rhaicos, her lover, pined away and died after the tree was
blasted.

758 _____. "Hercules, Pluto, Alcestis, Admetos," in Vol. 14,
Complete Works (1969), is presented entirely in dialogue
form but without any transition devices to indicate a change
of scene. Heracles has apparently entered the Underworld
to rescue Alcestis, but Admetos has accompanied him.
Pluto is reluctant to release Alcestis, but Persephone persuades him to do so.

759 _____. "Hippomenes and Atalanta," in Vol. 14, Complete Works (1969), is the traditional myth of the race that Atalanta lost to Hippomenes, subsequently becoming his wife. The trickery of dropping the golden apples along the way and so detaining Atalanta, who picked them up, figures greatly in this poem, and at the end the apples are dedicated to Eros and Aphrodite, and "to her who ratifies the nuptial vow"--that is, to Hera, who had given the apples to Hippomenes in the first place.

760 _____. "Hymn and Offering of Terpander to Juno," in Vol. 14, Complete Works (1969), is based on a semihistorical figure, a poet and musician of Lesbos who lived about 700 B.C. He is said to have added three strings to the lyre, which until then had only four. In Landor's poem he offers a richly woven garment to Hera and Prays to be free of the marriage "yoke."

761 _____. "Hymn to Proserpine," in Vol. 15, Complete Works (1969), is a plea to the "consort of a king whose realm is wider than the earth," to intercede on behalf of the brave souls who are falling in a modern, unheroic war.

762 _____. "Icarios and Erigone," in Vol. 14, Complete Works (1969), tells the story of the man who was favored by Dionysus and devotedly set about trying to win followers of the god by sharing the wine that he had taught Icarios and his daughter Erigone to make. The peasants drank of the wine, and repaid Icarios by brutally killing him. Zeus retaliates by setting the drunken peasantry to kill each other.

763 _____. "Iphigeneia," in Vol. 14, Complete Works (1969), is narrated primarily by Iphigeneia, the daughter of Agamemnon who was sacrificed at Aulis. At first she does not believe that Calchas, the prophet, heard "distinctly what the goddess spake," but the look on her father's face says that something is amiss. She turns then to pleading for her future, but is still met with no response from Agamemnon. At the end Iphigeneia surrenders herself to her doom.

765 _____. "The Last of Ulysses," in Vol. 13, Complete Works (1969), is a long narrative in three parts. In Part I Ulysses returns to Ithaca, where he is loved and welcomed by Penelope. Later he departs, telling Penelope that he is going to Dodona to make sacrifice to Jupiter. He goes instead to Argyripa, where Diomedes is now king. Part II begins with a long conversation between Diomedes and Ulysses in which they each relate their experiences since Troy. Ulysses then reveals that he has left Ithaca because of a dream in which Circe tells him that he will be killed by his son. Ulysses is thinking only of Telemachos. In Part III Telegonus, Ulysses' son by Circe, comes searching for his father. In an altercation between Telegonus and some of Diomedes' men, Ulysses intervenes and is killed by a stake thrown by Telegonus. He dies thinking he has averted the death prophesied by oracle.

765 _____. "Leda," in Vol. 16, Complete Works (1969), praises the beauty of the woman who could bring Zeus to abandon his Olympian grandeur and become a swan: the eagle had lost his fierceness.

766 _____. "The Marriage of Helena and Menelaos," in Vol. 14, Complete Works (1969), presents Helena at the age of sixteen, when Menelaos visits her home in company with Castor and Pollux, Helen's brothers. The young Menelaos captures Helen's heart immediately, but she made excuses, such as saying that she was too young. When she finally accepts the proposal of marriage, Menelaos thinks that he has captured "simplicity and innocence!" At the wedding the gods Hymen, the god of marriage, and Eros, the god of Love, quarrel bitterly, and Eros laughs in Hymen's face and twitches his "saffron robe. "

767 _____. "Menelaus and Helen at Troy," in Vol. 14, Complete Works (1969), portrays the traditional view of what happened when Menelaus confronted Helen at the fall of Troy. He first would have killed her, but then saw how beautiful she was and delayed, saying they would return to Sparta and he would punish her there.

768 _____. "Niobe," in Vol. 14, Complete Works (1969), is a scene in which the mother stands amid "nine daughters slain by Artemis," and prays that the goddess will now strike her.

769 _____. "Ode to Miletus," in Vol. 16, Complete Works (1969), is addressed to the city of Crete, the "beloved town" that Landor calls "parent of me and mine. " Miletus was established by the son of Jove, or some say the son of Apollo.

770 _____. "Pan," in Vol. 14, Complete Works (1969), is an invitation to the poet from Pan to sit with him awhile and listen to the story of how Boreas, the north wind, competed for the love of Pitys and how, when he lost, he changed her into a pine-tree.

771 _____. "Pan and Pitys, " in Vol. 14, Complete Works (1969), is the story that Pan refers to in the poem above. The nymph Pitys was loved by Boreas, the north wind, and the god Pan. She preferred Pan and scorned Boreas, who then dashed her against a rock and she became a pine-tree. Pan mourned deeply for his love, and thereafter wore a pine-wreath to honor her.

772 _____. "Peleus and Thetis, " in Vol. 14, Complete Works (1969), is a conversation in which the goddess speaks with

her mortal husband and tells him that their son, Achilles, has sailed for Troy. They have been separated, but now in their mutual sorrow they are reunited. Thetis knows that Achilles will not survive the war, and she grieves that her only son is fated to die at such an early age.

773 _____. "Penelope and Pheido," in Vol. 14, Complete Works (1969), is a conversation between Penelope and a serving woman called Pheido. They talk of Odysseus' departure for the Trojan War, how the Greeks needed him, despite his not wanting to go, and how he will win glory for them. Then the conversation becomes domestic, and they discuss picking and drying figs. Penelope tells the maid to busy herself, that "idleness ill befits a royal house."

774 _____. "The Phocaeans," in Vol. 13, Complete Works (1969), consists of two fragments with a connecting link and a short sequel. The story is told by a minstrel, who develops the theme of Liberty and glory in war when one's homeland is threatened. With the Persian invasion of Ionia the Phocaens sail to Iberia and seek aid from the king of Tartessus. Here they learn of the troubles that Tartessus has recently had, and how these brave ones fought until the country was returned to its rightful owners. Fragment II is a reply to the Tartessian's story, and recounts all the difficulties that the Phocaens have had with the invading Persians. The mythology of Hercules is interwoven into the story of the King of Tartessus.

775 _____. "The Shades of Agamemnon and Iphigeneia," in Vol. 14, Complete Works (1969), is in the Underworld after Agamemnon has been murdered by his wife, Clytemnestra. Here the daughter who was sacrificed and the father who was murdered meet and talk, with all human emotion purged away. In the kingdom of the dead there "are no wrongs to vindicate, no realms to overthrow." Iphigeneia says that Pluto is the "gentlest brother of the three," and all things are serene. Ultimately the poem focuses on the differences between life, when all things matter and are important, and death, when all things are the same.

776 _____. "Silenus," in Vol. 14, Complete Works (1969), is a picture of the elderly, satyrlike companion of Dionysus, as he sits down to converse with and teach the young satyrs in their following of the young god Dionysus.

777 _____. "Sophron's Hymn to Bakkos," in Vol. 14, Complete Works (1969), refers to Sophron of Syracuse, a poet who lived about 480 B.C. This poem--or hymn, as Landor calls it--praises the glory and power of the god Dionysus, and recalls some instances of the god being scorned and the resultant punishment.

157

778 _____ . "Theseus and Hippolyta," in Vol. 14, Complete
        Works (1969), is a conversation between Theseus, who with
        Hercules conquered and killed the Amazon women, and Hip-
        polyta, the queen of the Amazonians whom Theseus captured
        for his bride. The conversation is a spirited one, with
        Hippolyta vowing revenge and hatred, and Theseus promising
        her that his country shall be hers, and her estate royal.

779 _____ . "To Apollo," in Vol. 16, Complete Works (1969),
        is a six-line address to the god, with the poet wishing that
        he might follow Apollo's course around the earth, and al-
        ways be filled with light and song. However, he most de-
        sires to be always young, but this Apollo cannot provide.
        In view of this the poet asks that those who love him will
        stay near him.

780 _____ . "The Trial of Aeschylos," in Poems (1965), is a
        conversation among a judge, citizens, Aeschylus, and his
        brother Amyntos. The charge is that Aeschylus has be-
        trayed the mysteries of Eleusis, a charge that he denies.
        At the end the playwright is acquitted of all charges, on
        the grounds that he did not know that what he said was for-
        bidden knowledge. The historical facts of his trial and ac-
        quittal are rather vague, one source saying he was absolved
        by proving that he had not been initiated into the Mysteries.

LANG, Andrew (1844-1912, English)

781 "Ballade of the Voyage to Cythera," in XXII Ballades in Blue
        China. London: Kegan Paul, 1880.
        Cythera was an island sacred to Aphrodite, and according
        to one myth was the island where the goddess washed ashore
        after being born of the sea-foam. In Lang's poem the is-
        land is now desolate and the goddess is no longer there,
        but the narrator pushes on in his voyage and quotes Tenny-
        son's "Ulysses," saying, "It may be we shall touch the
        happy isle!"

782 _____ . "Cameos: Sonnets from the Antique," in Rhymes
        à la Mode. London: Kegan Paul, Trench, and Trübner,
        1890.
        This work consists of thirteen sonnets, each of which re-
        creates a scene from classical literature. The original work
        is followed rather closely in content, but the language is
        shaped into the form of a completed sonnet. The most not-
        able of these sonnets are "Helen on the Walls" (derived
        from the Iliad), "The Isles of the Blessed" (based on sev-
        eral fragments of Pindar), "Colonus" and "The Passing of
        Oedipus" (both from Sophocles' "Oedipus at Colonus"), "The
        Taming of Tyro" (from a fragment by Sophocles), "To

Artemis" (based on Euripides' "Hippolytus"), and "The Cannibal Zeus" (from a passage in Pausanias).

783   . "The Fortunate Islands," in Rhymes à la Mode (1890), is referred to as a "dream in June" prompted by the author's reading of the poet Lucian. His vision or dream is a visit to the Isles of the Blessed. Here he sees Helen and "all true Greeks and wise," including Socrates and his followers. The place is described as a paradise of nature, and those who inhabit it are truly at peace. In conclusion, however, the narrator realizes that he is with the dead, and he comes back to the living.

784   . Helen of Troy: Her Life and Translation. London: Bell, 1892.
This work consists of six books of varying lengths, with a Historical Note by the author. The eight-line stanzas of rhymed iambic pentameter is somewhat tiresome in spots, but creates an overall readable style. The story begins with the coming of Paris to Sparta, where he tells of his past life, including his decision with regard to the three goddesses. The story continues with the flight of Helen and Paris to Troy, and the subsequent war, with all the details of the Iliad, the Odyssey, and the Posthomerica of Quintus of Smyrna. At the end Menelaus would have stoned Helen to death, but was prevented from doing so by Aphrodite. Instead she returned to Sparta, and she and Menelaus beheld "the counted years of mortal life go by." When her life came to an end, she did not die, but with Menelaus was translated to Elysium, and on earth she became a kind of goddess, worshiped as "a kinder Aphrodite," a goddess of love and beauty.

785   . "Herodotus in Egypt," in Grass of Parnassus: Rhymes Old and New. London: Longmans, Green, 1888.
Although not specifically related to a particular myth, this sonnet does deal with a subject that is associated with mythology. Lang says that Herodotus left the "smiling gods of Greece," and sought the land of the Nile. He did not mock the animal forms of gods in Egyptian mythology, because he knew that "behind all creeds the Spirit is One."

786   . "Hesperothen," in Grass of Parnassus (1888), means relating to the Hesperides, or Hesperia, which signified the farthermost western lands, the land of the setting sun. Phaeacia is also identified as one of the far western islands. The seven lyrics comprising this work sing of adventures that certain mariners embarked upon after the war at Troy, adventure having become a part of their natures. The titles of these poems somewhat indicate their substance: "The Seekers for Phaeacia," "A Song of Phaeacia," "The Departure from Phaeacia," "A Ballad of Departure," "They Hear the Sirens for the Second Time," "Circe's Isle Revisited," and "The Limit of Lands."

787 _____. "Homer," in Ballades and Verses Vain. New York: Scribner, 1884.
This pays tribute to the poet in terms of two metaphors: Lang says the poet's work has been compared to the sea, all-encompassing, but he would compare it to a river whose source is unknown, the Nile of Egypt whose "flood makes green our human shore."

788 _____. "Homeric Unity," in Ballades and Verses Vain (1884), begins with an account of how the artifacts of the ancient world--of Troy, Mycenae, etc.--are scattered abroad to art museums and collectors. Everything has become a show, separated from its rightful habitat. In the reference to Homer, Lang is no doubt referring to a theory that the poet did not write the Iliad and the Odyssey. That contro-versy was never given strong support, and Lang certainly does not subscribe to it.

789 _____. "Iliad," in The Iliad of Homer. Done into English Prose by Andrew Lang, Walter Leaf, and Ernest Myers. New York: Modern Library, 1929.
This work consists of three sonnets, one each by the three translators. In the first (by Andrew Lang) Homer is re-garded as the indisputable sovereign of song, and unlike other forms of treasure he cannot be divided, carted away, and put into a museum. In the second poem (by Ernest Myers) Achilles is sung as the great hero and warrior of the Iliad, and his doom and tragedy is foreshadowed as a giant darkness that lies about him. In the third sonnet (by Walter Leaf) the subject is Priam and the majesty of his sorrow when he bowed before Achilles and sought the body of his dead son Hector. The figure of Andromache, Hector's widow, makes a forlorn and desolate image.

790 _____. "In Ithaca," in Ballades and Verses Vain (1884), this sonnet expresses the feelings of Odysseus, who, now that he has returned to Ithaca, regrets leaving the island of Calypso. "His sad heart followed after, mile on mile, / Back to the Goddess of the magic wile," the poet says, and concludes with the observation that such is generally the case.

791 _____. "Lost in Hades," in Ballads and Lyrics of Old France with Other Poems. Portland, Me.: Mosher, 1873.
Although this sonnet does not embody any particular myth, it does create an atmosphere similar to all classical de-scriptions of Hades or the Underworld. It is a personal love poem, the narrator searching for his loved one and not finding her. It is similar to the Orpheus figure search-ing for Eurydice.

792 _____. "The Mystery of Queen Persephone," in XXII
Ballades (1880), is a dialogue in which St. Paul and the
Devil argue about the immortality of the soul. St. Paul's
argument is reinforced by the arrival of Persephone (the
Queen of Death in classical mythology), Hela (a goddess of
death in Norse mythology), and St. Lucy (of the Christian
faith), all of whom verify that the soul continues to live
after the body dies.

793 _____. "The Odyssey," in Ballades and Verses Vain (1884),
is a sonnet of praise in the form of a Homeric simile, in
which the Odyssey itself is compared to one of its episodes.
The poet here says that readers turn "from the songs of
modern speech" and feel as Odysseus felt when he escaped
from "the song of Circe and her wine," in their response
to the "surge and thunder of the Odyssey."

794 _____. "Pisidice," in Ballades and Verses Vain (1884), is
the story of the daughter of Methymna, king of Lesbos.
The story is told that before he went to Troy, Achilles
made war against Lesbos, and Pisidice fell madly in love
with him. She delivered the city into his hands on the
promise that he would marry her, but when the city was
captured Achilles ordered her stoned to death for the betrayal of her father.

795 _____. "The Shade of Helen," in Ballades and Verses Vain
(1884), is based on the story that Helen never went to Troy
but remained in Egypt during the war (the gods had fashioned
a woman out of clouds and shadows and sent her to be the
wife of Paris). This poem, narrated by the shade that went
to Troy, expresses great weariness of the whole thing, longing for the peace of death. She remarks also that the men
who are fighting and dying are pawns of the gods as well,
although they believe themselves to be free-acting and responsible for what they are doing.

796 _____. The Story of the Golden Fleece, with Illustrations
by Mills Thompson. Philadelphia: Altemus, 1903.
Although this work is clearly written for young people, it
is a charming version of Jason's story, and may be enjoyed by any reader. It is told in three parts, beginning
with Phrixus and Helle, who fled from their stepmother on
the back of the Golden Ram. They came to the country of
Colchis, whose king had the Golden Fleece preserved. In
time Jason, the son of Aeson, was sent by King Pelias to
get the Fleece. Pelias intended to send his nephew on an
errand from which he would never return. After the long
and dangerous voyage, however, Jason returned with the
Golden Fleece and became King of Iolcus.

797 _____. Tales of Troy and Greece. New York: Longmans,
Green, 1928. First published in 1907.

161

This prose work is presented in a style with appeal to young people, but should be of interest to any reader. The sources for Lang's work are Homer, Quintus of Smyrna, the play- wrights, and whatever other scraps of mythological tradition were available on the lives of some of these heroes. The first part, "Ulysses the Sacker of Cities," covers the Tro- jan War, beginning with the boyhood and parents of Ulysses. In this telling of the story it is Ulysses and not Agamemnon or Achilles who is the hero. This part ends with the sack of Troy and the saving of Helen. Part two, "The Wander- ing of Ulysses," is based largely on the Odyssey, and ends with the hero returning to Ithaca and slaying the suitors. Part three tells the story of Meleager, the hero of the Calydonian Boar Hunt, about whom there is only scattered and fragmentary information. Lang's narrative begins with the strange curse under which Meleager was born--that he should live as long as a particular brand was not burned-- and ends with his death, when his mother sought revenge for her brothers' deaths by throwing the brand into the fire. In part four the story of Theseus, the king of Athens, is told in some detail up to the slaying of the Minotaur in Crete. The remainder of the king's long life is summarized quickly. Part five concludes the work with the story of Perseus, his slaying the Medusa, his rescuing Andromeda from the monster, and finally his avenging Danae, his mother, who had been ill treated by Polydectes, the king of Seriphos.

798 _____. "Two Sonnets of the Sirens," in Ballades and Verses Vain (1884), is based on the myth that the Sirens were orig- inally maiden companions of Persephone, the daughter of Demeter. Upon Persephone's disappearance Demeter changed them into monstrous shapes for not keeping watch on her daughter. They were also doomed to sing their magic song, which meant death to anyone who listened and succumbed to their charm.

799 _____, with H. Rider Haggard. The World's Desire. Lon- don: Longmans, Green, 1890. Reprinted New York: Ballantine Books, 1972.
When this novel was published it was called a "tortuous and ungodly jumble of anarchy and culture." This criticism is somewhat justified, but if readers will concentrate on the main line of the story, and ignore as best they can some of the endless digressions into Egyptian mythology and leg- endary paraphernalia, the work is not without interest. Basically it is the story of Odysseus after he returned to Ithaca, set sail again, and finally returned for the second time. There is little mythological tradition to support these events, but such as there is the authors make use of. Ac- cording to a lost epic, the Telegonia, Odysseus met his

death at the hands of his son Telegonus, whose mother was Circe. There is also a tradition that Odysseus was one of Helen's suitors, and that perhaps she loved him better than any of the others. "The world's desire" is Helen, and the last adventure of Odysseus is into Egypt, where Helen has become a goddess. However tedious some of this novel may be, the closing scenes are highly effective, as Odysseus realizes that "Fate is upon him," and that the end of his life is near.

LATTIMORE, Richmond (1906-   , American)

800 "Atlantis Now," in Poems from Three Decades. New York: Scribner, 1972.
The title of this poem is derived from the idea that whatever Atlantis might have been, whatever culture and life that might have thrived on the continent, it is now entirely in the hands of the "old myth makers," who deliberate, assess, "drink coffee, and compose the tale."

801 _____. "Demeter in the Fields," in Three Decades (1972), portrays the goddess as the inner life force that creates the green of the spring and the gold of the harvest. Her daughter, Persephone, the wife of the god of the dead, is the death-rebirth symbol. Thus Demeter is related to a trinity consisting of Life, Death, and Rebirth.

802 _____. "Glaukos," in Three Decades (1972), is in this poem the fisherman who was transformed into a sea-deity by Oceanus and Tethys. He fell in love with the Nereid Scylla, and Circe fell in love with him. Out of jealousy and spite the goddess changed Scylla into a monstrous shape that Glaukos could not love.

803 _____. "Hercules at the Crossroads," in Three Decades (1972), is a modern version of the traditional legend that Hercules was confronted with two maidens, each promising him gifts for the choosing. On the left was a fair maiden promising him a beautiful life, filled with sunshine and fair progress; on the right a dark maiden promised him rocky gorges, dry bread, and hazards. He chose the dark maiden, and the question is why he did so. At the end of his story he became an immortal and married Hebe. So the question remains: did he really choose the hard way?

804 _____. "Notes from the Odyssey," in Three Decades (1972), consists of four parts in which the author presents four interior monologues of characters from the Odyssey: Elpenor, Circe, Penelope, and Odysseus. These characters reveal themselves as they do not in Homer's work, presenting their "real story." Elpenor, who died when he drunkenly stepped off the roof at Circe's palace, now demands a grave, and

he has never demanded anything before. Circe is not the evil sorceress but a woman who loves her animals and forest, and is glad the sailors are gone. Penelope is sickened by the sight of all her slain suitors and hanged waiting maids, and Odysseus now that he is at home is haunted by ghosts of all that he has done and all that he has been.

805 _____. "Pandora," in Three Decades (1972), refers to the mythological figure, the woman who opened a box and allowed all the ills of humankind to escape. Lattimore interprets this figure as a form of Eve, in the Christian religion, who ate the apple and thus brought evil into the world. However, these so-called evils are in fact the conditions of being human, or the conditions necessary for life.

806 _____. "Remember Aphrodite," in Three Decades (1972), employs the imagery surrounding the birth of the goddess-- the sea, the foam, the shell beneath her feet--rising out of the depths into life, but is an intensely personal poem. The narrator remembers someone he loved, and time they spent near the sea. He remembers his love as a symbolic Aphrodite.

807 _____. "Sirens in the Aegean," in Three Decades (1972), describes an old fisherman at the oars of his boat. His passengers are two girls and a man. The blue and gold of the water was too much for the girls, and they responded by taking off their clothes and going over the side. The old man hated the temptation of the girls with him. They had indeed become Sirens to him.

LEDWIDGE, Francis (1891-1917, Irish)

808 "The Departure of Proserpine," in The Complete Poems of Francis Ledwidge, with Introduction by Lord Dunsany. London: Jenkins, 1919.
This poem is based on imagery of Autumn--the falling leaves, dying flowers, gloomy days, "a weary change from light to darkness." Persephone must return to her dark realms and wishes she might die rather than do so. She delays, and finally goes, knowing that "no secret turning leads from the gods' way."

809 _____. "A Dream of Artemis," in Complete Poems (1919), is narrated in first-person by a man who dreams of the goddess Artemis. They wander the forests together, hunting and enjoying the beauties of nature. He begs her to love him, pointing out that her existence is forever, whereas his is "no more than a morning" to her. He says, "taste with me the love of earth ... / Though for so short a while

on lands and seas. " At the end it becomes apparent why
the narrator speaks with such urgency when he says "I hear
the rolling chariot of Mars!" As a matter of record, the
poet in this instance lost his life in World War I.

810 _____. "Pan," in Complete Poems (1919), is a simple
statement describing Pan as he acts as shepherd, guiding
the lambs to safety, bedding them down for the night, and
playing a restful tune on his pipes.

LEWIS, C. S. (Clive Staples, 1898-1963, English)

811 "The Queen of Drum," in Narrative Poems, ed. by Walter
        Hooper. New York: Harcourt, Brace, Jovanovich,
        1969.
Regarded by the editor as Lewis's best poem, Hooper speculates that in 1919 Lewis was writing a poem, "Hippolytus,"
which later became identified as "Wild Hunt." This work
subsequently became The King of Drum, and this in turn
was incorporated into the finished The Queen of Drum.
Poems with these earlier titles have not been located. In
its final form Lewis has not created a mythological parallel,
although the story line strongly suggests that the "queen"
is a devotee of "great Artemis." The conflict is drawn between the world of Day--or Reality, or Christianity--in
which the queen lives, and the world of "the pure Huntress"
of Night--or fantasy, or mythological gods--into which the
queen sleepwalks. In conclusion the narrator says, "She
has tasted elven bread ... " and "she passed away / Out of
the world. "

812 _____. "Ten Years After," in Of Other Worlds: Essays
        and Stories, ed. by Walter Hooper. London: Bles,
        1966. Reprinted in The Dark Tower and Other Stories,
        ed. by Walter Hooper. London: Collins; New York:
        Harcourt Brace Jovanovich, 1977.
In this thirty-page fragment of a novel the story is far from
complete, but something of the characters begins to emerge,
and the reader can picture them quite clearly: Menelaus,
the Yellowhead, confronted by the question of what to do
with Helen at the fall of Troy; Helen, ten years later, now
old and fat, with "knuckley" hands; and Agamemnon, still
playing "the older brother" and advising Menelaus to take
Helen and slip away and leave everything to him. Agamemnon laughs at the predicament of finding Helen as the old
hag she has become, and he laughs especially loud when
Menelaus suggests that they fought the war for Helen. Agamemnon, the realist, says they fought the war to destroy
the power of Troy and make the waterways safe for Greek
shipping.
        What direction the story would have taken is indicated
by a disconnected fragment at the end. Helen and Menelaus

have landed in Egypt, and it is said that the "woman" whom
Menelaus has brought with him is an "Eidolon," a phantom,
and that the real Helen never left Egypt. In a note to
Lewis's work Roger Lancelyn Green says he believes, had
Lewis completed the novel, that the conflict would have de-
veloped around the question of what constitutes Reality, the
Eidolon who came with Menelaus or the vision of beauty
that remained in Egypt.

813   _____. Till We Have Faces. London: Bles, 1956; New
          York: Harcourt, Brace, 1957.
Although having many elements in common with the traditional Eros-Psyche story, Lewis's work is not a simple
retelling of the myth. The names have been changed, except for Psyche, and the conflict is more clearly drawn
between the forces of good and evil, between the beautiful
and the ugly. The story is told by Orual, the ugly sister
of Psyche, who is unloved and therefore seeks to destroy
all those who are loved. She blames Psyche for the evils
that beset the kingdom, and persuades their father, with the
blindly pitiless Ungit, to sacrifice Psyche to the Mountain
God, "the He-who-is-not-to-be seen."
       In the end, however, Orual triumphs over all the
ugliness in her nature, removing the veil and understanding
that only the worthy of spirit are admitted to the presence
of the gods. Lewis's work has been called a "religious
classic," a "powerful novel," and "a provocative psycholog-
ical drama."

LONGFELLOW, Henry Wadsworth (1807-1882, American)

814 "Chrysaor," in The Complete Poetical Works of Henry Wads-
          worth Longfellow. Boston and New York: Houghton,
          Mifflin, 1893. Reprint of Riverside edition, 1886.
Chrysaor, whose name means "golden sword," was the son
of Medusa and Poseidon and brother to the flying horse
Pegasus. When this poem was first published, Longfellow
called it "The Evening Star," which title would serve equally
well, since it is about the bright star or planet of Venus.
Callirrhoe, the Nereid wife of Chrysaor, is referred to.
The name Chrysaor is not usually applied to the star, but
might be because of the bright image that the star makes.

815   _____. "Enceladus," in Poetical Works (1893), is the giant
          son of Gaea who tried to assault the gods and was crushed
          under Mt. Etna. In this work he is regarded as some force
          or spirit that will arise and bring justice to the Italian peo-
          ple who in 1859 were fighting a war for deliverance of Italy
          from Austrian rule. There is no mythological basis for re-
          garding Enceladus as a deliverer.

816   . "Endymion," in Poetical Works (1893), is a romanticized version of the youth who was loved by the Moon.
Endymion is portrayed as one who lives a desolate, unloved
existence until the Moon awakens him with a kiss, and says
"Where hast thou stayed so long?"

817   . "Epimetheus," in Poetical Works (1893), refers to
the brother of Prometheus, whose name means "Afterthought."
Here the poet regrets some of the poetry which he has
written, but takes heart because he knows there is still
Hope, the jewel that did not escape from Pandora's box.
In mythology Pandora was the wife of Epimetheus.

818   . "The Masque of Pandora," in Poetical Works (1893),
was adapted for the stage, set to music by Alfred Cellier,
and produced in the Boston Theatre in 1881. The play begins in the workshop of Hephaestus, who has fashioned a
woman whom the gods call Pandora. She is beautiful in
every respect, and the Graces bestow even further gifts
upon her. In the next two scenes Hermes delivers the
woman to Prometheus, who suspects the gods of treachery
and deception. Prometheus refuses to accept the gift, and
Pandora is delivered to Epimetheus, the brother of Prometheus, who does not always behave wisely. In time they
are married. One day when Pandora is left alone, she can
no longer restrain her curiosity about a box that Epimetheus
has told her she must not open. She opens it, and unleashes
all the evils to which humanity is heir. Only Hope remains
in the box. At the end both Epimetheus and Pandora pray
that the gods will punish them for their disobedience, but of
course their actions reflected the will of the gods from the
beginning.

819   . "Pegasus in Pound," in Poetical Works (1893), is
based on the myth of the flying horse. In this narrative he
comes into a village, and is immediately put into pound.
It is given out that he is for sale, but that night he escapes
and soars to the stars. The only thing left of him was a
fountain flowing "from the hoof-marks in the sod." It is
said that the fountain of Hippocrene on Mt. Helicon was
created in this manner.

820   . "Prometheus," in Poetical Works (1893), although
based slightly on the myth of the god who stole fire from
the gods, is here created as a symbol of the Poet, Prophet,
Seer. It is the inspired creation of the poet that tells humankind where it is going, that looks ahead as a prophet,
and forewarns. The name Prometheus means "forethought,"
in contrast to his brother Epimetheus, whose name means
"afterthought."

LOWELL, James Russell (1819-1891, American)

821 "Endymion," in Vol. 5, <u>The Poetical Works of James Russell Lowell</u>, 5 vols. Boston: Houghton, Mifflin, 1904.
In this version of the Endymion myth it is Endymion himself who falls in love with the Moon Goddess, and fervently prays that she will love him. This she ultimately does, but in doing so she leaves the sky and comes to his mortal level. Afterward Endymion regrets her love for him, and beseeches her to "reclimb thy heaven, and be once more/ An inaccessible splendor to adore."

822 _____. "Eurydice," in Vol. 1, <u>Poetical Works</u> (1904), uses the name of the mythological figure, but has little to do with mythology. The name is used by Lowell to refer to another woman who went away and did not return. He says that Eurydice was not "swallowed by a gloomier Orcus."

823 _____. "The Finding of the Lyre," in Vol. 4, <u>Poetical Works</u> (1904), is a rather moralistic version of the tortoise-shell, which became the lyre. It lay empty and unattractive upon the shore until the god Mercury saw it and thought that with strings it would be the "thing of things/ In shape, material, and dimension!" The poet concludes that had we "eyes like Mercury's," what wondrous "songs should waken."

824 _____. "Hebe," in Vol. 1, <u>Poetical Works</u> (1904), is a lyric commemorating the lovely goddess of youth. The images of twinkling white feet, the flash of robes, the goblet filled with wine, entice the narrator to grasp the beauty of the goddess, but then the cup falls and splinters and Hebe flees.

825 _____. "Invita Minerva," in Vol. 4, <u>Poetical Works</u> (1904), is a version of the flute-playing story told of the goddess Minerva. A young would-be poet came looking for a reed on which to play his music, but after ruining a thousand reeds he was still unable to bring forth any music. Then came the goddess Minerva, who so much delighted in playing the reed that she fashioned into a flute. She was invited to play before the gods, but they laughed at her puckered-up face and she threw the instrument away, declaring that any who played it would come to a miserable end. Marsyas had the misfortune to find the cast-off flute.

826 _____. "Prometheus," in Vol. 1, <u>Poetical Works</u> (1904), is a long, diffuse monologue delivered by Prometheus and addressed primarily to Jove, whom he calls a tyrant and a "hated name." Some details of the Prometheus myth are included in the poem--the chaining to a rock in the Caucasus, the liver-eating vulture, the theft of the sacred fire--but these details seem incidental to the principal theme of warning against Jove, or any other tyrannical being, that his

name will pass into oblivion and all strength, except Love, will crumble.

827 _____. "Rhoecus," in Vol. 1, Poetical Works (1904), is simply referred to as a youth. His story is moral-ridden and is nearly lost under the weight of sermonizing details. While walking in the woods one day Rhoecus was spoken to by a lovely dryad, and she told him to meet him again an hour before sunset. Later he became involved in a game of dice and forgot about the dryad. A worrisome bee came through the window and he injured its wings. In conclusion he learns too late that the dryad had sent the bee to remind him, and he reacted harshly and cruelly. He begged forgiveness, which the dryad gave, but says she cannot cure his blindness of spirit. Thereafter Rhoecus was doomed to be alone.

828 _____. "The Shepherd of King Admetus," in Vol. 1, Poetical Works (1904), is a reference to Apollo, who was sentenced by Zeus to serve a mortal for one year. Apollo served Admetus as a shepherd, and increased the king's wealth by threefold. The imagery of this poem, however, is rather clearly related to Christ, who in a sense was sentenced to serve humanity for a term, and then die. Like Apollo, he too was unrecognized as a god.

829 _____. "The Sirens," in Vol. 1, Poetical Works (1904), creates a mood of loneliness and weariness to those who are cast upon the sea. The Sirens, with their lovely soothing voices, speak of rest and peace. They are more than persuasive, but their songs are dangerous, and if they promise rest and peace, they also represent death.

LOWELL, Robert (1917-1977, American)

830 "Falling Asleep over the Aeneid," in Poems: 1938-1949. London: Faber and Faber, 1949.
    In an introductory note the poet says: "An old man in Concord forgets to go to morning service. He falls asleep, while reading Vergil, and dreams that he is Aeneas at the funeral of Pallas, an Italian prince." Much of the poem derives from Book XI, lines 15-99, of the Aeneid, in which Aeneas observes and comments on the funeral preparations for Pallas, son of Evander, who has been slain by Turnus. Certain elements of the phrasing in Lowell's poem are from Virgil, but the bird imagery, set going in the first reference to "yellowhammers mating" is altogether Lowell's, and gives the poem its rich texture as well as supports the mythological theme.

831 _____. The Oresteia of Aeschylus. New York: Farrar, Straus, Giroux, 1978.

169

Although two parts of this trilogy were written in the 1960s, it was not until the last year of his life that Lowell was able to complete "The Furies." He hoped his version of the story would be performed at Lincoln Center, but Lowell never saw his play produced, and it was not published until after his death. Although this work is called a translation, it is less a translation than an adaptation. First of all, it is based on existing translations of the Aeschylus trilogy, and the quality of verse is distinctly Lowell's. The story does not depart from the original, and the language and action are simple and direct, and designed, as Lowell said, for a modern theater audience.

832 _____. "Phaedra," in Phaedra and Figaro. New York: Farrar, Straus, and Giroux, 1960. Reprinted in Phaedra and Hippolytus: Myth and Dramatic Form, ed. by James L. Sanderson and Irwin Gopnik. Boston: Houghton Mifflin, 1966.
This work is an English version of Jean Racine's drama "Phèdre," which in turn was based on Euripides' play "Hippolytus." Lowell's English version follows the French drama closely, and perhaps is rightly called a simple translation.

833 _____. Prometheus Bound. New York: Farrar, Straus, and Giroux, 1969.
This work is described as "derived from Aeschylus," but it is not a translation. Lowell says, "Half my lines are not in the original. But nothing is modernized." By using prose instead of verse, he was thus "free to tone down the poetic eloquence" and create something between the old play and a new one. The plot does not change from the traditional version of the myth. The theme is the punishment of the Titan Prometheus for his crime of stealing fire for humankind, and this act is regarded as a fight for intelligence and justice.

834 _____. "Ulysses and Circe," in Day by Day. New York: Farrar, Straus, and Giroux, 1977.
This poem is presented in a free verse, stream-of-consciousness style in six parts, beginning with a short introduction in which Ulysses is characterized as the one who "ended the ten years' war." By means of fraud he did what the great heroes could not do nor the "Greeks with their thousand ships." The same character is portrayed in the episode with Circe, in which a conniving, deceptive Ulysses uses the goddess to his own purposes and then leaves her on his journey back to Ithaca.

LYTTON, Sir Edward Bulwer (1803-1873, English)

835 "The Athenian and the Spartan," in Vol. III, The Poetical and
        Dramatic Works of Sir Edward Bulwer Lytton. London:
        Chapman and Hall, 1853.
        This brief composition is a dialogue in which each partici-
        pant stands for an opposing viewpoint. At the end Time
        says,

        Discuss, ye symbols of twain
        Great Creeds--THE STEADFAST AND IMPROVING:
        The one shall rot that would remain,
        The one wear out in moving.

    The Athenian stands for moving; the Spartan for holding on.

836 _____. "Bridals in the Spirit Land," in The Lost Tales of
        Miletus. New York: Sturgis and Walton, 1909. New
        edition; contains 1865 Preface.
        In a note to this work the author cites Pausanias, Book III,
        Section 19, in which the story is told that at their deaths
        Helen and Achilles were married and lived in a kind of im-
        mortal state on the Blessed Isles. They stand for Fame
        and Beauty, and it is appropriate they be wedded.

837 _____. "Corinna; or the Grotto of Pan at Ephesus," in
        Lost Tales (1909), is based on a legend that near Ephesus
        was a grotto in which there was a statue of Artemis. It
        was here that Pan dedicated a reed to the goddess as a
        peace-offering. It was said that any maiden charged of
        misconduct could clear her name by passing a test in the
        grotto: if the reed sang, she was innocent; if not, the
        maiden disappeared into the cave and was never seen again.
        In this poem Corinna vows her innocence to her betrothed
        Claucon and tries to prove herself with the test of the grotto.
        She disappears, however, and Glaucon dies thereafter.

838 _____. "Cydippe; or, the Apple," in Lost Tales (1909),
        tells with plentiful details the story of the maiden Cydippe
        and the hunter Acontius, both devoted to Artemis. At the
        festival on Delos, Acontius fell in love with Cydippe, but
        she scorned him because he was not her equal. An old
        woman gave him a golden apple inscribed with the words,
        "I at the altar Artemis hallows, vow to wed Acontius."
        He threw it into Cydippe's bosom, and she read aloud the
        words, thereby binding herself to a vow. In the time that
        followed neither Cydippe nor her father honored the vow,
        and one disaster followed another. Finally, Acontius and
        Cydippe were reunited, and Artemis was appeased.

839 _____. "Death and Sisyphus," in Lost Tales (1909), is a
        complete retelling of the story of Sisyphus. At the begin-
        ning Zeus is beseeched by mortals to help them from the
        thievery and tricks of Sisyphus. Zeus sends Hermes to
        tell Death to go for the rascal, and so he does. However,

when Death comes for him, Sisyphus manages to trap Death
in a cage.   Thereafter Zeus wonders why mortals no longer
pray to the gods, complain, or make any effort to communi-
cate.   He then learns that Sisyphus has caged Death, and
without Death human beings care about nothing.   Hermes
tricks Sisyphus into freeing Death, and Sisyphus dies.   But
he is left unburied and therefore cannot cross the River
Styx into the Underworld.   Hades allows Sisyphus to return
to earth and order his wife to bury him.   Once on earth,
however, Sisyphus decides it would be foolish to return to
Death, and proceeds to enjoy life.   In due time Hermes is
sent to get him, and this time Sisyphus is indeed doomed.
He is sentenced to an eternal punishment of rolling a rock
up the hill only to see it roll down again.

840   _____ .   "Euripides," in Poetical and Dramatic Works
(1853), is a study of the last of the three great tragedians,
who wrote not so much about the gods as about humanity
and its sorrowful struggles.   The poet concludes: "Genius
can / Fill with unsympathising Gods, the Scene, / But Grief
alone can teach us what is Man!"

841   _____ .   "The Fate of Calchas," in Lost Tales (1909), is
based on the myth that the famous soothsayer Calchas would
die when he found another soothsayer "with wisdom more
heaven-gifted than his own."   This came about when a
stranger challenged Calchas to drink the wine from his own
grapes.   The harvest came and Calchas watched the wine-
makers with anticipation.   Then he poured a glass of wine
and prepared to drink but was distracted and started laughing.   His laughter became so violent that the wine was
spilled, and he knew he had met a wiser man than himself.
Calchas died, and it was suspected that some god had a
hand in the matter.

842   _____ .   "Ganymede," in Poetical and Dramatic Works
(1853), is a brief account of taking the Trojan youth to
Olympus.   In the process of being transported into the
heavens, he let fall the reed that he dearly loved to play
on earth.   The theme is best pointed up in the line "What
charm'd thee most on earth is cast away. /   To soar--is
to resign."

843   _____ .   "Memnon," in Poetical and Dramatic Works (1853),
refers to the son of Aurora, the Dawn, who was killed at
Troy.   The poet here reflects that although he died, his
mother still honors her son with each new day, and that he
is the inspiration for music and song and other "glorious
things / With joyous songs, and rainbow-tinted wings."

844   _____ .   "The Oread's Son," in Lost Tales (1909), is the

story of Daphnis, the son of Hermes and an oread, or mountain-nymph. He is credited with having invented pastoral poetry, so great was his love of nature and all the creatures of the forests in which he grew up. He fell in love with a mortal princess, and was stricken blind because the Fates intended him for a naiad whom he had earlier scorned. In the end he and the naiad became "one pure soul for ever. "

845 _____. "The Secret Way, " in Lost Tales (1909), is an overly embellished tale of a Persian prince, Zariades, who is offered the hand of a Scythian king's daughter, Argiope, in marriage, but rejects the offer because he is constantly beset by a dream in which he sees the face of a beauty whom he will love and marry. After much war against the Scythian king, Zariades sees Argiope and knows she is the lady he loves. The work has some claim to mythology in that several figures are referred to, principally Medea, who is said to have been the mother of the Medes, or Persians, as they were later called.

846 _____. "The Wife of Miletus, " in Lost Tales (1909), is based on a custom of allowing the husband of a captured Miletian wife to ransom her. In this case it is Xanthus, a poor farmer, who sells "his house, his herds, his fields, and vineyards, " and goes to pay for Erippe, his captured wife. After she is freed, however, the woman tries to persuade her captor to kill the husband and rob him of all his money. The captor is tempted, but in the end slays the woman because she has tried to persuade him to violate the law of honor of his country and kill one who trusted him.

LYTTON, Edward Robert Bulwer (later the Earl of Lytton; pseudonym "Owen Meredith"; 1831-1891, English)

847 "Clytemnestra, " in Clytemnestra and Poems Lyrical and Descriptive. London: Chapman and Hall, 1867. New edition.
The details of this drama are mostly drawn from the "Agamemnon" of Aeschylus, but there are at least two notable differences: Electra and Orestes are characters in Lytton's work, and Cassandra is not killed. Most significantly, however, this play is lacking all the grand qualities that make Aeschylus great tragedy, and reduce the sordid story of Clytemnestra to a melodrama of hate and passion. This Clytemnestra kills her husband because she hates him and loves another man; very little of her heroic motivation is present, and the girl Electra is equally unattractive. Aegisthus is presented as something of a coward, but content to go along with Clytemnestra because he is greedy and ambitious, and Agamemnon's death will benefit him.

848 _____. "Tales from Herodotus," in Vol. 1, Chronicles and
            Characters, 2 vols. London: Chapman and Hall, 1868.
      This work consists of a Prelude and three tales: "Opis and
      Arge," "Croesus and Adrastus," and "Gyges and Candaules."
      The first tale is an elaboration of Herodotus, Book IV, para-
      graph 35, in which is briefly mentioned the two sisters Opis
      and Arge, Hyperborean maidens who are said to have first
      brought into Greece the images of the gods and introduced
      them at Delos. In a note to this work Robert Lytton says
      that he has used this story as a means to comment on the
      general debt that Western literature owes to Greek mythol-
      ogy. The story of "Croesus and Adrastus," based on
      Book I, paragraphs 35-45, of Herodotus, occurred around
      540 B.C. Croesus, who passed for the richest of all men,
      received a stranger into his court, Adrastus, who had ac-
      cidentally killed his brother and sought asylum and purifica-
      tion for his deed. Croesus received him graciously and
      put him in charge of his son, Atys. In time a great boar
      ravaged the country and was hunted by Atys, aided by Ad-
      rastus, who finally killed the animal. In the process, how-
      ever, Adrastus accidentally killed Atys. In despair, and
      knowing he could not escape his fate, Adrastus killed him-
      self. The tragedy of "Gyges and Candaules" is told in
      Book I, paragraphs 8-12, of Herodotus. Candaules, ob-
      sessed with the beauty of his own wife, boasted to a guard,
      Gyges, that she was the most beautiful woman in the world
      and wanted him to see for himself. The concept of looking
      upon a woman naked was forbidden, and Gyges tried to avoid
      this act. Candaules, however, would not be denied. The
      wife knew that her husband had conspired to have Gyges
      view her naked and vowed revenge. She conspired with
      Gyges to kill Candaules, and then the two of them took con-
      trol of the kingdom.

MacLEISH, Archibald (1892-1982, American)

849 "Calypso's Island," in Collected Poems: 1917-1952. New
            York: Houghton Mifflin, 1952.
      The speaker here is Odysseus, and he is responding to
      Calypso's pleas that he stay with her. His answers are
      mostly concerned with Penelope, and form a comparison
      between the goddess and the mortal woman: Penelope is
      not as beautiful as Calypso, and she will grow old and die
      while Calypso will live forever. Nevertheless, Odysseus
      says, he longs for the "cold, salt, restless, contending
      sea," and for the island "where the grass dies and the sea-
      sons alter." Most of all he longs for the one who "wears
      the sunlight for a while."

850 _____. "Excavation of Troy," in Act Five and Other Poems.
            New York: Random House, 1948.

This poem is a series of images in which the narrator asks the "Girl" if she ever thinks of him, or is he "buried under the many nights layer on layer / Like a city ... fallen in antique wars and forgotten?" The images form a continuous unpunctuated line and convey the mood of desolation and indifference.

851 _____. Herakles, a Play in Verse. Boston: Houghton Mifflin, 1967.

This long play deals with the myth of Herakles killing his sons. It is cast in a modern form, with Act I taking place in Athens, "now." Professor Hoadley and his family are visitors in Athens and discuss the past, but not with any sense of real urgency: for them it is mere history and myth. They display idiotic and superficial natures. Act II takes place in a high deserted ruin on a hilltop, with Professor Hoadley and his family as sightseers. Megara, the wife of Herakles, appears, and Herakles kills their sons. Mrs. Hoadley pleads with him not to do so, but there is no reversing the myth. The killing goes forward. Mrs. Hoadley screams at the end: "Oh, release me from this broken story," pleading to go back to whatever her life has been.

852 _____. "Jason," in Tower of Ivory, with a Foreword by Lawrence Mason. New Haven: Yale University Press, 1917.

This short composition explores the difference between dream and reality. Jason, who sailed in search of the Golden Fleece, is the archetypal example of one who made dream into reality, who sailed into the unknown and found what he sought.

853 _____. "Odysseus--Elpenor," in Poems, 1924-1933. Boston: Houghton Mifflin, 1933.

This poem is based on the Odyssey, Book XI, in which Odysseus goes to the Underworld to learn how he must find his way home. He speaks to Elpenor, who had fallen to his death by drunkenly stepping through a window, thinking it was a door. Elpenor comments on the various characters he sees in the Underworld, and urges Odysseus to take the way forward, to take to the sea, and cast his lot with freedom instead of comfort, to depend upon himself.

854 _____. "Our Lady of Troy," in Tower of Ivory (1917), is a retelling of the Faust legend in which the hero barters his soul for unlimited power and knowledge. At the end, the students call for him to conjure up Helen of Troy, and she appears. She explains what she is, "a rose the world has dreamed."

855 _____. The Pot of Earth. Boston: Houghton Mifflin, 1925. Reprinted in Collected Poems: 1917-1952 (1952).

The basis for this complicated work is the myth of the

175

Adonis gardens. Sir James G. Frazer, in The Golden Bough, writes: "These were baskets or pots filled with earth in which wheat, barley, lettuces, fennel, and various kinds of flowers were sown and tended for eight days, chiefly or exclusively by women. Fostered by the sun's heat, the plants shot up rapidly, but having no root they withered as rapidly away, and at the end of eight days were carried out with the images of the dead Adonis and flung with them into the sea or into springs. " In the three parts of his poem MacLeish has used this myth to portray a girl's youth, motherhood, and death, and to relate the human condition of building, maturity, and decay to the ancient myth in the world of plants. The parts of MacLeish's poem indicate the stages of production in the Adonis gardens: "The Sowing of the Dead Corn, " "The Shallow Grass, " and "The Carrion Spring. "

856 _____. "Selene Afterwards, " in Poems: 1917-1952 (1952), is anything but a romanticized version of the moon and its relation to lovers. The moon is described as a dead woman's face, "a long dead skull. " Other ghastly images mark the poem, and yet this is "the thing that made you love, that maddened you!" One reference is made to the moon as she who "climbed through the woods of Latmos to the bad / Of the eternal sleeper. "

857 _____. The Trojan Horse: A Play. Boston: Houghton Mifflin, 1952. Reprinted in Collected Poems: 1917-1952 (1952).
In a headnote to this work MacLeish writes that "this play is intended for reading without scenery or for radio: that is, for a presentation in which the scene is created by the imagination. " The events referred to are familiar, being derived from Homer (Odyssey, Book IV) and Virgil (Aeneid, Book II). The Greeks, almost ready to abandon the war, devised the Wooden Horse, and the Trojans were deluded into taking it inside their walls. The Horse stands for deceit, treachery, and corruption from within, a thing presented to save but designed to destroy.

MASEFIELD, John (1878-1967, English)

858 A King's Daughter: A Tragedy in Verse. New York: Macmillan, 1923.
This lengthy play is chiefly concerned with the Biblical story of Jezebel, the queen of Samaria, who with King Ahab brought about the destruction of their kingdom. The wrath of God descended upon the wickedness of Ahab and Jezebel and they both died in violence and bloodshed. For some reason Masefield weaves the story of Helen and Paris

into the maiden choruses of A King's Daughter. In addition
to serving practically no purpose in this play, this story of
Helen and Paris is manufactured almost entirely by Masefield. It involves an obscure character, Nireus, one of Helen's
rejected suitors and a trusted friend of Paris. Nireus went
to Troy, and according to this version, killed Paris. Years
later, after Menelaus was dead, Nireus finally claimed Helen,
and the gods restored all their youth and beauty.

859 _____. "Nireus," in Poems: Complete Edition. New York:
Macmillan, 1941.
This work uses the same material, and for the most part
the same language, as that used in the choruses of A King's
Daughter. The choric aspects of the first composition have
been removed, however, and the story is told in straight
narrative form.

860 _____. "Penelope," in Poems (1941), recreates the scene
in the Odyssey (Book XIV) in which Odysseus returns to
Ithaca as a stranger. Penelope, although not recognizing
her husband, is drawn to this stranger and tells him how
she has suffered for so many years. The old nurse does
recognize Odysseus but does not betray him. Odysseus
makes plans to slay the suitors and restore his house to
order.

861 _____. "The Taking of Helen," in The Taking of Helen
and Other Prose Selections. New York: Macmillan,
1924.
This is a prose account of the story that Masefield tells in
the poem "Nireus" and in the choruses of A King's Daughter.
However, this version is limited to the events of Helen's
escape from Menelaus. Nireus, the friend of Paris and a
former suitor of Helen, plans most of the action in helping
the lovers escape from an aging and unloving husband. The
work ends with the ship bearing Helen and Paris away to
Troy.

862 _____. "A Tale of Troy," in Poems (1941), consists of a
series of short tales, each told by a different narrator,
which together form an overall view of the Trojan War.
The tale begins with "The Taking of Helen" and is followed
by "The Going to Troy." In a section called "Klytaimnestra"
the story of Iphigenia is told and the death of Agamemnon is
planned. The war itself is fought for ten years, with the
quarrel of Achilles and the deaths of Hector, Achilles, and
Paris being emphasized. All this is told in a long section
by "The Spearman." Nearly beaten and knowing they will
not win, the Greeks devise the Wooden Horse and scheme
to make their entry through the great wall of Troy. These
events are recorded in "The Horse," "Sthenelus' Daughter"
(the daughter of one of the Greek warriors who tells the
story as her father told it to her after the war), and "The

Trojans About the Horse. " This narrative is interrupted by
"Kassandra, " who warns the Trojans that their doom is
near. In "The Surprise, " Troy is taken, the city plundered
and burned. The "Epilogue" is spoken by Kassandra, who
is nearing her own death at the hands of Klytaimnestra.

863 _____. "The Wild Swan, " in Minnie Maylow's Story and
Other Tales and Scenes. New York: Macmillan, 1931.
Although the events and characters of this story have no
basis in classical mythology, Masefield has created a charming romantic tale that makes a Trojan son of Priam the
founder of Britain, just as Aeneas came to stand at the head
of Roman history. The story takes place in Britain, "three
thousand years" ago, at the court of a king who had no heir,
but only a daughter, the Princess Wild Swan. On this occasion eight young Lords have come to race for the hand of
the Princess. One of them is Brutos, who has come from
a great distance over the sea. The king's counselor, Lykaon, recognizes Brutos and his attendants as Trojans, and
the story is told that Brutos is a son of Priam who escaped
the city with the horses of the god Apollo. Lykaon then
reveals himself as another son of Priam, the eldest, who
was captured and sold into slavery thirty years before.
The race for the princess goes forward, and Brutos wins
with the help of the godlike horses. In the Epilogue it is
said that Brutos married the Princess and in time became
king. He was so great a king that when he died England
was named "Britain from him ... or so it has been claimed. "

MASTERS, Edgar Lee (1868-1950, American)

864 "Apollo at Pherae, " in The Great Valley. New York:
Macmillan, 1917.
The basis for this poem is mythological, but some of the
details are of Masters's own devising. After Apollo destroyed the cyclops who had killed the god's son Aesculapius,
Zeus sentenced him to serve as a shepherd on earth for one
year (Masters says nine). Apollo chose to serve Admetus,
the king of Pherae, who was a good master. So much is
based on myth. In Masters's poem, however, the story revolves around Apollo falling in love with a girl named Chione,
being forced into marriage by the girl's father, and living
the next nine years as the shepherd husband of a wife who
bears one child after another. When they are bored, the
other gods on Olympus look down and laugh at what has happened to Apollo. At the end of nine years Apollo returns
to Olympus, and Chione is left alone with all her children.
She confesses to her father that her husband was not a mer-
chant but a shepherd, and the father points out rather ob-
viously that he has deceived Chione. At the end the father

prays that the gods may note this deception and avenge the wrong done his daughter.

865 _____. "The Apology of Demetrius," in The Great Valley (1917), is narrated by Demetrius, a Greek silver- and gold-smith, at about the time that St. Paul visited Athens. This Demetrius has created in silver and gold all the gods in the Greek and Roman pantheon, in exchange for money. He has quite literally given them life. But now comes "this Paul" and Athens has erected a stone "To the Unknown God." How is he to fashion this god in silver and gold? Perhaps he should sell his tools and worship this god in a safer way.

866 _____. "The Furies," in The Great Valley (1917), are pro-jected in this poem as the spirits of guilt, and the "way of freedom" is to act. Whatever you have done or not done can be expiated by action directed toward the future. The poet reminds man that he was a "dry weed when a Great Hand seized and bore him as a carrier of fire."

867 _____. "Helen of Troy," in Songs and Satires. New York: Macmillan, 1935.
The scene described in this poem is the flight of Helen as she and Paris are depicted on an ancient vase. The poet sees Helen as the symbol of freedom, the desire that besets all human beings to escape and go free of obligations and responsibilities, to know relief from the round of routine duties.

868 _____. "Invocation to the Gods," in The Open Sea. New York: Macmillan, 1921.
Here the poet expresses extreme dissatisfaction with the Christian religion, accusing the "Prince of Peace" of divid-ing humankind with "the sword/ Even as he prophesied." The ancient deities--Aphrodite, Pallas Athena, Apollo, and most of all Zeus, whose "mood was wine and love"--are called upon to return.

869 _____. "Marsyas," in The Great Valley (1917), begins with Athena's throwing away her flute, and with it her magical power of playing it. The satyr Marsyas picks it up, think-ing that it will play for him as it played for the goddess, and challenges the god Apollo to a musical contest. When Marsyas loses the contest, Apollo ties him to an oak-tree and flays him alive. He turns his blood to water and it be-comes the river Marsyas.

870 _____. "Pallas Athene," in Starved Rock. New York: Macmillan, 1920.
This composition repeats most of the sentiment expressed in "Invocation to the Gods," but limits the appeal to Pallas Athene, whom the poet sees as the symbol of power and wis-dom, order and law. She is much needed in a land where

injustice is the way of life, where beauty is trod under foot, where force, fanaticism, ignorance, and superstition rule the day.

871 _____. "Pentheus in These States," in The Open Sea (1921), involves the myth of Pentheus, the king of ancient Thebes, who denied the godhood of Dionysus, and was finally a victim of the maenads, who tore him limb to limb. Masters, however, has written a poem about America and sees Pentheus as a kind of American symbol who would discourage life and creativity.

872 _____. "Persephone," in Invisible Landscapes. New York: Macmillan, 1935.
The myth of Persephone is treated in very near the same way as the Christian religion's belief in the Resurrection. Persephone is viewed as returning from the dead, and her return to life in Spring is the symbol that humanity will "rise up after the winter of death / With joy and love and life reborn. "

873 _____. "Prometheus," in The Serpent in the Wilderness. New York: Sheldon Dick, 1933.
This long treatment of the Prometheus myth does not gain much distinction. It is narrated by the Titan himself, who does not repent of giving fire to mortals. Humanity evolved from the laws of nature: the stone made a plant, the plant made a beast, and the beast made a man, but Prometheus "stole fire in order to give men wisdom. " He will not ask to be released from his mountain, for in time men and women will send all gods into oblivion, and be their own gods.

874 _____. "Song for the Dead Gods," in The Serpent (1933), is an enthusiastic tribute to the old gods--to Apollo, Athene, Hermes, Aphrodite, and to high Olympus, the home of song and beauty. The narrator expresses a vehement dislike for Christianity, which he says is responsible for injustice and bigotry.

875 _____. "Terminus," in Songs and Satires (1935), refers to the Roman god who presided over boundaries and limits of property. This poem speaks of the end of a friendship, the two be separated in life or in death. All things must have an end, the poet says, and the heart resigns itself to the loss.

876 _____. "Ulysses," in The Open Sea (1921), is a conversation in which Telemachus asks his father, "Why did you stay so long from Ithaca?" Ulysses attempts to answer the question, not believing that his son will really understand. There

were so many adventures, the wide world to explore, but
mostly there was Calypso, the beautiful goddess who promised him youth and immortality if he would marry her and
remain on the island of Ogygia. This offer was too tempting to resist, but Ulysses knew that she made empty promises, and even if kept he would weary and could not return
to Ithaca. As Ulysses expected, Telemachus thinks his
father foolish to have left the goddess.

MEREDITH, George (1828-1909, English)

877 "Antigone," in The Poetical Works of George Meredith, with
notes by G. M. Trevelyan. London: Constable, 1912.
The speaker in this monologue is Polynices, the brother of
Antigone. For him she has defied Creon, the ruler of
Thebes, and buried her brother. In his remarks to Antigone,
Polynices tells her that she will be honored by the gods for
obeying their law and giving him a burial.

878 _____. "The Appeasement of Demeter," in Poetical Works
(1912), is based on the usual myth of Demeter sorrowing
for her lost daughter Persephone, but the conclusion of the
poem is somewhat original with Meredith. Whereas Demeter
is traditionally appeased by Zeus, who arranges for Persephone to spend part of the year in the world with her mother,
in this poem the earth-goddess gives up her tragic mood
when laughter breaks the spell. The sight of a near-starved
horse and mare trying to express themselves in mating
causes the "Great Mother" to laugh, and the laughter was
the "reviver of sick Earth!"

879 _____. "Bellerophon," in Poetical Works (1912), is a portrait of the hero after he attempted to climb to Mt. Olympus
and was struck down by the gods. Now he is "maimed,
beggared, grey; seeking an alms." He goes about the village, and is an object of pity to those who "dole him fruit
and crust," and pay little attention to what he is saying.
He talks of his heroic days, how he killed a monster, how
he tamed "the lightning steed," but the villagers have only
remotely heard of these brave feats, and they regard this
old man as crazy.

880 _____. "The Cageing of Ares," in Poetical Works (1912),
is based on an event referred to in the Iliad (Book V, lines
385-387), in which the Giants Ephialtes and Otus capture the
god of war and hold him in a cage for thirteen months.
The blessing does not last long, but while it does earth
prospers, and it always remembers the brief time of peace.

881 _____. "Cassandra," in Poetical Works (1912), is a recrea-
tion of the events as recorded in Part I, "Agamemnon," of
Aeschylus' "Oresteia." The King has arrived in Argos, and

his wife, Clytemnestra, is waiting for him to come into the
palace, where she and her lover, Aegisthus, will slay him.
Cassandra remembers all her dead family in Troy, her
unlistened-to prophecies, her life. She has now arrived at
her destiny, to die alongside Agamemnon. She calls on the
name of Apollo three times and prepares herself for death:
"Death is busy with her grave."

882 _____. "Daphne," in Poetical Works (1912), is a long poem
that tells the simple story of the girl who did not wish to
be loved by the god Apollo. She was changed the "lustrous
Laurel Tree," which graces the forest and is loved by all
creatures of the woodland.

883 _____. "The Day of the Daughter of Hades," in Poetical
Works (1912), is the story of Callistes, a youth of Enna,
who has a unique experience. One year in the Spring,
when Persephone returned to earth, her daughter slipped
into the carriage and came with her. Persephone was reunited with her mother, Demeter, but neither of the goddesses saw the child, who scampered out of the carriage
and lost herself among the flowers and woods of the countryside. She met Callistes, and they spent the whole day
roaming in the luxuriance of nature, she teaching him to
rejoice in light, in life, and in the loveliness of earth.
Finally she sings a joyous "Song of Days," and her voice
betrays her whereabouts to her father, Hades, who sends
his chariot to bring her back to the world of the dead.
Callistes is left with a vision of love and beauty that he
searches for the rest of his life.

884 _____. "Empedocles," in Poetical Works (1912), is a brief
treatment of the poet-philosopher who jumped into Aetna's
fiery depths and so perished. Meredith's poem, which takes
a most unheroic approach to suicide, questions whether there
is no "saner recipe/ For men at issue with despair."

885 _____. "Lucifer in Starlight," in Poetical Works (1912), is
a famous poem with slight mythological connections, Lucifer
being the name of the morning star. When this star, which
actually is the planet Venus, appears in the evening, it is
called Hesperus.

886 _____. "Melampus," in Poetical Works (1912), is the story
of one of the greatest, and perhaps the first, of Greek seers.
He was awakened one night by a brood of young snakes who
were licking his ears--the mother snake having been killed.
Melampus took care of them, and for this deed he received
divine knowledge of all living creatures and could understand
their languages. From Apollo he learned the gift of fore-
telling the future and also the healing art. Meredith calls

him "physician and sage," who loved humankind, by healing the sick or maimed or demented.

887 _____. "Periander," in Poetical Works (1912), is based on the historical career of the tyrant of Corinth who lived about 585 B.C. His savagery extended not only to the citizens of Corinth but to his own family: he put his wife, Melissa, to death and banished his son Lycophron for weeping and pitying the miserable end of his mother.

888 _____. "Phaethon," in Poetical Works (1912), tells the story of the son of Phoebus who insisted that he be allowed to take the fiery chariot of the sun across the heavens. When the fierce horses became too much for him, and the chariot went out of control, he nearly burned up the world, but Zeus intervened and killed the youth with a thunderbolt. Meredith's poem is distinguished by the emotion that is developed in Phoebus when he cannot persuade his son to relinquish his wish to drive the chariot, knowing that it will be fatal to the youth.

889 _____. "Phoebus with Admetus," in Poetical Works (1912), sings the praises of the god for all the blessings that he brought to mortals during the year of his exile from Olympus. Apollo, furious with Zeus for killing Asclepius, retaliated by killing the cyclopes who furnished Zeus with the thunderbolts. For this Zeus sentenced Phoebus (Apollo) to spend one year among mortals as a common laborer. Phoebus chose to serve Admetus, king of Pherae, and received such good treatment that he repaid Admetus with many blessings.

890 _____. "The Rape of Aurora," in Poetical Works (1912), is a short lyric describing the Dawn (Aurora or Eos) as she emerges from night to announce the day, but in this case is caught and ravished by the Sun (Apollo).

891 _____. "A Reading of Life," in Poetical Works (1912), is a sequence of four mythological poems. "The Vital Choice" poses the question, "Shall we run with Artemis / Or yield the breast to Aphrodite ... ?" and warns that "each can torture if derided." In "With the Huntress," the case for Artemis is debated, this goddess standing for virgin purity, intellect, and spirit. In "With the Persuader," by far the longest of the poems, the cause of Aphrodite is presented, this goddess representing the forces of life itself, in the sex drive, in reproduction, in fertility. Hers is a powerful persuasion, and one that cannot be denied without severe penalty. "The Test of Manhood" argues that devotion to either Artemis or Aphrodite alone means destruction, and it is the union of intellect and body that points the way to advancement.

892 _____. "The Shipwreck of Idomeneus," in Poetical Works

(1912), refers to the king of Crete who took ships to Troy and aided Agamemnon and Menelaus in their war against the Trojans. In the Odyssey Homer says that Idomeneus returned to Crete without incident. Virgil in the Aeneid says that he returned to find his wife and daughter murdered and his kingdom usurped, and so set sail for Italy to found a new land. Meredith's poem deals with a near-disaster that the king had on his way home. A savage storm was sent by Poseidon to destroy the ships, but Idomeneus prayed to the god and vowed that once on the shores of Crete, he would sacrifice the first living thing to the god. This sacrifice turned out to be his own son, but the king was then so much hated by his subjects that he left Crete and set sail for Italy. In Meredith's work the king does not reach Crete, but all is fated, and the boy, an innocent youth, is doomed.

893 _____. "Solon," in Poetical Works (1912), treats the great lawgiver of Athens, who lived about 550 B.C. After devoting himself to philosophy and political studies, he became a benefactor of his native city and could have become king had he so wished. Instead, he became lawgiver and succeeded in unifying the people and bringing prosperity to the state. He then left Athens, making the Athenians swear an oath that they would follow his laws for a hundred years. He returned to Athens within ten years only to find that all he had taught had been cast aside, and that his countrymen were under the iron yoke of a tyrant.

MERTON, Thomas (1915-1968, American)

894 "Ariadne," in The Collected Poems of Thomas Merton. New York: New Directions, 1977.
    The theme of this poem emerges from a consideration of the casual, ordinary afternoon that Ariadne of Crete is spending, and the extraordinary event of her life, which takes place when Theseus arrives. She goes to the window to observe the crowd gathered around his "Greek ship," and "Arrows of light/ Resound within her like the strings of a guitar." Later Theseus would take Ariadne from her home in Crete and then abandon her on the island of Naxos.

895 _____. "Ariadne at the Labyrinth," in Collected Poems (1977) contains the story of how the Cretan princess "solves the maze's cruel algebra"--that is, provides the means by which Theseus, whom she loves wildly, enters the labyrinth, kills the Minotaur, and returns to her safely. By giving him a ball of thread that he unwound as he went into the labyrinth, Theseus was able to accomplish his heroic deed, and then follow "the cotton thread" back to Ariadne.

896 _____. "Calypso's Island," in Collected Poems (1977),
portrays the goddess as Odysseus comes ashore to her
island. Until now she has lived alone, but with his coming
she will fall in love and he will stay with her seven years.
She is described as having lived in a dreamlike state until
Odysseus arrives, and then awakes to all the treasures of
life.

897 _____. "The Greek Women," in Collected Poems (1977),
are those whom the war at Troy has left widowed; "all
your men are sleeping in the alien earth," the poet says.
All, that is, except for one: Clytemnestra, for whom the
soldier-leader Agamemnon "bleeds in her conscience, twisting like a root." Ironically, Clytemnestra is not a widow
at the end of the long war, but she will be a widow when
she kills the husband who comes home.

898 _____. "Iphigenia: Politics," in Collected Poems (1977),
is narrated by Clytemnestra, Iphigenia's mother, who never
forgave the brutal sacrifice of her daughter at Aulis by a
father who was commanded to do so by the prophet Calchas.
Clytemnestra sees the entire event as a political move, the
prophet avenging himself on Agamemnon, whom he despised,
and Agamemnon killing his own child to retain the honor
and prestige of leading the army. The story that Iphigenia
was spirited away, alive, from the altar, to "Diana's
Tauris," seems concocted, designed to gloss over the horrible facts. The simple truth is that Iphigenia is gone,
and the "world has become a museum."

899 _____. "The New Song," in Collected Poems (1977), involves references to various mythological singers: Amphion
the Theban, whose song is said to have moved stones;
Arion, who "charmed a dolphin"; Orpheus, "who tamed the
wild animals with nothing but song." The subject of this
poem, however, is the Christian God, and "the new song."
It is this power who has "tamed the hardest of animals to
subdue--man." The new song has changed "beasts into
men," "has brought to life a God-fearing seed sensitive to
virtue." As the Master Musician, the poet says:

... He has structured the whole universe musically
And the discord of elements He has brought together
    in an ordered symphony
So that the whole Cosmos is for Him in harmony.

MEYNELL, Alice (1847-1922, English)

900 "The Love of Narcissus," in The Poems of Alice Meynell.
        London: Burns, Oates and Washbourne, 1923. Com-
        plete edition.
    The Narcissus myth is used in this poem as a metaphor

185

for the poet who sees himself reflected "through the changing nights and days" of Nature. Like Narcissus, the poet
must pursue her own dreams, her own voice, and her own
"lonely heart with piercing love and pain. "

MILLAY, Edna St. Vincent (1892-1950, American)

901 "Alcestis to her husband ..." in Collected Poems of Edna St.
Vincent Millay, ed. by Norma Millay. New York:
Harper & Row, 1956.
This sonnet presents an original view of the myth of Alcestis, who traditionally is said to have taken, out of love,
her husband's place when Death came for him. Millay's
poem creates an Alcestis who says she "despises" Admetus,
and dies "for her own sake, " because she no longer loves
her husband and wishes to be free of him.

902 _____. "Daphne, " in Collected Poems (1956), is a slight
treatment of the Daphne-Apollo myth, in this case spoken
by Daphne, who tells Apollo to chase as long as he likes--
she can change quickly into a tree and give him a branch
of leaves to embrace.

903 _____. "Oh, Sleep Forever in the Latmian Cave, " in
Collected Poems (1956), refers to Endymion, loved by the
Moon. The poem examines the difference between mortality
and immortality and concludes that the Moon "wanders mad, "
unfit for mortal love, and yet cannot die of it.

904 _____. "Prayer to Persephone, " in Collected Poems (1956),
is one section of a memorial to a friend of the poet, someone who died in her youth. In this prayer the poet pleads
with Persephone, the Queen of the Dead, to be kind to her
friend, and say to her, "It is not so dreadful here. "

905 _____. "Sappho Crosses the Dark River into Hades, " in
Collected Poems (1956), incorporates the few details believed to be true of Sappho. She loved the youth Phaon,
and when he refused her passion, she threw herself into
the sea. In Millay's poem she has killed herself, and is
being ferried across the Acheron to the Underworld. She
talks to the old ferryman Charon, and hopes that she will
find a peace she has long sought.

MOODY, William Vaughn (1869-1910, American)

906 The Fire-Bringer. Boston: Houghton, Mifflin, 1904.
Moody's dramatic poem in three acts is based on the story
of the Great Flood as given in Apollodorus, and was in-

tended to be the first part of a trilogy on the Promethean
theme. The entire work was to demonstrate the concept
of power behind the human scene, that humanity is irre-
vocably linked with unknown forces. The play begins at
the end of the Flood, which had been sent by Zeus to destroy the human race, and only Deukalion, his wife, Pyrrha,
and their children have escaped. Themis, the mother of
Prometheus, instructs them to throw "the bones of their
mother" over their shoulders, and by this action to repopu-
late the earth. At first they do not understand, and then
it comes to them that the goddess means to throw stones
over their shoulders. Thus the world is once again filled
with men and women, but they live in darkness and squalor.
Prometheus gave them fire, "bringing it secretly from the
gods in a fennel stalk." At the end of the play Zeus com-
mands Hephaestos, with the aid of Force and Violence, to
bind Prometheus upon Mt. Caucasus. With the departure
of Prometheus the human beings are disconsolate, but they
understand that he has made the sacrifice for them.

MOORE, Marianne (1887-1972, American)

907 "Cassandra," in Complete Poems of Marianne Moore. New
          York: Viking, 1959.
     In this poem Cassandra is the "mad girl with the staring
     eyes and long white fingers," "the storm-wrack hair and
     the screeching mouth." She is the daughter of Priam and
     Hecuba who labored under Apollo's curse that she would
     always be able to foresee the future, but that no one would
     believe her. It is for this that she symbolizes the prophet
     who rants and raves but is unheeded.

908 _____. "The Labors of Hercules," in Complete Poems
          (1967), poses the question, What was the true value of the
     labors of Hercules? The poet argues that the labors were
     to demonstrate that the common man had a voice in things,
     that superstition and "snake-charming" were no longer
     sacred, and that truth has a way of prevailing. Hercules
     was a hero of the people, and most of his Labors consisted
     of destroying the sacred idols of his day, cleaning out the
     "pigsty" of snobbishness and stupidity.

909 _____. "Phoebus and Boreas," in Fables of La Fontaine,
          trans. by Marianne Moore. New York: Viking, 1954.
     Although a translation, the poem bears the wit and charm
     of Marianne Moore, and is thus included here. The story
     deals with a contest between Phoebus, the Sun, and Boreas,
     the North Wind, to see which one can first induce a trav-
     eler to take off his cloak. The North Wind tries first, go-
     ing headlong to blow the cloak off, but the traveler merely
     hugs it closer. Then the Sun comes out and warms up so
     rapidly that the cloak comes off, and thus the Sun wins the
     contest in an unexpected way.

MOORE, continued

910 _____ . "The Staff of Aesculapius," in Complete Poems
(1967), refers to the god of healing, called Asclepius by
the Greeks, who was the mortal son of Apollo until he became a deity sometime after his death. He was widely
worshiped by the Romans, who associated him with the
snake--hence the serpent-wreathed staff, the Caduceus,
which is a rod entwined at one end by two serpents.
Moore's poem is in praise of research and medicine,
which search for answers. It is fitting that the "symbol
of medicine" be an animal that "by shedding its skin/ is
a sign of renewal."

MOORE, Thomas (1779-1852, English)

911 "Cephalus and Procris," in The Poetical Works of Thomas
Moore, ed. by A. D. Godley. London: Oxford University Press, 1929.
Moore's brief poem captures the pathos of the Cephalus
and Procris myth, in which a hunter mistakenly shoots
Procris, his young wife, thinking her bridal veil was the
"white-horn'd doe" that he had tracked all day.

912 _____ . "Cupid and Psyche," in Poetical Works (1929), details the scene in which Psyche, unable to bear the mystery
of her lover, succumbs to the taunting of her sisters that
she has married a demon, and looks at the face of Cupid.
When the god awakens and sees what his bride has done,
he bids her farewell, for it was in violation of a divine
law that she should not look upon him.

913 _____ . "The Fall of Hebe," in Poetical Works (1929), is
based on the myth that on a festival occasion Hebe fell as
she was carrying the cup of nectar to the gods. The
sparkling drink was said to spill over the heavens and
form the constellation Lyra. Because of her careless act,
Hebe was subsequently replaced as cupbearer by the youth
Ganymede.

914 _____ . "Hero and Leander," in Poetical Works (1929), is
the story of Leander's death as he tried to swim for the
last time to the island where Hero waited for him. The
lovers had been together by means of Hero's holding a
torch for Leander to guide himself to her tower, but on
this occasion the bitter wind blew out the light and he was
drowned.

915 _____ . "Song of Hercules to His Daughter," in Poetical
Works (1929), is based on an obscure myth that Hercules
searched the Indian Ocean to find a pearl with which he
adorned his daughter by Pandama, an Indian girl who bore
Pandaea.

188

916 _____. Addenda: Other poems by Moore that have very
slight mythological value are "Evenings in Greece," "From
the High Priest of Apollo," "The Grecian Girl's Dream of
the Blessed Islands," "Hymn of a Virgin of Delphi," and
"Ode to the Goddess Ceres"--all in Poetical Works (1929).

MORRIS, Sir Lewis (1833-1907, English)

917 "Clytemnestra in Paris," in The Works of Sir Lewis Morris.
London: Kegan Paul, Trench, and Trübner, 1898.
The story in this narrative is that of "a lonely woman,
soft of voice and mild of eye," who has been sentenced
to spent the rest of her life in prison. Her story is similar to that of the Greek tragic heroine who conspired with
her lover and killed her husband, Agamemnon. Morris's
story, however, is lacking in any semblance of tragedy,
and is merely a sordid tale of a woman who helped kill
her husband.

918 _____. "The Epic of Hades," in Works (1898), consists
of three major parts: Tartarus, Hades, and Olympus.
Within each part is a sequence of dramatic monologues
dealing with appropriate characters. In Tartarus are Tantalus, Phaedra, Sisyphus, Clytaemnestra; in Hades are
Marsyas, Andromeda, Actaeon, Helen, Eurydice, Orpheus,
Deianeira, Laocoön, Narcissus, Medusa, Adonis, Persephone, Endymion, Psyche; on Olympus are Artemis, Heracles, Aphrodite, Athene, Hera, Apollo, Zeus. At the end
the narrator awakens from his long dreamlike trance, and
finds himself on earth, "dreaming the dream of Life again."
The stories told about these characters are the traditional
ones, with nothing innovative or ironically interpreted.

919 _____. "Icarus," in Works (1898), derives its title from
the young son of Daedalus who built wax wings to escape
from the labyrinth in Crete. Icarus fell into the sea and
was lost, although Daedalus managed to survive by not
flying too close to the sun. In Morris's short poem the
subject is a young bird whose parents are teaching him to
fly. He falls to the earth and is snatched up and eaten by
a cat.

920 _____. "Nemesis," in Works (1898), refers to the goddess
of retribution, usually conceived of as an abstraction. The
retribution could be for evil deeds or for undeserved good
fortune, or as in this poem for failure to oppose evil.

921 _____. "Niobe on Sipylus," in Works (1898), is spoken by
the mother whose children were killed by Artemis and
Apollo. Overwhelmed with grief, Niobe could not stop
weeping and was turned to stone on Mt. Sipylus. As a
fountain, she continued weeping. In this poem it is emphasized that turning Niobe to stone did not allay her grief.

MORRIS, William (1834-1896, English)

922 "Atalanta's Race," in Vol. 3, The Collected Works of William
        Morris, 24 vols., ed. with Introduction by May Morris.
        London: Longmans, 1910-1915. Reprinted New York:
        Russell and Russell, 1966.
        This telling of the story of Atalanta is straightforward nar-
        rative, with the traditional account of the events. Atalanta,
        the virgin huntress, did not wish to be married, and so
        challenged every suitor to a foot-race. If they lost, their
        lives were forfeit. When Milanion, or Hippomenes as he
        is sometimes called, raced with her, he tricked her with
        the help of Venus by casting down three golden apples,
        which Atalanta could not resist picking up. This retarded
        her progress, and she lost the race. However, by the end
        she was glad to do so, and the poet says, "she weeps glad
        tears for all her glory done."

923 _____. "Bellerophon at Argos," in Vol. 6, Collected Works
        (1966), tells how Hipponous, the son of Glaucus, king of
        Corinth, accidentally killed his brother Beller. He fled to
        Proetus, king of Argos, who purified him of the crime and
        gave him lands and many other gifts. Thereafter Hipponous
        was called Bellerophon, which means Beller-killer. Later
        Sthenoboea, the wife of Proetus, fell in love with Bellerophon,
        but he would not succumb to her advances. She then told
        her husband, the king, that Bellerophon had attempted to
        rape her. Not wanting the blood of a guest on his hands,
        Proetus sent Bellerophon to the court of King Iobates of
        Lycia with a concealed message that Iobates was to have
        Bellerophon killed.

924 _____. "Bellerophon in Lycia," in Vol. 6, Collected Works
        (1966), continues the story of Bellerophon as he moves from
        Argos to Lycia. Here the king, reluctant to shed the blood
        of a guest himself, tries to have Bellerophon killed by set-
        ting him a dangerous and impossible task to fulfill: the
        slaying of the dangerous Chimera. With the help of the
        gods and the supernatural horse Pegasus, Bellerophon ac-
        complishes this act, and instead of death wins the admira-
        tion of Iobates, who realizes that the hero is protected by
        the gods. King Iobates gives his daughter Philonoe to
        Bellerophon, and in addition many lands and honors. Mor-
        ris's poem ends at this point, and does not go further into
        Bellerophon's life, which ended tragically because he offended
        the gods by trying to ride Pegasus into the heavens.

925 _____. "The Death of Paris," in Vol. 5, Collected Works
        (1966), begins with the wounding of Paris by Philoctetes,
        who possessed the bow and arrows of Heracles. He was
        taken to Mt. Ida, where Oenone, his first wife, could have
        healed him had she chosen to do so. Her only request was
        that Paris renounce Helen and stay with her on Mt. Ida.

Paris would have done so, falsely, to save his life, but at
the last minute Paris called out "Helen! Helen! Helen!"
and Oenone allowed him to die. The poem ends at this
point and does not tell how Oenone, stricken with remorse,
killed herself on Paris' funeral pyre.

926 _____. "The Doom of King Acrisius," in Vol. 3, Collected
Works (1966), like the story of Oedipus, illustrates the inevitability of fate, and that whatever course one takes to
avoid it is only the means to the doom. Acrisius, the king
of Argos, was told by a prophet that he would die by the
hand of his grandson, the son of Danae. He therefore took
means to see that the daughter had no children and shut her
up in a tower. Zeus, however, visited her in the form of
sun-rays, and she conceived a son, Perseus. Acrisius set
them afloat on the sea, hoping that they would meet death,
but instead they came ashore on the island of Seriphos.
Perseus grew to manhood, set out to win the Medusa's head,
and in the process freed and married the girl Andromeda.
On his way home he stopped at Larissa in Thessaly, where
funeral games were being held. Acrisius, having heard that
his grandson was alive, had fled to Larissa for sanctuary.
At the games, Perseus threw a discus and accidentally hit
Acrisius, unaware of whom he had slain. Thus the prophecy
was fulfilled. Perseus never ruled in Argos, but founded
the city of Mycenae, and died there after a long and just
reign.

927 _____. "Flora," in Vol. 9, Collected Works (1966), is a
slight lyric sung by the goddess of flowering plants. The
poem emphasizes the beauty that this goddess brings to
earth, but the ancients worshiped her as a deity of fertility.

928 _____. "The Golden Apples," in Vol. 6, Collected Works
(1966), is the story of Heracles and his Eleventh (or, according to some accounts, the Twelfth) Labor. This was
to bring back the apples of the Hesperides, which grew in
a grove somewhere at the ends of the earth and were tended
by the daughters of Hesperus and a hundred-headed snake
named Ladon.

929 _____. "The Hill of Venus," in Vol. 6, Collected Works
(1966), is the story of a man who spent his life with the
goddess of love, believing that nothing else was worth existence. As he said, "A world made to be lost--a bitter life
'twixt pain and nothing tossed!" At the end, however, he
is rejected by the goddess and by humanity. As he becomes
an old man "with high puckered brow, thin lips, long chin,
and wide brown eyes," he seeks the comforts of religion.
Although based on a mythological theme, and containing a
wide range of references to famous lovers--Orpheus and
Eurydice, Helen and Paris, Pyramus and Thisbe, Ariadne,
etc.--the poem is highly moralistic.

930 _____. The Life and Death of Jason, in Vol. 2, Collected
Works (1966), comprises seventeen books of well over ten
thousand lines. It is based on Ovid, Apollodorus, and
Apollonius of Rhodes. Morris has also used Lemprière's
Dictionary (1788) to fill in details. It is told in a medieval,
troubadour--rather than classical--fashion, in first-person.
The style is overly fluent, and the work as a whole lacks
drama and intensity. It is basically a retelling of the Jason
and the Golden Fleece story, but includes the episode of
Medea tricking Pelias to his death by promising to restore
his youth. This story, not in the Argonautica, appears in
the long Book 15. The last book is devoted to the tragedy
of Medea, and the death of Jason by falling beams of the
old ship Argo:

> ... when the day dawned, still on the same spot,
> Beneath the ruined stem did Jason lie
> Crushed, and all dead of him that here can die.

One of the most charming aspects of this work is the lyrics
that are attributed to Orpheus, one of the crew members,
that occur in Books 4 and 12, "O Bitter Sea," "A Garden
by the Sea," and "O Death, That Maketh Life so Sweet."

931 _____. "The Love of Alcestis," in Vol. 4, Collected
Works (1966), is the traditional account of how Alcestis
died in her husband's place when Death came for him.
However, this poem does not end happily, as in the original myth, for Alcestis does not return from the dead to
rejoin her husband and children.

932 _____. "Pomona," in Vol. 9, Collected Works (1966), is
a short lyric in first-person by the goddess of fruit-trees,
or the "ancient Apple-Queen" as she calls herself. She
comes year after year, past the "grave of Troy," past all
human events, to gladden the "heart of Summer's joy."

933 _____. "Pygmalion and the Image," in Vol. 4, Collected
Works (1966), tells the story, without any departure from
the basic myth, of the sculptor who made an image of a
woman and fell in love with it. He prayed to Venus, who
brought the statue to life, and thereafter married her with
great love.

934 _____. "The Ring Given to Venus," in Vol. 6, Collected
Works (1966), is a long moralistic tale not unlike "The
Hill of Venus," discussed above. A young man, Laurence
by name, gives his engagement ring to Venus, the goddess
of love. She will not return it, and until she does, Laurence cannot wed the maid to whom he is betrothed. Finally
after many trials and the death of his good friend, the ring

is recovered, and Laurence is free to marry the pure maid he loves.

935 _____. "Scenes from the Fall of Troy," in Vol. 24, Collected Works (1966), begins with the scene in which Helen arms Paris to go out and fight the Greeks. Later he is joined by Hector and they go out to battle. In the second scene Talthybius, the herald of the Greek kings, brings a message to Priam: give Helen back to Menelaus and the city will be spared. Priam rejects the offer and gives him a golden cup as a memento of the meeting. The next scene is Hector's last battle, at the end of which he is killed by Achilles. In scene four Hector's body is brought back to Troy, and there is some contention among Paris, Troilus, and Aeneas as to the leadership of Troy now that Hector is dead. In scene five a letter is received by the Trojans from Achilles, who asks for the hand of Polyxena in marriage. He says he can save Troy, and will do so if the maiden be given to him; otherwise he will take her anyway. Paris vows that he will see Achilles dead for this foul offer. Scene six takes place in Helen's chamber, where she and Paris talk of life as it used to be and will not be again. At the end Paris goes out to fight Achilles, and Helen wonders if she will ever see him again. Scene seven picks up the story after a considerable lapse of time: Achilles is dead, slain by Paris, who himself was slain by Philoctetes, and the Wooden Horse has been brought into the gates of Troy. In this scene the Greeks come pouring out of the Horse, ready to overthrow the city. The scene concludes with Helen and Menelaus confronting each other at last, and in the background Troy is being burned and sacked. Menelaus brutally kills Deiphobus, the son of Priam, who became Helen's lover after the death of Paris, and orders Helen to the ships. At the end Aeneas and a few other Trojans are escaping to their own ships, and Troy is in ruins, the men slain and the women herded into captivity.

936 _____. "The Son of Croesus," in Vol. 4, Collected Works (1966), illustrates, as do several other myths, the inevitability of fate. Croesus, the king of Lydia, dreamed that his son would die by means of an iron weapon. The king took all care to protect the boy, refusing to allow him to play in games or to go near any type of iron weapon. Finally the son persuaded his father to at least allow him to hunt the wild boar in the forest; here he would be safe. Accompanied by a close friend, the son wounded a boar of great size, and the friend threw a spear to finish him. The son intervened, and was killed.

937 _____. "The Story of Acontius and Cydippe," in Vol. 5, Collected Works (1966), is a love story with a happy, although ironic, conclusion. Acontius fell in love with Cydippe, a lady of noble birth, but was not allowed to marry her

because of his own lack of important family. The goddess
of love provided him with a golden apple, inscribed "Acontius will I wed to-day." At the festival of Diana, the young
man tossed the apple into the folds of Cydippe's bosom,
and in clasping the golden fruit she felt that she had bound
herself to an oath. They were therefore married amid
great festivities and rejoicing.

938 _____. "The Story of Aristomenes," in Vol. 24, Collected
Works (1966), is based in part on a semihistorical figure
who is said to have died about 671 B.C. The poem is the
life story of Aristomenes the Messenian, who strove for
thirty years to free his people and nation from Sparta. In
this he was unsuccessful, but his behavior with regard to
the Spartan women won their gratitude and thanks, and he
gradually came to move among them without fear. When
he died, Sparta honored him as greatly as did his own
country.

939 _____. "The Story of Cupid and Psyche," in Vol. 4, Collected Works (1966), is the traditional account of the beautiful princess who was loved by Eros, the god of love, until
she lost him by insisting that she must look on his face.
The greater part of Morris's poem is given to Psyche's
wanderings, persecuted by Venus, until finally she is received into the company of the gods and made a goddess
herself.

940 _____. "The Story of Orpheus and Eurydice," in Vol. 24,
Collected Works (1966), begins shortly before the death of
Eurydice and focuses on the grief that Orpheus felt with
her loss. Refusing to believe that Death could not be persuaded to release his bride, Orpheus went into the Underworld, and Eurydice followed him out again. When he
looked back, however, she was not there, and he wondered
if all this had been a dream. Thereafter he wandered the
earth, the loneliest of men, until finally he was killed by a
band of drunken maenads. The long narrative form of this
poem is lightened by numerous lyrics interspersed throughout, lyrics by Orpheus for his lost love.

941 _____. "The Story of Rhodope," in Vol. 5, Collected Works
(1966), is less mythology than fairy tale based on the Cinderella theme. Rhodope is a country girl, poor but exceed-
ingly beautiful. An eagle carries off one of her sandals
while she is bathing and drops it near the throne of an
Egyptian king. After a long search the owner of the other
sandal is found, and the king marries her. Rhodope is
mentioned in Lemprière's Dictionary (1788), but here she
is called a famous courtesan.

MUIR, Edwin (1887-1959, Scottish)

942 "Ballad of Hector in Hades," in Collected Poems. London:
Oxford University Press, 1965.
The narrator of this poem is Hector, who is now a spirit
and remembers the day he died in Troy. The details of
his recollection are drawn from the Iliad, but the mood of
indifference to and detachment from human affairs is created
solely by Edwin Muir. Hector refers to himself and Achilles
as "two shadows racing on the grass," and then one shadow
falls on the other--Achilles kills Hector, and Hector says,
"The race is ended. Far away/ I hang and do not care."

943 _____. "The Charm," in Collected Poems (1965), refers
to a drug "that Helen knew." When dropped into a wine-
cup, it could bring release from the cares and unhappiness
of life. This is referred to in the Odyssey, Book IV, when
Telemachus visits Helen and Menelaus in Sparta.

944 _____. "The Grave of Prometheus," in Collected Poems
(1965), is described as the spot on which the great Titan
was chained after he stole fire, "heaven's dangerous treasure." When the other gods were exiled from Olympus,
Prometheus simply "turned to common earth"--symbolically
appropriate, since his defiance of the gods was in the interest of mortals, who turn to common earth when they die.

945 _____. "The Labyrinth," in Collected Poems (1965), is
narrated by Theseus, the Athenian prince who killed the
Minotaur in the labyrinth at Crete. Since that day, Theseus
says, he has never been sure of reality. In the world outside he still hears his footstep echoing through the maze,
he still sees the high walls, he no longer knows if he is
living or dead. He comes to see the entire world as a
labyrinth, in which there is no exit, "no place to come to,"
and "you'll end where you are/ Deep in the centre of the
endless maze."

946 _____. "Oedipus," in Collected Poems (1965), is spoken
by the king after he has blinded himself. Details of his
tragic story--the killing of his father and marriage with
his mother--are revealed, but the emphasis is on the theme
of light and darkness: with his sight Oedipus walked the
world in darkness, with his sight now gone, light is all
about him.

947 _____. "Orpheus' Dream," in Collected Poems (1965),
creates a dreamlike atmosphere in which Orpheus regains
Eurydice. Sleep is described as a little boat "coasting the
zones of oblivion and despair," and somehow Eurydice is
there. Then she is gone, "the poor ghost of Eurydice ... /
Alone in Hades' empty hall."

948 _____. "The Other Oedipus, " in <u>Collected Poems</u> (1965),
is a description of Oedipus in old age, "white-headed and
light-hearted, " roaming the streets of the world, in a "time
without a yesterday or a to-morrow. " And why not? The
gods had inflicted all the punishment possible upon him,
and they can no longer hurt him. He has transcended tragedy, and is now happy.

949 _____. "Penelope in Doubt, " in <u>Collected Poems</u> (1965),
is a view of Penelope as she approaches Odysseus for the
first time in twenty years. Was this indeed Odysseus,
"this stranger, who had seen too much, / Been where she
could not follow"? She had identified the "brown scar, "
but twenty years of "drifting snow" had passed between
them, and she did not know this stranger.

950 _____. "Prometheus, " in <u>Collected Poems</u> (1965), is a
contemporary statement by the god who befriended humankind by stealing fire from the gods, and was subsequently
chained to a mountain where an eagle pecked out his liver
for all eternity. He is still suffering his punishment, but
the gods have left Olympus, and it is now a world without
gods. Prometheus has heard of another god who "came
down from another heaven, " not in rebellion, "but in pity
and love" for humanity. In conclusion, Prometheus says,
"If I could find that god, he would hear and answer. "

951 _____. "The Return of Odysseus, " in <u>Collected Poems</u>
(1965), is a description of Penelope as she waits for the
return of Odysseus. She does not know whether he is living or dead; she has not had word for ten years. Her life
has grown meaningless, she weaves and unweaves, "making
an emptiness amid disorder. " She waits and questions,
"will you ever return? Or are you dead... ?"

952 _____. "Telemachos Remembers, " in <u>Collected Poems</u>
(1965), portrays the son of Odysseus as he remembers his
mother, endlessly weaving and unweaving "a jumble of
heads and spears/ Forlorn scraps of her treasure trove, "
that is, her memories of Odysseus. The mood of the poem
is somber. Telemachos grieves for his mother, now dead,
and reflects that had Penelope woven a true pattern and
finished it, "she would have worked a matchless wrong. "
He expresses no sympathy for his father, who was absent
from Ithaca for twenty years.

953 _____. "A Trojan Slave, " in <u>Collected Poems</u> (1965), is
narrated by an old man, thirty years after the fall of Troy.
He was a slave in the Trojan world, and now he is "shackled
to a Grecian dolt. " He questions why the slaves of Troy
were not allowed to fight in the war. Although they did not

own any part of Troy, "but were owned by it," the slaves would still have fought for the city. It was all they had, and now it is gone, burned and lying in ruins.

954 _____. "Troy," in Collected Poems (1965), is a picture of desolation and ruin, described in a "rat-grey" atmosphere of an old man who survived the fall of Troy and "lived among the sewers / Scouring for scraps." He is mad, of course, and still fights the war, screaming to his ghosts, "Coward, turn and fight." At the end scavengers come seeking treasure in the ruins. They torture the old man, asking, "Where is the treasure?" until he dies.

NOYES, Alfred (1880-1958, English)

955 "Actaeon," in Vol. 2, Collected Poems, 2 vols. New York: Stokes, 1913.
This version of the Actaeon myth emphasizes that the time of year was Spring, and that the hunter in stumbling upon Diana in her bath, has actually tracked the mystery of Nature to "her woodlands lair." The tragedy of Actaeon goes forward: he is changed into a stag and his hounds kill him. Diana continues her bath, and Nature is unchanged.

956 _____. "Bacchus and the Pirates," in Vol. 2, Collected Poems (1913), is a narrative loosely based on the myth that at one time Bacchus was kidnapped by a band of pirates who attempted to sell him into slavery. This band of pirates--fifty, as Noyes tells the story--happen to raise Bacchus out of the sea, and are overjoyed because they now have the god of wine and drink, and will never be thirsty again. Bacchus, of course, wrecks their ships and escapes.

957 _____. "Echo and Narcissus," in The Loom of Years. London: Richards, 1902.
The story is told by Echo, the nymph who loved Narcissus, but was doomed never to speak any word of her own. She could merely repeat what she heard. Narcissus, the beautiful youth, who pined away because he could not obtain the object of his desire--his own reflection seen in a pool--repeated over and over "Narcissus," and Echo resounded "Narcissus, Narcissus."

958 _____. "Enceladus," in Vol. 1, Collected Poems (1913), refers to a son of Earth, the most powerful of all the giants, who tried to assault the gods on Olympus. They overpowered him, and crushed him beneath Mt. Etna.

959 _____. "Euterpe," in Songs of Shadow-of-a-Leaf and Other Poems. Edinburgh and London: Blackwood, 1924.
In mythology Euterpe was the Muse of poetry and song, and was said to have invented the flute and other wind instruments.

Noyes sees her as having "vanished, into the dusk, a moth-like dream." But then he looks into his "true love's face" and knows that she left the sky to be his "comrade on the road."

960 _____. "Helicon," in Shadow-of-a-Leaf (1924), is a mountain sacred to the Muses, who had a temple there. The fountain Hippocrene, the source of poetic inspiration, flowed from the mountain.

961 _____. "The Inn of Apollo," in The Elfin Artist and Other Poems. New York: Stokes, 1920.
The title of this poem is a metaphor for the sunset, as the poet envisions the god, "the Lord of the sun," retiring for the night. The description is gorgeous, with images of flame and gold pouring over the world like wine.

962 _____. "The Last of the Titans," in The Golden Hynde and Other Poems. New York: Macmillan, 1917.
The story in this poem is based on mythology, but Noyes has supplied his own version of the events. Atlas, the last of the Titans, has been condemned to support the world on his shoulders for all eternity. He has no relief from his punishment, and cannot look forward to any hope of reprieve. In time Perseus, the son of Zeus and Danae, comes his way, equipped with magic sword and shield from Athene, flying sandals from Hermes, and the cap of Hades, which renders him invisible. Atlas begs him to return, once the Medusa has been slain, and Perseus agrees. When Perseus returns, he is now bearing the awful head of the Medusa, and Atlas looks upon it and becomes a "granite mountain." His labor was over, and "everlasting quiet sealed his eyes."

963 _____. "Mount Ida," in Vol. 2, Collected Poems (1913), does not contain a mythological story, but was written to the memory of a young Englishman who went up into Mt. Ida and was not seen again. Mt. Ida and the range of mountains to which it belongs is in the vicinity of Troy, and is referred to frequently in the Iliad.

964 _____. "The Net of Vulcan," in Vol. 1, Collected Poems (1913), is based on the myth that Vulcan, who was married to Venus, devised a means of entrapping the goddess with her lover Mars. He caught them in a giant net, and the other gods were invited to come and see. Venus, however, is shameless in her infidelity, and regards the net as giving her and Mars "one more hour of bliss."

965 _____. "Niobe," in Vol. 1, Collected Poems (1913), the mother of seven daughters and seven sons who were killed by Artemis and Apollo, is presented in this work as the

embodiment of human grief. The poet says, "Through that fair face the whole dark universe speaks." Her anguish transcends all the spiteful meanness of the gods, and "the majesty of grief is eternal." Neither god nor mortal can usurp her crown.

966 _____. "Orpheus and Eurydice," in Vol. 1, Collected Poems (1913), is an elaborate and unusual view of the story of these two ill-starred lovers. It begins with their marriage and the happy carefree days they spent together. In the meantime Orpheus deserts his music, and his lyre rusts in disuse. Apollo sends the snake that bites and kills Eurydice, and Orpheus returns to his music, enlisting its aid as he goes into the Underworld to regain his bride. When he fails to bring her forth again into the sunlight, Orpheus turns entirely to his music, and Eurydice returns to his heart and is embodied in all his music and song.

967 _____. "The Ride of Phaethon," in The Golden Hynde (1917), begins as Phaethon, the son of Apollo (or Helios), is taking the four immortal steeds from their stalls to traverse the heavens. The poem progresses as the foolish youth loses more and more control of the chariot of the sun, and brings destruction and havoc over the entire world, burning it up in spots and freezing it in others. Ultimately the Father of Gods must intervene, and Phaethon is hurled from the sky, sinking into the sea on "the ultimate verge of the world."

968 _____. "Venus Disrobing for the Bath," in Poems, with an Introduction by Hamilton W. Mabie. New York and London: Macmillan, 1912.
The description in this poem is apparently a metaphor for the sunrise as seen on the waters of a sea. This process is presented as Venus might be viewed disrobing for her bath. She slips from her thin white robe, dips one foot into the water, and the world is covered with "a wild golden gleam."

969 _____. "The Venus of Milo," in Vol. 1, Collected Poems (1913), is a description of the famous statue found on the island of Milo, believed to have been created in the second century B.C., and recovered in 1820.

O'NEILL, Eugene (1888-1953, American)

970 "Desire Under the Elms" in Vol. I, The Plays of Eugene O'Neill, 3 vols. New York: Random House, 1955.
This play has been variously interpreted as Biblical allegory, as Freudian in its implications, and as a New England version of the Hippolytus-Phaedra-Theseus myth. Whatever merits the former versions may have, it is without question

mythological in plot: the father (Ephraim-Theseus) returns to his farm bringing with him a young wife (Abbie-Phaedra), who is immediately attracted to her stepson (Eben-Hippolytus.) Like Phaedra, Abbie conceals her growing passion for Eben, and asks that the son be banished, and for the same reason. As the play moves toward its tragic conclusion, Ephraim utters a curse against his sons, particularly against Eben, and at the end, like Theseus, is left alone surveying the wreck of his kingdom.

971 _____. Mourning Becomes Electra, a trilogy of plays, in Vol. II, The Plays (1955), is based on the Greek tragedy of Electra and her brother, Orestes. The time of O'Neill's story is the end of the Civil War, as the Greek story is set at the end of the Trojan War. The characters in O'Neill's play each have their counterparts in Greek myth: Ezra Mannon, a Civil War general, is Agamemnon, killed by his wife Christine, who has all the hatred and violence of a Clytemnestra in her nature. Lavinia Mannon is more than a match for the ancient Electra, with an irrational hatred of her mother and a determination to avenge the death of her father, which she strongly suspects is murder. Orin, the brother who falls under the dominance of Lavinia, shares much with Orestes, although he does not kill his mother. He kills her lover, and then she kills herself, thereby creating the guilt that drives him mad. At the end Orin dies as the result of an accident, or self-inflicted shot from his pistol. Lavinia, like Electra, alone survives to live with the ruin that she is largely responsible for. In addition to the characters and action following a parallel development of the mythology, O'Neill has succeeded in creating an atmosphere of doom and dark fatality as the background of his drama.

PATMORE, Coventry (1823-1896, English)

972 "Eros," in The Poems of Coventry Patmore, ed. with an Introduction by Frederick Page. London: Oxford University Press, 1949.
Although bearing a mythological title, Patmore's poem is a sonnet praising love itself, particularly "the first love of all," which he calls a "Radiance of Eden unquench'd by the Fall."

973 _____. "Eros and Psyche," in Poems (1949) is a dialogue between Psyche and her lover Eros as he is preparing to leave her for another day. She does not know his identity, but she is sure of his love, and therefore can bear taking leave of him until the night comes again.

974 _____. "Eurydice," in Poems (1949), is a lament of a husband for his dead wife, and makes slight use of the Orpheus-Eurydice myth. Like Orpheus, this husband-narrator seeks his beloved wife in spirit, and is thankful for the brief periods when he feels she is near him.

975 _____. "Orpheus," in Poems (1949), draws a comparison between Odysseus and Orpheus and the occasions on which each of them heard the fatal song of the Sirens. Odysseus had to be bound with strong cords to prevent his destruction by the Sirens; on the other hand, Orpheus defeated them by singing a more beautiful song than they were able to sing, and thus his was a more genuine triumph. The poet here says that he will try to pursue the way of Orpheus, and defeat folly by "pursuit of the Poet's sacred task."

976 _____. "Psyche's Discontent," in Poems (1949), expresses Psyche's feelings of frustration in not knowing who her lover is, and in feeling that he is a god whereas she is simply a mortal. She yearns for the immortality that Eros has, "for ether and infinitude."

977 _____. "Semele," in Poems (1949), refers to the young woman who insisted that her lover Zeus reveal himself to her in his godlike form, and so perished in the heat and fire of his radiance. In this poem Semele does not regret her choice, even though it was her destruction. At least she had a clear vision of deity before she died.

978 _____. "To the Unknown Eros," in Poems (1949), is a romanticized version of the awakenings to love as known by human beings. The Eros referred to here is not unlike the Eros of which Hesiod speaks, the beautiful primeval force that presides over the creation of all things.

979 _____. "Venus and Death," in Poems (1949), is a brief study of the image of death, and a prayer that Venus, or love, will preserve the loved one.

PHILLIPS, Stephen (1868-1915, English)

980 "Christ in Hades: A Phantasy," in Poems by Stephen Phillips. New York and London: Lane, 1905.
This work is based on the myth that Hermes goes into the Underworld each spring to guide the returning Persephone back to the earth. In this instance it becomes Christ who sojourns to the dark regions and beholds all the dead and those who have suffered unjustly. In keeping with the Christian religion Christ is symbolic of resurrection and immortality of all humankind.

981 _____. "Endymion," in New Poems. London: Lane, 1907.
At the beginning Endymion is created as a totally carefree,
happy young man, simply content to be alive, to breathe,
to live in the world of nature. With the coming of Selene,
the moon-goddess who loved him, all this changed, and
Endymion became keenly aware of the sorrows of the world,
seeing as the goddess sees from her height in the sky all
the unhappy nightly vigils of men and women.

982 _____. "Helen to Paris," in Panama and Other Poems:
Narrative and Occasional. New York and London:
Lane, 1915.
Helen reflects on her relation to Paris, fearing that he
does not really love her and that she is about to abandon
everything--country, husband, child--for one who has
"nothing of faith and steadfastness." She is also fearful
that they "are rousing the dread gods to strife." But she
is helpless to save herself; when Paris says "Come," she
will follow to the "earth's end."

983 _____. "Iole," in New Poems (1907), is called a "tragedy
in one act," and is based on a half-myth, half-historical
story. The scene is the city of Corinth at the time be-
seiged by the Spartans. The temple of Juno is in the background. Pelias, a Corinthian general, is begged by the
citizens of Corinth to save the city. After consulting the
Priestess of Juno, Pelias agrees, but the price of victory
will be for him to sacrifice the first one he sees after returning from battle. This turns out to be his young daughter Iole. Reluctantly, but in fear of the gods, he puts her
to the sword, and becomes the king of Corinth, saying he
has given everything to the city and it is his own.

984 _____. "Marpessa," in Poems (1905), involves the god
Apollo, the mortal Idas, and the beautiful maiden Marpessa.
She has been offered her choice of the god or mortal for
husband, and she chooses the mortal. The poem consists
largely of a debate between Idas and Apollo as to what each
can give her. Apollo offers immortality and divine love;
on the other hand Idas can offer only himself. He will
never leave her, and they will grow old together and finally
leave the world together, caring only for each other. At
the end Marpessa chooses Idas, and the god leaves in anger.

985 _____. "Orestes," in New Poems (1907), is a monologue
by Orestes after he has killed his mother. It begins with
his saying that Justice called him to do the deed, and at
that time he was strong and filled with high idealism to do
that which was just. At the end, however, he is broken
with grief over the death of a mother he loved, and knows
he must henceforth be called a murderer.

986 _____. "The Passing of Julian," in Panama (1915), refers
to the Roman emperor (A.D. 331-363), who was the last
great opponent of Christianity. It is said that he died on
the battlefield, exclaiming, "Thou hast conquered, O Galilean." He had tried to restore the authority of the gods
of Greece and Rome.

987 _____. "Penelope to Ulysses," in Panama (1915), is spoken
by Penelope on the first night after her husband's return
from a twenty-year absence. She welcomes him, but en-
treats his patience and help in helping her to adjust to his
reality instead of her dreams and imagination during the
long years of absence. She admits that he is somewhat
less than her imagination had made him out to be, and
much older.

988 _____. "Semele," in Panama (1915), is a telling of the
story in which Semele, the mother of Dionysus, begs her
lover Zeus to reveal himself in his divine form. He reluctantly must grant her wish, although warning her that
she will die. She replies, "Then if I die, I die a dazzling
death."

989 _____. "Ulysses," in Collected Plays. New York:
Macmillan, 1921.
The material in this play is all derived from the Odyssey,
but is not an attempt to retell the epic in dramatic form.
The episodes of Calypso and the visit to Hades are used
in the play, but the emphasis is on the action after Odysseus reached Ithaca. The cast of characters involved is
immense and includes all the major gods of Olympus, who
are either taking part in the events or observing with great
interest the affairs of human beings. A minor, but interesting, aspect of the gods is that they appear with their
symbolic emblem: Zeus with thunderbolt; Athene with
spear, shield, and aegis; Apollo with lyre; Aphrodite with
roses and doves; Artemis with bow and quiver; and Hermes
with caduceus and winged sandals.

POWYS, John Cowper (1872-1963, English)

990 "Ares and Aphrodite," in Poems. London: Rider, 1899.
The stories of the romantic adventures of Ares and Aphrodite are quite numerous, but most of them are basically
the same: Ares pursues the goddess until she gives in,
and she shamelessly allows his advances. Such is the case
in Powys's brief work, which is effective for the description
of the vast expanses of the universe over which Ares chases
Aphrodite.

991 _____. "Calypso," in Poems (1899), is narrated at the
time Odysseus leaves the goddess on her magic island.

She pleads with him not to leave her, tempting him to ignore the will of the gods. She promises him immortality,
but in spite of her arguments, he wishes to return to the
land of his fathers and die, as all mortals must, where
his roots are deep. He rejects immortality for the right
to "fall asleep, and at the last have rest."

992 _____. "The Hermes of Praxiteles," in Poems (1899), is
praised for the expression that the sculptor was able to
capture on the face of this god. He was the messenger
from gods to mortals, and the one who guides the human
beings into the dark abode of Hades. In short, he was the
god with human characteristics.

993 _____. "Ode to Proserpine," in A Selection from the
Poems of John Cowper Powys, ed. with Introduction
by Kenneth Hopkins. Hamilton, N.Y.: Colgate University Press, 1964.
The daughter of Demeter is addressed in the Winter, the
season of death when it is easy to wish to have done "with
pleasure and with pain," to forget "the foolishness of mortal breath."   But so long as the heart can long for Spring,
Persephone has not fled forever.

994 _____. "Saturn," in A Selection (1964), is based on the
story of Saturn, the elder god who was something of the
equivalent of Cronus in Greek mythology. Cronus, or
Saturn, was overthrown in the war of the Titans and gods,
and his son Zeus, or Jupiter, became the supreme god.

995 _____. "To Apollo," in A Selection (1964), is a good summary statement of all that the god Apollo stands for: god
of the golden bow, lord of the lyre, master of sunbeams,
god of truth and prophecy. Only one gift is lacking, "Godlike Pity for Human wrong."

996 _____. "To Diana," in Poems (1899), is based on the myth
that Diana, Artemis, and Persephone are three aspects of
the same deity. Sometimes Persephone is identified as
Hecate. In either case she is the goddess of the "triple
throne," and is powerful on earth, in the heavens, and in
hell.

997 _____. "The Venus of Milo," in Poems (1899), is phrased
in rather general terms, and could easily apply to any piece
of art that has escaped "the dark and hurrying stream" of
time. The title refers to the exquisite statue that was discovered on the island of Melos in the 1800s, believed to
have been created in the second century B.C. This "deathless child of Art" has escaped the "universal doom."

PRESTON, Margaret Junkin (1820-1897, American)

998   "Alcyone," in Old Song and New.   Philadelphia: Lippincott,
            1870.
        This poem tells the story of the great love that King Ceyx
        and his wife, Alcyone, held for each other.   She pleads
        that he not go to sea, but he must go, and so leaves her
        in deep sadness.   After a long while Thetis, the Nereid,
        appears to Alcyone and tells her that Ceyx is dead and
        will not return.   In despair Alcyone throws herself into
        the waves of the ocean, crying that since her husband can-
        not come to her she will come to him.   It is said that
        the gods took pity and changed Ceyx and Alcyone to king-
        fishers, or halcyon birds, which build their nests on the
        sea, and for seven days the waters remain calm while
        they are nesting.

999   _____.   "Erinna's Spinning," in Old Song (1870), has slight
        mythological value, the only relation being the poet of
        Lesbos who was one of the girls Sappho loved.   In this
        poem Erinna's mother forbids her to go to a town festival,
        saying that it is foolish and a waste of time.   The girl
        is kept at her spinning, but she would rather go free as
        her idol Sappho is free, than to become a good housewife.
        Ironically Sappho leaves Erinna when the youth Phaon comes
        along.

1000   _____.   "The Flight of Arethusa," in Old Song (1870), is
        the story of the naiad who went bathing in the River Al-
        pheus.   The god of the river fell in love with her, and
        assuming a mortal shape, he chased her until she fell into
        a spring and drowned.   She still did not escape him, how-
        ever, for the river was the origin of the spring, and after
        Arethusa's transformation, the waters of the River Alpheus
        and the spring "met and mingled into one."

1001   _____.   "Hestia," in Colonial Ballads, Sonnets and Other
            Verse.   Boston: Houghton, Mifflin, 1887.
        While paying tribute to the "gentle Goddess of the Grecian
        hearth," Hestia, this poem also pays tribute to the poet's
        fond memories of her childhood home, her parents' love,
        the warmth and comfort of the household.   At the end
        there is a note of pain and dejection at having lost the
        world of her childhood.

1002   _____.   "Keats's Greek Urn," in Colonial Ballads (1887),
        is a sonnet praising the "Ode on a Grecian Urn."   In
        Preston's sonnet the poem becomes the metaphor for an
        urn, and is permanent and unwasting.   Had Keats known
        what generations would "appease their thirsts," in his
        poetry, he would not have died in despair.

1003   _____.   "Persephone," in Colonial Ballads (1887), celebrates

the coming of Spring with a lengthy catalogue of flowers,
birds, butterflies, clover, budding trees, and all the lovely
facets of nature associated with the season. The goddess
Persephone, who returns to earth at this season, is equated
with the season itself.

1004 _____. "Prince Deucalion," in Colonial Ballads (1887),
was written to commemorate a performance of the play
by Bayard Taylor. He died about a month after the publication of the work. Preston believes that the play was
prophetic of Taylor's death in the closing line: "Not
mine, I deem full well, / To dare divine that future known
to none."

1005 _____. "The Quenched Brand," in Old Song (1870), is in
three parts and deals with the birth of Meleager, his years
of heroic action, and finally his death. At his birth the
Fates gave his mother, Althaea, a brand and told her that
her son would live as long as the brand was not burned.
After the Calydonian Boar Hunt, Meleager became involved
in a quarrel with Althaea's brothers and killed them. His
mother was so enraged that she threw the brand into the
fire, and her son's life was ended. The emphasis in this
poem is on the fate of Meleager, and the role of the brand
in bringing his life to an end.

1006 _____. "Rhodope's Sandal," in Old Song (1870), is a version of the Cinderella story, but does not identify the
Rhodope referred to. One source relates the sandal story
to the Rhodope who was the famous courtesan. At any
rate, in Preston's poem Rhodope went bathing in a river,
leaving her clothes and sandals on the bank. An eagle
flew over, dipped low, and made off with one of her sandals. He carried it to his master the King and dropped
it in his lap. The King was so impressed with the dainty
sandal that he declared that he would wed the woman it
belonged to. Messengers went forth and soon brought
Rhodope to the King. They were soon married.

RANDALL, Dudley (1914- , American)

1007 "Hail, Dionysus," in Cities Burning. Detroit: Broadside,
1968.
In this poem the god is ironically addressed as the patron
of drunkenness. The imagery of the poem is ugly, creating disgusting forms of animal-like behavior: a man snores
on the sofa, a girl staggers among the chairs, a man vom-
its on the rug, another girl wets her panties.

RANSOM, John Crowe (1888-1974, American)

1008 "Philomela," in Poems and Essays. New York: Vintage, 1955.
The poet begins with a brief history of the nightingale, referring to the tragic story of Procne, Philomela, and Itylus, a story that he--as an American--does not really understand. The story is told in Ovid, and this somewhat alleviates the dreadful pain of the events. Philomela also came to England, where the poets have attempted to write about her often enough, but never to America, "this other Thrace." In conclusion the poet here resigns himself to being unable to experience the Greek sense of tragedy, the really dark shadows that the story of Philomela so much typifies.

1009 _____. "Prometheus in Straits," in Chills and Fever. New York: Knopf, 1924.
The title sets the tone for a humorous, ironic account of the Titan who stole fire from the gods and gave it to mortals. It suggests a Prometheus not in tragic circumstances, but in a state of embarrassment for having acted so foolishly. His faith in humanity has been unwarranted, and the poem ends with Prometheus aspiring to build an altar to "the Unknown Man." Known Man is a failure, but Prometheus believes that his shallowness and stupidity were not inevitable.

READ, Sir Herbert Edward (1893-1968, English)

1010 "Daphne," in Collected Poems of Sir Herbert Read. London: Faber and Faber, 1966.
The story of the nymph who eluded the god Apollo by being changed into a laurel tree is embodied in this poem, but the story of her escape is secondary to the idea of what she became. Daphne is the Greek name for the true laurel, a beautiful tree with dense grey-green foilage, usually an evergreen. The poet praises the beauty and permanence of the tree, and says in conclusion: "The nymph that from Apollo fled/ lives long after he is dead...."

1011 _____. "Mycene," in Collected Poems (1966), refers to the city that was regarded as the capital of Argolis during the time of Agamemnon and other great kings. It was defeated and laid in ruins by 568 B.C., and the site all but lost. In 1876, however, the ruins were discovered and excavated by Schliemann. This poem describes the current scene where so much pride and arrogance was enacted and is now inhabited by a grazing herd of goats, whose indifferent hooves tread the ground.

1012 _____. "Sappho," in Collected Poems (1966), is a slight
poem, making but a single point. Sappho collects the
material of her poetry from nature itself--the stone steps,
the golden sunlight, the electric air. She will "elicit
lyric analogues of the rocky kingdom."

1013 _____. "Sappho and Atthis," in Collected Poems (1966),
refers to one of the lovers of Sappho with whom it is
said the poet had a rather violent relationship. This
monologue could be narrated by Sappho or Atthis, and
examines their relationship. At the end an image of a
fishing net is created, and the narrator says that she
wishes the fishermen could "unravel the intricate mesh"
of their love.

1014 _____. "The White Isle of Leuce," in Collected Poems
(1966), is based on the myth that at their deaths Helen
and Achilles went to Leuce Island, a kind of Elysium,
where they were married and enjoyed a kind of immortality. Here Helen remains beautiful forever, and Achilles
remains the brave young warrior.

REED, Henry (1914- , English)

1015 "Chrysothemis," in A Map of Verona. London: Cape, 1946.
This daughter of Agamemnon and Clytemnestra is presented, as a minor character, only in Sophocles' "Electra." In this play she is sympathetic to her sister's
loyalty to their murdered father, but is opposed to defying Clytemnestra and Aegisthus. In Reed's poem, narrated by Chrysothemis herself, she is the haunted sur-
vivor of the many tragedies that befell the House of
Atreus. She is haunted by the memory of her father's
murder at the hands of her mother and Aegisthus; she
remembers her brother, Orestes, who later killed Clytemnestra and Aegisthus; she recalls Orestes and Electra
fleeing for their lives--she alone remains, to protect and
watch over the innocent children of Clytemnestra and
Aegisthus. She declares herself "not guilty of anybody's
blood," and yet the conclusion of the poem raises the
question of her guilt: was she guilty by means of asso-
ciation, by what she did not do rather than what she did?
Finally, the all-important question, will she protect the
innocent children, or will the old avenging fury fall on
them also? There is little mythology concerning these
children--a son, Aletes, and a daughter, Erigone. One
source says that Orestes killed them when he returned
from exile after his mother's death.

1016 _____. "Philoctetes," in A Map (1946), is a lengthy mono-

logue in which the hero reviews his past life and tries
to analyze his future. Ten years ago he had been put
ashore on the island of Lemnos by Odysseus and other
men of the ship because they could no longer bear the
stinking wound that Philoctates had incurred. With him
they also put ashore his bow and arrows, the gift that
he had inherited from Heracles. Through all these years
he has suffered--mentally, from the isolation and loneliness, and physically, from the great wound that would
not be healed. He grew bitter and rancorous, but always
he knew that Troy could not be taken without him and his
bow and arrows. Now they have come for him, and he
says, "I have changed my mind; or my mind is changed
in me." He prepared to depart with Neoptolemus, the
son of Achilles, and Odysseus, whom he has hated above
all others. "The wound is quiet, its death/ Is dead within me," he says.

RENAULT, Mary (pseudonym of Mary Challans, 1905- , English)

1017 Bull from the Sea. New York: Pantheon, 1962.
      This novel, the sequel to The King Must Die, covers the
      later years in the life of Theseus, king of Athens. It
      begins after his experiences in Crete, with the death of
      his father, Aegeus. It covers the Ariadne story, with
      Theseus deserting her on the island of Naxos; his love
      for the Amazon Hippolyta and the son she bore him; and
      his marriage to Phaedra, the younger sister of Ariadne.
      Finally it embraces the story of Hippolytus, the ill-fated
      son who was destroyed by Phaedra, his stepmother, and
      his father's curse for Poseidon to send a "bull from the
      sea" and mangle the son who Theseus believed and se-
      duced his own wife. The novel ends with Theseus resign-
      ing his kingship and going into exile to meet his death.
      For the most part the reviewers rated this novel as a
      very high performance, but perhaps lacking in the color
      and excitement of The King Must Die.

1018 _____. The King Must Die. New York: Pantheon, 1958.
      The focus of this work is on the youth of Theseus, begin-
      ning with the first time he left Athens and was crowned
      king at Eleusis. This kingship proved to be of short
      duration, for in a year he was challenged, and he had to
      kill the challenger or be killed. He killed the challenger,
      but chose not to continue as their king. The bulk of the
      novel is a recreation of the Minotaur episode, in which
      Theseus kills the bull-man and escapes Crete with the
      daughter of Minos. This part of the novel has been well
      researched, and the events of the Bull Court and the Bull
      Dancers are realistic and highly detailed. The reviewers
      felt that this mythological novel was altogether excellent
      in form and presentation, with sharply outlined characters
      and realistically explained events.

1019 _____. Last of the Wine. New York: Pantheon, 1956.
The setting of this work is in Athens during the time of
Socrates, and the hero-narrator is a fictional friend and
disciple of the philosopher. Through Alexias' eyes we
see the huge scenes of battle, in the days of the Third
Peloponnesian War, and the closeup views of Socrates
and his friends--Alcibiades, Plato, Phaedo--as they walk
in the shadow of the Acropolis. The slender plot revolves around Alexias and his lover, the half-fictional
character Lysis, and their deep involvement with each
other. The reviews were not too enthusiastic, regarding
the novel as somewhat loosely put together and boring
with too many details.

1020 _____. The Mask of Apollo. New York: Pantheon, 1966.
Here the setting is Syracuse and Athens in the fourth century B.C., during the struggle for power between Dion--
philosopher, soldier, and friend of Plato--and the tyrant
Dionysios the Younger. Against this background is set
the main character, the actor Nikeratos, and the rise of
his career. The title derives from a mask of Apollo that
the actor carries with him as he travels about, and gradually this mask becomes the alter ego for Nikeratos' ar-
tistic conscience. One of the most interesting and best
researched aspects of this novel is the portrayal of dramatic activities during this period, the last before classical drama would decline. The reviews of this work
were not too favorable, with most reviewers feeling that
the novel was too slow is getting started and never too
certain of itself once it did.

RICE, Cale Young (1872-1943, American)

1021 "An Ancient Greek, Dying, " in Selected Plays and Poems.
London: Hodder and Stoughton, 1926.
Although consisting of only five lines, this simple poem
conveys quite vividly the sense of death as the man steps
into Charon's boat and says farewell to his loved one.

1022 _____. "The Dead Gods, " in Song-Surf. New York:
Doubleday, Page, 1910.
The narrator sets the mood of this poem from the outset
with images of oblivion and void: he has lain ten thousand years "blind, deaf, and motionless." Then he senses
the presence of phantoms and discovers them to be gods--
Persephone, Pluto, Jove, and many others from Egyptian
and primitive mythologies. Lifeless they "huddle in despair until a mighty voice calls out "God alone is God!"

1023 _____. "The Faun Repents, " in Plays and Poems (1926),

portrays an example of hasty and irrational behavior that the
faun later regrets. In the Spring he is seized with an uncontrollable desire for the nymph he loves, but succeeds
only in losing her, becoming "shunned and hated." He
blames it on the Spring, "with her wanton kiss."

1024 _____. "A Lydian Bacchanal," in Plays and Poems (1926),
pays tribute to the "vine-god," and the free life that his
worshipers enjoy in the Spring. The poem captures some
of the frenzy and utter abandonment of his followers, the
bacchants, as they dance with "naked limbs," reeling in
a trancelike world of "Bacchus, god of the grape."

1025 _____. "A Maenad to a Young Panther," in Plays and
Poems (1926), portrays the young animal whose mother
has been killed by a spear, hungry and fearful. The
woman offers to nurse it, saying that only courage "counts
with the fearless gods." The courage here is both hers
and the young panther's: she afraid of the animal and the
animal afraid of her.

1026 _____. "Mycenaean Revenge," in Plays and Poems (1926),
is a grim story not unlike the tragedies of the House of
Atreus. It is narrated by a woman who was raped by
Pharon, and bore his son "in hatred." She waited many
years for revenge, and finally it came. The son became
a man and raped Pharon's daughter. With her revenge
complete the woman set sail with her son and ten slaves
and "a cask of gold," and left the Cretan king to rave in
hopelessness and despair.

1027 _____. "Sappho's Death Song," in Plays and Poems (1926),
is sung as she is preparing to go over the sea-cliff in
Leucadia. It is principally an appeal to Persephone, the
goddess of the Underworld, for freedom from all the madness that was life. Images of loss and transience pervade
the poem, and Sappho prays for peace and cessation of
desire.

1028 _____. "A Vision of Venus and Adonis," in Plays and
Poems (1926), is based on the myth that Venus loved the
beautiful youth Adonis more than any god or mortal.
Adonis was killed at an early age by a boar, and his death
is commemorated in the Spring by planting the "Adonis
gardens," plants that grow up quickly and then die in shallow soil. Rice's poem consists of a dreamlike vision in
which he sees Adonis and Venus sitting together expressing
their love for each other.

RICH, Adrienne (1929-   , American)

1029 "I Dream I Am the Death of Orpheus," in Adrienne Rich's

211

Poetry, ed. by Barbara C. and Albert Gelpi. New York: Norton, 1975. Norton Critical edition. The imagery of this poem, although based upon a familiar mythological figure, is of a very eccentric nature. Jean Cocteau (1889-1963) wrote and directed a motion picture, Orphée (1950), in which he modernized the story of the legendary Thracian poet Orpheus, who went into the Underworld to recover his dead wife, Eurydice. In Cocteau's movie Death, a woman riding in a Rolls Royce guarded by motorcyclists with black leather jackets, comes for Orpheus and carries him through a mirror into the Underworld on the other side. These scenes and images are used in Adrienne Rich's poem, with "Hell's Angels" being a reference to a motorcycle club that originated in Oakland, California.

1030 _____. "Orion," in Rich's Poetry (1975), is a constellation that becomes prominent in the northern hemisphere during the winter. It was named for a mythical hunter of gigantic size and great beauty, and the belt and sword are stars in the constellation. The poet here regards the great star as a source of inspiration and permanence.

ROBINSON, Edwin Arlington (1869-1935, American)

1031 "As a World Would Have It," in The Collected Poems of Edwin Arlington Robinson. New York: Macmillan, 1954.
Robinson's poem is based on the Alcestis myth in which the wife, Alcestis, takes her husband's place when it is time for him to die. According to legend she was brought back from death and happily reunited with her husband, Admetus. This poem portrays an Alcestis and Admetus who did not live so happily thereafter. Alcestis reproaches her husband for the coldness of their relation since the episode of her death, and does not understand why he has so changed. Eventually she pries the truth out of him: he cannot rejoice at her return as a man might who loved his wife; he must maintain the aspects of a king, for only a king would have allowed his wife to die in his place. A man would have been considered cowardly and unheroic.

1032 _____. "Cassandra," in Collected Poems (1954), is aimed at a materialistic society, possibly America, whose "only Word" is the Dollar, and whose only fear is an economic one. "Are you to pay for what you have/ With all you are?" This "Cassandra" asks, but "none heeded and few heard." As with Cassandra of Troy, no one pays attention to her warnings.

212

1033 _____ . "The Chorus of Old Men in 'Aegeus, ' " in Collected Poems (1954), is imitative of the Greek chorus,
and is in effect a lament for the untimely death of King
Aegeus, who plunged into the sea when he saw the black
flag that signaled that his son Theseus was dead. His
death, however, was a tragic accident; Theseus was alive
but had forgotten to change the flag to signal victory over
the Cretans.

1034 _____ . "Demos and Dionysus, " in Collected Poems (1954),
contains slight mythology, and is a propagandistic approach
to the problem of Equality and Reason in a Democracy, in
this instance a "miscalled democracy" which infringes upon
the rights of the individual and upon personal liberty.

1035 _____ . "Dionysus in Doubt, " in Collected Poems (1954),
is a continuation of the debate between the rights of the
individual (Dionysus) and the rights of the state (Demos),
as begun in the above poem. Here Dionysus affirms
that he will continue to exist, and when there is a need
for him in human affairs he will return.

ROSSETTI, Dante Gabriel (1828-1882, English)

1036 "Aspecta Medusa, " in Complete Poetical Works, ed. by
William M. Rossetti. Boston: Little, Brown, 1903.
This short composition was written for a design from
which Rossetti intended to paint a picture of Perseus
allowing Andromeda to look at the severed head of Medusa
as it was reflected in a tank of water. The picture, however, was never painted. Medusa was one of the Gorgons,
monsters with snaky hair, and faces that turned the be-
holder to stone. Perseus had overcome danger and cut
off Medusa's head by looking at its reflection in his shield.
Later he rescued Andromeda from a monster that was
ravaging her father's land, and married her.

1037 _____ . "Cassandra, " in Poetical Works (1903), is for a
drawing that depicts Cassandra prophesying among her
kindred, as Hector leaves them for his last battle. Helen
is arming Paris, Priam comforts Hecuba, and Andromache
clutches her infant son, Astyanax, to her bosom. The
Trojan troops are marching out to battle.

1038 _____ . "Death's Songsters, " in Poetical Works (1903),
treats two incidents derived from mythology: when Helen
was forced to walk around the Trojan Horse and "sing the
songs of home, " hoping to find out if there were men inside; and when the Sirens sang to Ulysses and his men.
These are examples of "death's songsters, " but in both
instances Ulysses listened to the sweetness of the calling,

but did not succumb: he and the men sat very still inside the horse when Helen called out deceptively, "Friends, I am alone; come, come!" and he was "lashed to his own mast," his men with wax in their ears, when the deadly Sirens sang to him and his men.

1039 _____. "For 'The Wine of Circe, ' " in Poetical Works (1903), was written for a picture by Edward Burne-Jones, an English painter who lived 1833-1898. The picture is a contrast of light and dark, of gold and black, and depicts Circe, the sorceress, robed in gold, pouring the deadly wine that will change men into beasts.

1040 _____. "Hero's Lamp," in Poetical Works (1903), is based on the legend that after the deaths of Leander, by drowning in the Hellespont, and Hero, by throwing herself off the cliff into the sea, the signal-lamp that she had used to light his way across the water was dedicated to Anteros, with the edict that no man should light it unless his love had proved fortunate.

1041 _____. "Pandora: For a Picture," in Poetical Works (1903), depicts Pandora standing over the box from which escaped all the ills that would plague humankind. What she is doing, "she dare not think." She does not even know if Hope, still in the box, be alive or dead.

1042 _____. "Proserpina," in Poetical Works (1903), was written for a picture, and portrays the goddess in the Underworld reflecting on the dreary aspects of her existence--gray, cold, night--as compared with her life-- flowers, sun, warmth, day. The picture is, of course, a contrast in life and death.

1043 _____. "Troy Town," in Poetical Works (1903), is based on a legend told by Pliny (A.D. 23-79), a Roman historian and naturalist, that Helen of Sparta dedicated to Venus (Aphrodite), the goddess of love, a golden goblet molded in the shape of her breast. Woven into the poem is the story of the elopement of Helen with Paris, son of Priam, king of Troy. At the wedding of Peleus and Thetis the goddess of discord had thrown among the guests a golden apple inscribed "To the Fairest." Juno (Hera), Minerva (Athena), and Venus all claimed it, but Paris, called upon to judge, awarded it to Venus. In return she gave him Helen, with the ultimate result that Troy was besieged, sacked, and burned by the angry Greeks under the leadership of Helen's husband, Menelaus, king of Sparta. Throughout Rossetti's poem the refrain "O Troy's down/ Tall Troy's on fire," runs like a dire prophecy, hauntingly beautiful, and tragic.

1044 _____. "Venus Verticordia," in Poetical Works (1903), is an epithet applied to the goddess in her capacity to "turn the hearts" of women to cultivate chastity. This poem, which was written for a picture, shows Venus with an apple in her hand as she approaches Paris. Yet she holds back, seeing him at peace and knowing what will happen if she offers it to him, and what will happen to Helen.

1045 _____. "Venus Victrix," in Poetical Works (1903), means Venus Victorious, and is used in a very personal manner in this poem. The narrator compares his lady to Juno, Pallas, and Venus, and questions which goddess most deserves the prize. Like Paris, he chooses Venus--that is, the qualities in his lady represented by Venus.

RUSKIN, John (1819-1900, English)

1046 "Aristodemus at Plataea," in The Poems of John Ruskin, collected and ed. by James Osborne Wright. New York: Wiley, 1882.
This poem is based on a story found in Herodotus (Book VII, paragraph 229, and Book IX, paragraph 71), in which two Spartans, Eurytus and Aristodemus, were prevented from taking part in the battle of Thermopylae because of illness. They were consequently degraded to the level of helots (henchmen), and Eurytus killed himself. Aristodemus later fought at the battle of Plataea, in which 33,000 allied Greeks stood against 300,000 Persians. He charged into the enemy's rank, calling "follow the coward." After the Greeks had slaughtered 200,000 Persians, Aristodemus was found lying dead on the field. He was refused the honors of burial, however, because they said he was courageous only in despair.

1047 _____. "The Last Song of Arion," in The Poems (1882), is related in Herodotus (Book I, paragraphs 23-24), and tells how the poet Arion of Methymna escaped from a crew of sailors who would have killed him for his money. Arion asked that he be allowed to sing one song before they cast him into sea. Upon completion of his song he leapt into the sea, where a dolphin took Arion on its back and carried him ashore.

1048 _____. "A Scythian Banquet Song," in The Poems (1882), is based on a custom of these half-savage people as told in Herodotus (Book IV, paragraphs 64-65). When they killed an enemy, they scalped him and made a drinking cup of the skull, which they gilded with gold and flowers. At feasts the wine was served in such cups, and the Scythians frequently drank a toast to the enemy who had provided them with a head.

RUSKIN, continued

1049 _____ . "The Scythian Grave," in The Poems (1882), is another poem based on a grisly custom of the Scythians as related by Herodotus (Book IV, paragraph 71). When a king died, he was accompanied by an assortment of cupbearers, grooms, lackeys, coachmen, and cooks, all slaughtered and put into his grave. Then they built a mound over him, trying to make it as large as possible. Finally they strangled fifty of the king's men and fifty of his horses, and mounted the men in a circle around the king's mound.

1050 _____ . "The Scythian Guest," in The Poems (1882), is based on yet a third custom recounted by Herodotus (Book IV, paragraph 73). When the master of a Scythian family died, he was placed in his chariot and carried to visit each one of his blood relations. Each house gave him a splendid feast, at which the dead man sat at the head of the table. He was showered with gifts and treasures, which he took with him the next morning. This round of visits lasted forty days, at which time he was buried with all the goods that his kin had bestowed upon him.

1051 _____ . "The Tears of Psammenitus," in The Poems (1882), is based on a story in Herodotus (Book III, paragraph 14). Psammenitus, the king of Egypt, was defeated by Cambyses, the son of Cyrus, and his sons were sentenced to death, his daughters to slavery. He saw his children pass under the sword and to dishonor without emotion, but wept on observing a noble, who had been his companion, ask alms of the Persians. Cambyses was puzzled by this behavior and sent to inquire the reasons. The answer was a simple one but enough to shake the victor: the noble had once been one of the world's greatest men, but now he had fallen into old age and poverty and was a beggar. The wheel of fortune spins and does not regard the position of a man in this world. Cambyses and his men were moved to compassion and fear.

RUSSELL, George William ("A. E.," 1867-1935, English)

1052 "Aphrodite," in Collected Poems by A. E. London: Macmillan, 1920.
In this poem the goddess Aphrodite is revealed through the face of a much-loved woman, and the narrator sees her as the "ancestral face which lighted up the dawn," and "one fiery visitation of the love the gods desire."

1053 _____ . "Ares," in Collected Poems (1920), refers to the god of war, "the mighty hunter," who in later history has become an outcast. In his own words, however, he was the force that moved humanity forward to conquer the evil forces of the early world, "the might that made man unafraid," until the earth was won.

1054 _____. "The Childhood of Apollo," in The Mask of Apollo and Other Stories. London: Macmillan, 1904.
This tale is based on the myth that the god Apollo was sentenced to serve a mortal for a period of time. He chose Admetus, and assumed the form of a young shepherd. In this poem Admetus consults the sybil, who tells him that "the pale boy" is in reality a god, and that from time to time the gods choose to walk among mortals in the most unrecognizable forms. "Nature herself will adore you, and sing through you her loveliest song," the sybil says.

1055 _____. "Exiles," in Voices of the Stones. London: Macmillan, 1925.
The first line, "the gods have taken alien shapes," expresses the main theme of the poem, and the remaining lines simply explain this statement: the gods have become human beings, "driving swine," toiling "under grey skies," "huddled at night within low, clay-built cabins." They do not know that they are gods, but they "carry with them diadem and sceptre."

1056 _____. "Gods of War: 1914," in Collected Poems (1920), has slight mythological value, but draws an interesting parallel between ancient wars and World War I. It is more fitting, the poet says, that Zeus and Thor or Ares claim our allegiance than to make empty prayers to the "Prince of Peace."

1057 _____. "The Grey Eros," in Collected Poems (1920), is a sad tribute to love by one who says he is "so old" and "so feeble now." He remembers love over a wide expanse of time and space, and hardly remembers it at all; it is now shadowed and gray in his memory.

1058 _____. "Janus," in Collected Poems (1920), pays tribute to the god of doorways, the god with two faces to look forward and backward. The poem, however, emphasizes the "thin veil that lies/ Between the pain of hell and paradise," how we go through one door "to life or death."

1059 _____. "The Mask of Apollo," in The Mask (1904), is a tale of the god who disguises himself as an old priest and speaks to several members of the village. Being a god, Apollo has great wisdom to impart to the people, but his principal theme is that beauty and love, and reverence for the gods is something that arises from within the human heart, and is not a show from without.

SANTAYANA, George (1863-1952, American)

1060 "Aphrodite's Temple," in The Complete Poems of George
Santayana, ed. with Introduction by William G. Holz-
berger. Lewisburg, Pa. : Bucknell University Press,
1979.
Aphrodite speaks, describing the awe with which her followers come to the temple. She breathes upon them, and
they bow their heads. Then they pass their way, and she
remembers them.

1061 _____. "Apollo in Love," in Complete Poems (1979), is
a personal reflection by the narrator on his choice of
vocations. In the subtitle, "The Poet Lost in the Platonist," the idea is made clear that the poet became the
philosopher.

1062 _____. "Before a Statue of Achilles," in Complete Poems
(1979), is largely a description of the warrior-hero, the
perfect specimen of human being, a half-god, and yet
doomed to die. The statue, which could have been created
by Phidias or Polyclitus, is a "fair immortal form no
worm shall gnaw. "

1063 _____. "The Dioscuri," in Complete Poems (1979), refers
to the twins Polydeuces and Castor, sons of Leda and
brothers of Helen. According to the myth Polydeuces was
the son of Zeus, and therefore a demigod, and Castor was
the son of Tyndareus, the mortal husband of Leda. Because the brothers were so devoted to each other and could
not bear to be separated in death, Zeus granted them both
a form of immortality and made them the Gemini Twins
constellation.

1064 _____. "The Flight of Helen," in Complete Poems (1979),
is a fragment in which Helen talks to her brother Polydeuces about the stranger who has come from the north.
She says he is a god, which the brother doubts, and sets
about to find him. While Polydeuces hunts the trails and
roads of the forest for this stranger, Paris returns for
Helen telling her that his ship is hidden in the "leafage of
the shelving shore," and she must come with him.

1064a _____. "Lucifer," in Complete Poems (1979), is not based
upon a mythological story, but does make use of figures
derived from Greek mythology and the Christian religion.
Hermes, the son of Maia, one of the Seven Sisters, goes
into the heavens searching for his mother. In his travels
he encounters the star Lucifer, which at one time was the
brightest star in all the heavens, but is now black and
cold. Lucifer explains to Hermes that he tried to rebel
against the King of Gods and was cast down from Heaven.
Hence the name sometimes applied to the devil of the
Christian religion.

SHAPIRO, Karl (1913-   , American)

1065   "The Rape of Philomel," in Collected Poems, 1940-1978.
         New York: Random House, 1978.
         This work is presented in ten sections, each narrated by
         one of the individuals involved in the myth: Procne,
         Philomel, and Tereus.   In turn they reveal one of the
         most violent and barbarous stories in all mythology, and
         at the end the poet says, "The feathers of these birds
         are stained with murder."   Procne, the daughter of Pan-
         dion of Athens, was married to Tereus, a king of Thrace.
         After five years Procne desired to see her sister, Philo-
         mel, and Tereus brought her to Athens for a visit.   Mad-
         dened by an uncontrollable lust, Tereus raped Philomel
         and then cut out her tongue to prevent the truth from be-
         ing told.   He locked her away and gave out the news that
         Philomel had drowned on the voyage back to Thrace.   In
         time Philomel wove her story into a tapestry and sent it
         to Procne.   In the last act of this tragedy Procne killed
         her son, Itys, and served his flesh to Tereus.   In rage
         and disgust Tereus tried to kill both Procne and Philomel,
         but they were changed into a swallow and a nightingale.
         Tereus was changed into a hawk.   The imagery of Shapiro's
         poem is appropriately ugly and realistic, and blends easily
         into the grisly story.

1066   _____. "Scyros," in Collected Poems (1978), also spelled
         Scyrus and Skyros, is an Aegean island northeast of Euboea.
         It is sometimes called the birthplace of Achilles, but actu-
         ally it was to the court of Lycomedes of Scyros that Achil-
         les' mother, Thetis, took him to avoid going to the Trojan
         War.   It was here that Achilles was reared and later had
         his son, Neoptolemus.   The allusion in this poem is ironic,
         Scyros being used to suggest the great and heroic, the
         epiclike unreality of Achilles' role in the Trojan War in
         contrast to the real holocaust of World War II.   All of
         the references in the poem are to the history of this mod-
         ern war, which was far from being glorious or heroic.

SILL, Edward Rowland (1841-1887, American)

1067   "The Lost Magic," in The Poetical Works of Edward Rowland
         Sill.   Boston and New York: Houghton, Mifflin, 1906.
         Reprinted New York: Arno, 1972.
         The magic referred to is that which Pygmalion used to
         bring the lovely woman out of the "snowy stone," which
         he had sculpted into a statue.   The narrator says that he
         too has "loved a heart of stone," but expresses no hope
         that she will turn into a lovable woman.

1068   _____. "Semele," in Poetical Works (1972), is told of the
         mother of Dionysus, who at her death descended into Hades
         but later was brought up to Olympus under the name

Thyone. The story of her death is incorporated into Sill's poem--how she secured Jupiter's oath to come to her in his godlike form, and perished as a result. Even so, she expresses no regret, and feels honored that she has indeed looked upon true divinity.

1069 _____. "The Venus of Milo," in Poetical Works (1972), refers to the statue of Venus created by Praxiteles in the fourth century B.C. A copy of this work was found on the island of Melos (or Milo) about 1820. It is said that Praxiteles made two statues of Venus, one naked and the other veiled. The Venus referred to in this poem was the one chosen by the people of Cos, the veiled Venus.

SQUIRES, Radcliffe (1917- , American)

1070 "A Letter to Pausanias," in Fingers of Hermes. Ann Arbor: University of Michigan Press, 1965.
This poem is addressed to Pausanias, a Greek travel writer who lived perhaps in the second half of the second century A.D. and wrote a voluminous work in ten books called Description of Greece. This work, although tedious and pedantic, is nonetheless a valuable source of information on mythology, religious customs, temples and statues, art, and the history of ancient Greece. In Squires's composition the point is made that Pausanias wrote about dead ruins, and that generations of archaeologists have excavated in these ruins, but only "life is alive," and the living "are the play to be played."

STEVENS, Wallace (1879-1955, American)

1071 "The World as Meditation," in Collected Poems of Wallace Stevens. New York: Knopf, 1954.
The subject of this poem is Penelope, the wife of Odysseus, who has waited for him twenty years--ten during the Trojan War, and another ten during his adventures in getting home. She has lived in a world of meditation, composing in her mind day after day a self "with which to welcome" her husband home again. When the warmth of the sun came through the window and struck her pillow, she felt Odysseus to be there. The days wore on, and she never ceased "repeating his name with its patient syllables," never forgot "him that kept coming constantly so near."

STICKNEY, Joseph Trumbull (1874-1904, American)

1072 "The Death of Aischylos," in The Poems of Trumbull Stickney,

ed. with Introduction by Amberys R. Whittle; Foreword by Edmund Wilson. New York: Farrar, Straus and Giroux, 1972.
According to one legend the dramatist Aeschylus was killed by an eagle dropping a tortoise on his head, thus fulfilling a prophecy that he would die from a blow from heaven. In this poem he prays for death, feeling that he has outlived his time and place in the dramatic competitions. At the end he dies, after a long painful suffering: "What sick, slow pain," he says.

1073 _____. "Kalypso," in The Poems (1972), is a study of the sea-goddess and Odysseus in a scene before the gods commanded her to let him go. He is asleep, and she sings lovingly and gently, hoping that he will stay with her. When he awakes, he sees her as a "gaoler of Fate," and hopes that before he dies he will see even "the smoke of tree-clad Ithaca."

1074 _____. "Mnemosyne," in The Poems (1972), is a reference to mother of the Muses, the Titan Memory, but the poem has little mythological background. It is a first-person recollection of someone who returns to "the country" of former life and remembers the way it was: "warm wind," "long sun-sweetened summer days," "yellow cattle," as compared with the way it is: "empty" and "dark," with "slushed path" and "twisted stumps." The last line: "It rains across the country I remember," summarizes the gloomy atmosphere of the entire poem.

1075 _____. "Prometheus Pyrphoros," in The Poems (1972), is presented in dramatic form with the characters of Pandora, Prometheus, Deukalion, Pyrrha, Epimetheus, and the Voices of Zeus. At the beginning the scene is dark, the characters speaking but not being seen. They talk mostly about the lack of light and warmth, fearful and argumentative over whether Prometheus should again confront the wrath of Zeus and bring fire to them. Ultimately Prometheus makes the decision to do so, saying that Justice will be served. As the play comes to its conclusion, the Voices of Zeus announce that they have come for Prometheus. He says, "We'll die in battle," but they remind him that he cannot die, he must struggle everlastingly. As Prometheus is dragged away, Pandora is singing of hope that each new day brings.

STODDARD, Richard Henry (1825-1903, American)

1076 "Arcadian Hymn to Flora," The Poems of Richard Henry Stoddard: Complete Edition. New York: Scribner, Sons, 1880.
Although principally a hymn to nature in general, a romantic praising of the beauties of Spring, Stoddard's poem

does contain the myth of Flora, the Roman goddess of flowering plants. According to the myth Flora was a mortal girl who was loved by Zephyrus, the West Wind. He pleaded with Jupiter to make her an immortal, and thus she became a goddess and was worshiped as one of the fertility deities.

1077 _____. "Arcadian Idyl," in Complete Edition (1880), is mythological only in that it makes several references to gods and poets who were associated with music: Apollo, Hermes, Pan, Theocritus, and the shepherd Lycidas.

1078 _____. "The Captives of Charon," in The Lion's Cub with Other Verse. New York: Scribner, 1890.
This poem creates an unpleasant scene in which Charon, the ferryman of the River Styx, hurries the dead along and does not wait for mothers to say good-bye to their children, husbands to their wives, or any other human consideration. He drives his captives forward toward the gloomy shores of Hades, and has no regard for youth or age.

1079 _____. "The Children of Isis," in Complete Edition (1880), are Typhon and his brother, Osiris. This mythology belongs especially to the Egyptians, but connects with Greek mythology in that Isis was called a daughter of Saturn and Rhea who went to Egypt. Her sons fought over the empire, and finally Typhon destroyed his brother and scattered parts of his body throughout the land. These parts became embodied in statues, and thus Osiris became the supreme god who existed throughout the land. He is more particularly associated with fertility of the soil and is something of the same as Dionysus in Greek mythology.

1080 _____. "The Fisher and Charon," in Songs of Summer. Boston: Ticknor and Fields, 1857.
This work is a lengthy narrative of an old fisherman Diotimus and his wife, Doro. They lived a life of poverty and hard toil, and finally Doro died. After her death the fisherman lost all interest in living, and tried constantly to find a means of dying and crossing the river Styx without paying Charon a fee. In desperation he stole one of Charon's boats and rowed furiously until he reached the other side. Charon was outraged, but Diotimus rejoined Doro, and together "the smiling spirits go to meet their judge." In addition to the story it tells, the poem is interesting for its simple portrayal of two old people devoted to each other.

1081 _____. "The Search for Persephone," in Songs of Summer (1857), is a section of the Demeter myth that seems to require a beginning and an end. This poem encompasses most of the search for Demeter's missing daughter as she asks the various spirits of earth for information. No one has seen her, or knows anything. Finally the grieving mother asks Polyphemus, the cyclops. and he too has no information. The poem ends here, without resolution.

1082 _____. "The Song of the Syrens," in Complete Edition (1880), is a simple but effective lyric in which the Sirens invite sailors to come to their island and rest "on the happy shore." There is no danger, they insist, and if there is it is they who will suffer, not the men who come there.

1083 _____. "The Wine-Cup," in Complete Edition (1880), is an ironic story of Lycius, a king of Crete who neglected his kingdom and would gladly lay down his sceptre for the wine-cup. Angered by the warnings of Philocles, his old teacher and a prophet, Lycius ordered the old man to be silent, and threw the wine-cup out the window. It struck his young son and killed him instantly, "slain by the wine-cup from his father's hand!"

SWINBURNE, Algernon Charles (1837-1909, English)

1084 "Anactoria," in Vol. 1, The Complete Works of Algernon Charles Swinburne, ed. by Sir Edmund Gosse and Thomas James Wise. London: Heinemann, 1925-1927. Bonchurch edition. Reprinted New York: Russell and Russell, 1968.
The subject of this poem is a woman of Lesbos who was loved by Sappho. Although Anactoria loves Sappho, the poem is also passionate with a kind of remorse and hatred of the love relationship.

1085 _____. "At Eleusis," in Vol. 1, Complete Works (1968), is a dramatic monologue spoken by Demeter. In the course of her remarks she painfully recalls the abduction of her daughter, Persephone, and also discourses on the slight treatment she has received at the hands of human beings. At Eleusis, however, she was welcomed by the King and Queen, and in return she taught their son, Trip-tolemus, the arts and secrets of agriculture.

1086 _____. "Atalanta in Calydon," in Vol. 7, Complete Works (1968), is a tragedy in which Swinburne attempted, he said, to write an original English drama in the manner of a Greek play. The story covers the entire series of events referred to as the Calydonian Boar Hunt, although the play concentrates on the personal tragedy that befell Meleager. At Meleager's birth the Fates told his mother Althaea that her son would live so long as a particular brand were not consumed by fire. After this Meleager became a heroic figure, and his mother took all care to preserve the brand. At the height of his powers Meleager invited all the heroes of the day and the beautiful huntress Atalanta to participate in the hunting of an enormous boar that was laying the country in waste. Atalanta killed the boar, and Meleager, who had fallen in love with her, gave her the prize. This provoked his kinsmen, who objected to giving the prize to a woman. War broke out between the two factions, and Meleager killed his mother's brothers. In revenge his mother threw the brand into the fire, and Meleager's life came to an end. Later in remorse Althaea ended her own life, and the tragedy was complete.

1087 _____. "The Ballad of Melicertes," in Vol. 6, Complete Works (1968), was written in memory of Théodore de Banville, a French poet who lived 1823-1891. Much admired by Swinburne, Banville is compared to the mythological figure of Melicertes, a son of Athamas and Ino, who leapt to his death in the sea and became a sea-deity known as Palaemon. In a similar manner the poet died and continued to live in his poetry.

1088 _____. "Delphic Hymn to Apollo," in Vol. 6, Complete Works (1968), is a song of praise for the god of the Delphic oracle. The Muses, Apollo's sisters, are called upon to chant his praises.

1089 _____. "Erechtheus," in Vol. 7, Complete Works (1968), is a tragedy presented in the Greek manner with Chorus, Messenger, and high poetic language. Although interminable, the story is somewhat simple: Erechtheus, a king of Athens, is threatened with invasion by Eumolpus, and the oracle pronounces that only the human sacrifice of a virgin maid can save the city. The king's daughter, Chthonia, freely and even gladly offers her life for the cause. Other maidens follow her in the sacrifice, and Athens is saved.

1090 _____. "Eros," in Vol. 5, Complete Works (1968), is a hymn of praise for the god of love, "the soul in all things born or framed." The winged god is addressed in many glowing terms: "a fire of heart untamed," "higher than transient shapes or shows," and "pure as fire or flowers or snows."

1091 _____. "Eurydice," in Vol. 2, Complete Works (1968), is a sonnet dedicated to Victor Hugo, who is addressed as Orpheus in the composition. The narrator admonishes him to wait, and "see hell yield up Eurydice."

1092 _____. "The Garden of Proserpine," in Vol. 1, Complete Works (1968) is narrated by a world-weary Roman pagan, who does not believe in Christianity and who has lost any significant belief in the gods. The entire tone and mood of the poem is one of hopelessness and weariness. The mythological basis of the poem is the story of Proserpine's abduction by Hades, who carried her off to be the queen of the Underworld. Her mother, Demeter, goddess of the harvest, wandered the world over looking for her daughter, and when she did not find her threatened to lay waste the soil and crops. Zeus could not allow this catastrophe, and told Demeter that Proserpine could spend six months of the year as her daughter, and six months as the wife of Hades. Her alternate periods on earth and in the Underworld indicate the cycle of growth and dormancy or life and death. Swinburne, however, does not see in the Proserpine myth the concept of immortality, or recurring life, but rather uses the story to comment on the weariness of life, the comfort in knowing that it will end, and when life ends, it will not come again.

1093 _____. "Hermaphroditus," in Vol. 1, Complete Works (1968), refers to a son of Hermes and Aphrodite who was loved by the nymph Salmacis. While he was bathing in her spring, she clung to his body and prayed to the gods that they might never be separated. Thus he became a half-man with the body of a woman and a man's genitals.

1094 _____. "Hymn to Proserpine," in Vol. 1, Complete Works (1968), is spoken by a noble pagan who regrets the overthrow of the Greek deities after the Proclamation in Rome of the Christian faith, possibly the Edict of Milan given by the Roman emperors Constantine and Licinius in A.D. 313. The epigraph, "Vicisti Galilae"--Thou hast conquered, Galilean--is attributed to Emperor Julian (331-363) who renounced Christianity but is said to have died with these words on his lips.

1095 _____. "Itylus," in Vol. 1, Complete Works (1968), is narrated by Philomela, the nightingale, to her sister the swallow, and the subject of the poem is Itylus, "the small slain body," who was the son of Procne the swallow. When Procne learned that her husband, Tereus, had raped Philomela, she killed Itylus and served him to his father. As Philomela and Procne fled from the wrath of Tereus, they were changed into the nightingale and swallow.

1096 _____. "The Last Oracle," in Vol. 3, Complete Works (1968), is a commentary on the event that occurred in A.D. 361, when Apollo's oracle on Delphi was closed forever, and the Roman emperor Julian said as he was dying, "Thou hast conquered, Galilean." The narrator, a poet of the modern era, is still sad that the gods are gone, and honors Apollo as the "father of all of us."

1097 _____. "Laus Veneris," in Vol. 1, Complete Works (1968), means "in praise of Venus," and refers to the goddess as a symbol of pagan beauty and sensuality. The narrator prefers her type of love to the Christian model of love, which is passionless and abstract.

1098 _____. "The Palace of Pan," in Vol. 6, Complete Works (1968), is a tribute to nature as it manifests itself in September, "glorious with gold," and "outsweetening the spring." The palace of Pan, is indeed the entire year of nature, all seasons building on each other to produce the perfect whole.

1099 _____. "Pan and Thalassius," in Vol. 3, Complete Works (1968), is a lyrical dialogue between Pan, who symbolizes the land, and Thalassius, who stands for the sea. They each make claims for their own importance.

1100 _____. "Phaedra," in Vol. 1, Complete Works (1968), is a fragment of a drama based on the Phaedra-Hippolytus myth. This work develops the scene in which Phaedra makes her feelings for Hippolytus known. He scorns her advances, and she passionately pleads with him to become her lover. When he ultimately refuses, she curses him.

1101 _____. "Sapphics," in Vol. 1, Complete Works (1968), are love lyrics in the manner of Sappho, in which Aphrodite is praised. Aphrodite, however, does not respond favorably to women who love women.

1102 _____. "Thalassius," in Vol. 3, Complete Works (1968), is based largely on Swinburne's imagination, and has no real basis in mythology. Thalassius, the sea, is the source of health and well-being to a child of the Nereid Cymothoe and the sun-god Apollo. The long poem consists of very little story, and a great deal of praise for the blessings of the sea.

1103 _____. "Tiresias," in Vol. 2, Complete Works (1968), is narrated by the blind prophet of Thebes, who ironically sees all the past and the future. In this poem he is weary and would gladly die, for he has seen nothing but evil in the city of Thebes since the day it was founded by King Cadmus, who took Harmonia for his bride. Tiresias reviews the Oedipus story, his marriage to Jocasta, his mother, the death of Antigone, and the approaching war between the sons of Polynices and Eteocles. He is a very old, very tired man, but sees no end to his life.

SYMONDS, John Addington (1840-1893, English)

1104 "Callicrates," in Many Moods: A Volume of Verse. London:
Smith, Elder, 1878.
The story told in this work is based in part on Herodotus
(Book IX, paragraph 72). Callicrates, known for his ex-
ceptional beauty, was loved by Aristodemus, the Spartan
who suffered the disgrace of cowardice at the battle of
Thermopylae. Callicrates then turns on his friend and
refuses to show him kindness. Later both men fought
and died at the battle of Plataea. Symonds's poem deals
with the two friends coming into the gates of Hades before
the judgment of Minos. Aristodemus tells his story,
pleading his case that he was not a coward. At the end
Minos agrees, and sentences the two friends to spend
eternity in each other's company, telling heroic tales and
singing of brave deeds.

1105 _____. "An Episode," in New and Old: A Volume of
Verse. London: Smith, Elder, 1880.
The narrator of this poem is Phaidon, a disciple of Socrates, and "the episode" is the occasion of Socrates' death.
In the depth of despair over his teacher's approaching
death, Phaidon weeps and cannot be comforted. Socrates
tries to comfort him, saying merely, "Oh, Phaidon,
Phaidon!" In old age these words still haunt Phaidon,
and he realizes that everything was said in this simple
phrase.

1106 _____. "Hesperus and Hymenaeus," in New and Old
(1880), is a narrative in which Hesperus, who was regarded as a god, tells a simple shepherd a love story.
The shepherd is on his way to visit another shepherd
whom he loves in friendship, and Hesperus tells him of
Hymenaeus, also a shepherd, who was changed into an
immortal and now roams the skies with Hesperus.

1107 _____. "Leuké," in New and Old (1880), refers to what
has been called White Island, a place not unlike the Elysian fields where certain heroes dwelled in immortality.
Among the most celebrated of heroes was Achilles, who
lives there with Helen (or according to one story Iphigenia),
and his friends Ajax and Patroclus.

1108 _____. "The Lotos-Garland of Antinous," in Many Moods
(1878), is the story of a youth who was dearly loved by
the emperor Hadrian (A.D. 138). There are several versions of the death of Antinous, but in this poem he offers
himself as a sacrifice in the Nile river to save the Emperor's life. At his death the Emperor built a temple to
Antinous and wanted it believed that the youth had been
changed into a constellation.

1109 _____. "Love and Death" in Many Moods (1878), is the
story of Cratinus and Aristodemus, two Athenian friends
who offered themselves as sacrifices during a plague of
Athens. The soothsayer Epimenides from Crete told the
people of Athens that they must purge themselves "for the
crime of Megacles," who had sacrificed many Athenians
in a battle against the Cylons. The two friends, Cran-
tinus and Aristodemus, handsome and in the prime of
youth, go to their deaths without hesitation, knowing their
deed will remain in legend forever.

1110 _____. "The Myrtle Bough," in New and Old (1880), is a
statement of the ancient symbolism of the myrtle, which
stood for both love and death. In this poem the two are
also parts of the same thing: love for "thy friend and
thou," through life, and death, "who waits for both."

1111 _____. "Pantarkes," in New and Old (1880), is a monologue spoken by Phidias, a celebrated sculptor of Athens,
who lived in the fourth century B.C. He made a thirty-
nine-foot statue of Athena on which he carved his own portrait and that of Pericles in the shield of the goddess.
For this he was banished, and fled to Elis, where he pro-
ceeded to avenge the ill-treatment of the Athenians. He
carved the Olympian Zeus and the statue of Victory. Between the knees of the god, he created a portrait of Pantarkes, his young friend. The point of this work is that
Pantarkes has been given life and immortality by the great
statue of marble.

1112 _____. "Prometheus Dead," in New and Old (1880), retells
a dream in which the narrator travels to the Caucasian
mountains and sees Prometheus still chained to his crag,
"still enduring for us the perpetual disaster." He reflects
that surely death would have been better for the Titan than
this everlasting torment, and then he awakens and realizes
that the old gods are dead, those "who groaned and bled
for men" are no more. We can remember them in visions
and dreams only, and cannot bring back the dead.

1113 _____. "The Sacrifice," in New and Old (1880), is a fragmentary version of the Cratinus and Aristodemus story,
the two friends who sacrificed themselves for the good of
Athens. This fragment, however, creates a very effective
scene in which the two young men go to their deaths, as
they approach "the awful shrine, the altar, and the knife."
They hear the sound of singing as night closes over them,
and "they slept."

SYMONS, Arthur (1865-1945, English)

1114   "The Chimaera," in <u>Poems by Arthur Symons</u>, 2 vols. New
York: Lane, <u>1911.</u>
The Chimaera in mythology was a creature who had three
heads--that of a lion, a goat, and a dragon. It was known
for its ability to outwit its pursuers by changing its shapes
and colors. Symons's poem is about change, the pursuit
of one goal or ambition, and then watching desire for it
change into something else.

1115   _____. "Faustus and Helen." in <u>Poems</u> (1911), is a dialogue in which Faustus expresses great dissatisfaction with
life, and the fetters of "eternal change." He would have
that which is changeless, and finds nothing but change.
He conjures up what appears to be Helen, the image of
perfect love and beauty that man may dream of but never
quite attain. Faustus knows she is not reality and sends
her back to oblivion, meanwhile waiting "cruel old age,
and kinder death, and sleep."

1116   _____. "Wine of Circe," in <u>Poems</u> (1911), is spoken by
an Odysseus-like narrator, one who has lived and experienced much. This poem, however, is a plea for oblivion,
which he hopes to find in the magic of the "wine of Circe,"
a powerful draught that will bring forgetfulness of everything, including "another woman."

TATE, Allen (1899-1979, American)

1117   "Aeneas at New York," in <u>Collected Poems, 1919-1976.</u>
Farrar, Straus, Giroux, 1977.
The implication in this chaotic poem is that heroism is
a matter of economics, and that all wars are fought for
the acquisition of materialistic goods. Take the war at
Troy, for example, fought primarily in the interest of
trade. New York is used as the imagery of New World
wealth and commerce, trade, and economics--a kind of
American Troy.

1118   _____. "Aeneas at Washington," in <u>Collected Poems</u> (1977),
is narrated by the character as created in Virgil's <u>Aeneid,</u>
and most of the mythological references in Section 1 are
derived from Book II of the <u>Aeneid.</u> Aeneas is seen here
as the archetypal explorer-colonizer, who, even as he
watches the demise of his city, Troy, already dreams of
another world and other walls that he will build. In the
second movement of the poem Aeneas is now in Washington,
"by the Potomac," "four thousand leagues" from the buried
city of Troy. He has become cynical and wonders why humanity keeps building towers when they are inevitably
doomed to destruction. A similar theme is expressed in
John Peale Bishop's poem "Experience of the West" (<u>Col-
lected Poems</u>, 1948), edited by Allen Tate.

TAYLOR, Bayard (1825-1878, American)

1119 "Hylas," in Poetical Works of Bayard Taylor. Boston:
Houghton, Mifflin, 1890.
The story of the unfortunate youth is presented in a
straightforward narrative, beginning with the early morning when Hylas left the camp of the Argonauts to walk
near the river. The details of Hylas discovering himself
reflected in the water and subsequently being drowned are
especially effective, and occupy most of the poem. At
the end, which is also the end of the day, Hercules
searches for the lost youth, but all that remains is a
purple cloak that Hylas has left behind.

1120 _____. "Icarus," in Poetical Works (1890), is narrated
by the boy Icarus as he and his father, Daedalus, make
their escape from the Labyrinth on Crete. By means of
wings attached to their bodies with wax, Icarus and Daedalus flew over land and sea and thus gained freedom.
All might have gone well, but the youth dared to fly ever
higher and higher until the heat of the sun melted the wax
and he dropped out of the sky and drowned in the sea.
We experience these events with Icarus until the very end.

1121 _____. The Masque of the Gods. Boston: Osgood, 1872.
This dramatic work is presented in three scenes in only
forty or so pages. The first scene takes place at mid-
night, and the characters are Rocks, Caverns, Serpents,
Wolves, the gods Odin and Baal, a Voice from Space, and
Man. The argument is that Man has worshiped these gods
and now they are dead. Scene 2 is in a temple near the
Aegean Sea, and the characters here are Trees, Rivers,
Mountains, the gods of Greek mythology, Christ, and Man.
The gods debate their individual values, and each recom-
mends himself to Man. Scene three takes place in a vast
landscape and consists of a chorus of Spirits and Man.
The spirits sing of a God whose nature is single and in-
divisible, the perfect One. Man complains that he does
not understand, and in the closing line he is told, "Wait!
Ye shall know."

1122 _____. "Pandora," in Poetical Works (1890), creates the
imagery of Italy as a land on which the gods poured out
every conceivable gift: beauty of nature and climate,
great art, the sea and mountains. Pandora was the mythological character who carried a box of assorted ills and
goods and poured them out indiscriminately on humankind.
The one gift that Italy did not receive was permanence,
for most of her greatness is now in ruin.

1123 _____. "Passing the Sirens," in The Poet's Journal.
Boston: Ticknor and Fields, 1863.
The heroes most associated with the Sirens are Orpheus

and Odysseus, who lived at different times, and each met
the temptation in his own way. Taylor's poem brings the
two heroes together, as though on the same ship, and they
confront the Sirens, each presenting his scheme for dealing with the alluring women. Ulysses instructs his men
to bind him to the mast of his ship and to stop their own
ears with wool. Thus Ulysses will be able to hear the
Sirens, but will not be able to succumb to their temptation.
On the other hand Orpheus, as a true son of the god
Apollo, will defeat the Sirens with his own divinely inspired music; the lofty appeal of his music will overcome
the sensuous songs of the Sirens. At the end the ship's
crew judge the two points of view: they choose in favor
of Ulysses, saying it is the more human response.

1124 _____. Prince Deukalion: A Lyrical Drama. Boston:
Houghton, Osgood, 1878.
This work was published a month before Taylor died, and
thus the author did not live to see its critical acclaim.
It is generally regarded as Taylor's best work and, although far from being a perfect drama, is nonetheless an
important statement of the author's philosophical mind.
It is presented in four acts with the leading characters of
Prince Deukalion, the son of Prometheus, and Pyrrha, the
daughter of Pandora, representing Man and Woman. The
time covered by the work is well in excess of two thousand
years, the first act taking place in the fourth century A. D.,
and the last "sometime in the Future." The overall theme
of the work is the human search for fulfillment, which has
so far been principally a failure. First was the passing away
of the classical world, and the emergence of Christianity;
then in another thousand years the failure of Christianity
to allow men and women their freedom. The nineteenth
century is no better, for humanity is still encumbered by
superstition, creed, and organization. In the last act of
the work, Urania, representing Science, becomes a main
character and promises humankind a "new Era." Urania,
however, does not promise Immortality, and this contra-
dicts our essential need. It remains for Prometheus, the
Firegiver, to speak the closing lines:

> For Life, whose course not here began,
> Must fill the utmost sphere of Man,
> And, so expanding, lifted be
> Along the line of God's decree,
> To find in endless growth all good, --
> In endless toil, beatitude.
> Seek not to know him; yet aspire
> As atoms toward the central fire.

1125 _____. "The Sunshine of the Gods," in Poetical Works
(1890), is a lyrical expression on the subject of poetical
inspiration and composition. Taylor describes the poet

as a man walking through mist and fog, but then "the mist is blown from the mind," and "the sunshine of the Gods" breaks through uniting thought and word in "the hour of perfect Song."

TENNYSON, Alfred Lord (1809-1892, English)

1126 "Amphion," in Tennyson's Poetry, selected and ed. by Robert W. Hill, Jr. New York: Norton, 1971. Norton Critical edition.
In Greek mythology Amphion was a musician of such powers that the stones in the great walls of Thebes were drawn into place by the enchantment of his music. In Tennyson's poem he is given such power over all nature, and the poet laments that poetry has become such a poor thing in the modern world.

1127 _____. "The Death of Oenone," in Tennyson's Poetry (1971), is a sequel to "Oenone" (discussed below). This poem begins with Paris, now mortally wounded by Philoctetes' poisoned arrow, seeking Oenone, his former wife, who is the only one able to cure his wound. Oenone has now become a Fury of vengeance, and refuses to aid Paris. After his death she reverses her feelings, and kills herself on his funeral pyre.

1128 _____. "Demeter and Persephone," in Tennyson's Poetry (1971), is based on the myth that Persephone, while gathering flowers in the field of Enna, was carried away by Hades, king of the dead and the Underworld. In deep grief her mother Demeter failed to bring in the year until Zeus restored Persephone to her for at least six months of the year. This poem, however, goes beyond the Greek myth and in the last stanza envisions a new religion, Christianity, that will defeat the forces of death.

1129 _____. "Frater, Ave Atque Vale," in Tennyson's Poetry (1971), means "Brother, hail and farewell," and is from Catullus' elegiac lament for his brother. Tennyson wrote this poem in 1880 following the death of his own brother Charles in April 1879. Tennyson was visiting Desenzano, a town at the southern end of Lake Garda about three miles from Sirmione. Catullus, c. 87-54 B. C., maintained his country villa on Sirmione, the peninsula in Lake Garda.

1130 _____. "Hero to Leander," in The Complete Poetical Works of Alfred Tennyson. Boston: Osgood, 1877. This is a passionate cry of Hero to her lover, Leander, to stay with her. In her fears she foretells all the tragic events that are to befall the lovers. Leander will be

drowned in the Hellespont, and Hero will kill herself by
jumping off a cliff into the sea.

1131   _____. "The Hesperides," in Tennyson's Poetry (1971),
is based on the myth of the four daughters of the evening
star, Hesperus, who lived near the Atlas Mountains.
With the dragon Ladon they guarded the tree of the golden
apples given to Hera by Gaea on her wedding day to Zeus.
The eleventh labor of Hercules was to get the golden apples, which he did by slaying the dragon. The apples are
symbolic of happiness, love, and wisdom.

1132   _____. "The Lotos-Eaters," in Tennyson's Poetry (1971),
is derived from Homer in Book IX of the Odyssey. The
crew of Odysseus ate of the lotus, a "honied fruit," and
wished never to leave the ideal land, the euphoric influence was so great. Odysseus was hard pressed to get
the sailors back to ship. Much of Tennyson's poem, however, is not related to Homer, it being a personal record
of a trip that he and Arthur Hallam made through the
Pyrenees in 1830.

1133   _____. "Oenone," in Tennyson's Poetry (1971), begins the
story of Oenone, the nymph of Mt. Ida, who lived happily
with her husband, Paris, until the three goddesses offered
the unsophisticated shepherd a choice of three great boun-
ties. After choosing Aphrodite as the fairest of the goddesses, Paris was given the world's most beautiful woman
--Helen, the wife of Menelaus of Sparta. Oenone lost her
husband to the beautiful Helen, and was helpless to win
back his love. Although most people regarded Cassandra
as a madwoman, Oenone did not and knew that Paris' reck-
less actions would ultimately bring about the total destruction of Troy and the Trojans.

1134   _____. "Parnassus," in Tennyson's Poetry (1971), was a
mountain in Phocis, held to be sacred by the Muses.
Tennyson constructs a monument to the Muses, but admits
that most of his life he has struggled with the "terrible
Muses," astronomy and geology, sciences that do not
idealize humanity's position in the universe.

1135   _____. "Tiresias," in Tennyson's Poetry (1971), the blind
soothsayer of Thebes, is addressing Menoeceus, the son
of Creon, on the approaching war of the Seven Against
Thebes. The prophet has been informed in a vision that
Thebes can be saved only by one of the descendents of
Cadmus offering his own life freely in suicide in sacrifice
to Ares. Menoceus is urged to win glory for himself and
save his city from destruction by making this sacrifice.
In mythology the young Menoeceus gave himself for the
cause and the city was spared.

1136 _____. "Tithonus," in Tennyson's Poetry (1971), is the
story of the beautiful Trojan youth with whom Eos, the
Dawn, fell madly in love. She begged Zeus to grant
Tithonus eternal life, but forgot to ask for eternal youth.
Finally the gods took pity on the old man and changed him
into a grasshopper. Tennyson's poem points up the danger
inherent in the differences between mortal and immortal.

1137 _____. "To Ulysses," in Tennyson's Poetry (1971), is
mythological only in its title. The poem is addressed to
W. G. Palgrave, whose career as soldier, priest, mis-
sionary, and diplomat was not unlike that of the legendary
hero.

1138 _____. "To Virgil," in Tennyson's Poetry (1971), was
written in 1882 to commemorate the nineteenth centenary
of Virgil's death. Virgil was born near Mantua in 70 B. C.
and died in 19 B. C. For Tennyson, Virgil was always
the greatest of classical writers, and this poem, although
making use of several well-chosen allusions--Ilion, Dido,
Hesiod--is largely a praise for the great Roman poet.

1139 _____. "Ulysses," in Tennyson's Poetry (1971), is perhaps
the best known of Tennyson's mythological works, and well
it should be since it is compact in structure and theme,
and does not distract with overelaboration. It is based in
part on the Odyssey, Book XI, in which Odysseus learns
that after he reaches Ithaca he must still undertake a final
sea voyage. Dante's Inferno, Canto 26, also provides an
account of that voyage, in which Odysseus sails beyond the
Straits of Gibraltar, in ancient belief the end of the world.

WHEELOCK, John Hall (1886-1978, American)

1140 "Aphrodite, 1906," in Collected Poems, 1911-1936. New
York: Scribner, 1936. Reprinted in Atlantic, Vol.
117, April 1974.
This poem describes a modern girl in a bathing suit
emerging from the swimming area of the sea. The imagery is in terms of the myth in which Venus, or Aphrodite,
issues from the sea-foam near the island of Cyprus. The
poem is nostalgic in tone, and the girl described by the
poet is indistinct and shadowy, as are individuals remembered in dreams.

1141 _____. "The Bathing Beach," in Dear Men and Women:
New Poems. New York: Scribner, 1966.
The mythological basis of this poem is very slight, with
only passing references to Aphrodite and Poseidon. For
the most part it is a description of a modern beach,

crowded with boys and girls, swimming and laughing in
their happy youth. The tone and mood is similar to
"Aphrodite, 1906," with the narrator passively watching
the scene.

1142 _____ . "Helios," in Dear Men and Women (1966), is referred to as the "all-beholding father," whom the narrator
comes face to face with one day in the "bare solitude of
the beaches" and the "naked solitude of the sea." The
sun is regarded as the creator of all things, and has looked
upon all things, the Pharaohs of Egypt, the Crucifixion at
Golgotha, and "the passing generations of mankind."

1143 _____ . "Helios-Apollo," in The Gardener and Other Poems.
New York: Scribner, 1961.
The scene is once again "the bathing beach," with boys and
girls laughing and swimming in the water, and adults sitting or lying on the sandy shores. They are like sun-
worshipers, hushed and silent in the beams of light. The
sun is again regarded as a father, "life-giver, light-
bringer," by the narrator. In the final description Helios-
Apollo is called a god "whom none has dared look upon,"
the image of "terrible beauty."

WILLIS, Nathaniel Parker (1806-1867, American)

1144 "Parrhasius," in Poems: Sacred, Passionate and Humorous.
New York: Clark, Austin, and Smith, 1859.
Parrhasius, an Athenian painter who lived about 397 B.C.,
is used by Willis as a vehicle for sermonizing and moralizing on the subject of "unrein'd ambition." It is said that
Parrhasius was a very arrogant man who gave himself airs
by going about in purple and gold, boasting that as an ar-
tistic genius he had the right to do anything he pleased.
On one occasion he is said to have bought an old man, a
captive from Olynthus in Macedonia, and brought him to
his house where the fellow was put to death with extreme
torture, in order for Parrhasius to better express in his
art the pains and torture of Prometheus, whom he was
then about to paint. This episode is fully embodied in
Willis's poem, and not without effect, but then follows a
lengthy passage on ambition that seems thematically disconnected from the Parrhasius story except that certainly
the artist overstepped the boundary of human decency, no
matter how much a genius he was.

1145 _____ . "Psyche, Before the Tribunal of Venus," in Poems
(1859), is a form of debate in which the virtues of the
feminine, physical beauty that Venus can give, are opposed
to the beauties of soul and spirit represented by Psyche.
The weight of argument goes to Psyche, "for the soul is
better than its frame / The spirit than its temple."

WINTERS, Yvor (1900-1968, American)

1146   "Alcmena," in The Collected Poems of Yvor Winters, with
        Introduction by Donald Davie. Chicago: Swallow,
        1978.
        Although exceptionally brief, Winters's poem covers in great
        detail the life and death of Alcmena, one of the best known
        of mythological women. After her brothers were unjustly
        killed in a cattle raid, she sent Amphitryon to avenge the
        deaths, promising him marriage when he returned. Later
        she was visited by Zeus, and became the mother of Her-
        cules, called Alcides in this poem after his paternal
        grandfather, Alcaeus. Alcmena outlived her husband and
        her great son, "Hero of Symbolic War," and when she
        died Zeus made her the wife of Rhadamanthus to rule in
        the Underworld.

1147   _____. "Apollo and Daphne," in Collected Poems (1978),
        is the fable of how Daphne, whose name means laurel,
        was changed into a tree when she was pursued by Apollo.
        Angered and frustrated, the god then "withdrew into Eter-
        nity." The laurel became the plant sacred to Apollo.

1148   _____. "Chiron," in Collected Poems (1978), is the re-
        flection of an old teacher whose "head is bald and dried."
        He has been the teacher of Achilles and other great heroes,
        but now he sits "on the edge of naught," and waits for
        death.

1149   _____. "Heracles," in Collected Poems (1978), is a nar-
        rative spoken by Heracles, in which he relates his fate of
        being subservient to Eurystheus. He performs all the
        Labors set for him by the tyrant, but he was finally struck
        down by the evil of the centaur Nessus. Hercules killed
        Nessus, but before he died the centaur gave Dejanira,
        Hercules' wife, a poison that he tricked her into believing
        was a love potion. Late in life Hercules was unfaithful to
        Dejanira, and she sent him a robe treated with the love
        potion. It proved to be his death; in mortal pain his men
        built his funeral pyre, and he climbed onto it. At his
        death he was made "perfect, and moving perfectly."

1150   _____. "Midas," in Collected Poems (1978), describes the
        process by which the king turned everything he touched,
        including himself, into gold. Just before he dies he looks
        back, and knows a moment of meaning.

1151   _____. "Orpheus," in Collected Poems (1978), was written
        in memory of Hart Crane, the American poet who died
        very young. The comparison is between Crane and the
        mythological poet-singer Orpheus. At the end of his life
        Orpheus was killed and floated down a river; Hart Crane
        committed suicide by jumping overboard from a ship.

1152 _____ . "Satyric Complaint," in Collected Poems (1978),
is a stream-of-consciousness reflection by an animal-like
creature, presumably a satyr, the half-man, half-goat
creation. The point of Winters's poem is to show the conflict between flesh and mind, the agony of glaring "from
gray eyes" knowing the end is in the earth.

1153 _____ . "Socrates," in Collected Poems (1978), is narrated
in the first-person by the Athenian philosopher, just prior
to his drinking the hemlock. He has done his best, and
should someone follow him of "tougher thought in richer
phrase," then he would be "the vast foundation of a Western World." He concludes his life by reflecting on the
times and the Timeless into which he is returning.

1154 _____ . "Theseus: A Trilogy," in Collected Poems (1978),
tells the story of Theseus and his relation with three different women: Hippolyta, Ariadne, and Phaedra. In
Part I, Theseus and Hercules, in their raids against the
Amazon women, capture the beautiful queen, Hippolyta.
Theseus rapes her, and the son Hippolytus was born.
The goddess Artemis, protector of the Amazons, vows
vengeance for the rape of Hippolyta. In Part II Theseus
kills the Minotaur of Crete and escapes with Ariadne, the
daughter of Minos. Later he abandoned Ariadne, or killed
her, on the island of Naxos, and married Phaedra, Ariadne's very young sister. Part III brings Theseus' life
to its tragic conclusion. His son, Hippolytus, becomes
the object of Phaedra's illicit passion, and Theseus mistakenly prays to Poseidon for the destruction of his son.
Thus Artemis, who had never forgiven Theseus for his
abduction of Hippolyta, wreaks havoc on the house of Theseus, and he goes into exile, where he is treacherously
killed. Lycomedes, the king of Scyros, "cast him from
the rock to solitude, / To the cold perfection of unending
peace."

WOODBERRY, George Edward (1855-1930, American)

1155 "Agathon," in The North Shore Watch. New York: Macmillan,
1890. Reprinted in Poems. New York: Macmillan,
1903.
The title refers to the tragic poet who lived about 447-
400 B.C. and who is the subject of Plato's Symposium.
Woodberry's poem, cast in dramatic form, is an allegory
of love in which the poet Agathon passes from the love of
beauty in various physical forms to the love of a beauty
that exists beyond the realms of time and death.

1156 _____ . "Demeter," in The Flight and Other Poems. New
York: Macmillan, 1914.
This is a poem in a work called "A Day at Castrogiovanni,"

referring to a town in Sicily said to be the birthplace of
Demeter, where that goddess had her first temple. The
narrator reflects on the passage of time, the temple now
vanished, and the worshipers all gone their ways. Yet
he can still praise the great "Giver of the Corn," by whatever name, for the "summer's wealth, the winter's gar-
nered store."

1157 _____. "Proserpine," in The Flight (1914), celebrates the
beauty of nature as it appears in the Spring with flowers
and the song of birds. Proserpine, the daughter of Demeter, was snatched away on "such a morn in May" by the
"thunder-black horses," and carried to the "dark deep
under." In conclusion the poet reflects that all things
physical and beautiful will thus meet the same fate at the
hands of the "mightiest lover that the world has known,"
and asks, "Dark lover, Death,--was he not beautiful?"

WORDSWORTH, William (1770-1850, English)

1158 "Dion," in The Complete Poetical Works of Wordsworth.
Boston: Houghton Mifflin, 1932. Cambridge edition.
This poem, based chiefly on Plutarch, concerns Dion, a
Syracusian prince who lived at about the time of Plato.
He advised his kinsman, the tyrant Dionysius, to give up
the supreme power, but when he would not Dion organized
forces against Dionysius and drove him from Syracuse.
The tyrant fled to Corinth. Later Dion was betrayed by
one of his friends and died a shameful death. His death
was widely lamented by the Syracusians, who raised a
monument to his memory.

1159 _____. "Laodamia," in Poetical Works (1932), is a long
narrative in which the story of Protesilaus and Laodamia
is told. As foretold by the oracle, Protesilaus was the
first Greek who went ashore at Troy and was killed. Laodamia, his wife, grieved at his death and would not be
consoled. Finally her husband was granted a brief respite
to visit her, and when he did so he begged her to join
him in death. As he was taking leave, she clung to him
and so perished. However, she had died before her time
and did not join Protesilaus in the Underworld. Subsequently a knot of spiry trees grew out of the tomb of these
two lovers, but when the summits of the trees were within
sight of the walls of Troy, they withered.

1160 _____. "When Philoctetes in the Lemnian Isle," in Poetical Works (1932), is based on the myth of the hero who
was forsaken by his fellow Greeks and cast off on the island of Lemnos. The reason for this apparent heartless-

ness was a wound that Philoctetes had incurred, which
smelled bad and would not heal. Wordsworth's sonnet
deals only with the act of casting him off, an act that the
poet sees as an example of human cruelty. There is also
a reference to the French Bastille, another symbol for
what man is capable of doing to his "brother man."

YEATS, William Butler (1865-1939, English)

1161 "Leda and the Swan," in Collected Poems of William Butler
        Yeats. New York: Macmillan, 1956.
        The poem is based on the myth of Zeus visiting Leda,
        the mother of Helen, Clytemnestra, Castor, and Pollux,
        disguised as a swan. The encounter is described in sen-
        suous terms, and presented as being far greater than
        merely the rape of a mortal by one of the gods: it is
        the beginning of Helen, The Trojan War, the death of
        Agamemnon.

1162 _____. "News for the Delphic Oracle," in Collected Poems
        (1956), begins with the reporter announcing that several
        figures of a widely assorted lot have all reached the Ely-
        sian Fields and are engrossed in activities of perpetual
        pleasure, each according to his own nature: Yeats's own
        mythical lovers Niamh and Oisin; the mathematician and
        philosopher Pythagoras and Plotinus; the Innocents slain
        at the order of Herod; and Peleus and Thetis of Greek
        mythology. The music of the god Pan accompanies the
        sensuous activities of the last section in which nymphs
        and satyrs perpetually "copulate in the foam." The poem
        gains much of its effect by the shocking contrasts of
        figures--real and mythical; and by the wide range of love
        images connected with these figures.

1163 _____. "No Second Troy," in Collected Poems (1956), is
        the portrait of a woman, a kind of modern Helen of Troy,
        who lives on strife and violence, and in any age is the
        source of misery and destruction. In modern times, how-
        ever, she merely makes those in her circle miserable,
        since there is not "another Troy for her to burn."

1164 _____. "Oedipus at Colonus," in The Variorum Edition of
        the Plays of William Butler Yeats, ed. by Russell K.
        Alspach and Catharine C. Alspach. New York:
        Macmillan, 1966.
        This adaptation follows the Sophocles play in its telling of
        the death and transfiguration of the king of Thebes, blind
        Oedipus, who has wandered a great many years in search
        of his grave. It is called a "version for the modern
        state" but does not make any significant changes in the
        order of events. The language is modern, though not
        common or vulgar.

1165 _____ . "Oedipus the King," in The Variorum Edition
(1966), is the companion to the above play, adapted in
much the same manner for the modern stage. The familiar story is unchanged, with only the language updated.

1166 _____ . "The Resurrection," in The Variorum Edition
(1966), is a dramatic discussion of the Christian religion
as it compares and contrasts with the Hebrew, the Syrian,
and the Greek mythological religions.

APPENDIX

ANDERSON, John Redwood (1883-?, English)

1167 "Icarus," in Transvaluations. London: Oxford University
      Press, 1932.

1168 _____. The Legend of Eros and Psyche. Oxford: Thorn-
      ton, 1908.

ARENSBERG, Walter Conrad (1878-1954, American)

1169 "Atalanta," in Poems. Boston: Houghton, Mifflin, 1914.

1170 _____. "Chryseis," in Poems (1914).

1171 _____. "The Night of Ariadne," in Idols and Other Poems.
      Boston: Houghton Mifflin, 1916.

ARMSTRONG, Martin Donisthorpe (1882-1974, English)

1172 "The Naiad," in The Bird-Catcher. London: Secker, 1929.

1173 _____. "Phaethon," in Thirty New Poems. London:
      Chapman and Hall, 1918.

ASQUITH, Herbert (1881-1947, English)

1174 "Ares, God of War," in The Volunteer and Other Poems.
      London: Sidgwick and Jackson, 1915.

AUSTIN, Alfred (1835-1913, English)

1175 "At Delphi," in At the Gate of the Convent. London:
      Macmillan, 1885.

1176 _____. "Polyphemus," in A Tale of True Love. New York and London: Harpers, 1898.

1177 _____. "Sisyphus," in Sacred and Profane Love. London: Macmillan, 1908.

AUSTIN, Arthur Williams (1807-1884, American)

1178 "Jupiter and Hebe," in The Woman and the Queen. Cambridge, Mass.: Wilson, 1875.

BABCOCK, Charlotte Farrington (?-?, American)

1179 "Nausicaa," in Echoes. Boston: Four Seas, 1927.

BALL, Benjamin West (1823-1896, American)

1180 "Ionia," in Elfin Land. Boston: Munroe, 1851.

1181 _____. "Pan and Lais," in Elfin Land (1851).

1182 _____. "The Song of Eneas' Men," in Elfin Land (1851).

BEERS, Henry Augustin (1847-1926, American)

1183 "Narcissus," in Odds and Ends. Boston: Houghton, Osgood, 1878.

1184 _____. "The Rise of Aphrodite," in Odds and Ends (1878).

BENNETT, Alfred Gordon (1901-?, English)

1185 "Ulysses," in Collected Poems, 1920-1930. London: Duckworth, 1930.

BENNETT, William Cox (1820-1895, English)

1186 "Ariadne," in Queen Eleanor's Vengeance and Other Poems. London: Chapman and Hall, 1857.

1187 _____. "Cassandra," in Queen Eleanor (1857).

1188 _____. "The Judgment of Midas," in Queen Eleanor (1857).

1189 _____. Prometheus, the Fire-Giver. London: Chatto

and Windus, 1877. An attempt to restore the third play in Aeschylus' trilogy, of which only "Prometheus Bound" is extant.

1190 _____. "Pygmalion, " in Queen Eleanor (1857).

1191 _____. "The Triumph for Salamis, " in Poems. London: Chapman and Hall, 1850.

BERESFORD, Dudley (1876-?, English)

1192 "Io and Jupiter, " in Lyrics and Legends. London: George Allen, 1908.

BODE, John Ernest (1816-1874, English)

1193 "Aristagoras at Sparta, " in Ballads from Herodotus. London: Longmans, Brown, Green, and Longmans, 1853.

1194 _____. "Atys and Adrastus, " in Ballads (1853).

1195 _____. "Cleobis and Biton, " in Ballads (1853).

1196 _____. "Croesus on the Pyre, " in Ballads (1853).

1197 _____. "The Fate of Polycrates, " in Ballads (1853).

1198 _____. "The Feast of Attaginus, " in Ballads (1853).

1199 _____. "A Glance at the Pyramids, " in Ballads (1853).

1200 _____. "A Legend of Macedon; or, the Tale of Perdiccas, " in Ballads (1853).

1201 _____. "The Nasamonian Tale About the Nile, " in Ballads (1853).

1202 _____. "The Olive of Minerva, " in Ballads (1853).

1203 _____. "Pactyas and Aristodicus, " in Ballads (1853).

1204 _____. "Psammenitus; or, The Grief Too Deep for Tears, " in Ballads (1853).

1205 _____. "The Purple Cloak; or, the Return of Styloson to Samos, " in Ballads (1853).

1206 _____. "The Samian Oasis, " in Ballads (1853).

1207 _____. "The Temple of Bubastis, " in Ballads (1853).

BODE, continued

1208 _____. "Thermopyle," in Ballads (1853).

1209 _____. "The Wooing of Agarista," in Ballads (1853).

BOKER, George Henry (1823-1890, American)

1210 "The Vision of the Goblet," in The Podesta's Daughter and
      Other Poems. Philadelphia: Hart, 1852.

BOTTOMLEY, Gordon (1874-1948, English)

1211 "Atlantis," in Poems and Plays, with Introduction by Claude
      Colleer Abbott. London: Bodley Head, 1953.

1212 _____. "The Dairy-Maids to Pan," in The Gate of
      Smaragdus, with Decorations by Clinton Balmer. London:
      At the Sign of the Unicorn, 1904.

1213 _____. "Daphne," in The Gate (1904).

1214 _____. "Kassandra Prophesies," in Poems and Plays
      (1953).

1215 _____. "Laodice and Danae," in Poems and Plays (1953).

1216 _____. "The Last of Helen," in The Gate (1904).

1217 _____. "Phillis," in The Gate (1904).

1218 _____. "The Stealing of Dionysus," in The Gate (1904).

BOURDILLON, Francis William (1852-1921, English)

1219 "Chryseis," in Preludes and Romances. London: Allen,
      1908.

1220 _____. "The Debate of the Lady Venus and the Virgin
      Mary," in Preludes and Romances (1908).

1221 _____. "Eurydice," in Sursum Corda. London: Unwin,
      1893.

1222 _____. "Helen," in Sursum Corda (1893).

1223 _____. "A Lost God," in Sursum Corda (1893).

1224 _____. "The Statue," in Preludes and Romances (1908).

BRADLEY, Katherine Harris (1848-1914), and Edith Cooper (?-?,
"Michael Field," pseudonym, English)

1225   "Eros," in A Selection from the Poems of Michael Field,
         with Introduction by Thomas Sturge Moore.   Boston:
         Houghton Mifflin, 1925.

1226   _____.   "Eros Does Not Always Smite," in A Selection
         (1925)

1227   _____.   "Frozen Rushes," in A Selection (1925).

1228   _____.   "Gold Is the Son of Zeus," in A Selection (1925).

1229   _____.   "Hades Is Tongueless," in A Selection (1925).

1230   _____.   "Jason," in A Selection (1925).

1231   _____.   "Not Aphrodite," in A Selection (1925).

1232   _____.   "Onycha: Pan to Eros," in A Selection (1925).

1233   _____.   "Pan Asleep," in A Selection (1925).

1234   _____.   "Penetration: Syrinx to Pan," in A Selection
         (1925).

1235   _____.   "Shepherd Apollo," in A Selection (1925).

1236   _____.   "Tiresias," in A Selection (1925).

1237   _____.   "When high Zeus first peopled earth ...," in
         Underneath the Bough, by Michael Field.   Portland, Me.:
         Mosher, 1898.

BRANCH, Anna Hempstead (1875-1937, American)

1238   "Selene," in A Rose of the Wind and Other Poems.   Boston:
         Houghton Mifflin, 1910.

1239   _____.   "A Song from Ganymede," in Sonnets from a Lock
         Box and Other Poems.   Boston: Houghton Mifflin, 1929.

BRENT, John (1808-1882, English)

1240   "Atalanta," in Atalanta, Winnie, and Other Poems.   London:
         Knight, 1873.

BROWN, Alice (1857-1948, American)

1241 "Love Denied," in The Road to Castaly. New York:
Macmillan, 1896. Reprinted 1917. About Endymion.

1242 _____. "Mnemosyne," in Fable and Song. Boston:
Privately printed for the author, 1939.

1243 _____. "Pan," in The Road (1896).

1244 _____. "Penelope," in Fable and Song (1939).

1245 _____. "The Shepherds," in The Road (1896). About
Admetus.

1246 _____. "To Circe," in The Road (1896).

BROWN, Thomas Edward (1830-1897, English)

1247 "Euroclydon," in The Collected Poems of T. E. Brown, with
Introduction by William Ernest Henley. London and New
York: Macmillan, 1901.

1248 _____. "Israel and Hellas," in Collected Poems (1901).

1249 _____. "Roman Women," in Collected Poems (1901).

1250 _____. "Triton," in Collected Poems (1901).

BUTLER-THWING, Francis Wendell (?-?, American)

1251 "The Death of Penelope," in First Fruits. New York:
Privately printed for the author, 1914.

CALDCLEUGH, William George (?-?, American)

1252 "Alcyon," in The Branch and Other Poems. Philadelphia:
Challen, 1862.

1253 _____. "Echo," in The Branch (1862).

1254 _____. "Pan, the Wood God," in The Branch (1862).

1255 _____. "Sappho," in The Branch (1862).

1256 _____. "Thessalia," in The Branch (1862).

CALDWELL, Howard Hayne (1831-1858, American)

246

1257 "Artemisia," in <u>Oliatta and Other Poems</u>. New York: Redfield, 1855.

1258 _____. "Evadne," in <u>Oliatta</u> (1855).

CAMPBELL, Archibald Young (1885-?, English)

1259 "The Fall of Troy," in <u>Poems</u>. London: Longmans, Green, 1926.

CAMPBELL, Ivar (1891-1916, English)

1260 "Odysseus and Calypso," in <u>Poems</u>, with Memoir by Guy Ridley. London: Humphreys, 1917.

CAMPBELL, William Wilfred (1858-1918, English)

1261 "The Dryad," in <u>Beyond the Hills of Dream</u>. Boston and New York: Houghton, Mifflin, 1899.

1262 _____. "Pan the Fallen," in <u>Beyond the Hills</u> (1899).

1263 _____. "Phaethon," in <u>Beyond the Hills</u> (1899).

CARPENTER, Maurice (1911-?, English)

1264 "Venus on a Sea Horse," in <u>IX Poems</u>. London: Phoenix, 1935.

CARRUTH, Hayden (1921- , American)

1265 "The Birth of Venus," in <u>The Crow and the Heart: 1946-1959</u>. New York: Macmillan, 1959.

1266 _____. "A Word for Apollo in the Spring," in <u>The Crow</u> (1959).

CHALMERS, Patrick Reginald (1872-1942, English)

1267 "Daphne," in <u>Green Days and Blue Days</u>. Dublin: Maunsel, 1912.

1268 _____. "Pan-Pipes," in <u>Green Days</u> (1912).

1269 _____. "Pomona," in <u>Green Days</u> (1912).

1270 _____. "A Song of Syrinx," in <u>Green Days</u> (1912).

247

CHAPMAN, John Jay (1862-1933, American)

1271 Cupid and Psyche. New York: Gomme, 1916.

1272 _____ . Homeric Scenes: Hector's Farewell and the Wrath of Achilles. New York: Gomme, 1914.

CHIVERS, Thomas Holley (1809-1858, American)

1273 "Apollo," in Virginalia: or, Songs of My Summer Nights. Philadelphia: Lippincott, 1853. Reprinted New York: Arno, 1972.

1274 _____ . "Astarte's Song to Endymion," in Virginalia (1972).

1275 _____ . "Ganymede," in Virginalia (1972).

1276 _____ . "The Lost Pleiad," in The Lost Pleiad and Other Poems. New York: Jenkins, 1845.

COATES, Mrs. Florence Earle (1850-1927, American)

1277 "Dryad Song," in Poems. Boston: Houghton, Mifflin, 1898.

1278 _____ . "Hylas," in Poems (1898).

1279 _____ . "Psyche," in Poems (1898).

CONKLING, Grace Walcott Hazard (1878-1958, American)

1280 "Proserpine and the Sea-Nymphs," in Afternoons of April. Boston: Houghton, Mifflin, 1915.

1281 _____ . "To Hermes," in Afternoons of April (1915).

COUTTS, Frances (Francis Burdett Latymer; "F. B. Money-Coutts," pseudonym, 1852-1923, English)

1282 "Butes," in Poems. London: Lane, 1896.

1283 _____ . "Hercules and Hylas," in Poems (1896).

1284 _____ . "Tithonus," in Poems (1896).

COX, Ethel Louise (?-?, American)

1285 "Circe," in Poems Lyrical and Dramatic. Boston: Badger, 1904.

1286 _____. "The Hamadryad," in Poems (1904).

1287 _____. "Hymn to Diana," in Poems (1904).

1288 _____. "Narcissus," in Poems (1904).

1289 _____. "Prometheus," in Poems (1904).

CROWLEY, Aleister (Edward Alexander, 1875-1947, English)

1290 "The Argonauts," in The Works of Aleister Crowley, 3 vols. Foyers, England: Society for Propagation of Religious Truth, 1905-1907.

1291 _____. "Orpheus, a Lyrical Legend," in The Works (1905-1907).

1292 _____. "The Tale of Archais," in The Works (1905-1907).

DAVIE, Donald (1922-?, English)

1293 "Agave in the West," in Events and Wisdom. Middletown, Conn.: Wesleyan University Press, 1965.

1294 _____. "Creon's Mouse," in New and Selected Poems. Middletown, Conn.: Wesleyan University Press, 1961.

DE LA MARE, Walter John (1873-1956, English)

1295 "Alexander," in The Sunken Garden. London: Constable, 1917.

1296 _____. "The Birth of Venus," in Collected Poems. London: Faber and Faber, 1979.

1297 _____. "Sorcery," in Collected Poems (1979).

1298 _____. "They Told Me," in Collected Poems (1979). Earlier published as "Tears," in Poems: 1901-1908. London: Constable, 1920. This poem and "Sorcery" both about Pan.

DE TABLEY, Lord (John Byrne Leicester Warren. William P. Lancaster and George F. Preston, pseudonyms, 1835-1895, English)

1299 "Agamemnon," in Ballads and Metrical Sketches, by George F. Preston. London: Kent, 1860.

1300 _____. "Anchises," in The Collected Poems of Lord de Tabley. New York and London: Macmillan, 1903.

1301 _____. "Ariadne," in <u>Collected Poems</u> (1903).

1302 _____. "Ariadne," in <u>Ballads and Sketches</u> (1860). Not the same as poem listed above.

1303 _____. "Children of the Gods," in <u>Poems: Dramatic and Lyrical,</u> First Series. London: Mathews and Lane, 1893.

1304 _____. "Circe," in <u>Poems: Dramatic and Lyrical,</u> Second Series. London: Lane, 1895.

1305 _____. "Circe," in <u>Ballads and Sketches</u> (1860).

1306 _____. "Daedalus," in <u>Collected Poems</u> (1903).

1307 _____. "Daphne," in <u>Poems</u> (First Series, 1893).

1308 _____. "A Daughter of Circe," in <u>Orpheus in Thrace and Other Poems.</u> London: Smith, Elder, 1901.

1309 _____. "The Death of Phaethon," in <u>Poems</u> (Second Series, 1895).

1310 _____. "An Eleusinian Chant," in <u>Orpheus in Thrace</u> (1901).

1311 _____. "Endymion," in <u>Ballads and Sketches</u> (1860).

1312 _____. "Eros and Psyche," in <u>Ballads and Sketches</u> (1860).

1313 _____. "Hero and Leander," in <u>Ballads and Sketches</u> (1860).

1314 _____. "Hymn to Aphrodite," in <u>Poems</u> (Second Series, 1895).

1315 _____. "Hymn to Astarte," in <u>Poems</u> (First Series, 1893).

1316 _____. "Iphigeneia," in <u>Collected Poems</u> (1903).

1317 _____. "The Island of Circe," in <u>Poems</u> (First Series, 1893).

1318 _____. "Lament for Adonis," in <u>Poems</u> (First Series, 1893).

1319 _____. "Lament for Echo," in <u>Orpheus in Thrace</u> (1901).

1320 _____. "Lament for Phaethon's Sisters," in <u>Ballads and Sketches</u> (1860).

1321 _____. "Lament for Phaethon's Sisters," in <u>Collected Poems</u> (1903).

1322 _____. "Medea," in <u>Collected Poems</u> (1903).

1323 _____. "Memnon," in <u>Ballads and Sketches</u> (1860).

1324 _____. "Minos," in <u>Collected Poems</u> (1903).

1325 _____. "Niobe," in <u>Collected Poems</u> (1903).

1326 _____. "Ode to Pan," in <u>Poems</u> (First Series, 1893).

1327 _____. "Ode to the Sun," in <u>Collected Poems</u> (1903).

1328 _____. "Orestes," a play, in <u>Collected Poems</u> (1903).

1329 _____. "Orpheus in Hades," in <u>Poems</u> (Second Series, 1895).

1330 _____. "Orpheus in Thrace," in <u>Orpheus in Thrace</u> (1901).

1331 _____. "Pandora," in <u>Poems</u> (First Series, 1893).

1332 _____. "Phaethon," in <u>Poems</u> (First Series, 1893).

1333 _____. "Philoctetes," in <u>Collected Poems</u> (1903).

1334 _____. "Philoctetes," a play, in <u>The Selected Poems of Lord de Tabley</u>, ed. by John Drinkwater. London: Oxford University Press, 1924.

1335 _____. "Proserpine at Enna," in <u>Ballads and Sketches</u> (1860).

1336 _____. "Pygmalion," in <u>Ballads and Sketches</u> (1860).

1337 _____. "Romulus," in <u>Ballads and Sketches</u> (1860).

1338 _____. "Semele," in <u>Collected Poems</u> (1903).

1339 _____. "Semele," in <u>Ballads and Sketches</u> (1860). Not the same as poem listed above.

1340 _____. "The Siren to Ulysses," in <u>Collected Poems</u> (1903).

1341 _____. "The Spear of Achilles," in <u>Orpheus in Thrace</u> (1901).

1342 _____. "Zeus," in <u>Collected Poems</u> (1903).

DEUTSCH, Babette (1895- , American)

1343 "Epistle to Prometheus, " in Collected Poems, 1919-1962. Bloomington: Indiana University Press, 1963.

1344 _____. "Twentieth Century Hymn to Isis, " in Collected Poems (1963).

DEVLIN, Denis (1908-1959, Irish)

1345 "Bacchanal, " in Collected Poems. Dublin: Dolmen, 1964.

1346 _____. "A Dream of Orpheus, " in Collected Poems (1964).

1347 _____. "Tantalus, " in Collected Poems (1964).

1348 _____. "Venus of the Salty Shell, " in Collected Poems (1964).

DICKEY, James (1923- , American)

1349 "Orpheus Before Hades, " in Into the Stone. New York: Scribner, 1957.

DILLON, George (1906-1968, American)

1350 "Weep, Aphrodite, for Adonis Dead, " in The Flowering Stone and Other Poems. New York: Viking, 1932.

DOW, Dorothy (1903-?, American)

1351 "Echo, " in Black Babylon. New York: Boni & Liveright, 1924.

1352 _____. "Eternal Diana, " in Black Babylon (1924).

1353 _____. "To Atalanta, " in Black Babylon (1924).

DOWDEN, Edward (1843-1913, English)

1354 "The Heroines, " in Poems. London: King, 1876. Helen, Atalanta, Europa, Andromeda, Eurydice, etc.

DOWSON, Ernest (1867-1900, English)

1355 "Libera Me, " in The Poems of Ernest Dowson, ed. by Mark

Longaker. Philadelphia: University of Pennsylvania
Press, 1962.

1356 _____ . "Villanelle of Acheron," in The Poems (1962).

DRINKWATER, John (1882-1937, English)

1357 "The Death of Leander," in The Death of Leander and Other
Poems. Birmingham, England: Cornish, 1906.

1358 _____ . "A Ghost Speaks on the Styx," in New Poems.
Boston: Houghton Mifflin, 1925.

1359 _____ . "Persephone," in Summer Harvest: Poems 1924-
1933. London: Sidgwick and Jackson, 1933.

1360 _____ . "Venus in Arden," in Collected Poems, 2 vols.
London: Sidgwick and Jackson, 1923.

1361 _____ . "X=0: A Night in the Trojan War," in Pawns:
Four Poetic Plays, with Introduction by Jack R. Craw-
ford. Boston: Houghton Mifflin, 1920.

DUNCAN, Robert (1919- , American)

1362 "An Apollonian Elegy," in The Years as Catches: First
Poems, 1939-1946. Berkeley, Calif.: Oyez, 1966.

1363 _____ . "Atlantis," in The Opening of the Field. New
York: Grove, 1960.

1364 _____ . "The Chimeras of Gerard de Nerval," translations
based on the work of Gerard Labrunie; pseudonym Gerard
de Nerval (1808-1855, French), in Bending the Bow. New
York: New Directions, 1968.

1365 _____ . Medea at Kolchis: The Maiden Head, a play.
Berkeley, Calif.: Oyez, 1965.

1366 _____ . "Persephone," in The Years as Catches (1966).

DUNKIN, William (1709-1765, English)

1367 "The Judgment of Hercules," in Select Poetical Works.
Dublin: Jones, 1769.

EBERHART, Richard (1904- , American)

1368 "Kaire," in The Quarry: New Poems. New York: Oxford
University Press, 1964.

EBERHART, continued

1369 _____. "Oedipus," in Collected Poems, 1930-1960. New
York: Oxford University Press, 1960.

1370 _____. "Prometheus," in The Quarry (1964).

1371 _____. "The Return of Odysseus," in Collected Poems
(1960).

ELIOT, George (Mary Ann Evans, 1819-1880, English)

1372 "Arion," in The Poems of George Eliot. New York: Hurst,
1900. Refers to a Greek poet of the seventh century A.D.

EMPSON, William (1906-?, English)

1373 "Arachne," in Poems. New York: Harcourt, Brace, 1956.

1374 _____. "Bacchus," in Collected Poems of William Empson. New York: Harcourt, Brace, 1949.

FARJEON, Eleanor (1881-1965, English)

1375 "Apollo in Pherae," in Pan-Worship and Other Poems.
London: Mathews, 1908.

1376 _____. Ariadne and the Bull. London: Joseph, 1945.

1377 _____. "Pan-Worship," in Pan Worship (1908).

FARLEY, Jean (1928-1974, American)

1378 "Kore to Co-ed," in Figure and Field. Durham: University
of North Carolina Press, 1970.

FAUST, Frederick (1892-1944, American)

1379 Dionysus in Hades, a play. Oxford: Blackwell, 1931.

FICKE, Arthur Davison (1883-1945, American)

1380 "Cytherea," in From the Isles: A Series of Songs Out of
Greece. Norwich, England: Samurai, 1907.

1381 _____. "Demeter," in From the Isles (1907).

254

1382 _____. "Dionysus," in From the Isles (1907).

1383 _____. "The Elder Gods," in From the Isles (1907).

1384 _____. "Foam Around Delos," in From the Isles (1907).

FIELD, Edward (1924- , American)

1385 "Icarus," in Stand Up, Friend, with Me. New York: Grove, 1963.

FIELD, Eugene (1850-1895, American)

1386 "Pan Liveth," in Songs and Other Verses. New York: Scribner, 1896.

FIELDS, Mrs. Annie Adams (Mrs. J. T. Fields, 1834-1915, American)

1387 "Achilles," in Under the Olive. Boston: Houghton, Mifflin, 1881.

1388 _____. "Antinous," in Under the Olive (1881).

1389 _____. "Artemis," in Under the Olive (1881).

1390 _____. "Clytia," in The Singing Shepherd and Other Poems. Boston: Houghton, Mifflin, 1895.

1391 _____. "Helena," in Under the Olive (1881).

1392 _____. "Herakles," in Under the Olive (1881).

1393 _____. "The Lantern of Sestos," in Under the Olive (1881).

1394 _____. Orpheus: A Masque. Boston: Houghton, Mifflin, 1900.

1395 _____. The Return of Persephone, a dramatic sketch. Cambridge, Mass.: Privately printed for the author, 1877.

FINKEL, Donald (1929- , American)

1396 "The Sirens," in The Clothing's New Emperor and Other Poems. New York: Scribner, 1959.

FLEETWOOD, Frank (Frances Fleetwood, pseudonym, 1902-?, English)

1397 "Antigone," in The Threshold. London: Selwyn and Blount, 1926.

1398 _____. "Electra," in The Threshold (1926).

1399 _____. "Pan," in The Threshold (1926).

1400 _____. "Sappho," in The Threshold (1926).

FRANK, Florence Kiper (1885-1976, American)

1401 "Hymn to the Wingéd Nike," in The Jew to Jesus and Other Poems. New York: Kennerley, 1915.

1402 _____. "Tennyson's 'The Lotos Eaters,'" in The Jew to Jesus (1915).

FRENEAU, Philip (1752-1832, American)

1403 "A Bacchanalian Dialogue," in Vol. III, The Poems of Philip Freneau, ed. by Fred Louis Pattee. Princeton, N.J.: Princeton University Press, 1902-1907. Reprinted New York: Russell and Russell, 1963.

1404 _____. "Mars and Hymen," in Vol. I, Poems (1963).

1405 _____. "Mars and Venus," in Poems Written Between 1768 and 1794. Monmouth, N.J.: Privately printed, 1795.

1406 _____. "Minerva's Advice," in Poems Written (1795).

1407 _____. "The Monument of Phaon," in Vol. I, Poems (1963).

1408 _____. "The Prayer of Orpheus," in Vol. I, Poems (1963).

FROST, Robert (1875-1963, American)

1409 "Pan with Us," in Complete Poems. New York: Holt, 1949.

FROTHINGHAM, Nathaniel Langdon (1793-1870, American)

1410 "Odysseus and Calypso," in Metrical Pieces. Boston: Crosby, Nichols, 1855.

FULLER, Roy (1912- , English)

1411 "The Centaurs," in Collected Poems: 1936-1961. Philadel-
       phia: Dufour, 1962.

1412 _____. "Faustian Sketches," in Collected Poems (1962).

1413 _____. "The Ides of March," in Collected Poems (1962).

1414 _____. "Mythological Sonnets," in Collected Poems (1962).

FULLER, Sarah Margaret (Countess Ossoli, 1810-1850, American)

1415 "Ganymede to His Eagle," in At Home and Abroad, ed. by
       Arthur B. Fuller. New York: Tribune Association, 1869.

GALSWORTHY, John (1867-1933, English)

1416 "Botticelli's 'The Birth of Venus,'" in The Collected Poems
       of John Galsworthy. New York: Scribner, 1934.

1417 _____. "Botticelli's 'Primavera,'" in Collected Poems
       (1934).

GARRETT, George (1929- , American)

1418 "Narcissus," in The Sleeping Gypsy and Other Poems. Aus-
       tin: University of Texas Press, 1958.

1419 _____. "Tiresias," in The Sleeping Gypsy (1958).

1420 _____. "Underworld," in The Sleeping Gypsy (1958).

GASCOYNE, David (1916- , English)

1421 "Orpheus in the Underworld," in Collected Poems, ed. with
       Introduction by Robin Skelton. London: Oxford University
       Press, 1965.

1422 _____. "Venus Androgyne," in Collected Poems (1965).

GAY, John (1685-1732, English)

1423 "Achilles," an opera, in Poetical Works of John Gay, ed. by
       G. C. Faber. London: Oxford University Press, 1926.

1424 _____. "Acis and Galatea: An English Pastoral Opera,"
       in Poetical Works (1926). Libretto for music by Handel.

GIBSON, Charles Dana (1867-1945, American)

1425 "Hero and Leander," in The Spirit of Love and Other Poems.
Boston: Privately printed for the author, 1906.

1426 _____. "Orpheus and Eurydice," in Spirit of Love (1906).

GLOVER, Richard (1712-1785, English)

1427 The Athenaid, A Sequel to Leonides. Dublin: Byrne,
McKenzie, and Moore, 1788.

1428 _____. Boadicea, a Tragedy. London: Bell, 1778.

1429 _____. Jason, a Tragedy. London: Debrett, 1799.

1430 _____. Leonidas. Dublin: Smith and Bruce, 1737.

1431 _____. Medea, a Tragedy. Dublin: Chamberlaine, 1761.

GOETHE, Johann Wolfgang von (1749-1832, German).

1432 "Ganymede," in The Permanent Goethe, ed. with Introduction
by Thomas Mann. New York: Dial, 1948. Translated
from German by Theodore Martin.

1433 _____. "Phoebus and Hermes," in The Permanent (1948).

1434 _____. "Prometheus," in The Permanent (1948).

GOGARTY, Oliver St. John (1878-1957, Irish)

1435 "Europa and the Bull," in Selected Poems. London: Constable, 1933.

1436 _____. "Leda and the Swan," in Selected Poems (1933).

GOODMAN, Paul (1911-1972, American)

1437 "Alcestis's Speech," in The Lordly Hudson: Collected Poems.
New York: Macmillan, 1962.

1438 _____. "Ballade to Venus," in Lordly Hudson (1962).

1439 _____. "Danae (After Titian)," in Lordly Hudson (1962).

1440 _____. "In Lydia," in Lordly Hudson (1962).

1441 _____. "Io Pan!" in Lordly Hudson (1962).

1442 _____. "Orion," in Collected Poems, ed. by Taylor
Stoehr, with Memoir by George Dennison. New York:
Vintage, 1977.

1443 _____. "Orpheus and Mozart," in Lordly Hudson (1962).

1444 _____. "Orpheus in the Underworld," a short story, in
A Ceremonial: Stories 1936-1940, Vol. II of the Collected
Stories, ed. by Taylor Stoehr. Santa Barbara, Calif.:
Black Sparrow, 1978.

1445 _____. "Phaethon," a short story, in The Break-up of
Our Camp: Stories 1932-1935, Vol. I of the Collected
Stories, ed. by Taylor Stoehr. Santa Barbara, Calif.:
Black Sparrow, 1978.

1446 _____. "Philoctetes," in Lordly Hudson (1962).

1447 _____. "Reading 'Adonais,'" in Collected Poems (1977).

1448 _____. "Sirens," in Collected Poems (1977).

1449 _____. "A Sphinx," in Collected Poems (1977).

1450 _____. "A Statue of Nestor," a short story, in A Ceremonial (1978).

1451 _____. "Theseus," in Lordly Hudson (1962).

1452 _____. "Venus and Mars," in Lordly Hudson (1962).

GORE-BOOTH, Eva (1870-1926, English)

1453 "The Death of Orpheus," in The Agate Lamp. London:
Longmans, Green, 1912.

1454 _____. "Narcissus," in The Three Resurrections and The
Triumph of Maeve. London: Longmans, Green, 1905.

1455 _____. "Proserpine," in The One and the Many. London:
Longmans, Green, 1904.

1456 _____. "The Three Resurrections: Lazarus, Alcestis,
and Psyche," in The Three Resurrections (1905).

GOULD, Gerald (1885-1936, English)

1457 "Helen," in Collected Poems. London and New York: Pay-
son and Clarke, 1929.

GOULD, Wallace (?-?, American)

1458 "Aphrodite," in Aphrodite and Other Poems. New York:
      Macaulay, 1928.

1459 _____. "Drunken Heracles," in Aphrodite (1928).

1460 _____. "Endymion," in Aphrodite (1928).

GRANT, Percy Stickney (1860-1927, American)

1461 "Hero at Sestos," in A Fifth Avenue Parade. New York:
      Harper, 1922.

1462 _____. The Return of Odysseus: A Poetic Drama in
      Four Acts. New York: Brentano, 1912.

GRAVES, Arnold F. (?-?, English)

1463 Clytaemnestra, a Tragedy, with Preface by Robert Y. Tyr-
      rell. London: Longmans, Green, 1903.

GUTHRIE, William Norman (1868-1944, American)

1464 "The Coming of Dionysus," in Songs of American Destiny:
      A Vision of New Hellas. Cincinnati: Clarke, 1900.

1465 _____. "Orpheus Today," in Orpheus Today, Saint Francis
      of the Trees and Other Verse. Cincinnati: Western
      Literary Press, 1907.

1466 _____. "The Vision of Demeter," in Songs (1900).

HAGEDORN, Hermann (1882-1964, American)

1467 "The Great Maze," in The Great Maze and the Heart of Youth.
      New York: Macmillan, 1916. Refers to Clytemnestra.

HAYDEN, Robert (1913-1980, American)

1468 "O Daedalus, Fly Away Home," in Selected Poems. New
      York: October House, 1966.

HAYNE, Paul Hamilton (1830-1886, American)

1469 "Aethra," in Poems of Paul Hamilton Hayne. Boston:
      Lothrop, 1882.

260

1470 _____. "Ancient Myths," in <u>Poems</u> (1882).

1471 _____. "Cambyses and the Macrobian Bow," in <u>Poems</u> (1882).

1472 _____. "Daphles," in <u>Poems</u> (1882).

1473 _____. "The Dryad of the Pine," in <u>Poems</u> (1882).

1474 _____. "Hera," in <u>Poems</u> (1882).

1475 _____. "Isles of the Blest," in <u>Poems by Paul Hamilton</u>
Hayne. Boston: Ticknor and Fields, 1855.

1476 _____, "Lethe," in <u>Poems</u> (1882).

1477 _____. "Song of the Naiads," in <u>Poems</u> (1882).

1478 _____. "The Story of Glaucus the Thessalian," in <u>Poems</u>
(1882).

1479 _____. "The Temptation of Venus: A Monkish Legend,"
in <u>Poems</u> (1855).

1480 _____. "The Vengeance of the Goddess Diana," in <u>Poems</u>
(1882).

HEATH-STUBBS, John Francis Alexander (1918- , English)

1481 "The Dark Planet," in <u>Selected Poems</u>. New York and London: Oxford University Press, 1958.

1482 _____. "The Sphinx," in <u>The Blue-Fly in His Head:</u>
<u>Poems</u>. London: David Higham, 1962. Reprinted in
<u>Selected Poems</u> (1958).

HENDERLAND, George (?-?, English)

1483 "Marsyas," in <u>Dawn and Other Poems</u>. London: Mathews,
1929.

1484 _____. "Sarpedon," in <u>Dawn</u> (1929).

HENLEY, William Ernest (1849-1903, English)

1485 "The Gods Are Dead," in <u>Poems</u>. New York: Scribner, 1926.

HEPPENSTALL, John Rayner (1911- , English)

1486 "Actaeon," in <u>Poems: 1933-1945</u>. London: Secker and Warburg,
1946.

HERVEY, Thomas Kibble (1799-1859, English)

1487 "Aeneas and Dido," in Poems, ed. by Mrs. T. K. Hervey.
      Boston: Ticknor and Fields, 1866.

1488 _____. "Arethusa," in Poems (1866).

1489 _____. "Diana," in Poems (1866).

1490 _____. "Erato: The Muse of Love," in Poems (1866).

1491 _____. "Hebe," in Poems (1866).

1492 _____. "Mercury and Pandora," in Poems (1866).

1493 _____. "Prometheus," in Poems (1866).

1494 _____. "The Sleeping Nymph," in Poems (1866). Refers
      to Echo.

1495 _____. "Venus," in Poems (1866).

1496 _____. "Venus Weeping for Adonis," in Poems (1866).

HIGGINS, Alexander George McLennon Pearce (?-?, English)

1497 "Hecuba," Part I, in Marcellus and Other Poems. Oxford:
      Blackwell, 1926.

1498 Hecuba, Parts I and II. London: Benn, 1928.

HILL, Eleanor Deane (?-?, English)

1499 "Demeter," in Demeter and Other Poems. Oxford: Black-
      well, 1918.

1500 _____. "The Jest on Marsyas," in The Jest on Marsyas
      and Other Poems. London: Mathews and Marrot, 1929.

1501 _____. "Polyphemus," in The Questing Prince. London:
      Methuen, 1923.

1502 _____. "Song of Bacchanals," in The Questing Prince
      (1923).

HILL, Geoffrey (1932- , English)

1503 "Orpheus and Eurydice," in For the Unfallen: Poems, 1952-
      1958. London: Dufour, 1959.

1504 _____. "The Rebirth of Venus," in For the Unfallen (1959).

HILL, George (1796-1871, American)

1505 "Circe and Telemachus," in Titiana's Banquet: Pictures of
 Woman. New York: Appleton, 1870. Third edition.

HILLYER, Robert Silliman (1895-1961, American)

1506 "Antinous," in Sonnets and Other Lyrics. Cambridge, Mass.:
 Harvard University Press, 1917.

1507 _____. "The Lost Music," in The Relic and Other Poems.
 New York: Random House, 1957. Refers to Orpheus.

HOLE, W. G. (?-?, English)

1508 The Chained Titan: A Poem of Yesterday and Today. London: Bell, 1910.

1509 _____. "Gyges Replies to the Queen," in Poems Lyrical
 and Dramatic. London: Mathews, 1902.

1510 _____. "The Naiad to the Hamadryad," in Poems Lyrical
 (1902).

1511 _____. "Procris," in Procris and Other Poems. London:
 Kegan Paul, 1886.

HOLLANDER, John (1929- , American)

1512 "The Great Bear," in A Crackling of Thorns, with Introduction by W. H. Auden. New Haven, Conn.: Yale University Press, 1958.

1513 _____. "Helicon," in Visions from the Ramble. New
 York: Athenaeum, 1965.

HOLLOWAY, John (1920- , English)

1514 "Apollonian Poem," in The Minute and Longer Poems. East
 Yorkshire, England: Marvell, 1956.

1515 _____. "Hephaistos," in The Minute (1956).

1516 _____. "Ulysses," in The Minute (1956).

HOLMES, Oliver Wendell (1809-1894, American)

1517 "The First Faun," in The Poetical Works of Oliver Wendell
 Holmes. Boston: Houghton, Mifflin, 1880.

HOLMES, continued

1518 _____. "The Meeting of the Dryads," in Poetical Works
       (1880).

HOOD, Thomas (1759-1845, English)

1519 "Flowers," in The Complete Poetical Works of Thomas Hood,
     ed. with Notes and Introduction by Walter Jerrold and
     Humphrey Milford. London: Oxford University Press,
     1920. Refers to Clytie.

1520 _____. "Hero and Leander," in Poetical Works (1920).

1521 _____. "Lamia," in Poetical Works (1920).

1522 _____. "Lycus the Centaur," in Poetical Works (1920).

1523 _____. "Ode to the Moon," in Poetical Works (1920).

1524 _____. "Sonnet: Written in Keats' 'Endymion,'" in
     Poetical Works (1920).

HOUSMAN, Laurence (1865-1959, English)

1525 "Antaeus," in The Collected Poems of Laurence Housman.
     London: Sidgwick and Jackson, 1937.

1526 _____. "Apollo in Hades," in The Wheel: Three Poetic
     Plays on Greek Subjects. New York: French, 1920.

1527 _____. "The Death of Alcestis," in The Wheel (1920).

1528 _____. The Death of Orpheus, a play. London: Sidgwick
     and Jackson, 1921.

1529 _____. The Death of Socrates, a dramatic scene. Boston:
     Small, Maynard, 1925.

1530 _____. "The Doom of Admetus," in The Wheel (1920).
     Published in 1916 as "The Return of Alcestis."

1531 _____. "The New Narcissus," in Collected Poems (1937).

1532 _____. "Orpheus and the Phoenix," in The Love Concealed.
     London: Sidgwick and Jackson, 1928.

HOVEY, Richard (1864-1900, American)

1533 "The Faun," in Along the Trail: A Book of Lyrics. Boston:
     Small, Maynard, 1898.

HOWES, Barbara (1914- , American)

1534 "Chimera," in Light and Dark. Middletown, Conn.: Wes-
      leyan University Press, 1958. Reprinted in A Private
      Signal. Middletown: Wesleyan University Press, 1977.

1535 _____. "Danae," in Light and Dark (1958). Reprinted in
      A Private Signal (1977).

HUNTINGTON, Channing Moore (?-?, American)

1536 "A Day in the Homeric Age," in A Bachelor's Wife and Other
      Poems. Utica, N.Y.: Kelly and Bostwick, 1889.

HUNTINGTON, Elizabeth (1893-1928, American)

1537 "Endymion," in The Playground of the Gods. Boston: Four
      Seas, 1921.

1538 _____. "Proserpine," in The Playground (1921).

1539 _____. "Psyche in Cupid's Palace," in The Playground
      (1921).

IGNATOW, David (1914- , American)

1540 "Oedipus," in Figures of the Human. Middletown, Conn.:
      Wesleyan University Press, 1964. Reprinted in Earth
      Hard. London: Rapp and Whiting, 1968.

1541 _____. "The Sphinx," in Figures of the Human (1964).

JEFFREY, William (1896-1946, English)

1542 "Andromeda," in The Wise Men Come to Town. London:
      Gowans and Gray, 1923.

1543 _____. "The Doom of Atlas," in The Doom of Atlas and
      Other Poems. London: Gowans and Gray, 1926.

1544 _____. The Nymph. Edinburgh: Porpoise, 1924.

1545 _____. "Prometheus Returns," in Prometheus Returns
      and Other Poems. London: Macdonald, 1921.

KAVANAGH, Patrick Joseph Gregory (1905-1967, Irish)

1546 "Pegasus," in A Soul for Sale. London: Macmillan, 1947.

KEMP, Harry (1883-?, American)

1547 "Calypso," in Boccaccio's Untold Tale and Other One-Act Plays. New York: Brentano, 1924.

1548 _____. "Cresseid," in The Passing God and Other Poems. New York: Brentano, 1919.

1549 _____. "Helen," in The Sea and the Dunes. New York: Brentano, 1926.

1550 _____. "Helen in Hades," in The Passing God (1919).

1551 _____. "The Mirrored Venus," in The Passing God (1919).

1552 _____. "The Passing God," in The Passing God (1919).

1553 _____. "To Atthis," in The Passing God (1919).

KENDALL, Henry Clarence (1839-1882, Australian)

1553a "Daphne," in Leaves from Australian Forests. Melbourne: Robertson, 1869.

1554 _____. "Merope," in Leaves (1869).

1555 _____. "Ogyges," in Leaves (1869).

1556 _____. "Syrinx," in Leaves (1869).

1557 _____. "The Voyage of Telegonus," in Leaves (1869).

KUNITZ, Stanley (1905- , American)

1558 "The Flight of Apollo," in The Poems of Stanley Kunitz: 1928-1978. Boston: Little, Brown, 1979.

1559 _____. "For Proserpine," in Poems (1979).

LANGLAND, Joseph Thomas (1917- , American)

1560 "Fall of Icarus: Brueghel," in The Green Town: Poems. New York: Scribner, 1956.

LATHROP, George Parsons (1851-1898, American)

1561 "Helen at the Loom," in Rose and Roof Tree. Boston: Osgood, 1875.

LAW, Alice (1886- ?, English)

1562 "Cupid and Psyche," in Cupid and Psyche and Other Poems.
London: Mathews, 1919.

1563 _____. Iphigenia: A Tragedy. Altham, Accrington,
England: Old Parsonage, 1931.

LAWRENCE, D. H. (David Herbert, 1885-1930, English)

1564 "The Argonauts," in Complete Poems of D. H. Lawrence,
2 vols., ed. by Vivian de Sola Pinto and Warren Roberts.
New York: Viking, 1964.

1565 _____. "The Greeks Are Coming," in Complete Poems
(1964).

1566 _____. "Hymn to Priapus," in Complete Poems (1964).

1567 _____. "Leda," in Complete Poems (1964).

1568 _____. "Middle of the World," in Complete Poems (1964).
Mainly refers to Dionysus.

LAZARUS, Emma (1849-1887, American)

1569 "Admetus," in Admetus and Other Poems. New York: Hurd
and Houghton, 1871.

1570 _____. "Aphrodite," in Poems and Translations. Boston:
Hurd and Houghton, 1867.

1571 _____. "Clytie," in Poems and Translations (1867).

1572 _____. "Daphne," in Poems and Translations (1867).

1573 _____. "Orpheus," in Admetus (1871).

1574 _____. "Penelope's Choice," in Poems and Translations
(1867).

LEDOUX, Louis Vernon (1880-1948, American)

1575 "Persephone: A Masque," in The Shadow of Aetna. New
York and London: Putnam, 1914.

1576 _____. The Story of Eleusis: A Lyrical Drama. New
York: Macmillan, 1916. Refers to Demeter.

267

LE GALLIENNE, Richard (1866-1947, English)

1577 "Alma Venus," in The Lonely Dancer and Other Poems.
      London: Lane, 1914.

1578 _____. "The House of Venus," in English Poems. Lon-
      don: Mathews and Lane; New York: Cassell, 1892.

1579 _____. Orestes: A Tragedy. New York: Kennerley,
      1910.

1580 _____. Perseus and Andromeda: The Story Retold.
      New York: Russell, 1902.

LINKLATER, Eric (1899-1974, Scottish)

1581 "Silenus," in A Dragon Laughed and Other Poems. London:
      Cape, 1930.

LITCHFIELD, Grace Denio (1849-1944, American)

1582 "Icarus," in Collected Poems. New York and London:
      Putnam, 1913.

1583 _____. "Narcissus," in Collected Poems (1913).

1584 _____. "Semele," in Collected Poems (1913).

1585 _____. The Song of the Sirens. New York and London:
      Putnam, 1917. Reprinted in Collected Poems. New
      York: Putnam, 1922.

LODGE, George Cabot (1873-1909, American)

1586 "The Greek Galley," in Poems: 1899-1902. New York:
      Cameron and Blake, 1902.

1587 _____. "Herakles," a drama, in Poems and Dramas of
      George Cabot Lodge, 2 vols. Boston: Houghton Mifflin,
      1911.

1588 _____. "Kalypso," in The Great Adventure. Boston and
      New York: Houghton Mifflin, 1905.

1589 _____. "Odysseus," in The Great Adventure (1905).

1590 _____. "Tannhauser to Venus," in Poems (1902).

LOW, Benjamin Robbins Curtis (1880-1941, American)

1591 "Galatea," in The Sailor Who Sailed. New York: Lane, 1911.

1592 _____. "Penelope," in The Sailor (1911).

1593 _____. "Pygmalion to Galatea," in Broken Music. New York: Dutton, 1920.

LOWE, Helen (?-?, English)

1594 "Cephalus and Procris," in Poems, Chiefly Dramatic. London: Pickering, 1840.

LOWELL, Amy (Lawrence, 1874-1925, American)

1595 "Hippocrene," in The Complete Poetical Works of Amy Lowell, with Introduction by Louis Untermeyer. Boston: Houghton Mifflin, 1955.

1596 _____. "The Pleiades," in Poetical Works (1955).

1597 _____. "The Sibyl," in Poetical Works (1955).

1598 _____. "Venus Transiens," in Poetical Works (1955).

LUCAS, Frank Laurence (1894-1967, English)

1599 Ariadne. London: Cambridge University Press, 1932.

1600 _____. "Coresus and Callirrhoe," in Time and Memory. London: L. and V. Woolf, 1929.

1601 _____. "The Destinies," in Marionettes. New York: Macmillan, 1930.

1602 _____. "The Elms of Protesilaus," in Time and Memory (1929).

1603 _____. "Pygmalion to Galatea," in Marionettes (1930).

MACAULAY, Thomas Babington (1800-1859, English)

1604 Lays of Ancient Rome, ed. with Notes and Introduction by Arthur Beatty. New York: Scribner, 1912. Consists of "Horatius," "The Battle of Lake Regillus," "Virginia," and "The Prophecy of Capys."

McCLYMONT, James Roxburgh (?-?, English)

1605 "The Golden Age," in Metrical Romances and Ballads. London: Ouseley, 1912.

1606 _____. "Hera in the Hesperides," in The Land of False Delight. London: Heath, Cranton, and Ouseley, 1913.

1607 _____. "Theseus in Crete," in Metrical Romances (1912).

McCULLOCH, Hugh (1869-1902, American)

1608 "Antinous," in The Quest of Heracles. Cambridge and Chicago: Stone and Kimball, 1894.

1609 _____. "The Death of Pan," in Written in Florence. London: Dent, 1902.

1610 _____. "Hermaphroditus," in The Quest (1894).

1611 _____. "Phaeton," in The Quest (1894).

1612 _____. "The Quest of Heracles," in The Quest (1894).

1613 _____. "The Triumph of Bacchus," in Written in Florence (1902).

McGIFFERT, Gertrude Huntington (?-?, American)

1614 "A Greek Cycle," in Cast in Bronze. Portland, Me.: Mosher, 1929.

MACKAIL, John William (1859-1945), Henry Charles Beeching (1859-1919), and Bowyer Nicholas (1859-1939, English)

1615 "In Scheria," 2 parts, in Love in Idleness (by Beeching). London: Kegan Paul, 1883. Reprinted as "Nausicaa" and "The Return of Ulysses," in Love's Looking Glass (by Beeching, Mackail, and Nicholas). London: Percival, 1891.

MacKAYE, Percy (1875-1956, American)

1616 "The Chase," in Poems and Plays, 2 vols. New York: Macmillan, 1916. Refers to Diana.

1617 _____. "Dionysus," in Poems and Plays (1916).

1618 _____. "Lethe," in Poems and Plays (1916).

270

1619 _____. Sappho and Phaon, a tragedy. New York:
        Macmillan, 1907. Reprinted in Poems and Plays (1916).

MacNEICE, Louis (1907-1964, Irish)

1620 "Autolycus," in The Collected Poems of Louis MacNeice,
        ed. by E. R. Dodds. New York: Oxford University
        Press, 1967.

1621 _____. "Charon," in Collected Poems (1967).

1622 _____. "Circe," in Collected Poems (1967).

1623 _____. "The grey ones ...," in Collected Poems (1967).

1624 _____. "Perseus," in Collected Poems (1967).

1625 _____. "The Stygian Banks," in Collected Poems (1967).

1626 _____. "Thalassa," in Collected Poems (1967).

1627 _____. "Thyestes," in Collected Poems (1967).

1628 _____. "Venus' Speech," in Poems: 1925-1940. New
        York: Random House, 1940.

MALONE, Walter (1866-1915, American)

1629 "The Fallen Gods," in Selected Poems by Judge Walter
        Malone, ed. by Ella Malone Watson (sister). Louisville,
        Ky.: Morton, 1919.

1630 _____. "The Greek Boy," in Selected Poems (1919).

1631 _____. "Homer," in Selected Poems (1919).

1632 _____. "Narcissus," in Narcissus and Other Poems.
        Philadelphia: Lippincott, 1893. Reprinted in Selected
        Poems (1919).

1633 _____. "Orpheus and the Sirens," in Narcissus (1893).

1634 _____. "Song of the Dying Orpheus," in The Outcast and
        Other Poems. Cambridge, Mass.: Riverside, 1886.

MANIFOLD, John (1915- , Australian)

1635 "Bellerophon," in Collected Verse. Queensland, Australia:
        University of Queensland Press, 1978.

MANIFOLD, continued

1636 _____. "Helen and Theseus," in Collected Verse (1978).

1637 _____. "The Sirens," in Collected Verse (1978).

MANNING, Frederic (1887-1935, Australian)

1638 "Danae," in Eidola. London: Murray, 1917.

1639 _____. "Demeter Mourning," in Eidola (1917).

1640 _____. "The Faun," in Eidola (1917).

1641 _____. "Kore," in Poems. London: Murray, 1910.

1642 _____. "Pythagoras," in Scenes and Portraits. New
         York: Putnam; London: Murray, 1909.

1643 _____. "Theseus and Hippolyta," in Poems (1910).

MARKHAM, Edwin (1852-1940, American)

1644 "Divine Aphrodite," in New Poems: Eighty Songs at Eighty.
         Garden City, N.Y.: Doubleday, Doran, 1932.

1645 _____. "Hellas Again," in New Poems (1932).

1646 _____. "Pan Encountered," in New Poems (1932).

1647 _____. "A Prayer at the Altar of Hermes," in New
         Poems (1932).

1648 _____. "The Story of Bacchus," in Lincoln and Other
         Poems. New York: McClure, Phillips, 1901.

MAVROGORDATO, John (1882- , English)

1649 Cassandra in Troy, a prose drama. London: Secker, 1914.

MEREDITH, William (1919- , American)

1650 "After Greece," in Water Street. New York: Atheneum,
         1967.

1651 _____. "Orpheus," in The Wreck of the Thresher and
         Other Poems. New York: Knopf, 1965.

MERWIN, W. S. (1927- , American)

1652 "December of Aphrodite, " in The Dancing Bears. New
Haven, Conn.: Yale University Press, 1954.

1653 _____. "Odysseus: For George Kirstein, " in The Drunk
in the Furnace and Other Poems. New York: Macmillan,
1956.

1654 _____. "Proteus, " in The Dancing Bears (1954).

1655 _____. "When I Came from Colchis, " in The Dancing
Bears (1954).

MIDDLETON, Richard Barham (1882-1911, English)

1656 "Hylas, " in Poems and Songs: Second Series, ed. with
Preface by Henry Savage. London: Unwin, 1912.

1657 _____. "Pan, " in Poems and Songs (1912).

1658 _____. "To Diana, " in Poems and Songs (1912).

MILLER, Vassar (1924- , American).

1659 "The New Icarus, " in Wage War in Silence. Middletown,
Conn.: Wesleyan University Press, 1960.

1660 _____. "Note of Apology to Medea, " in My Bones Being
Wiser. Middletown, Conn.: Wesleyan University Press,
1963.

MONRO, Harold Edward (1879-1932, English)

1661 "Ariadne in Naxos, " in Collected Poems. London: Duckworth, 1906.

1662 _____. "Clytie, " in Collected Poems (1906).

1663 _____. "Pausanias, " in Collected Poems (1906).

MONTGOMERY, Roselle Mercier (?-1933, American)

1664 "Atalanta, " in Many Devices. New York: Appleton-Century,
1929.

1665 _____. "Daedalus, " in Many Devices (1929).

MONTGOMERY, continued

1666 _____. "Marpessa," in Many Devices (1929).

1667 _____. "Ulysses Returns," in Ulysses Returns and Other Poems. New York: Brentano, 1925.

MOORE, Charles Leonard (1854-?, American)

1668 "Herackles," in Poems: Antique and Modern. Philadelphia: Potter, 1883.

1669 _____. "Prometheus," in Poems (1883).

MOORE, Thomas Sturge (1870-1944, English)

1670 "Agathon to Lysis," in The Sea Is Kind. Boston: Houghton Mifflin, 1914.

1671 _____. "Alcestis," in The Vinedresser and Other Poems. London: At the Sign of the Unicorn, 1899.

1672 _____. Aphrodite Against Artemis, a tragedy. London: At the Sign of the Unicorn, 1901.

1673 _____. "A Chorus of Dorides," in The Vinedresser (1899).

1674 _____. "A Chorus of Greek Girls," in The Sea Is Kind (1914).

1675 _____. "Daimonassa," in Mystery and Tragedy: Two Dramatic Poems. London: Cayme, 1930.

1676 _____. "Danae," in Danae and Other Poems. London: Richards, 1903. Revised edition, 1920.

1677 _____. "Daphne," in The Vinedresser (1899).

1678 _____. "A Daughter of Admetus," in Poems: Collected Edition, 4 vols. London and New York: Macmillan, 1931-1933.

1679 _____. "The Home of Helen," in The Sea Is Kind (1914).

1680 _____. "Io," in The Sea Is Kind (1914).

1681 _____. "Lines on Titian's 'Bacchanal,'" in The Gazelles and Other Poems. London: Duckworth, 1904.

1682 _____. "Medea," in Tragic Mothers. London: Richards, 1920.

274

1683 _____ . "Niobe, " in Tragic Mothers (1920).

1684/5 _____ . "Omphale and Heracles, " in Poems (1931-1933).

1686/7 _____ . "Psyche in Hades, " in Mystery and Tragedy
(1930).

1688 _____ . "Pygmalion, " in The Vinedresser (1899).

1689 _____ . The Rout of the Amazons.   London: Duckworth,
1903.

1690 _____ . "Sappho's Death, " in The Vinedresser (1899).

1691 _____ . "Semele, " in The Sea Is Kind (1914).

1692 _____ . "The Song of Cheiron, " in The Sea Is Kind (1914).

1693 _____ . "Theseus, " in Poems (1931-1933).

1694 _____ . "The Thigh of Zeus, " in The Sea Is Kind (1914).

1695 _____ . "To Leda, " in To Leda and Other Odes.   London:
Duckworth, 1904.

MORGAN, Evan (1860-?, English)

1696 "An Incident in the Life of Ganymede, " in The City of Canals.
London: Routledge, 1929.

1697 _____ . "The Lament, " in The City of Canals (1929).

1698 _____ . Psyche, a fragment.   Oxford: Blackwell, 1920.

MORGAN, Frank (?-?, English)

1699 "Daphne, " in The Quest of Beauty.   London: Parsons, 1926.

1700 _____ . "Hero and Leander, " in The Quest (1926).

1701 _____ "Jason and Medea, " in The Quest (1926).

1702 _____ . "Theseus and Ariadne, " in The Quest (1926).

NEMEROV, Howard (1920- , American)

1703 "Antigone, " in The Collected Poems of Howard Nemerov.
Chicago: University of Chicago Press, 1977.

1704 _____ . "Mars, " in Collected Poems (1977).

275

NEMEROV, continued

1705 _____. "A Predecessor of Perseus," in Collected Poems
(1977).

1706 _____. "To Clio, Muse of History," in Collected Poems
(1977).

NEWSON, Ranald (?-?, English)

1707 "Apollo in Galilee," in Interrupted Serenade. London: New
Temple, 1932.

1708 _____. Apollo and Marsyas, an idyl. London: New
Temple, 1930.

1709 _____. "Helen of Argos," a play in 2 parts, in Opus
Eight. London: New Temple, 1932.

1710 _____. "Procris and the Faun," in For Saxophone and
Harpsichord. London: New Temple, 1932.

1711 _____. Sappho, a Lyrical Drama. London: New Temple,
1929.

NOEL, Roden Berkeley Wriothesley (1834-1894, English)

1712 "Ganymede," in Beatrice and Other Poems. London:
Macmillan, 1868.

1713 _____. "Pan," in Beatrice (1868).

1714 _____. "The Triumph of Bacchus," in A Modern Faust.
London: Kegan Paul, 1888.

NORMAN, Charles (1904-?, American)

1715 "Telemachus," in The Bright World and Other Poems.
New York: Morrow, 1930.

OLLIER, Edmund (1827-1886, English)

1716 "Bacchus in the East," in Poems from the Greek Mythology.
London: Hotten, 1867.

1717 _____. "Eleusinia," in Poems (1867).

1718 _____. "Pan," in Poems (1867).

1719 _____. "Proserpina in the Shades," in Poems (1867).

1720 _____. "Proteus," in Poems (1867).

PALGRAVE, Francis Turner (1824-1897, English)

1721 "Alcestis," in Lyrical Poems. London: Macmillan, 1871.

1722 _____. "Pausanias and Cleonicé," in Amenophis and Other Poems. London: Macmillan, 1892.

PARNELL, Thomas (1679-1718, English)

1723 "Bacchus; or, The Drunken Metamorphoses," in Poetical Works of Thomas Parnell, with "Life of the Author," by Rev. John Mitford. London: Bell and Doldy, 1866.

1724 _____. "Elysium," in Poetical Works (1866).

1725 _____. "Hesiod; or, The Rise of Woman," in Poetical Works (1866).

1726 _____. "The Judgment of Paris," in Poetical Works (1866).

PATCHEN, Kenneth (1911-1972, American)

1727 "Anubis," in Cloth of the Tempest. New York: Padell, 1948.

1728 _____. "Niobe," in The Collected Poems of Kenneth Patchen. New York: New Directions, 1968.

PATER, Walter Horatio (1839-1894, English)

1729 "The Bacchanals of Euripides," in Greek Studies: A Series of Essays. London: Macmillan, 1895. Reprinted as Vol. 7, Works of Walter Pater, 8 vols. London: Macmillan, 1901.

1730 _____. "Hippolytus Veiled: A Study from Euripides," in Greek Studies (1895).

1731 _____. The Marriage of Cupid and Psyche, illustrated by Edmund Dulac. New York: Heritage, 1951. "The story as first set down by Lucius Apuelius in his 'Transformations' which is called The Golden Ass and then retold by Walter Pater in the pages of his novel Marius the Epicurean."

1732 _____. "The Myth of Demeter and Persephone," Parts I and II, first appeared in Fortnightly Review, 25 (1876). Reprinted in Greek Studies (1895).

1733 _____. "A Study of Dionysus: The Spiritual Form of Fire and Dew," in Greek Studies (1895).

PATON, Sir Joseph Noel (1821-1901, English)

1734 "Actaeon in Hades," in Spindrift. Edinburgh: Blackwood, 1867.

1735 _____. "Ariadne," in Poems by a Painter. Edinburgh and London: Blackwood, 1861.

1736 _____. "Circe," in Poems by a Painter (1861).

1737 _____. "Hymn to Aphrodite," in Poems by a Painter (1861).

1738 _____. "Narcissus," in Poems by a Painter (1861).

1739 _____. "Pan and Syrinx," in Poems by a Painter (1861).

1740 _____. "The Song of Silenus," in Poems by a Painter (1861).

1741 _____. "Syrinx," in Poems by a Painter (1861).

1742 _____. "Ulysses in Ogygia," in Spindrift (1867).

PATTERSON, J. E. (?-?, English)

1743 "Daughters of Nereus," in The Lure of the Sea. New York: Doran, 1912.

PAYNE, John (1842-1916, English)

1744 "Anchises," in The Poetical Works of John Payne, 2 vols. London: Printed for the Villon Society by J. E. Brill-Leyden, 1902.

1745 _____. "The Death of Pan," in Carol and Cadence. London: Printed for the Villon Society, 1908.

1746 _____. "Hector," in Carol and Cadence (1908).

1747 _____. "The Last of Hercules," in Poetical Works (1902).

1748 _____ . "The Wrath of Venus," in <u>Carol and Cadence</u>
(1908).

PEACOCK, Thomas Love (1785-1866, English)

1749 "The Death of Oedipus," in Vol. 7, <u>The Works of Thomas</u>
<u>Love Peacock</u>, 10 vols., ed. by H. F. B. Brett-Smith,
and C. E. Jones. London: Constable, 1924-1934. Reprinted New York: AMS, 1967.

1750 _____ . "Ode to Love," in Vol. 7, <u>Works</u> (1967).

1751 _____ . "Phaedra and the Nurse," in Vol. 7, <u>Works</u>
(1967).

1752 _____ . "Polyxena to Ulysses," in Vol. 7, <u>Works</u> (1967).

1753 _____ . "Rhododaphne: or, the Thessalian Spell," in
Vol. 7, <u>Works</u> (1967).

PERCIVAL, James Gates (1795-1856, American)

1754 "Greece from Mt. Helicon," in <u>Clio</u>, No. 3. New York:
Carvill, 1827. <u>Clio</u>, Nos. 1 and 2. Charleston, S. C.:
Babcock, 1822.

1755 _____ . "The Mythology of Greece," in <u>Clio</u> (1827).

1756 _____ . "Prometheus," Parts I and II, in <u>Poems</u>. New
York: Wiley, 1823.

PERCY, William Alexander (1885-1942, American)

1757 "Calypso to Ulysses," in <u>Enzio's Kingdom and Other Poems</u>.
New Haven, Conn.: Yale University Press, 1924.

1758 _____ . "A Legend of Lacedaemon," in <u>Selected Poems</u>.
New Haven, Conn.: Yale University Press, 1930. Refers
to Castor and Pollux.

1759 _____ . "Medusa," in <u>Selected Poems</u> (1930).

1760 _____ . "Phaon in Hades," in <u>Sappho in Leukas and Other</u>
<u>Poems</u>. New Haven, Conn.: Yale University Press,
1915.

1761 _____ . "Sappho in Leukas," in <u>Sappho</u> (1915).

1762 _____ . "Siren Song," in <u>Enzio's Kingdom</u> (1924).

PERKINS, William Rufus (1847-1895, American)

1763 "Bellerophon," in Eleusis and Lesser Poems. Chicago: McClurg, 1892.

1764 _____. Eleusis, a Narrative Poem. Chicago: Privately printed for the author, 1890.

1765 _____. "Hadrian's Lament over Antinous," in Eleusis (1892).

PETERSON, Henry (1818-1891, American)

1766 "Helen After Troy," in Poems: Second Series. Philadelphia: Lippincott, 1883.

PHELPS, Mrs. Elizabeth Stuart (Mrs. H. D. Ward, 1844-1911, American)

1767 "Eurydice," in Songs of the Silent World. Boston: Houghton, Mifflin, 1885.

1768 _____. "Galatea," in Songs (1885).

PHILLIMORE, John Swinnerton (1873-1926, English)

1769 "Mantis," in Poems. Glasgow: MacLehose, 1902.

1770 _____. "Pan," in Things Old and New. London: Oxford University Press, 1918.

PICKTHALL, Margorie Lowry Christie (1883-1922, English)

1771 "The Little Fauns to Proserpine," in The Drift of Pinions. Montreal: Montreal University Press, 1913.

1772 _____. "To Alcithoe," in The Drift (1913).

PIERCE, Henry Niles (1820-1899, American)

1773 "The Death Chant of Orpheus," in The Agnostic and Other Poems. New York: Whittaker, 1884.

1774 _____. "Eurydice," in The Agnostic (1884).

PIKE, Albert (1809-1891, American)

1775 Hymns to the Gods. Philadelphia: Privately printed, 1854.

PINKNEY, Edward Coote (1802-1828, American)

1776 "Cleonice," in Life and Works of Edward Pinkney, ed. by
Thomas O. Mabbott and Frank Pleadwell. New York:
Macmillan, 1926.

PITTER, Ruth (1897- , English)

1777 Persephone in Hades. New York: Privately printed for the
author, 1931.

1778 _____. "Urania," in Poems: 1926-1966. London:
Barrie and Rockcliff, 1968. Published as Collected
Poems, New York: Macmillan, 1969.

PLATH, Sylvia (1932-1963, American)

1779 "Medusa," in Ariel and Other Poems. New York: Harper
and Row, 1966.

PLOMER, William (1903-c. 1977, English)

1780 "The Archaic Apollo," in Collected Poems. London: Cape,
1960.

1781 _____. "Two Abductions," in Collected Poems (1960).
Refers to Europa and Ganymede.

POE, Edgar Allan (1809-1849, American)

1782 "To Helen," in Collected Works of Edgar Allan Poe: Vol. I,
Poems, ed. by Thomas Mabbott. Cambridge, Mass.:
Belknap, 1969.

POUND, Ezra (1885-1972, American)

1783 "Canto I," in Cantos of Ezra Pound. New York: New Directions, 1948. About Odysseus in the Underworld and Elpenor.

1784 _____. "An Idyl for Glaucus," in Collected Early Poems
of Ezra Pound. New York: New Directions, 1976.

1785 _____. "Pan Is Dead," in Collected Early Poems (1976).

1786 _____. "A Virginal," in Collected Early Poems (1976).

1787 _____. Women of Trachis, an adaptation from Sophocles,
with Introduction by S. V. Jankowski. New York: New
Directions Press, 1957.

PRAED, Winthrop Mackworth (1802-1839, English)

1788   "Athens," in Vol. II, The Poems of Winthrop Mackworth
       Praed, 2 vols., ed. by Derwent Coleridge. London:
       Moxon, 1864.

1789   _____. "Cassandra," in Vol. I, Poems (1864).

PRIOR, Matthew (1664-1721, English)

1790   "Cupid and Ganymede," in Poems on Several Occasions, ed.
       by A. R. Waller. Cambridge: Cambridge University
       Press, 1905. Reprinted 1941.

1791   _____. "Cupid Mistaken," in Several Occasions (1941).

1792   _____. "The Female Phaeton," in Dialogues of the Dead
       and Other Works, ed. by A. R. Waller. Cambridge:
       Cambridge University Press, 1907. Reprinted 1941.

1793   _____. "Hymn of Callimachus to Jupiter, First," in
       Several Occasions (1941).

1794   _____. "Hymn of Callimachus to Apollo, Second," in
       Several Occasions (1941).

1795   _____. "The Judgment of Venus," in Dialogues of the
       Dead (1941).

1796   _____. "Mercury and Cupid," in Several Occasions (1941).

1797   _____. "Pallas and Venus," in Several Occasions (1941).

1798   _____. "Venus Mistaken," in Several Occasions (1941).

PROCTER, Bryan Waller ("Barry Cornwall," pseudonym, 1787-1874,
English)

1799   "Bacchanalian Song," in The Poetical Works of Barry Corn-
       wall, 3 vols. London: Colburn, 1822.

1800   _____. "The Death of Acis," in A Sicilian Story. Lon-
       don: Ollier, 1820.

1801   _____. "The Dream," in Dramatic Scenes. London:
       Ollier, 1819.

1802   _____. "The Fall of Saturn," in The Flood of Thessaly
       and Other Poems. London: Colburn, 1823.

1803   _____. "The Flood of Thessaly," in The Flood (1823).

282

1804 _____. "Gyges," in A Sicilian Story (1820).

1805 _____. "Lysander and Ione," in Dramatic Scenes (1819).

1806 _____. "On the Statue of Theseus," in Poetical Works (1822).

1807 _____. "The Rape of Proserpine," in Poetical Works (1822).

1808 _____. "Tartarus," in The Flood (1823).

1809 _____. "The Worship of Dian," in A Sicilian Story (1820).

QUENNELL, Peter Courtney (1905- , English)

1810 "In Aulis," in Masques and Poems. Waltham St. Lawrence, Berkshire, England: Golden Cockerel, 1922.

1811 _____. "The Lion in Nemea," in Masques and Poems (1922).

1812 _____. "Procne," in Masques and Poems (1922).

RAINE, Kathleen (1908- , English)

1813 "The Goddess," in The Pythoness and Other Poems. London: Hamilton, 1949.

1814 _____. "The Marriage of Psyche," in Collected Poems of Kathleen Raine. London: Hamilton, 1968.

1815 _____. "Medea," in The Oracle in the Heart and Other Poems. London: Allen and Unwin, 1980.

1816 _____. "The Oracle in the Heart," in The Oracle (1980).

1817 _____. "The Pythoness," in The Pythoness (1949).

1818 _____. "Transit of the Gods," in Collected Poems (1968).

1819 _____. "Venus," in Collected Poems (1968).

1820 _____. "Winged Eros," in Collected Poems (1968).

RANDALL, John Witt (1813-1892, American)

1821 "The Dream of Orestes," in Poems of Nature and Life, ed. by Francis Ellingwood Abbott. Boston: Ellis, 1899.

1822 _____. "Lament of Orpheus," in Consolations of Solitude.
Boston: Jewett, 1856.

RANDALL, Julia Sawyer (1923- , American)

1823 "Danae," in The Puritan Carpenter. Chapel Hill: University
of North Carolina Press, 1972.

READ, Harriette Fanning (?-?, American)

1824 "Medea," in Dramatic Poems. Boston: Crosby and Nichols,
1848.

READ, Thomas Buchanan (1822-1872, American)

1825 "Endymion," in Poems. London: Delf and Trübner, 1852.

1826 _____. "Hero and Leander," in Sylvia: or, The Last
Shepherd. Philadelphia: Parry and Macmillan, 1857.

READE, John Edmund (1800-1870, English)

1827 "Achilles' Description of Hector," in The Deluge. London:
Saunders and Otley, 1839.

1828 _____. "Arethusa," in The Deluge (1839).

1829 _____. "The Dance of the Nereids," in The Deluge (1839).

1830 _____. "Prometheus," in The Deluge (1839).

1831 _____. "Prometheus Bound," in The Deluge (1839).

1832 _____. A Record of the Pyramids, a drama in 10 scenes.
London: Saunders and Otley, 1842.

RENWICK, James (?-?, English)

1833 "Ariadne at Naxos," in Poems and Sonnets. Paisley, Scot-
land: Gardner, 1897.

1834 _____. "Aristomenes," in Poems (1897).

REXROTH, Kenneth (1905- , American)

284

1835 "Adonis in Summer, " in The Collected Shorter Poems of Kenneth Rexroth. New York: New Directions, 1966.

1836 _____. "Adonis in Winter," in Shorter Poems (1966).

1837 _____. "Andromeda Chained to Her Rock ...," in Shorter Poems (1966).

1838 _____. "Homer in Basic, " in Shorter Poems (1966).

1839 _____. "Leda Hidden, " in Shorter Poems (1966).

1840 _____. "When We with Sappho, " in Shorter Poems (1966).

RICHARDSON, Jack Carter (1935- , American)

1841 The Prodigal, a play based on the Agamemnon-Orestes story. New York: Dutton, 1961. Reprinted in Force, William M., ed., Orestes and Electra: Myth and Dramatic Form. Boston: Houghton Mifflin, 1968.

RILKE, Rainer Maria (1875-1926, German)

1842 "Orpheus, Eurydice, and Hermes, " adapted from Rilke by Robert Lowell. The Hudson Review, 12 (Spring 1959). Reprinted in Flores, Angel, ed., An Anthology of German Poetry from Holderlin to Rilke. Garden City, N. Y.: Doubleday/Anchor, 1960.

1843 _____. Sonnets to Orpheus, 55 sonnets in two parts, trans. by Mrs. M. D. Herter Norton. New York: Norton, 1942. Published in German, 1923.

ROBERTS, Cecil (1892-1976, English)

1844 "Andromache," in Poems, with Preface by John Masefield. New York: Stokes, 1920.

1845 _____. "Helen of Troy," in Poems (1920).

1846 _____. "Strayed Hylas, " in Poems (1920).

ROBERTS, Sir Charles George Douglas (1860-1943, Canadian)

1847 "Actaeon, " in In Divers Tones. Boston: Houghton, Mifflin, 1886.

1848 _____. "Ariadne," in Orion and Other Poems. Philadelphia: Lippincott, 1880.

ROBERTS, continued

1849 _____. "Memnon," in Orion (1880).

1850 _____. "Off Pelorus," in In Divers Tones (1886).

1851 _____. "Orion," in Orion (1880).

1852 _____. "The Pipes of Pan," in In Divers Tones (1886).

1853 _____. "Sappho," in Orion (1880).

ROBERTS, Michael (1902-1948, English)

1854 "Diomed, Diomed," in Collected Poems, with Introductory
Memoir by Janet Roberts. London: Faber and Faber,
1958.

1855 _____. "Dionysos," in Collected Poems (1958).

ROBERTSON, Louis Alexander (1856-1910, American)

1856 "The Dead Calypso," in The Dead Calypso and Other Poems.
San Francisco: Robertson, 1901.

1857 _____. "Helen," in Through Painted Panes. San Francisco: Robertson, 1907.

1858 _____. "Orpheus and Eurydice," in Through Painted
Panes (1907).

1859 _____. "Phryne," in Through Painted Panes (1907).

RODGERS, W. R. (1909-1969, Ireland)

1860 "Europa and the Bull," in Europa and the Bull and Other
Poems. London: Secker and Warburg; New York:
Farrar, Straus, and Cudahy, 1952.

ROGERS, Robert Cameron (1862-1912, American)

1861 "Blind Polyphemus," in The Wind in the Clearing and Other
Poems. New York: Putnam, 1894.

1862 _____. "Charon," in For the King. New York: Putnam,
1899.

1863 _____. "The Dancing Faun," in The Wind (1894).

286

1864 _____. "The Death of Argus," in The Wind (1894).

1865 _____. "Hylas," in The Wind (1894).

1866 _____. "Odysseus at the Mast," in The Wind (1894).

ROGERS, Samuel (1763-1855, English)

1867 "On the Torso of Hercules," in The Poetical Works of Samuel
       Rogers. London: Routledge, 1867.

1868 _____. "A Temple Dedicated to the Graces," in Poetical
       Works (1867).

ROSCOE, William Caldwell (1823-1859, English)

1869 "Ariadne," in Poems and Essays, 2 vols., ed. by R. H.
       Hutton. London: Chapman and Hall, 1860.

ROSENBERG, Isaac (1890-1918, English)

1870 "Psyche's Lament," in The Collected Poems of Isaac Rosen-
       berg, ed. by Gordon Bottomley and Denys Harding, with
       Foreword by Siegfried Sassoon. New York: Schocken,
       1949.

ROSSETTI, Christina (1830-1894, English)

1871 "Ariadne's Farewell to Theseus," in Poems of Christina
       Rossetti, ed. with Introduction by Alice Meynell. Lon-
       don: Blackie, 1923.

1872 _____. "The Lotus-Eaters," in The Poetical Works of
       Christina Georgina Rossetti, with Memoir and Notes by
       William Michael Rossetti. London: Macmillan, 1908.

1873 _____. "Sappho," in Poems (1923).

1874 _____. "Venus's Looking Glass," in Poetical Works (1908).

RUKEYSER, Muriel (1913-1980, American)

1875 "The Birth of Venus," in Waterlily Fire: Poems 1935-1962.
       New York: Macmillan, 1963.

1876 _____. "The Minotaur," in Beast In View. New York:
       Doubleday, 1944. Reprinted in Selected Poems. New
       York: New Directions, 1951.

287

RUKEYSER, continued

1877 _____ . "Orpheus," in Orpheus and Other Poems. New York: Centaur, 1949. Reprinted in Selected Poems (1951).

RUSSELL, Thomas (1762-1788, English)

1878 "Sonnet suppos'd to be written at Lemnos," in Sonnets and Miscellaneous Poems. Oxford: Prince, 1789.

SABIN, Arthur Knowles (1879-1959, English)

1879 "Clymene," in Typhon and Other Poems. London: Stock, 1902.

1880 _____ . "Circe," in Medea and Circe and Other Poems. East Sheen, Surrey, England: Temple Sheen, 1911.

1881 _____ . "The Death of Icarus," in The Death of Icarus and Other Poems. Glasgow: MacLehose, 1906.

1882 _____ . "Ida," in Typhon (1902).

1883 _____ . "Medea," in Medea and Circe (1911).

1884 _____ . "Orion," in Typhon (1902).

1885 _____ . "Typhon," in Typhon (1902).

SAMPSON, Martin Wright (1866-1930, American)

1886 "Odysseus," in Voices of the Forest. Ithaca, N.Y.: Cayuga, 1933.

1887 _____ . "Pan," in Voices (1933).

1888 _____ . "Voices in the Forest," in Voices (1933).

SANDBACH, Mrs. Henry Roscoe (1812-1852, English)

1889 "Antigone," in Aurora and Other Poems. London: Pickering, 1850.

1890 _____ . "Aurora," in Aurora (1850).

1891 _____ . "Penthesilea," in Aurora (1850).

288

SAXE, John Godfrey (1816-1887, American)

1892 "The Choice of King Midas," in Poems: Travesties. Boston: Houghton, Mifflin, 1861.

1893 _____. "Icarus," in The Poetical Works of John Saxe. Boston and New York: Houghton, Mifflin, 1900. Also in Selections from the Poems of John Godfrey Saxe. Boston: Houghton, Mifflin, 1905.

1894 _____. "Orpheus," in Poetical Works (1900).

1895 _____. "Orpheus and Eurydice," in Poems (1861).

1896 _____. "Pan Immortal," in The Masquerade and Other Poems. Boston: Ticknor and Fields, 1866.

1897 _____. "Phaethon," in Poems (1861).

1898 _____. "Polyphemus and Ulysses," in Poems (1861).

1899 _____. "Pyramus and Thisbe," in Poems (1861).

1900 _____. "The Spell of Circe," in Poetical Works (1900).

SCHMITT, Gladys (Mrs. Simon Goldfield, 1909-1972, American)

1901 The Gates of Aulis, a novel. New York: Dial, 1942.

SCHWARTZ, Delmore (1913-1966, American)

1902 "Abraham and Orpheus, Be with Me Now," in Summer Knowledge: New and Selected Poems, 1938-1958. Garden City, N.Y.: Doubleday, 1959.

1903 _____. "Cupid's Chant," in Summer Knowledge (1959).

1904 _____. "In the Naked Bed, in Plato's Cave," in Summer Knowledge (1959).

1905 _____. "Once and for All," in Summer Knowledge (1959). Refers to Apollo and Dionysus.

1906 _____. "Paris and Helen: An Entertainment," in The Last and Lost Poems of Delmore Schwartz, ed. by Robert Phillips. New York: Vanguard, 1979.

1907 _____. "Psyche Pleads with Cupid," in Summer Knowledge (1959).

SCHWARTZ, continued

1908 _____. "Socrates' Ghost Must Haunt Me Now," in <u>Summer Knowledge</u> (1959).

1909 _____. "The Studies of Narcissus," in <u>Last and Lost Poems</u> (1979). Similar to shorter poem "Narcissus," in <u>Summer Knowledge</u> (1959).

SCOLLARD, Clinton (1860-1932, American)

1910 "The Dancing Faun," in <u>Italy in Arms and Other Poems</u>. New York: Gomme and Marshall, 1915.

1911 _____. "The Death of Orion," in <u>With Reed and Lyre</u>. Boston: Osgood, 1886.

1912 _____. "The Dryad," in <u>With Reed and Lyre</u> (1886).

1913 _____. "Memnon," in <u>The Singing Heart</u>. New York: Macmillan, 1934.

1914 _____. "Off Chios," in <u>The Singing Heart</u> (1934).

1915 _____. "On a Copy of Heats' 'Endymion,'" in <u>Lyrics from a Library</u>. Portland, Me.: Mosher, 1917.

1916 _____. "Pomona," in <u>With Reed and Lyre</u> (1886).

1917 _____. "The Sphinx," in <u>The Singing Heart</u> (1934).

SCOTT, William Bell (1812-1892, English)

1918 "Eurydice," in <u>Poems by William Bell Scott</u>. London: Smith and Elder, 1854.

1919 _____. "Iphigeneia at Aulis," in <u>Poems</u> (1854).

1920 _____. "The Sphinx," in <u>Poems, Ballads, and Studies</u>. London: Longmans, Green, 1875.

SEAMAN, Owen (1861-1936, English)

1921 "The Dirge of the Amateur Maenad," in <u>Owen Seaman: A Selection</u>, with Introduction by C. L. Graves. London: Methuen, 1937.

1922 _____. "Marsyas in Hades," in <u>Owen Seaman</u> (1937).

1923 _____. "Pan of the Pointed Ears," in <u>Interludes of an Editor</u>. London: Constable, 1929.

1924 _____. "To Venus Shot in Her Tracks," in Owen Seaman
        (1937).

SEEGER, Alan (1888-1916, American)

1925 "Antinous," in Poems, ed. with Introduction by William
        Archer. New York: Scribner, 1916.

1926 _____. "Tithonus," in Poems (1916).

SEXTON, Anne (1928-1974, American)

1927 "To a Friend Whose Work Has Come to Triumph," in All
        My Pretty Ones. Boston: Houghton Mifflin, 1962.
        Refers to Icarus.

SHAW, George Bernard (1856-1950, English)

1928 Pygmalion, a play. London: Constable, 1913. Reprinted
        in Four Plays by Bernard Shaw. New York: Random
        House, 1953.

SHELLEY, Mary (1797-1851, English)

1929 "Midas," in Proserpine and Midas: Two Unpublished Mytho-
        logical Dramas, ed. by A. H. Koszul. London: Milford,
        1922.

1930 _____. "Proserpine," in Proserpine and Midas (1922).

SHELLEY, Percy Bysshe (1792-1822, English)

1931 "Adonais," in Complete Poetical Works, ed. by Thomas
        Hutchinson. London: Oxford University Press, 1934.

1932 _____. "Arethusa," in Poetical Works (1934).

1933 _____. "Hellas, a Lyrical Drama," in Poetical Works
        (1934).

1934 _____. "Hymn of Apollo," in Poetical Works (1934).

1935 _____. "Hymn of Pan," in Poetical Works (1934).

1936 _____. "Merope," in Poetical Works (1934).

1937 _____. "Oedipus Tyrannus: or Swellfoot the Tyrant," in
        Poetical Works (1934).

1938 _____ . "On the Medusa of Leonardo da Vinci," in Poetical Works (1934).

1939 _____ . "Orpheus," in Poetical Works (1934).

1940 _____ . "Prometheus Unbound," in Poetical Works (1934).

1941 _____ . "Song of Proserpine," in Poetical Works (1934).

1942 _____ . "To Night," in Poetical Works (1934).

1943 _____ . "The Witch of Atlas," in Poetical Works (1934).

SHENSTONE, William (1714-1763, English)

1944 "The Judgment of Hercules," in Poetical Works, ed. by George Gilfillan. Edinburgh: Nichol, 1854.

SILL, Louise Morgan (?-?, American)

1945 "Pan and Echo," in In Sun and Shade. New York: Harper, 1906.

SIMCOX, George Augustus (1841-1905, English)

1946 "The Cumaean Sibyl," in Poems and Romances. London: Strahan, 1869. Reprinted in The Decadent Consciousness: An Archive of Late Victorian Literature, 36 vols., ed. by Ian Fletcher and John Stokes. New York: Garland, 1978.

1947 _____ . "The Daughters of Pandarus," in Poems and Romances (1978).

1948 _____ . "Hypsipyle," in Poems and Romances (1978).

1949 _____ . "The Love of Sophocles," in Poems and Romances (1978).

1950 _____ . "The Masque of Nemesis," in Poems and Romances (1978).

1951 _____ . "Mnemosyne," in Poems and Romances (1978).

1952 _____ . "Oedipus," in Poems and Romances (1978).

1953 _____ . "Polyxene," in Poems and Romances (1978).

1954 _____. Prometheus Unbound: A Tragedy. London: Smith and Elder, 1867.

1955 _____. "Thoas," in Poems and Romances (1978).

1956 _____. "The Troades," in Poems and Romances (1978).

1957 _____. "When Nemesis and Aidos Heard None Pray," in Poems and Romances (1978).

SIMPSON, Louis (1923- , American)

1958 "The Flight to Cytherea," in Selected Poems. New York: Harcourt, Brace, and World, 1965.

1959 _____. "Orpheus in America," in Selected Poems (1965).

1960 _____. "Orpheus in the Underworld," in Selected Poems (1965).

SITWELL, Edith (1887-1964, English)

1961 "Daphne," in The Collected Poems of Edith Sitwell. New York: Vanguard, 1954.

1962 _____. "Dido's Song," in Collected Poems (1954).

1963 _____. "Dionysus of the Tree," in Collected Poems (1954).

1964 _____. "Eurydice," in Collected Poems (1954).

1965 _____. "Gardener Janus Catches a Naiad," in Collected Poems (1954).

1966 _____. "Hymn to Venus," in Collected Poems (1954).

1967 _____. "Medusa's Love Song," in Collected Poems (1954).

1968 _____. "Prometheus' Song," in Collected Poems (1954).

1969 _____. "The Road to Thebes," in Collected Poems (1954).

1970 _____. "A Sylph's Song," in Collected Poems (1954).

SITWELL, Osbert (1892-1969, English)

1971 "Bacchanalia," in Out of the Flame. London: Duckworth, 1923.

1972 _____ . "The Jealous Goddess," in Out of the Flame (1923).

1973 _____ . "Neptune in Chains," in Out of the Flame (1923). Reprinted in Selected Poems: Old and New. London: Duckworth, 1943.

1974 _____ . "Song of the Fauns," in Argonaut and Juggernaut. London: Duckworth, 1919.

SITWELL, Sacheverell (1897- , English)

1975 "Aeneas Hunting Stags upon the Coast of Libya," in Canons of Giant Art: Twenty Torsos in Heroic Landscapes. London: Faber and Faber, 1933.

1976 _____ . "Agamemnon's Tomb," in Giant Art (1933).

1977 _____ . "Bacchus in India," in Giant Art (1933).

1978 _____ . "Battles of the Centaurs," in Giant Art (1933).

1979 _____ . "Cephalus and Procris," in Giant Art (1933).

1980 _____ . "Daphne," in The Thirteenth Caesar. London: Duckworth, 1924.

1981 _____ . "Eurydice," in Thirteenth Caesar (1924).

1982 _____ . "The Farnese Hercules," in Giant Art (1933).

1983 _____ . "The Hermes of Praxiteles," in Giant Art (1933).

1984 _____ . "Landscape with the Giant Orion," in Giant Art (1933).

1985 _____ . "The Laocoon of El Greco," in Giant Art (1933).

1986 _____ . "Pindar," in The People's Palace. London: Blackwell, 1918. Reprinted in Selected Poems, with Preface by Osbert Sitwell. London: Duckworth, 1948.

1987 _____ . "The River God," in Thirteenth Caesar (1924).

1988 _____ . "The Royal Hunt and Storm in the Forest: Aeneas and Dido," in Giant Art (1933).

1989 _____ . "The Sea God," in Thirteenth Caesar (1924).

1990 _____ . "Variation on a Theme by John Lyly: Pan and Syrinx," in Thirteenth Caesar (1924).

1991 _____. "The Venus of Bolsover Castle," in Thirteenth
  Caesar (1924).

SMITH, Arthur James Marshall (1902-?, Canadian)

1992 "Choros," in Poets Between the Wars, ed. by Milton Wilson.
  Toronto: McClelland and Stewart, 1969. Poets of Canada
  series.

1993 _____. "The Plot Against Proteus," in Between the Wars
  (1969).

SMITH, Chard Powers (1894-1977, American)

1994 The Quest of Pan. New York: Coward-McCann, 1930.
  First book of a trilogy on evolution.

SNODGRASS, William DeWitt (1926- , American)

1995 "An Archaic Torso of Apollo," a free translation from Rainer
  Maria Rilke, in After Experience: Poems and Translations. New York: Harper and Row, 1968.

1996 _____. "Orpheus," in Heart's Needle. New York:
  Random House, 1954.

1997 _____. "Sonnets to Orpheus" (selections from), by Rainer
  Maria Rilke, in After Experience (1968).

SOTHEBY, William (1757-1833, English)

1998 Orestes, a tragedy in five acts. Bristol, England: Mills,
  1802.

SOUTHESK, James Carnegie, Earl of (1827-1905, English)

1999 "Andromeda: A Ballad," in The Burial of Isis. Edinburgh:
  Douglas, 1884.

2000 _____. "Theseus: A Ballad," in The Burial (1884).

SOUTHEY, Robert (1774-1843, English)

2001 "Aristodemus," a mono-drama, in Poems of Robert Southey,
  ed. by M. H. Fitzgerald. London: Oxford University
  Press, 1909.

2002 _____. "Hymn to the Penates," in Poems (1909).

SOUTHEY, continued

2003 _____. "Lucretia," in Poems (1909).

2004 _____. "Othryades," a mono-drama, in Poems (1909).

2005 _____. "Sappho," a mono-drama, in Poems (1909).

SPENDER, Stephen (1909- , English)

2006 "Icarus," in Selected Poems. New York: Random House,
     1964

SPEYER, Leonora (1872-1956, American)

2007 "Again, Medusa," in The Naked Heel. New York: Knopf,
     1931.

2008 _____. "The Maid Medusa," in Naked Heel (1931).

2009 _____. "Sappho in Crete," in Slow Wall. New York:
     Knopf, 1946.

SQUIRE, Sir John C. (1884-1958, English)

2010 "Artemis Altera," in Collected Poems by J. C. Squire, with
     Preface by John Betjeman. London: Macmillan; New
     York: St. Martin, 1959.

2011 _____. "To a Lady Beginning to Learn Greek," in
     Collected Poems (1959).

2012 _____. "To a Roman," in Collected Poems (1959).

STEDMAN, Edmund Clarence (1833-1908, American)

2013 "Alectryon," in The Poems of Edmund Clarence Stedman.
     Boston: Houghton Mifflin, 1908.

2014 _____. "Apollo," in The Poems (1908).

2015 _____. "Crete," in The Poems (1908).

2016 _____. "Hebe," in The Poems (1908).

2017 _____. "Hylas," in The Poems (1908).

2018 _____. "Hypatia," in The Poems (1908).

2019 _____. "News from Olympia," in The Poems (1908).

2020 _____. "Pan in Wall Street," in The Poems (1908).

2021 _____. "Penelope," in The Poems (1908).

STERLING, George (1869-1926, American)

2022 "The Death of Circe," in Selected Poems. New York:
    Holt, 1923.

2023 _____. "The Lost Nymph," in Selected Poems (1923).

STERLING, John (1806-1844, English)

2024 "Aphrodite," in Poems. London: Moxon, 1839. Reprinted
    in The Poetical Works of John Sterling. Philadelphia:
    Hooker, 1842.

2025 _____. "Daedalus," in Poems (1839). Reprinted in
    Poetical Works (1842).

STORK, Charles Wharton (1881-?, American)

2026 "Actaeon," in The Queen of Orplede. Philadelphia: Lippin-
    cott, 1910.

2027 _____. "Ganymede," in Day-Dreams of Greece. Phila-
    delphia: Lippincott, 1908.

2028 _____. "Philemon and Baucis," in Day-Dreams (1908).

2029 _____. "The Wanderings of Psyche," in Day-Dreams
    (1908).

STORY, William Wetmore (1819-1895, American)

2030 "Artemis," in Poems: Parchments and Portraits. Boston:
    Houghton, Mifflin, 1856.

2031 _____. "Cassandra," in Poems by William Wetmore Story,
    2 vols. Boston: Houghton, Mifflin, 1896.

2032 _____. "Chersiphron," in Poems (1896).

2033 _____. "Clytie," in Poems. Boston: Little, Brown,
    1847.

2034 _____. "Europa," in Poems (1896).

STORY, continued

2035 _____. "Nemesis," in Poems (1896).

2036 _____. "Orestes," in Poems (1896).

2037 _____. "Pan in Love," in Poems (1896).

2038 _____. "Praxiteles and Phryne," in Poems (1896).

2039 _____. "Prometheus," in Poems (1847).

2040 _____. "Sappho," in Parchments and Portraits (1856).

2041 _____. "Tantalus," in Parchments and Portraits (1856).

STRINGER, Arthur John Arbuthnott (1874-1950, Canadian-American)

2042 "Hephaestus," in Hephaestus and Other Poems.   Toronto:
        Methodist Book and Publishing House, 1903.

2043 _____. "Persephone at Enna," in Hephaestus (1903).

2044 _____. "Sappho in Leucadia," in Hephaestus (1903).

SUTHERLAND, Howard Vigne (1868-?, American)

2045 "Acis and Galatea," in Idylls of Greece: First Series.
        Boston: Sherman and French, 1908.

2046 _____. "Idas and Marpessa," in Idylls of Greece: Third
        Series.   New York: Desmond and Fitzgerald, 1914.

2047 _____. "Melas and Anaxe," in Idylls: First (1908).

2048 _____. "Oeme and Oeonus," in Idylls: First (1908).

2049 _____. "Orpheus and Eurydice," in Idylls of Greece:
        Second Series.   New York: Desmond and Fitzgerald,
        1910.

2050 _____. "Pan and Pitys," in Idylls: Second (1910).

2051 _____. "Phyllis and Demophoon," in Idylls: Second
        (1910).

2052 _____. "Praxis and Narcissus," in Idylls: Second (1910).

2053 _____. "Procris and Cephalus," in Idylls: First (1908).

2054 _____. "Rhodanthe," in Idylls: Third (1914).

2055 _____. "Sappho and Phaon," in Idylls: Third (1914).

SWEETMAN, Elinor (?-?, English)

2056 "The Dancers," in The Wild Orchard. London: Herbert
       and Daniel, 1911.

2057 _____. "The Faun," in Wild Orchard (1911).

2058 _____. "The Footsteps of the Gods," in Footsteps of the
       Gods and Other Poems. London: Bell, 1893.

2059 _____. "Pastoral of the Faun," in Pastorals. London:
       Dent, 1899.

2060 _____. "Pastoral of Kyprios," in Pastorals (1899).

2061 _____. "Rhoecus," in Wild Orchard (1911).

SWIFT, Jonathan (1667-1745, English)

2062 "Apollo Outwitted," in Vol. I, Poems, 3 vols., ed. by
       Harold Williams. Oxford: Clarendon Press, 1937.

2063 _____. "Fable of Midas," in Vol. I, Poems (1937).

2064 _____. "Prometheus," in Vol. I, Poems (1937).

2065 _____. "The Story of Baucis and Philamon," in Vol. I,
       Poems (1937).

2066 _____. "To Janus," in Vol. III, Poems (1937).

TAGGARD, Genevieve (1894-1948, American)

2067 "Galatea Again," in Words for the Chisel. New York: Knopf,
       1926.

TAYLOR, Rachel Annand (1876-?, English)

2068 "Dirge for Narcissus," in Rose and Vine. London: Mathews,
       1909.

2069 _____. "The Dryad," in Rose and Vine (1909).

2070 _____. "Hades," in Rose and Vine (1909).

299

TEASDALE, Sara (1884-1933, American)

2071 "Anadyomene," in Helen of Troy and Other Poems. New
York: Putnam, 1911.

2072 _____. "Erinna," in Helen of Troy (1911). Reprinted
in Collected Poems of Sara Teasdale. New York:
Macmillan, 1938.

2073 _____. "Helen of Troy," in Helen of Troy (1911). Reprinted in Collected Poems (1938).

2074 _____. "Sappho," in Rivers to the Sea. New York:
Mcamillan, 1915. Reprinted in Collected Poems (1938).

2075 _____. "To an Aeolian Harp," in Collected Poems (1938).

2076 _____. "To Cleis: Daughter of Sappho," in Collected
Poems (1938).

2077 _____. "To Erinna," in Collected Poems (1938). Not
the same as "Erinna" listed above.

TENNYSON, Frederick (1807-1898, English)

2078 "Aeson," in Daphne and Other Poems. London and New
York: Macmillan, 1891.

2079 _____. "Alcaeus," in The Isles of Greece. London and
New York: Macmillan, 1890.

2080 _____. "Ariadne," in Daphne (1891).

2081 _____. "Atlantis," in Daphne (1891).

2082 _____. "Daphne," in Daphne (1891).

2083 _____. "Death and the Shepherd," in Days and Hours.
London: Parker, 1854.

2084 _____. Halcyone. London: Printed for private circulation, 1888. Reprinted in Daphne (1891).

2085 _____. "Hesperia," in Daphne (1891).

2086 _____. King Athamas. London: Printed for private
circulation, 1888. Reprinted in Daphne (1891).

2087 _____. "The Lament of the Wood-Nymphs," in The
Shorter Poems of Frederick Tennyson. London:
Macmillan, 1913.

2088 _____ . Niobe. London: Printed for private circulation,
        1888. Reprinted in Daphne (1891).

2089 _____ . Psyche. London: Printed for private circulation,
        1888. Reprinted in Daphne (1891).

2090 _____ . "Pygmalion," in Daphne (1891).

2091 _____ . "Sappho," in The Isles of Greece (1890).

2092 _____ . "Sappho and Alcaeus," in The Isles of Greece
        (1890).

TERRELL, Francis (Daniel Thomas Callaghan, 1846-1916, English)

2093 "Antiope," in Antiope and Other Poems. London: Provost,
        1871.

2094 _____ . Sappho: A Dream. London: Provost, 1881.

THAYER, Stephen Henry (1839-1919, American)

2095 "Aurora's Gift to Tithonus," in Songs from Edgewood.
        New York: Putnam, 1902.

THOMAS, Edith Matilda (1854-1925, American)

2096 "Apollo the Shepherd," in Lyrics and Sonnets. Boston and
        New York: Houghton, Mifflin, 1889.

2097 _____ . "Antaeus," in A Winter Swallow. New York:
        Scribner, 1896.

2098 _____ . "Anteros," in Fair Shadow Land. Boston and
        New York: Houghton, Mifflin, 1891.

2099 _____ . "At Athens Long Ago," in Selected Poems of
        Edith M. Thomas, ed. with Memoir by Jessie B. Ritten-
        house. New York and London: Harper, 1926.

2100 _____ . "Atys," in Fair Shadow Land (1891).

2101 _____ . "Demeter's Search," in A New Year's Masque
        New York: Scribner, 1885.

2102 _____ . "Fighting the Wind," in Lyrics and Sonnets (1889).
        Based on a tale from Herodotus.

2102a _____ . "Glaucus," in Lyrics and Sonnets (1889).

301

THOMAS, continued

2103 _____. "The Homesickness of Ganymede," in Lyrics and Sonnets (1889).

2104 _____. "The Kingfisher," in Lyrics and Sonnets (1889).

2105 _____. "Linus: A Lament at the Gathering of the Vintage," in Lyrics and Sonnets (1889).

2106 _____. "Marsyas," in Lyrics and Sonnets (1889).

2107 _____. "Moly," in Lyrics and Sonnets (1889).

2108 _____. "Persephone," in A New Year's Masque (1885).

2109 _____. "Psyche Laughs," in Selected Poems (1926).

2110 _____. "The Sphinx," in Lyrics and Sonnets (1889).

2111 _____. "Syrinx," in A New Year's Masque (1885).

2112 _____. "The Tears of the Poplars," in A Winter Swallow (1896).

2113 _____. "Thalassa," in Selected Poems (1926).

2114 _____. "Ulysses at the Court of Alcinous," in A Winter Swallow (1896).

2115 _____. "Vertumnus," in Selected Poems (1926).

2116 _____. "The Water of Dirce," in The Flower from the Ashes and Other Verse. Portland, Me.: Mosher, 1915.

2117 _____. "A Winter Swallow," in A Winter Swallow (1896). Refers to Leonidas, a king of Sparta.

THOMPSON, Edward John (1886-1946, English)

2118 "Child of Achilles," in John in Prison and Other Poems. London: Unwin, 1912.

2119 _____. "Pheidippes," in John in Prison (1912).

2120 _____. The Thracian Stranger, a narrative poem. London: Benn, 1929.

THOMPSON, Francis (1859-1907, English)

2121 "Daphne," in Poems of Francis Thompson, ed. with Biographical and Textual Notes by Rev. Terence L. Connolly. New York and London: Century, 1932.

2122 _____. "Hermes," in Poems (1932).

2123 _____. "Ode to the Setting Sun," in Poems (1932).

2124 _____. "Song of the Hours," in Poems (1932).

THOMPSON, James Maurice (1844-1901, American)

2125 "Atalanta," in The Poems of James Maurice Thompson. Boston: Houghton, Mifflin, 1892.

2126 _____. "Ceres," in Poems (1892).

2127 _____. "Diana," in Poems (1892).

2128 _____. "Eos," in Poems (1892).

2129 _____. "Garden Statues: Eros, Aphrodite, Psyche, and Persephone," in Poems (1892).

2130 _____. "The Orphic Legacy," in Poems (1892).

2131 _____. "Pan in the Orchard," in Poems (1892).

2132 _____. "To Sappho," in Poems (1892).

THURLOW, Lord Edward (1781-1829, English)

2133 Angelica; or, The Rape of Proteus. London: Booth, 1822.

2134 _____. "Ariadne," a narrative poem in three parts, in Poems on Several Occasions. London: Booth, 1822.

TIGHE, Mary (Mrs. Henry Tighe, 1772-1810, English)

2135 Psyche, or the Legend of Love. London: Printed for J. Carpenter by C. Whittington. Reprinted London: Clarke, 1843.

TODHUNTER, John (1839-1916, English)

2136 Alcestis, a dramatic poem. London: Kegal Paul, 1879.

2137 _____. "Helena in Troas," in A Sicilian Idyll. London: Mathews, 1890.

TODHUNTER, continued

2138 _____. "The Wooing of Artemis," in Trivium Amoris.
London: Dent, 1927.

TRENCH, Herbert (1865-1923, English)

2139 "Apollo and the Seaman," in New Poems. London: Methuen,
1907.

2140 _____. "Milo," in Poems with Fables in Prose. London:
Constable, 1918.

TREVELYAN, Robert Calverly (1872-1951, English)

2141 "Archilochus," in Mallow and Asphodel. London: Macmillan,
1898.

2142 _____. The Bride of Dionysus, a musical drama with
music by D. F. Tovey. Edinburgh: MacDonald, 1912.

2143 _____. Cheiron, a poetic drama. London: L. and V.
Woolf, 1927.

2144 _____. "Helen," in Poems. London: Macmillan, 1934.

2145 _____. "Lucretius," in The Deluge. London: L. and V.
Woolf, 1926.

2146 _____. Meleager, a poetic drama. London: L. and V.
Woolf at Hogarth Press, 1927.

2147 _____. "Orpheus," in Mallow and Asphodel (1898).

2148 _____. "Polyphemus," a dramatic poem, in Polyphemus
and Other Poems, with designs by R. E. Fry. London:
Johnson, 1901.

2149 _____. Sisyphus, an operatic fable. London and New
York: Longmans, Green, 1908.

2150 _____. "Sulla," in Three Plays. London: L. and V.
Woolf, 1932.

TROWBRIDGE, John Townsend (1827-1916, American)

2151 "Phaeton," in The Poetical Works of John Townsend Trowbridge. Boston: Houghton, Mifflin, 1903. Reprinted
New York: Arno, 1972.

2152 _____. "The Tragedy Queen," in Poetical Works (1972).

304

TURNER, Charles Tennyson (1808-1879, English)

2153 "Christ and Orpheus," in Sonnets. London: Macmillan, 1864.

2154 _____. "Orion," in A Hundred Sonnets, ed. by John
Betjeman and Sir Charles Tennyson. London: Rupert,
Hart-Davis, 1960.

2155 _____. "A Picture of the Fates," in Sonnets and Fugitive
Pieces. Cambridge, England: Bridges, 1830.

TURNER, Joseph Mallord William (1775-1851, English painter)

2156 "Apollo and Daphne," in The Sunset Ship: The Poems of
J. M. W. Turner, ed. with essay by Jack Lindsay.
Lowestoft, Suffolk, England: Scorpion, 1966.

2157 _____. "Apollo and Python," in Sunset Ship (1966).

2158 _____. "The Monstrous Python," in Sunset Ship (1966).

2159 _____. "Narcissus and Echo," in Sunset Ship (1966).

2160 _____. "Ode to Discord," in Sunset Ship (1966).

2161 _____. "The Parting of Hero and Leander," in Sunset
Ship (1966).

2162 _____. "Vision of Medea," in Sunset Ship (1966).

TURNEY, Robert (1900-?, American)

2163 Daughters of Atreus, a play. New York: Knopf, 1936.

VALERY, Paul (1871-1945, French)

2164 "Helen," trans. by Robert Lowell, in Imitations. New York:
Farrar, Straus, and Giroux, 1961.

2165 _____. "To Helen," trans. by Delmore Schwartz, in
Last and Lost Poems of Delmore Schwartz, ed. by Robert
Phillips. New York: Vanguard, 1979.

2166 _____. "Helen," trans. by Richard Wilbur, in Things of
This World. New York: Harcourt, Brace, 1956.

VAN DOREN, Mark (1894-1972, American)

2167 "Achilles," in Collected and New Poems: 1924-1963. New
York: Hill and Wang, 1963.

VAN DOREN, continued

2168 _____. "The Dinner," in Collected and New (1963). About Philamon and Baucis.

2169 _____. "Hector Dead," in Collected and New (1963).

2170 _____. "In Athens, Though," in Collected and New (1963).

2171 _____. "Odysseus," in Collected and New (1963).

2172 _____. "Proteus," in Collected and New (1963).

2173 _____. "Tiresias," in Collected and New (1963).

2174 _____. "To Homer," in Collected and New (1963).

VANSITTART, Sir Robert Gilbert (1881-1957, English)

2175 "The Gods of Yesterday," in Songs and Satires. London: Humphreys, 1909.

VAN ZANDT, George Harrison (?-?, American)

2176 "The Lotus-Eaters," in The Poems of George Harrison Van Zandt. Philadelphia: Jay, 1886.

2177 _____. "Semele," in Poems (1886).

2178 _____. "The Sirens," in Poems (1886).

2179 _____. "The Sleep of Endymion," in Poems (1886).

2180 _____. "Venus and Luna," in Poems (1886).

VAUGHAN, Virginia (?-1913, English)

2180a Orpheus and the Sirens, a drama in lyrics. London: Chapman and Hall, 1882.

VICKRIDGE, Alberta (?-?, English)

2181 "Goatfoot," in Goatfoot and Other Poems. Bradford, England: Beamsley House, 1931. About Pan.

2182 _____. "Tamer of Horses," in Goatfoot (1931). About Hector.

VOKES, William (?-?, English)

2183 The Labours of Heracles. London: Stockwell, 1924.

WALLER, Edmond (1606-1687, English)

2184 "Phoebus and Daphne," in The Poetical Works of Edmund
      Waller, ed. by Rev. George Gilfillan. Edinburgh: Nichol,
      1857.

2185 _____. "Stay Phoebus," in Poetical Works (1857).

2186 _____. "Thyrsis, Galatea," in Poetical Works (1857).

WASSON, David Atwood (1823-1887, American)

2187 "Orpheus," in Poems. Boston: Lee and Shepard, 1888.

WATKINS, Vernon Phillips (1906-1967, English)

2188 "Niobe," in The Lady with the Unicorn and Other Poems.
      London: Faber and Faber, 1948.

WATSON, Edward Willard (1843-1925, American)

2189 "The Cry of Prometheus," in Songs of Flying Hours. Phila-
      delphia: Coates, 1898.

WATSON, William (1858-1935, English)

2190 "Lachrymae Musarum," in Collected Poems. London: Lane,
      1899.

2191 _____. "On Landor's 'Hellenics,'" in Collected Poems
      (1899).

WATTS-DUNTON, Theodore (1832-1914, English)

2192 "The Deaf and Dumb Son of Croesus," in The Coming of Love.
      London: Lane, 1898.

2193 _____. "Ancestral Memory," in Coming of Love (1898).

2194 _____. "Apollo in Paris," in Coming of Love (1898).

WEISS, Theodore (1916-   , American)

2195   "The Fire at Alexandria," in Outlanders.   New York:
         Macmillan, 1960.

WESTERN, Hugh (Alfred Ernest Hamill, pseudonym, 1883-1953,
American)

2196   "Actaeon," in Serenade.   Chicago: Hill, 1926.

2197   _____.   "The Return of Dionysios," in Serenade (1926).

WHARTON, Edith (1862-1937, American)

2198   "Artemis to Actaeon," in Artemis to Actaeon and Other Poems.
         New York: Scribner, 1909.

2199   _____.   "The Eumenides," in Artemis to Actaeon (1909).

WHITMAN, Sarah Helen Power (1803-1878, American)

2200   "Proserpine to Pluto in Hades," in Poems.   Boston: Houghton,
         Osgood, 1879.

2201   _____.   "The Venus of Milo," in Poems (1879).

WILBUR, Richard (1921-   , American)

2202   "Gérard de Nerval: Anteros," in Advice to a Prophet.   New
         York: Harcourt, Brace, 1961.

2203   _____.   "The Sirens," in Ceremony and Other Poems.
         New York: Harcourt, Brace, 1950.

2204   _____.   "Under Cygnus," in Walking to Sleep: New Poems
         and Translations.   New York: Harcourt, Brace, 1969.

WILDE, Oscar (1854-1900, English)

2205   "The Burden of Itys," in Vol. I, The Complete Works of Oscar
         Wilde, 12 vols., with Introduction by Richard Le Gallienne.
         Garden City, N.Y.:   Doubleday, Page, 1923.

2206   _____.   "Charmides," in Vol. I, Complete Works (1923).

2207   _____.   "Endymion," in Vol. I, Complete Works (1923).

2208   _____.   "The Garden of Eros," in Vol. I, Complete Works
         (1923).

308

2209 _____. "The New Helen," in Poems by Oscar Wilde, with Biographical Introduction by Temple Scott. New York: Brentano, 1910.

2210 _____. "The Sphinx," in Vol. I, Complete Works (1923).

WILEY, Sara King (1871-1909, American)

2211 "Alcestis," in Alcestis and Other Poems. New York: Macmillan, 1905.

2212 _____. "Apollo and Daphne," in Poems Lyrical and Dramatic. London: Chapman and Hall, 1900.

2213 _____. "Clytie," in Poems Lyrical (1900).

2214 _____. "Endymion," in Poems Lyrical (1900).

2215 _____. "The Faun," in Poems Lyrical (1900).

2216 _____. "Iphigeneia," in Alcestis (1905).

2217 _____. "Iphigeneia Before the Sacrifice at Aulis," a poem for music by William Henry Humiston. New York: Breitkopf and Härtel, 1912.

WILLAN, Edmund (?-?, English)

2218 "Hector and Andromache," in Mary, Queen of Scots and Other Poems. London: Oxford University Press, 1919.

WILLIAMS, Alfred (1877-1930, English)

2219 "The Cyclops," in Aeneas in Sicily and Other Poems. London: MacDonald, c. 1905.

2220 _____. "Helen," in Songs in Wiltshire. London: MacDonald, 1909.

2221 _____. "Paris and Oenone," in Songs (1909).

2222 _____. "Penelope to Phemius," in Songs (1909).

2223 _____. "The Story of Acestes," in Nature and Other Poems. London: MacDonald, 1912.

WILLIAMS, Charles (1886-1945, English)

2224 "Proserpina," in Poems of Conformity. London: Oxford University Press, 1917.

309

WILLIAMS, continued

2225 _____. "Troy: Sonnets on Andromache, Helen, Hecuba, and Cassandra," in Poems of Conformity (1917).

WILLIAMS, William Carlos (1883-1963, American)

2226 "Landscape with the Fall of Icarus," in Pictures from Brueghel and Other Poems. New York: New Directions, 1959.

WILLIAMSON, David R. (?-?, English)

2227 "The Sacrifice of Iphigenia," in Collected Poems. London: Mitre, 1928.

WILLS, Alice (?-?, English)

2228 "Oenone," in Orpheus and Other Poems. London: Roberts, 1929.

2229 _____. "Orpheus," in Orpheus (1929).

2230 _____. "Ulysses," in Orpheus (1929).

WOLFE, Humbert (1885-1940, English)

2231 "Ilion," in This Blind Rose. London: Gollancz, 1928.

2232 _____. "Psyche," in This Blind Rose (1928).

2233 _____. "The Sicilian Expedition," in Shylock Reasons with Mr. Chesterton and Other Poems. Oxford: Blackwell, 1920.

2234 _____. "The Sirens," in This Blind Rose (1928).

2235 _____. "The Unknown God," in Shylock Reasons (1920).

2236 _____. "What the Sirens Sang," in This Blind Rose (1928).

2237 _____. Troy, with drawings by Charles Ricketts. London: Faber and Gwyer, 1928.

WOOLNER, Thomas (1825-1892, English)

2238 "Cytherea," in Tiresias and Other Poems. London: Bell, 1886.

2239 _____. "Pallas Athene," in Tiresias (1886).

2240 _____. Pygmalion. London: Macmillan, 1881.

310

2241 _____. Silenus. London: Macmillan, 1884.

2242 _____. "The Sphinx," in Tiresias (1886).

2243 _____. "Tiresias," in Tiresias (1886).

WORDSWORTH, Dame Elizabeth (1840-1932, English)

2244 "The Apple of Discord," in Poems and Plays. London:
     Oxford University Press, 1931.

WORSLEY, Philip Stanhope (1835-1866, English)

2245 "Narcissus," in Poems. Edinburgh and London: Blackwood,
     1863.

2246 _____. "Phaethon," in Poems and Translations, ed. by
     Rev. Edward Worsley. Edinburgh and London: Blackwood,
     1875.

WRIGHT, David (1920- , South African)

2247 "An Invocation to the Goddess," in Monologues of a Deaf Man.
     London: Peters, 1958. Refers to Venus.

WRIGHT, Merle St. Croix (1859-1925, American)

2248 "The Apparition of Pan," in Ignis Ardens. New York: Vinal,
     1926.

2249 _____. "Venus Anadyomene," in Ignis Ardens (1926).

YARDLEY, Edward (?-?, English)

2250 "Bacchus and Ariadne," in Supplementary Stories and Poems.
     London: Privately printed, 1870.

2251 _____. "Circe," in Supplementary (1870).

2252 _____. "Electra," in Melusina and Other Poems. London:
     Privately printed, 1867.

2253 _____. "Prometheus," in Melusina (1867).

YARNALL, Agnes (?-?, American)

2254 "Pandora," in Pandora and Other Poems. Philadelphia:
     Dorrance, 1926.

SUBJECT INDEX

[Items 1167 and following, listed in the Appendix, are not annotated.]

313

1145, 1184, 1220, 1231,
1264, 1265, 1274, 1296,
1314, 1315, 1348, 1350,
1355, 1360, 1380, 1384,
1405, 1416, 1422, 1438,
1452, 1458, 1479, 1481,
1495, 1496, 1504, 1551,
1570, 1577, 1578, 1590,
1598, 1610, 1628, 1644,
1652, 1672, 1737, 1748,
1795, 1797, 1798, 1819,
1874, 1875, 1924, 1958,
1966, 1991, 2024, 2060,
2071, 2129, 2140, 2180,
2201, 2238, 2247, 2249
Apollo (Phoebus, Helios, etc.)
  88, 118, 181, 201, 266, 272,
  293, 337, 341, 343, 394,
  422, 427, 431, 432, 440,
  542, 555, 585, 608, 663,
  696, 714, 719, 720, 779,
  828, 864, 889, 909, 916,
  961, 995, 1020, 1054,
  1059, 1061, 1077, 1088,
  1147, 1228, 1235, 1266,
  1273, 1327, 1362, 1375,
  1433, 1514, 1526, 1558,
  1707, 1708, 1780, 1794,
  1905, 1934, 1995, 2014,
  2062, 2096, 2123, 2139,
  2156, 2157, 2158, 2184,
  2185, 2194, 2212
Arachne 15, 687, 1373
Ares (Mars, etc.) 195, 880,
  990, 1053, 1174, 1404, 1405,
  1452, 1704
Arethusa 1000, 1488, 1828,
  1932
Ariadne 145, 178, 216, 313,
  619, 649, 650, 697, 702,
  730, 732, 894, 895, 1154,
  1171, 1186, 1301, 1302,
  1376, 1599, 1661, 1702,
  1735, 1833, 1848, 1869,
  1871, 2080, 2134, 2250
Arion 729, 899, 1047, 1372
Aristodemus 1109, 1113, 2001
Aristodemus (died at Plataea)
  1046
Aristomenes 938, 1834
Artemis (Diana, Phoebe, etc.)
  33, 36, 70, 168, 229, 273,
  345, 387, 468, 557, 600,

647, 651, 659, 663, 670,
683, 691, 782, 809, 811,
837, 891, 996, 1257, 1287,
1352, 1389, 1480, 1489,
1512, 1616, 1658, 1672,
1809, 2010, 2030, 2127,
2138, 2198
Atalanta 69, 393, 759, 922,
  1086, 1169, 1240, 1353,
  1354, 1664, 2125
Athamas 2086
Athena (Pallas, Minerva) 49,
  81, 221, 309, 418, 474,
  553, 825, 870, 1202, 1406,
  1797, 2239
Athens 1427, 1430, 1788,
  2099, 2170
Atlantis 100, 110, 296, 333,
  371, 395, 800, 1211, 1363,
  2082
Atlas 962, 1543, 1943
Atreus 2163
Attaginous 547
Attis 51, 1553
Atys (son of Croesus) 684,
  1194, 2100
Aurora see Eos (Dawn)
Autolycus 1620

Bellerophon 2, 160, 217, 879,
  923, 924, 1635, 1763
Blessed Isles (Fortunate Isles,
  Elysium) 573, 594, 640,
  782, 783, 1475, 1724
Boreas 909
Butes 1282

Cacus 120
Cadmus 121
Calchas 841
Callicrates 1104
Calliope 620
Callirhoe 747
Calypso 29, 438, 456, 731,
  849, 896, 991, 1073, 1260,
  1410, 1547, 1588, 1757,
  1856
Cassandra 231a, 302, 457,
  482, 628, 708, 881, 907,
  1032, 1037, 1187, 1214,
  1649, 1789, 2031, 2225

316

Lotus-Eaters 1132, 1402,
1872, 2176
Lucifer 58, 204, 885, 1064a
Lucretia 2003
Luna (see also Selene) 275a
Lycius 1083

Maenads (see also Dionysus)
596, 1024, 1025, 1921
Marathon 268, 549
Marpessa 984, 1666, 2046
Marsyas 175, 245, 323, 340,
869, 1483, 1500, 1708, 1922,
2106
Medea 60, 63, 148, 711, 712,
1322, 1365, 1431, 1660,
1682, 1701, 1815, 1824,
1883, 2162
Medusa 12, 112, 232, 528,
627, 1036, 1759, 1779,
1967, 2007, 2008
Melampus 886
Meleager 1005, 2146
Memnon 185, 439, 598, 843,
1323, 1849, 1913
Menelaus 261, 766, 767, 812
Menippe and Metioche 129
Merope (daughter of Pleione;
wife of Sisyphus) 93, 1276,
1554, 1936
Merope (wife of Cresphontes)
79
Metaneira 521
Midas 1150, 1188, 1892, 1929,
2063
Miletus 769, 846
Minos 130, 236, 653, 664,
1324
Minotaur 317, 692, 1876
Mnemosyne 282, 359, 1074,
1242, 1951
Moly 360, 2107
Muses 24, 48, 85, 103, 228,
487, 592, 1490, 1706, 2190
Mycenaean 1011, 1026
Myrtle 1110

Naiads (Nereids, Nereus) 3,
21, 157, 246, 283, 362, 736,
1172, 1477, 1510, 1673,
1829, 1965

Narcissus 152, 205, 256, 328,
335, 373, 536, 559, 656,
900, 957, 1183, 1288, 1418,
1454, 1531, 1583, 1632,
1738, 1909, 2068, 2159,
2245
Nausicaa 564, 1179, 1615
Nemea 499, 1811
Nemesis 511, 920, 1950,
1957, 2035
Nereus 1743
Nestor 1450
Night (Nyx) 1942
Nike (Victory) 56, 1401
Niobe 186, 374, 665, 768,
921, 965, 1325, 1683, 1728,
2088, 2188
Nireus 859
Nymphs 20, 43, 349, 369,
699, 1494, 1544, 2023, 2087

Odysseus (Ulysses) 115, 258,
358, 360, 376, 399, 438,
472, 500, 535, 622, 625,
631, 672, 764, 790, 793,
799, 804, 834, 853, 876,
951, 987, 989, 1038, 1123,
1137, 1139, 1185, 1260,
1340, 1371, 1410, 1462,
1516, 1589, 1615, 1653,
1667, 1742, 1752, 1757,
1783, 1866, 1886, 1898,
2114, 2171, 2230
Oedipus 8, 140, 212, 382,
383, 494, 529, 579, 706,
782, 946, 948, 1164, 1165,
1369, 1540, 1749, 1937,
1952, 1969
Oenone 189, 704, 748, 1127,
1133, 2221, 2228
Olympia 2019
Oracles (Sibyls, Prophets; see
also individual names) 65,
366, 448, 558, 614, 635,
677, 685, 1088, 1096, 1162,
1175, 1413, 1597, 1816,
1817, 1946
Orestes 64, 705, 713, 831,
985, 1328, 1579, 1821, 1841,
1998, 2036
Orion 129, 131, 473, 679,
1030, 1442, 1851, 1884,

1911, 1984, 2154
Orithyia 66, 666
Orpheus 18, 188, 213, 214,
274, 284, 384, 407, 435,
440, 461, 488, 501, 595,
629, 690, 695, 940, 947,
966, 975, 1029, 1123, 1151,
1291, 1329, 1330, 1346,
1349, 1394, 1408, 1421,
1426, 1443, 1444, 1453,
1465, 1503, 1507, 1528,
1532, 1573, 1634, 1651,
1773, 1822, 1842, 1843,
1858, 1877, 1894, 1895,
1902, 1939, 1959, 1960,
1996, 1997, 2049, 2130,
2147, 2153, 2180a, 2187,
2229
Othryades 550, 2004

Pan 28, 32, 247, 269, 270,
275a, 285, 301, 307, 323,
325, 326, 327, 336, 363,
368, 512, 523, 543, 565,
661, 667, 749, 770, 771,
810, 1098, 1099, 1181, 1212,
1232, 1233, 1234, 1243,
1254, 1262, 1268, 1297,
1298, 1326, 1377, 1386,
1399, 1409, 1441, 1609,
1646, 1657, 1713, 1718,
1739, 1745, 1770, 1785,
1852, 1887, 1896, 1923,
1935, 1945, 1990, 1994,
2020, 2037, 2050, 2131,
2181, 2248
Pandarus 1947
Pandora 19, 222, 805, 818,
1041, 1122, 1331, 1492,
2254
Pantarkes 1111
Paris 154, 189, 220, 518,
748, 925, 982, 1726, 1906,
2221
Parnassus 1134
Parrhasius 1144
Pasifae 615, 673
Pausanias 1070, 1663, 1722
Pegasus 160, 819, 1546
Peleus 534, 772
Pelops 132, 176, 391
Penates 2002

Penelope 286, 455, 489, 502,
687, 743, 773, 804, 860,
949, 987, 1071, 1244, 1251,
1574, 1592, 2021, 2222
Penthesilia 190, 515, 519,
617, 1689, 1891
Pentheus 710, 871
Periander 887
Persephone (Proserpina, Kore)
35, 150, 179, 191, 197,
329, 365, 398, 424, 437,
580, 674, 701, 761, 792,
808, 872, 904, 993, 1003,
1042, 1081, 1092, 1094,
1128, 1157, 1280, 1335,
1359, 1366, 1378, 1395,
1455, 1538, 1559, 1575,
1641, 1719, 1732, 1771,
1777, 1807, 1930, 1941,
2043, 2108, 2129, 2200,
2224
Perseus 133, 926, 1580, 1624,
1705
Persians 552
Phaeacia 535
Phaedra 319, 475, 477, 478,
709, 832, 970, 1100, 1154,
1751
Phaethon 4, 206, 888, 967,
1173, 1263, 1321, 1332,
1445, 1611, 1792, 1897,
2112, 2151, 2246
Philemon and Baucis 566,
2028, 2065, 2168
Philoctetes 46, 414, 581
1016, 1160, 1333, 1334,
1446, 1878
Philomela 82, 539, 599, 1008,
1065
Phineus 172
Phoenix (bird) 400, 1532
Phoenix (son of Amyntor) 6
Pindar 1986
Pisidice 794
Pitys 771, 2050
Plato 370, 1904
Pleiads 72, 96, 248, 642,
735, 1276, 1596
Polycrates 182
Polyidus 568
Polyphemus (the Cyclops) 177,
218, 287, 436, 443, 538,
1176, 1501, 1861, 1898, 2148

319